Strengthening the Parent–Child Relationship in Therapy

Strengthening the Parent–Child Relationship in Therapy

Laying the Foundation for Healthy Development

Larissa N. Niec

AMERICAN PSYCHOLOGICAL ASSOCIATION

Published by
American Psychological Association
750 First Street, NE
Washington, DC 20002
https://www.apa.org

Order Department
https://www.apa.org/pubs/books
order@apa.org

In the U.K., Europe, Africa, and the Middle East, copies may be ordered from Eurospan
https://www.eurospanbookstore.com/apa
info@eurospangroup.com

Typeset in Meridien and Ortodoxa by Circle Graphics, Inc., Reisterstown, MD

Printer: Gasch Printing, Odenton, MD
Cover Designer: Beth Schlenoff Design, Bethesda, MD

Library of Congress Cataloging-in-Publication Data

Names: Niec, Larissa N., author. | American Psychological Association.
Title: Strengthening the parent-child relationship in therapy : laying the foundation for healthy development / by Larissa N. Niec.
Description: Washington, DC : American Psychological Association, 2022. | Includes bibliographical references and index.
Identifiers: LCCN 2021060316 (print) | LCCN 2021060317 (ebook) | ISBN 9781433836664 (paperback) | ISBN 9781433840197 (ebook)
Subjects: LCSH: Parent and child. | Family psychotherapy. | Child development.
Classification: LCC HQ755.85 .N526 2022 (print) | LCC HQ755.85 (ebook) | DDC 306.874--dc23/eng/20211222
LC record available at https://lccn.loc.gov/2021060316
LC ebook record available at https://lccn.loc.gov/2021060317

https://doi.org/10.1037/0000304-000

Printed in the United States of America

10 9 8 7 6 5 4 3 2 1

To my parents, Al and Marie, who provided me with unconditional love, safe limits, and a secure base from which to explore.

We are unlikely to eradicate poverty and systemic discrimination in our time—or their negative impacts on children's development—but while we fight for social justice, if we can do just one thing to protect children from those adverse experiences, if we do just one thing to increase children's resilience and their chances of growing into healthy adults, we must help parents to be responsive and effective. We must strengthen the parent–child relationship.

CONTENTS

PREFACE

Psychotherapists have long appreciated the power of parenting and the influence the parent–child relationship has on the developing child. However, advances in brain imaging and genomic technologies, partnered with long-term (e.g., 13–30 years) longitudinal studies of the development process, have increased our understanding of the physiological and psychological mechanisms through which early experiences contribute to later functioning. The collected evidence demonstrates that parenting is a primary promoter of developmental cascades that begin in early childhood. That is, the quality of parenting sets into motion developmental processes that may lead to numerous negative or positive outcomes. Not only does higher quality parenting predict children's better emotional and behavioral health, but recent studies suggest that responsive and effective parenting buffers children from some of the negative impacts of exposure to adverse experiences (e.g., poverty, parent mental illness) on physiological development, including the structure and function of the brain.

The importance of a healthy parent–child relationship as a buffer cannot be overstated. Many families in the United States and globally are confronting serious and pervasive adversities. Exposure to violence, financial hardship, less access to education and employment opportunities, and systemic discrimination are harms that relate to increased health and mental health problems. Health problems are then compounded by difficulties accessing quality care, which in turn exacerbate health disparities, causing families who experience such harms to be burdened with poorer health and mental health outcomes relative to other families. As therapists, we can attack this issue by making meaningful and lasting changes for children and parents. The primary goal of this book is to support therapists in their work with young children, bringing a lens that shifts the therapeutic focus to the parent–child relationship.

Several excellent books have focused on the development of the parent–child relationship in infancy and on interventions targeting parents of infants (e.g., Cassidy & Shaver, 2016; Steele & Steele, 2018). In contrast, this volume focuses on children from toddlerhood (2 years) to early school age (7–8 years). These years are a foundational period during which children quickly develop emotionally, behaviorally, cognitively, and physically. At the same time, children have moved beyond the infancy period by 2 years of age, when the regulation of systems (e.g., emotional, behavioral, physical) is primarily maintained by the parent. During this early childhood period, children face developmental tasks related to self-regulation, language use, and the negotiation of social interactions that set the stage for later functioning.

In my many years of training mental health professionals in the community, I have often witnessed that even when therapists value the importance of the parent–child relationship, barriers exist that prevent them from addressing the relationship in a way that is likely to facilitate change. This three-part volume tackles some of those challenges. In Part I, I integrate current developmental and intervention science to provide practical knowledge about the parent–child relationship and healthy parenting. Chapter 1 reviews the initial development of the parent–child relationship, antecedents that influence the quality of parent–child attachment, and the child's internalization of the relationship in the early years of life. Chapter 2 focuses on the ways in which the parent–child relationship can initiate a positive cascade across developmental stages and domains. In Chapter 3, the discussion turns to risk factors at the individual, dyadic, and societal levels that can disrupt responsive and effective parenting. In each chapter, I consider concrete lessons and approaches that the developmental research offers to therapists.

Building on the foundational knowledge provided in the first three chapters, Part II includes a discussion of evidence-based assessment and intervention techniques valuable to therapeutic work with parents and children. Chapter 4 introduces a multimethod approach to the assessment of the parent–child relationship, reviewing standardized assessment tools across measurement domains. Chapters 5 and 6 focus on two of the core elements of parenting related to healthy child development: responsiveness and limit setting. In Chapter 7, I consider the strengths and limitations of four parent–child interventions that have been broadly disseminated and are frequently implemented in community mental health settings.

Part III shifts away from what is optimal in assessment and treatment to frankly consider some of the common barriers faced by therapists across systems (e.g., organization, client, individual). Chapter 8 discusses the importance of the father–child relationship and the neglected role of fathers in the treatment process. In this chapter, I provide strategies to "flip the script" to create an inclusive environment that welcomes fathers. Chapter 9 explores some of the challenges specific to working with parent–child dyads, the ways in which those challenges can lead to therapist burnout, and strategies for self-care. In the concluding chapter, I consider some of the societal-level challenges impeding the achievement of health equity for all parents and children, and I offer suggestions for areas in which therapists may be advocates for themselves and for families.

NOTES ON TERMINOLOGY

Across families from all backgrounds, the primary caregivers of a child may include many and varied relations who may or may not be biological parents. It is essential to recognize and welcome into treatment any caregiver who may be primary in a child's life. I frequently work with stepparents, grandparents, foster parents, aunties, uncles, and adult siblings. Throughout the book, however, I use the word *parent* to reduce redundancy, knowing it connotes any adult who plays an important role in caring for a child.

The mental health profession encompasses a diverse range of disciplines—psychology, psychiatry, social work, marriage and family therapy, licensed professional counseling, and so on. In the service of removing the superfluous and providing clarity, I use the terms *therapist* and *clinician* interchangeably to represent any mental health professional who provides psychotherapeutic services.

Finally, please note that client identities in the case discussions have been disguised to preserve families' confidentiality.

ACKNOWLEDGMENTS

I am extraordinarily grateful for the secure base provided to me in my early years of development as a therapist. With deep appreciation, I thank my mentors and supervisors during those years who provided a safe space within which I could struggle and grow, particularly Drs. Sandra Russ, Beverly Funderburk, and Jane Silovsky. Your responsive and effective support allowed me to flourish and provided a strong model for my own work with students and therapists-in-training.

I wrote much of this book during the COVID-19 pandemic. In the midst of converting courses, training workshops, and clinical services to remote formats; figuring out the HIPAA compliance of internet platforms; and worrying about the well-being of students and families, I sometimes wondered if the project would reach completion. I am grateful to Susan Reynolds, my editor at APA Books, for her tremendous patience as I struggled through the process.

Many thanks to my dear friends Drs. Sarah Domoff and Kris McDermott, who cheered me tirelessly, and to Mikaela Overton, who is on her way to becoming an excellent clinician in her own right and who kept my references organized from start to finish.

Finally, my gratitude and admiration to the therapists who daily collaborate with parents to put children on a path to healthy development and to the parents who take the difficult step of asking for help for themselves and their children, and then take the even more difficult step of engaging in the therapeutic work.

THE INFLUENCE OF THE PARENT–CHILD RELATIONSHIP ON CHILD DEVELOPMENT

1

When I Need You, You're Here

Initiation of the Parent–Child Relationship

"I'm right here, buddy!"

In response to his mother's voice behind him, the curly-haired 2-year-old giggled wildly and continued trotting down the airport concourse, absorbing the novel sights—restaurants, gift shops, and passing strangers—as he went. Not far behind him, his mother and father strode on, dragging luggage and maintaining visual contact with him. From time to time, the little boy slowed and glanced over his shoulder, his large dark eyes casting about among the crowd. Spotting his parents not far away, he would dart off again. Once in a while, mother or father would call out with a reassurance or a gentle caution.

I watched this game of eye tag continue all the way down the concourse—with the parents maintaining watch over their child and the child checking in visually with the parents, even as he careened through an unfamiliar environment. The pleasure evident in the toddler's exploration—his unfettered smile and enthusiastic giggling—was balanced by a level of wariness that increased as he ran farther from his parents. As his wariness increased, the toddler slowed and glanced back to find mother and father. In parallel, parents displayed vigilance but not anxiety as their child explored. They ensured he stayed within sight and offered him ongoing guidance in the form of verbal reassurance and caution.

A balance existed in the interaction, a gentle but persistent back-and-forth tugging from parents and child. On one side, the parents offered warmth,

https://doi.org/10.1037/0000304-001
Strengthening the Parent–Child Relationship in Therapy: Laying the Foundation for Healthy Development, by L. N. Niec

responsiveness, and concern in verbal and nonverbal cues, but they never let him draw too far away. On the other side, the child expressed delight in exploration and confidence in his parents' presence but grew cautious as he wandered farther, slowing and checking in.

The exquisite balance observed between these parents and child at the airport reflected many behaviors indicative of a secure attachment, a core aspect of a healthy parent–child relationship. It was a very different pattern than is often observed among families who seek mental health services or who have been identified by the child welfare system, where unpredictable, unavailable, or unsafe caregiving may have led to problematic attachment behaviors. Before considering the causes and consequences of pathogenic parent–child interactions, however, it is important to understand the process through which the parent–child relationship first develops. As for any developmental domain, it is necessary to define the typical trajectory in order to understand what is atypical and to create interventions to address problems. In other words, it is important to understand how these parents and their little one reached such a positive state that they could move happily and comfortably through a strange environment together.

This chapter begins with an overview of the initial growth of the parent–child bond and reviews antecedents of parent–child relationship quality. The discussion then turns to children's internalization of the relationship and the transformation into internal working models, which link the early parent–child relationship to later interpersonal functioning. I then review what is known about the stability of attachment patterns, before ending with a consideration of aspects of early relationship development that are particularly relevant in clinical settings. Some of the questions raised in this chapter are examined throughout the book: How does the parent–child relationship influence child development over the life course? What are the consequences of pathogenic parent–child interactions? In a clinical setting, what dimensions of the parent–child relationship are key to a valid and valuable assessment? What protective factors might be fostered through effective intervention?

WHAT IS ATTACHMENT?

The quality of attachment is one of the most basic aspects of the parent–child relationship. In the initial months of a child's life, an argument can be made that the attachment behaviors of parent and child are in fact the relationship. Although therapists, case managers, and health care providers often use the term *attachment* to refer to the quality of the parent–child relationship generally, attachment theory describes a specific set of systems, and behaviors within those systems, that encompass "attachment behaviors" (Ainsworth, 1989; Bowlby, 1969/1982; Sullivan et al., 2011). That is, attachment describes complementary systems operating between a caregiver and child that are activated by opposing pressures and that together support a dual purpose of enabling the child's survival and fostering the development of the child's autonomy (see Figure 1.1; Bowlby, 1969/1982; Marvin et al., 2016).

The first of those systems leads to attachment behaviors through which the child maintains proximity to the caregiver, obtaining protection and the fulfillment of basic needs. In the example of the parent–child interaction at the airport, as the toddler drew farther from his parents, he became wary, slowed his pace, and made eye contact with his attachment figures. The opposing system leads to exploration behaviors, through which the child begins to investigate the world and develop autonomy. Thus, with his parents nearby, the toddler trotted happily through a novel environment. Bowlby (1969/1982) proposed that (a) these systems are biologically based in humans, as in other animals in which the young are born helpless, because they allow for the survival of offspring; and (b) the behaviors within each system grow more complex across the phases of the development of the child and of the parent–child bond.

While Bowlby played a foundational role in the growth of attachment theory, Ainsworth (1969, 1989) made major contributions to the early understanding of individual differences in attachment patterns through her extensive naturalistic and lab observations of infants and their mothers. Based on the proposition that infants' attachment and exploration systems are activated in opposing circumstances (e.g., separation from caregiver or perceived threat vs. novel, safe environment), Ainsworth and her colleagues (1978) developed the Strange Situation procedure (SSP) to explore infants' reactions in both

FIGURE 1.1. Children's Attachment and Exploration Behaviors Are Activated by Opposing Environmental Situations

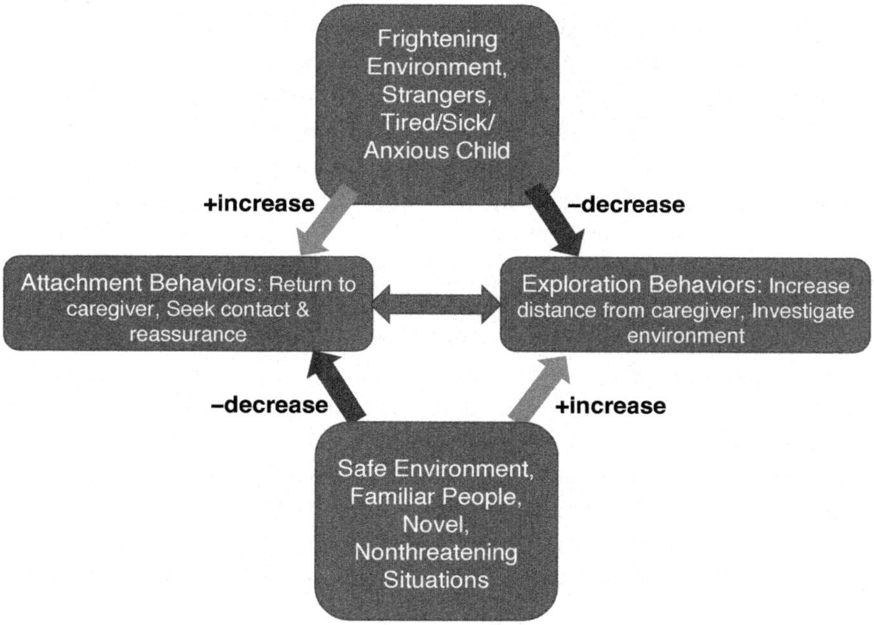

types of situations. The SSP is a 20-minute standardized behavioral observation measure with eight brief scenarios (e.g., parent and child alone in a room with toys, stranger with parent and child, stranger with child alone, parent return to child) designed to activate attachment and exploration behaviors in order to investigate patterns in parent–child interactions (Ainsworth et al., 1978). Of particular relevance is the child's willingness to explore the environment, responses to separation from parent, and reaction to parent upon reunion. The development of the SSP allowed for the testing of key hypotheses arising from attachment theory; for instance, can stable parent–child interaction patterns be identified, and are those patterns influenced by differences in the quality of the caregiving environment (Carlson et al., 2003)?

The answer to both questions is yes. Across samples of parent–child dyads, a number of consistent patterns emerged, which were categorized as *secure* or *insecure* patterns of attachment. Ainsworth and colleagues (1978) identified three primary patterns: secure (B), insecure/avoidant (A), insecure/resistant (C). Among a community sample without socioeconomic stressors, secure attachment quality is the most commonly observed pattern, with 60% to 65% of 1-year-olds falling within the secure classification (E. Waters, 1978). Infants with secure attachments demonstrate a balance between attachment and exploration behaviors and readily shift between the two systems, as observed in the adventurous toddler at the airport (Bowlby, 1988; Main et al., 2005). Infants whose attachment relationships are classified as insecure/avoidant tend to interact with the environment but display muted affect upon separation from and reunion with the parent, interacting with the toys instead of the parent and avoiding eye contact. They do not seek proximity to their caregiver or use their caregiver as a source of comfort. This avoidant strategy has been conceptualized as a way to minimize expressions of distress by a child who has experienced unresponsiveness and rejection by their caregiver (Ainsworth et al., 1978; Opie et al., 2021; Waters, 1978). In other words, confronted with a caregiver who does not provide responsive support, the infant avoids seeking support. In contrast, infants with insecure/resistant attachment patterns tend to exhibit high levels of distress upon separation from their caregiver and to show urgent proximity seeking upon reunion, often clinging to their caregiver and crying. Despite intense distress, infants in the resistant category are not easily comforted. They remain vigilant to the actions of the caregiver, who is inconsistent and unreliable in their availability. In the face of unpredictable care, the insecure/resistant strategy is to attempt to maintain proximity.

Subsequent to the initial studies of the SSP, later observations of children in pathogenic caregiving environments revealed a group of children who did not fit within the three classifications; a fourth category, *disorganized*, was identified (Main & Solomon, 1990). Children with disorganized attachments demonstrate a lack of coherent patterns in their responses to their caregivers and disordered shifting in their behavioral strategies. They tend to demonstrate fearful or confused reactions toward their caregivers that can be pervasive and intense. They do not appear to find comfort in proximity to their caregivers, but unlike the infants with avoidant attachment behaviors, neither do they find distraction from distress in the environment. Although the occurrence of disorganized attachment is low among low-risk samples (14%–18%), among children who have experienced abuse, as many as 80% may be classified as disorganized (McIntosh et al., 2021; van IJzendoorn et al., 1999).

All four primary attachment classifications (secure, insecure/avoidant, insecure/resistant, insecure/disorganized) can be reliably identified from children's behaviors during the SSP scenarios (Opie et al., 2021). The SSP remains the gold standard for the measurement of attachment behavior in children from 11 to 24 months.

ATTACHMENT IS LEARNED

Bowlby's formulation of attachment marked an important shift in the understanding of the development of the parent–child relationship. Prior to attachment theory, the psychoanalytic concept of the bond between mother and child was as an instinctive connection with which infants were born (Sullivan et al., 2011). The critical change included the understanding that infants and caregivers must learn about each other and that attachment develops through repeated interactions over time—beginning within days of birth but continuing over months to years (Bowlby, 1969/1982; Marvin et al., 2016). In other words, the process of attachment begins due to the biological predisposition of parent and child to bond but develops over time with the accumulation of learned experiences between the dyad (see Figure 1.2).

This shift was significant for the understanding of children's development—in particular, the ways in which the parent–child relationship influences development. The fact that attachment is learned through repeated parent–child interactions has implications for (a) the development of psychopathology in young children, (b) the design of interventions that target the parent–child relationship, and (c) the potential for positive change in problematic parent–child relationships. Each of these issues is considered further throughout this volume. The following section presents an overview of the attachment process.

DEVELOPMENT OF ATTACHMENT

Bowlby (1969/1982) suggested that attachment develops across four phases; the first three occur in the initial 12 to 18 months of life, and the fourth occurs in the 4th year. These phases are influenced by and must be considered within the context of other domains of development (e.g., sensorimotor, cognitive, language), as throughout the process, developmental gains allow for increases in the complexity of parent–child interactions and the increasing agency of the child. In the following sections, I discuss the four phases of attachment development, antecedents of the parent–child relationship, and the child's internalization of the relationship.

FIGURE 1.2. Parent–Child Attachment Develops Through Complex Interactions Among Biological Predispositions, Environmental Factors, and Learned Experiences

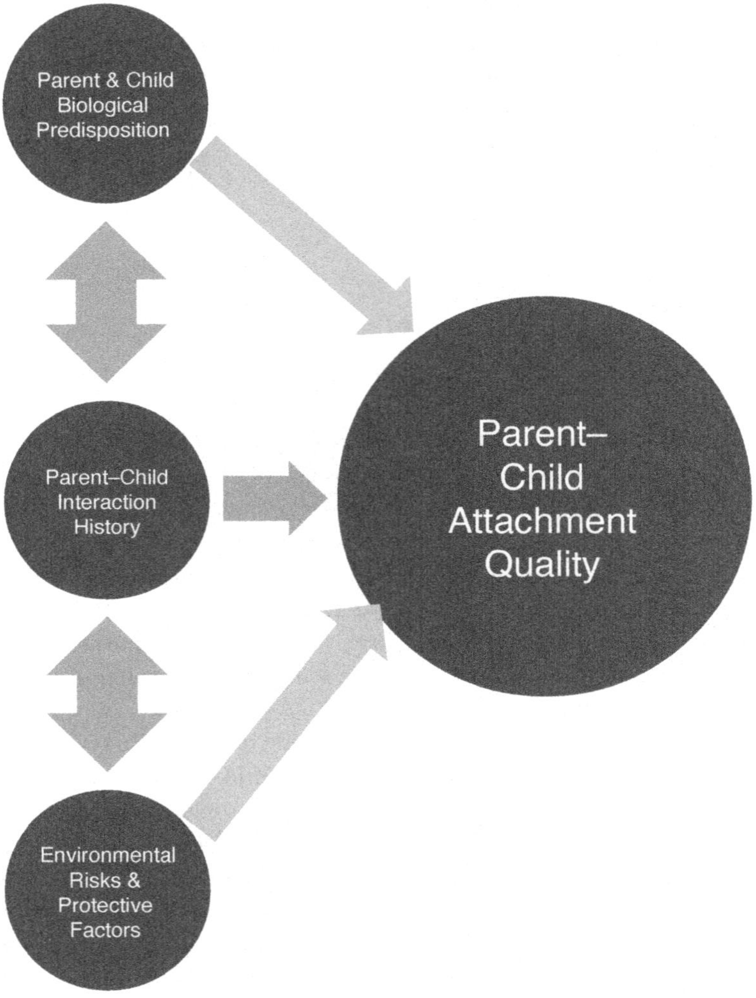

Early Years

During the first phase of attachment, the primary function of attachment behaviors in the infant is to signal need, which will elicit care. Infants' behaviors are reflexive—not goal oriented—and the infant tends to respond to other individuals generally rather than to specific people. During this time, chains of behaviors occur between parent and child and are frequently repeated. For instance, the infant cries, signaling hunger; a responsive parent picks up and cuddles the infant, leading the infant to root for the breast or the bottle. The parent provides food, meeting the infant's need, and crying stops. Proximity at this point is dependent on the parent, and signaling by the infant is reflexive rather than determined by a goal. Even in these early weeks, however, the responses of the caregiver influence the pattern of attachment that emerges toward the end of the 1st year (Beebe & Steele, 2013). A review of antecedents of infants' attachment, for example, found that infants whose mothers interacted less with them at 3 months were more likely to demonstrate insecure/ambivalent attachment patterns at 1 year (Cassidy & Berlin, 1994). In a more recent small, controlled trial, infants whose mothers carried them regularly (average of 5.9 hours a week in a close-contact infant carrier) during the first 3 months of life demonstrated more positive representations of their mothers' responsiveness at 7 months (L. R. Williams, 2020).

The second phase in the development of attachment begins in the 3rd to 4th month, as infants gain some control over their sensorimotor systems. With more control, behavior may begin to be directed and moves from purely reflexive to somewhat more complex. In parallel, infants begin to discriminate among people and to respond or signal to fewer people—specifically to attachment figures. For example, infants may smile in response to a parent's cuddling them, providing warmth and comfort, or they may reach toward a soft toy offered by a parent. As discrimination among attachment figures increases, infants' social behaviors also increase, and infants begin to initiate interactions (e.g., smiling, cooing, grasping at an attachment figure).

The third phase begins when the infant is between 6 and 9 months old. It is marked by the infant's increased mobility (e.g., rolling, scooting, crawling). Once infants can move of their own volition, they are capable of making their own efforts to maintain proximity to attachment figures (Marvin et al., 2016). Locomotion also allows infants to begin exploring the environment. Thus, the variety of behaviors infants may manifest within the two systems—attachment and exploration—begins to increase. This increase is due to not only infants' motor development but also changes in cognitive functioning that allow for the setting of a goal and the selecting of a behavior to achieve the goal (e.g., crawling across the kitchen to reach a parent). During this phase, communication skills also continue to develop, providing another channel through which infants can interact with others, increasing social interactions. It is during this phase, at approximately 8 months of age, that children's wariness of unfamiliar people increases and they demonstrate clear preferences for attachment figures (Kelmanson, 2012).

Bowlby (1969/1982) proposed that the first three phases of attachment develop within the child's 1st year and that around 12 months relatively stable patterns of parent–child interaction are established. Bowlby's fourth phase occurs around the child's 4th year (Marvin et al., 2016; E. Waters et al., 1994). This phase accompanies significant changes in a child's cognitive, language, and affective functioning. As a result of developmental advancements that allow the child to use language to communicate complex ideas, to delay the gratification of their own goals, and to negotiate and compromise with caregivers, Bowlby and others have described the fourth phase as a parent–child partnership or "emergent partnership" (Marvin et al., 2016). During this time, children begin to be able to consider their own and others' points of view and to shift their behaviors to address joint needs. Attachment behaviors (i.e., proximity seeking) need no longer involve only physical proximity, as the child has an increasingly sophisticated internal model of the attachment figure that can provide a representation of the relationship as ongoing and comforting outside of the immediate presence of the caregiver. Bowlby proposed that the parent–child partnership reached in the fourth phase is the ultimate stage of the development of the attachment relationship.

Antecedents of the Early Parent-Child Relationship

Investigations of the factors that influence the parent–child relationship have focused primarily on the quality of the caregiving environment. In the following sections, I consider the influence of three key factors related to caregiving: parental sensitivity, parenting style, and parents' internal representations. In addition, I discuss the recent research on the contributions of children's genetic makeup to the development of parent–child attachment.

Parent Sensitivity

From an attachment theory perspective, a young child's pattern of attachment develops in response to the quality of the caregiving (i.e., the history of parent–child interactions). Specifically, the sensitivity of caregiving within the context of children's distress is proposed to influence the child's selection of behavioral responses, which over time become organized into a pattern. Sensitivity from this perspective refers to a parent's ability to read the child's cues, interpret them correctly, and provide a developmentally appropriate response (Ainsworth, 1969). As predicted from theory, the link between sensitivity and attachment security has been found consistently: Parents who respond sensitively to their children's needs are more likely to have children who are securely attached (DeWolff & van IJzendoorn, 1997; Zeegers et al., 2017). This association remains true beyond infancy into early childhood and adolescence (Koehn & Kerns, 2018). High parental sensitivity is not only predictive of attachment security but also protective against children's disorganized attachment in the presence of social and environmental risk factors (McIntosh et al., 2021). The connection between parental sensitivity and child attachment patterns has been found across cultures that value a diversity of parenting practices (Y. H. Ding et al., 2012; Fuertes et al., 2016; Jin et al., 2012; N. J. Peterson et al., 2001; Zevalkink et al., 1999). Counter to expectations based on attachment theory, however, across numerous studies over several decades, the strength of the association is only modest. That is, sensitivity influences but does not exclusively determine the quality of attachment. Although from an attachment theory perspective this may be surprising, from a broader developmental perspective, the finding makes sense. Sensitivity, as a narrow and focused construct of parenting, contributes reliably but modestly to the development of the parent–child relationship. Evidence suggests that (a) the association between parent sensitivity and attachment is significantly impacted by risk factors such as socioeconomic stressors (Jeon & Neppl, 2019), and (b) other components of parenting related to a broader conceptualization of responsiveness may have additional or potentially stronger influences on attachment security (Koehn & Kerns, 2018; Woodhouse et al., 2020). In other words, parent sensitivity is important but not the sole or even primary determinant of children's attachment security. To gain a more comprehensive understanding of early relationship development, it is necessary to consider other aspects of parenting that may contribute to attachment quality and to the parent–child relationship more broadly defined.

Parenting Styles

The construct of parenting styles considers parents' interactions with their children along two primary dimensions: demandingness/control (e.g., level of confrontation, limit-setting, expectations of child behavior) and responsiveness (e.g., warmth, nurturance, supportiveness; Baumrind, 1966, 1991). Four classifications of parenting styles were originally defined depending on where parents' behaviors fell on a continuum of each dimension. The *authoritarian* parenting style reflects parents' high demandingness and low responsiveness with their children. A *permissive* parenting style reflects low demandingness and high responsiveness. The *rejecting/neglecting/uninvolved* style includes parents who demonstrate both low demandingness and low responsiveness. Finally, the *authoritative* style reflects a balance of moderate to high demandingness and high responsiveness (Baumrind, 1966, 1991). Parenting styles can be reliably measured in parents of children as young as 6 months of age (Wittig & Rodriguez, 2019) through adolescence (Pinquart, 2017) and into young adulthood (E. H. Steele & McKinney, 2019).

The association between parenting styles and children's socioemotional and interpersonal functioning has been explored in depth and is discussed further in Chapter 2. Fewer studies have specifically examined the link between parenting styles and the quality of the parent–child relationship. In a study of young adults, permissive and authoritarian parenting styles were negatively associated with secure attachment representations and positively associated with insecure/avoidant attachment representations (Ebrahimi et al., 2017). Similarly, among a sample of adolescents, parenting styles were significantly associated with quality of attachment, with authoritative styles positively associated with a positive emotional bond with mother and father (Nunes & Mota, 2017).

Parents' Representations of Attachment

Even prior to the development of reliable methods to measure adult representations of attachment, clinicians have observed continuity in parent–child relationship risk across generations, noting that adults who experience abuse in their childhood are at increased risk for unpredictable, aggressive, or emotionally frightening behaviors toward their own children. As scripts of interpersonal interactions that inform and organize expectations about new relationships, internal working models/internal representations are posited to provide a link across the generations from parent to child. Parents' representations of attachment, formed from their own early relationship experiences, are expected to influence the attachment quality of their children through their parenting behaviors.

Significant support exists for this mechanism of transmission (Hesse, 2016; van IJzendoorn, 1995; Verhage et al., 2016). In 78 studies across 30 years, significant associations were found between parents' representations of attachment as expressed in a standardized interview format and children's observed attachment quality (Verhage et al., 2016). Parents whose representations of attachment relationships are coherent, who express investment in and valuing of attachment relationships (e.g., missing lost attachment figures, depending on others), and who are able to acknowledge flaws and strengths in attachment figures are more likely to have children who are securely attached. In contrast, parents who are dismissive of the importance of attachment relationships and who minimize or deny hurt from past negative experiences are more likely to have children who display insecure/avoidant patterns of attachment. Parents whose representations reflect severely unresolved loss or trauma are more likely to have children who display disorganized attachment.

It is important to note that, for parent sensitivity, the association between parent representations and child attachment quality has been consistent but not fully explanatory. The transmission of attachment quality is also impacted by ecological risk factors such as low socioeconomic status and education, parent psychopathology, and adolescent parenthood (McIntosh et al., 2021; Verhage et al., 2018). Parents' representations of relationships can be viewed, therefore, as relevant to but not determinant of parent–child relationship quality.

Genetic Contributions

Over the past 20 years, clinicians and developmentalists have gained an appreciation for the complex interactions among an individual's biology, physical environment, and early life experiences as they influence child well-being. Although the question of the contributions of "nature versus nurture" is one that researchers have argued for more than a century, advances in methodologies, particularly as related to study of genetic influences, have led to more sophisticated explorations. To date, behavioral genetic studies examining potential genetic contributions to attachment quality have found more support for environmental influence than for genetic influence in early childhood for mother–child and father–child attachments (Bakermans-Kranenburg et al., 2004; Bokhorst et al., 2003; Picardi et al., 2020; Roisman & Fraley, 2008). In twin studies of young children, between 52% and 59% of the variance in attachment classification was attributable to shared environmental influences and 0% to a nonsignificant 17% was attributable to genetic makeup (Bakermans-Kranenburg et al., 2004; Bokhorst et al., 2003; Roisman & Fraley, 2008). In contrast, studies of adolescents and young adults have found a larger genetic contribution to representations of attachment, suggesting that influences on relationship quality may change across developmental stages (P. Fearon et al., 2014; Picardi et al., 2011).

Based on the consistency of findings, it is clear that environment plays a significant role in shaping the parent–child relationship, and quite possibly a larger role than genotype. However, it may be that the genetic influence on attachment security occurs through a third factor. For instance, arguments have been made for a differential susceptibility hypothesis in which children may have different levels of sensitivity to the caregiving environment depending on their genotype (Bakermans-Kranenburg & van IJzendoorn, 2007; Slagt et al., 2016; van IJzendoorn & Bakermans-Kranenburg, 2012). In other words, children with the genotype for susceptibility would demonstrate a stronger association between the quality of caregiving (positive or negative) and attachment security: The type of caregiving would affect them more. To date, molecular genetic studies attempting to identify genotypes that relate to susceptibility have had inconsistent results, and the most promising studies have not been replicated (Bakermans-Kranenburg & van IJzendoorn, 2016; R. M. P. Fearon & Belsky, 2016; Picardi et al., 2020). Calls for more rigorous methodology across studies may lead to clearer findings in the future.

Internal Working Models

The toddler racing through the airport demonstrated confidence that, even in a strange and bustling environment, he was safe to explore. His affect as he ran was bright, curious, and eager, and he was readily able to shift from exploration to a brief check-in with his parents. His behavior suggests that he possessed an internal model of his attachment figures as responsive and available. He had expectations, based on a history of previous interactions, that if he had need of his parents, they would be present to help. These expectations allowed him to select a goal—running through a setting filled with strangers—without fear.

Children's representations of the parent–child relationship develop over years based on repeated patterns of interaction (Bowlby, 1973; Bretherton, 2005). Bowlby named such representations *internal working models* (IWMs), but similar concepts in psychodynamic and cognitive theories are referred to as *internal representations* or *schema* (e.g., Levine & Tuber, 1993; Westen, 1991; Westen et al., 1991). The latter terms are typically considered broader constructs that include generalized expectations regarding interactions with multiple important others in a range of contexts in the child's life as well as emotional and cognitive perceptions of the self. A number of relevant cognitive and affective dimensions of internal representations that have implications for children's socioemotional functioning have been described: for example, the complexity with which the self and others are represented (unidimensional vs. multifaceted), the depth of understanding of cause and effect in social interactions (logical vs. confused/simplistic), the emotional investment in relationships (others exist only to gratify personal needs vs. deep, genuine regard), and the affect-tone of relationships (relationships are malevolent and painful vs. benign and safe; Graceffo et al., 2014; Urist, 1980; Westen, 1991). In contrast, *internal working model* refers more specifically to the representation of attachment figures, the expected responses from attachment figures, and the self in times of emotional or physical distress (Bretherton, 1987; Bretherton & Munholland, 2016). Such models are proposed to guide children's focus and the way in which new information about relationships is processed (Zimmermann & Iwanski, 2015).

Whether conceptualized as IWMs or internal representations, many dimensions are developmentally linked (Bretherton & Munholland, 2016; Niec & Russ, 2002; Sherman et al., 2015). That is, representations become more complex as children develop the ability to recognize that others have different perspectives, emotions, and goals from the self and from one another. Initial representations begin to form in the first weeks of life as an expression of an infant's experience in the moment (Bretherton & Munholland, 2016). Over time, those representations become a script that hold cognitive and affective information about the caregiver, the relationship, and the self. Such information allows the child to develop expectations about how a caregiver will respond in times of need and to select their own responses based on expectations. Children with healthy attachments demonstrate what has been named a "secure-base script" (Cassidy et al., 2013; H. S. Waters & Waters, 2006). Having experienced repeated interactions with their caregivers as responsive in times of need (e.g., hunger, illness) and distress (e.g., fear, pain), children possess a representation that says, "When in need, I can count on help from mother/father." With an internal model of the parent–child relationship established, children are able, in a sense, to carry the relationship with them. In other words, the IWM allows for a sense of continuity in the caregiving relationship even in the absence of the caregiver. The continuity provided by the IWM is believed be a primary link between the quality of early infant–parent interactions and children's later functioning.

One of the limitations in the study of IWMs is the lack of consensus regarding some of their fundamental characteristics. For instance, theorists have disagreed about the extent to which IWMs are primarily experienced at a conscious or unconscious level (R. A. Thompson, 2016). Whether children are aware or unaware of the internal scripts for attachment-related caregiving behavior has important implications for the ways they may organize their own behaviors. Advances in neuroimaging technology have begun to allow for deeper exploration into the brain structures and functions associated with the multi-sensory processing and encoding of social interactions, and thus of IWM, although much work is still needed (Bretherton & Munholland, 2016). Ultimately, identifying the structures that play a role in translating specific events into general scripts may help to illuminate how specific interactions with attachment figures are translated into IWMs and how those IWMs inform future interactions.

Continuity and Malleability

With a foundational understanding of the initial development of the parent–child relationship, two questions arise that are especially relevant in a clinical setting: (a) Do healthy parent–child relationships tend to remain healthy? and (b) When attachment patterns are problematic, is there malleability in the parent–child relationship that allows for positive change? Bowlby proposed that the development of the IWM of the early parent–child relationship would foster stability in the quality of the relationship across childhood, but that changes in the responsiveness of the caregiver would gradually bring about changes in the relationship. Investigations of stability became possible with the arrival of the SSP as a valid tool to classify the attachment relationship (Ainsworth et al., 1978; Vaughn et al., 1979; Waters, 1978). Since 1999, four meta-analyses have been conducted to synthesize the numerous findings (Fraley, 2002; Opie et al., 2021; Pinquart et al., 2013; van IJzendoorn et al., 1999). The most recent meta-analysis, and the most methodologically rigorous, examined all studies conducted up to 2019 that explored the stability of attachment classifications across early childhood (12–75 months) using the SSP or a developmentally appropriate adaptation of the SSP (Opie et al., 2021). Studies testing an intervention were excluded, as the goal was to explore rates of attachment stability without deliberate manipulation. Including the data from 63 studies, the overall stability of attachment classifications across early childhood was moderate, which is largely consistent with findings from earlier reviews. Of particular importance—and a reason for optimism in considering parent–child interventions—were the findings that when considering all four attachment patterns, (a) secure attachments were the most stable classification, (b) more children moved toward security than toward insecurity in their relationships with their caregivers, and (c) insecure classifications were the least stable (i.e., most malleable).

Exploring the stability of the parent–child relationship beyond early childhood becomes more challenging. As the parent–child relationship is internalized and IWMs grow more complex, children's attachment behaviors can no longer be activated with simple 3-minute separations from the caregiver, and attachment categories can no longer be captured with brief observational measures such as the SSP. Instead, in the exploration of attachment stability into later childhood and adolescence, the IWM is presumed to reflect the developmental equivalent of the relationship quality (Bretherton, 1987). In the past 30 years, valid and reliable methods for assessing children's and adolescents' representations of relationships have been developed (e.g., Niec & Russ, 2002; Shmueli-Goetz et al., 2008; Westen, 1995); however, the variety of assessment methods used, and range of dimensions examined make it difficult to compare outcomes across studies. One meta-analysis examined attachment stability from infancy into adulthood, with time-intervals ranging from 2 weeks to 29 years across 127 studies (Pinquart et al., 2013). Similar to the findings of Opie and colleagues, significant stability was observed across early childhood. However, attachment quality did not remain significantly stable across spans of 15 years or more. This finding may be due to the contribution of the myriad, more proximal factors that influence individuals' functioning in adulthood, but also may be related to the challenges of assessing attachment representations in consistent ways over a wide range of developmental levels. Overall, findings related to attachment stability in early childhood have been the most consistent and, as discussed next, have meaningful implications for the selection of interventions to address problems in the parent–child relationship.

CLINICAL IMPLICATIONS OF THE DEVELOPMENTAL LITERATURE

The process through which the parent–child relationship forms, deepens, and changes over time has implications for therapeutic work. In particular, the nature of the parent–child relationship has implications for the caregivers who should be included in therapy, the aspects of the relationship that are of importance as therapeutic targets, and the potential for positive change in the quality of the relationship.

Children Form Multiple Attachments

Children form attachments with caregivers other than their biological mothers, and multiple caregivers influence children's development (Ahnert et al., 2006; Fearon & Belsky, 2016). By 18 months, many toddlers have developed a set of key attachments that may include mothers, fathers, and nonparental caregivers such as grandparents, adult siblings, or daycare providers (Ahnert et al., 2006; Lucassen et al., 2011; Marvin et al., 2016). Although the overwhelming majority of attachment studies focus on mothers, significant evidence supports a link between the quality of the father–child relationship and children's socioemotional, cognitive, and behavioral functioning (see Chapter 8, this volume). In some cases, the father–child relationship may be more predictive of functioning than the mother–child relationship (Bureau et al., 2017; Malmberg et al., 2016). Evidence further suggests that children's secure relationships with multiple supportive adults may have a cumulative positive effect on functioning (Main & Weston, 1981). These findings emphasize the need for therapists to consider the caregiving system as a whole and to include in treatment all the key caregivers in a child's life, rather than maintaining a lens solely on the mother–child relationship.

The Parent–Child Relationship Beyond Attachment

The concept of attachment encompasses specific aspects of the parent–child relationship—those systems associated with the child's need to maintain proximity to the caregiver and to explore the environment. In the preschool years, as children develop more sophisticated representations of their caregivers and the parent–child relationship, attachment behaviors become more complex. Attachment is no longer readily assessed with brief separation and reunion episodes with the parent, such as those used in the SSP. The relationship itself becomes more complex. As has been noted, attachment is a relatively narrow construct and does not include all the important aspects of preschoolers' and early school-aged children's relationships with their caregivers. Other key parental roles, for example, include teacher, playmate, and limit-setter. Although attachment quality impacts children's functioning in a variety of developmental domains, the size of the associations between early attachment and areas of children's functioning such as self-regulation (Pallini et al., 2018), language (van IJzendoorn et al., 1995), peer relations (Pallini et al., 2014), and externalizing and internalizing socioemotional symptoms (Groh et al., 2017) are only small to moderate. That is, attachment status predicts an important but small component of children's well-being. Other aspects of the parent–child relationship—in particular, dimensions of parenting quality such as warmth/nurturance, supportiveness, and healthy limit setting—are also predictive, and sometimes more predictive, of children's health and socioemotional well-being than attachment status (Brody, Gray, et al., 2017; Brody et al., 2019; Greene et al., 2020; Rispoli et al., 2013). From a therapeutic perspective, then, it is critical to take a comprehensive view of the parent–child relationship—within which attachment quality is but one component. A more comprehensive perspective has implications for the assessment of a family's presenting problems as well as the selection of treatment models.

What Is Learned May Be Unlearned: Thoughts on Change

The parent–child relationship evolves as children develop and has the potential for positive change beyond infancy. Bowlby (1969/1982) proposed that the early months of life are a sensitive period for the development of attachment; that is, attachments are more readily formed within the child's 1st year. In fact, infants who are separated from early attachment figures after 1 year of age and are placed with new caregivers take longer to demonstrate attachment behaviors to the new caregivers (Dozier & Rutter, 2016). However, these children do form attachments in the new environments. Similarly, studies of infants placed in institutional care at or shortly after birth have found them to be at significant risk for developing insecure attachment patterns, but generally even these children demonstrate attachments, and when placed into responsive environments, such children often develop healthy attachment behaviors (McGoron et al., 2012; Zeanah, 2000).

Intervention studies offer further evidence that positive parent–child interactions can replace pathogenic interactions. Two meta-analytic reviews synthesized the impact of interventions specifically on attachment security (Bakermans-Kranenburg et al., 2003; Mountain et al., 2017). The first review integrated the findings of 70 studies that evaluated parent–child interventions for families with children younger than 54 months. Small but significant improvements were found in attachment quality (reduction of insecurity) and in parent sensitivity, with stronger effects found for studies that focused on parent sensitivity alone (Bakermans-Kranenburg et al., 2003). The second review included interventions for parent–child dyads with children 36 months or younger and included only four studies (Mountain et al., 2017). Results, however, were consistent with the earlier review.

Interventions developed for parent–child dyads with somewhat older children have also demonstrated positive changes in the parent–child relationship; for example, physically abusive parents who completed parent–child interaction therapy, an intervention for children 2 to 7 years of age, increased their warm, positive, and child-centered interactions and reduced toxic parent–child interactions (Chaffin et al., 2004). In a sample of parent–child dyads who completed the intervention child-parent psychotherapy, children were more likely to be securely attached than children who did not receive treatment (Toth et al., 2006).

Together, the findings support the concept of malleability in the development of the parent–child relationship and are a reason for optimism in clinical settings among families at risk for relationship disruptions.

A Key Target of Change Is Parenting Quality

Empirical and theoretical arguments both support the importance of parenting quality as key to strengthening the parent–child relationship. From a theoretical perspective, Bowlby (1969/1982) proposed that children's IWMs of the parent–child relationship shift in response to actual changes in the parent's responsiveness and subsequent parent–child interactions. In other words, by shifting the behavioral contingencies in the relationship (e.g., from "Mother rarely responds when I need her" to "Mother regularly responds when I need her"), the representation of the relationship will also gradually shift (e.g., from "I can never be sure if mother will be there when I'm distressed" to "Mother will be there when I'm distressed"), which will have a long-term influence on children's socioemotional functioning.

From an empirical perspective, as discussed in greater detail in upcoming chapters, interventions that target parenting quality have shown significant and meaningful effects in improving parent–child interactions. In the previously mentioned meta-analysis for children younger than 4½ years of age, parent–child interventions were more likely to reduce attachment insecurity when they were behaviorally based and focused only on fostering parent sensitivity (rather than including case management/support and/or a focus on parents' representations; Bakermans-Kranenburg et al., 2003). Interventions that included video feedback (allowing parents to observe their own interactions with their children and to receive constructive feedback) were more effective than interventions that did not include video feedback (e.g., provided information on child development or demonstrated infant massage). In sum, parenting quality is a critical target to improve the parent–child relationship. The following points provide a few of the questions to ask next:

- What dimensions of parenting quality are most influential in children's development, and which dimensions serve as protective factors against developmental risks?
- What mechanisms lead to positive change in parenting quality?
- How can key parenting dimensions be reliably assessed?
- What interventions have demonstrated efficacy in improving the most important aspects of parenting quality?

SUMMARY

The parent–child relationship is a multifaceted construct that begins to form within the first weeks of life and grows more complex in terms of behaviors, expressed emotions, and internal representations into early preschool years. The quality of the relationship is influenced by a learned history of parent–child interactions. Specifically, parenting quality and parents' own representations of attachment relationships contribute significantly to children's security of attachment. To date, no strong evidence exists to support a direct link between genetic makeup and attachment. Genotype may possibly relate to increased or decreased responsiveness to the caregiving environment; however, this hypothesis is in need of additional investigation.

Key Takeaways

1. *Attachment* refers not to the parent–child relationship as a whole but to a specific pair of behavioral systems that are activated in times of child distress and exploration.
2. Through repeated patterns of parent–child interactions, children form representations of others, relationships, and the self that contain cognitive and affective information. These internal representations, or IWMs, provide a set of expectations about interactions with others that guide behaviors in new interpersonal contexts.
3. Children form distinct relationships with multiple caregivers other than their biological mothers. Similar to the mother–child relationship, the father–child relationship is shaped by parenting quality. The father–child relationship influences children's functioning in multiple developmental domains. In some domains (e.g., child conduct problems) the quality of the father–child relationship is more predictive than the mother–child relationship.
4. Early caregiving experiences influence but need not determine children's developmental outcomes.

5. Although secure relationships tend to remain secure, the parent–child relationship is malleable.
6. Attachment theory proposes that improvements in parenting behaviors lead to children forming more positive IWMs of relationships and to children's improved socioemotional functioning.
7. Interventions that improve parenting quality result in improvements in attachment security specifically and the parent–child relationship generally.

Clinical Growth Questions

1. What aspects of the parent–child relationship do I currently consider important for children's healthy development?
2. How might understanding of the key antecedents of parent–child relationship quality influence my assessment and treatment of parent–child dyads?
3. To what extent do I view children's early caregiving histories (e.g., insensitive parenting, abuse, and neglect) as determining their developmental trajectories and future interpersonal relationships (e.g., that they are doomed to negative outcomes)? How does that influence my work with parent–child dyads?
4. Does my primary approach to the parent–child relationship target parent knowledge, parent and child internal structures (e.g., IWMs and internal representations), or observable parent–child interactions? Given Bowlby's prediction that improving parenting quality improves internal models and empirical evidence that improving parents' behavior improves children's functioning, how might I increase the emphasis on actual, observable parenting interactions?
5. Given the importance of multiple attachment figures to children's functioning, are there ways I might expand the focus of my interventions to include more members of each child's caregiving system?

2

Keep the First Domino Standing

How Healthy Parenting Builds Healthy Children

When Luna came in for treatment, she was distraught and afraid of harming her only child, a 2-year-old son named Marc.

"I want to be a good mom. I'm not doing that now. How am I going to do that?"

Luna, a 25-year-old single mother, reported that prior to Marc's birth, she had experienced intimate partner violence perpetrated by her boyfriend. Upon becoming pregnant, Luna left the boyfriend and moved to another state, where she had familial support. Although she was now in a safe environment, after Marc's birth she reported experiencing frequent periods of anxiety during which she would catch herself reliving moments of the abuse. Luna described herself as "zoning out" during those times, unable to complete daily tasks. Other times, she reported feeling irritable and so short-tempered that even small things, such as spilling her coffee or Marc's whining, made her angry. Luna related that Marc, who had been a sweet and easy baby, had begun to demonstrate challenging behaviors, such as frequent noncompliance, tantrums, and mild aggression.

"I'm not there for my son when I should be. I'm gonna mess him up because I'm a mess."

After assessing Luna's socioemotional functioning, Marc's functioning, and the parent–child relationship through interview, parent rating scales, and behavioral observation, the therapist identified a number of significant strengths in the dyad. Luna described her son as creative, happy, and caring.

https://doi.org/10.1037/0000304-002
Strengthening the Parent–Child Relationship in Therapy: Laying the Foundation for Healthy Development, by L. N. Niec

She expressed a desire to be a good parent and was aware that her current symptoms prevented her from meeting her son's needs. In a standardized observation of the parent–child interaction during a free play situation, Marc and Luna displayed positive affect with each other (e.g., smiles, playfulness), although their play was primarily parallel rather than interactive. When Luna asked Marc to clean up toys, he became oppositional and angry (e.g., pushing toys off the table, stomping on toys, and slapping at his mother). Luna quickly became frustrated with her son's behavior and told the examiner she didn't know what she was supposed to do. On the basis of the observation and parent rating scales, Marc's behaviors were in the clinical range of severity. Other risk factors in the relationship included Luna's history of trauma and related symptoms of posttraumatic stress disorder (PTSD) and her high level of parenting stress. The therapist recommended individual treatment for Luna to address her symptoms and an evidence-based parent–child intervention to strengthen her parenting skills and the parent–child relationship.

Luna and Marc participated in 17 sessions of treatment together, during which Luna learned how to interact with Marc in child-centered ways and to implement developmentally appropriate limits and noncorporal consequences. Luna also participated in cognitive behavior therapy with a component of exposure to reduce her PTSD symptoms, increase her understanding of the impact of trauma on her and her child's functioning, and enhance her ability to maintain a safe environment for herself and her son. Luna attended sessions consistently and participated actively in treatment. As she and Marc neared graduation from the parent–child intervention, Luna reported feeling confident in her ability to care for her son. Her interactions had become child centered and developmentally sensitive. Although Luna still experienced PTSD symptoms, she was able to provide available and consistent parenting to which Marc responded positively. His emotion regulation increased, and disruptive behaviors decreased. He actively sought his mother to share positive experiences (e.g., to share a favored toy) and when in need of comfort (e.g., when hungry or tired). Luna's responsive parenting provided a buffer for Marc against the influence of her psychopathology. After completing the parent–child intervention, Luna continued with individual therapy to address her PTSD.

In this case, a mother's insight that her symptoms were impacting her parenting was a strength that led her to seek support. Substantial evidence links parenting quality and the quality of the parent–child relationship to developmental outcomes in early childhood, adolescence, and young adulthood. Parenting quality has the potential to serve as either a protective factor or a risk factor in the developmental process. In Chapter 1 of this volume, I reviewed the early formation of the parent–child relationship and important antecedents of attachment. In this chapter, I review the concept of developmental cascades, considering the ways in which a healthy parent–child relationship may serve as a protective factor and is linked to a positive developmental trajectory. The impact of responsive and effective parenting on children's emotional, behavioral, and physical health is examined, including evidence that supportive parenting helps to buffer children against the influence of threats to healthy functioning—such as parents' mental health symptoms, family poverty, and marginalization. The chapter concludes with a look at the positive trajectories that can be initiated through parent–child interventions.

UNDERSTANDING THE IMPACT OF PARENTING ON CHILD DEVELOPMENT: DEVELOPMENTAL CASCADES

Did you ever play with dominoes as a child—setting them up in long chains, perhaps trying to contrive fancy sequences down stairs and over barriers? On the internet, one can find videos of sculptures made of hundreds of thousands of dominos—some sculptures include more than 1 million dominos. It takes many days to set up such sculptures. One complex design reportedly took 19 builders more than 1 week to create, yet it takes only an instant to knock down the first domino, causing the entire design to collapse over a span of tension-filled moments. Once every domino of the 1 million has fallen, imagine how long it takes to set them all upright again. In the process of child development, the parent–child relationship is a first domino.

The domino or cascading effect in which one condition or set of conditions push into motion a spreading chain of influence across developmental domains and systems of functioning is a *developmental cascade* (Masten & Cicchetti, 2010). Developmental cascade refers to the associated consequences that manifest across time (e.g., over different developmental stages) and/or across domains of functioning (e.g., social, behavioral, cognitive). Cascades help to explain the mechanisms by which early parent–child interactions impact functioning in later childhood, adolescence, and young adulthood. Through the pervasive influence on children's development, the parent–child relationship is an initiator of cascades. That is, the quality of parent–child interactions impacts proximal outcomes, such as children's behavior and emotion regulation, which in turn influence more distal outcomes such as adjustment to preschool, which then impact outcomes across developmental stages (e.g., school adjustment, health risk behaviors) and developmental domains (e.g., peer relationships, academic functioning; Figure 2.1).

Depending on the initiating factors, developmental cascades may be negative or positive. Parenting quality and parent–child interactions have a direct effect on certain developmental processes, such as children's level of conduct problems (Patterson et al., 1992). As illustrated by Luna's case, high-quality parenting may also act as a buffer—a protective support—against the impact of risks on children's development such as parent psychopathology and other adverse experiences (Greene et al., 2020).

The direction and shape of developmental cascades have significant implications for intervention (Doty et al., 2017; Masten & Cicchetti, 2010). By identifying early catalysts in the cascade and understanding the developmental timing of likely risk and protective factors, therapists can develop interventions

FIGURE 2.1. Example of a Developmental Cascade Across Time and Developmental Domains, Initiated by Quality of Parent–Child Interactions

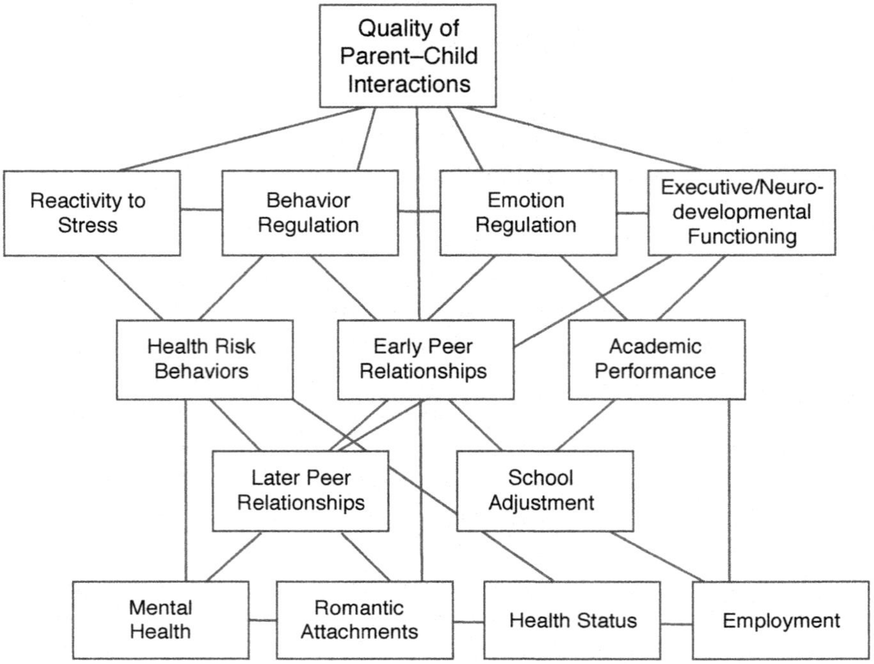

Note. Cascade links based on work of B. L. Blair et al. (2015), Diener et al. (2016), Ettekal et al. (2020), Flouri et al. (2019), Golm et al. (2020), Gonzales et al. (2017), Haller et al. (2010), Handley et al. (2017), Handley et al. (2019), T. M. Jones et al. (2016), S. Kim and Kochanska (2015), Masten et al. (2005), Murray et al. (2021), and Reyes et al. (2019).

to build resilience and reduce risk for children and families (Ettekal et al., 2020; Handley et al., 2017). As I discuss in detail in the next chapter, if negative developmental cascades continue without intervention, children are at risk to experience adverse outcomes that may have a lifelong impact. On the other hand, responsive parenting can foster a long-term positive developmental trajectory. The implication for intervention is clear: By keeping the first domino standing—enhancing parenting quality and strengthening the parent–child relationship—it is possible to reduce the chance that other key pieces in the developmental structure—cognitive, socioemotional, behavioral, neurobiological—will fall.

RESPONSIVE PARENTING: LINKS TO HEALTHY CHILD DEVELOPMENT

Much of the early work on sensitive parenting came out of the attachment literature, with a focus on identifying the types of parent behaviors that relate to secure attachment in infancy (Ainsworth, 1969; Ainsworth et al., 1978;

Atkinson et al., 2000; De Wolff & van IJzendoorn, 1997). Since that time, the terms *sensitivity, responsiveness,* and *sensitive responding* have been used beside one another, either interchangeably or with one term conceptualized as falling within the others (e.g., Bornstein et al., 2008; Caplan et al., 2019; Greene et al., 2020; Hill et al., 2008; Mesman & Emmen, 2013). In this volume, *responsiveness* refers to the broader term applied across theoretical approaches and conceptualized as a multidimensional construct encompassing a range of parenting behaviors such as warmth, validation of child emotional and behavioral needs, scaffolding, and engagement in positive parent–child interactions (see Chapter 5 for a detailed description). *Sensitivity* is used to describe the specific set of behaviors originally described by Ainsworth (1969). *Responsive and effective parenting* refers to child-centered interaction in concert with developmentally healthy and appropriate strategies for necessary limit-setting. As supported in the work on parenting styles and discussed next, children do better in a range of developmental domains when they experience parenting that includes responsive and effective interactions.

Cognitive and Academic Functioning

Cognitive functioning is a broad construct that encompasses children's general intelligence along with particular dimensions such as working memory, planning ability, and problem-solving skills. How children perform academically can also be understood as a component of cognitive functioning. Overall cognitive functioning is a foundational characteristic that contributes to an individual's success or failure in many domains of daily life. Thus, insofar as parenting and the parent–child relationship influence children's cognitive development, they impact children's lifelong well-being. In longitudinal studies from infancy to early childhood, responsive and effective parenting contributes to children's general cognitive development, with higher responsiveness predicting greater cognitive growth or higher cognitive functioning relative to children with less responsive parents (Landry et al., 2001; Malmberg et al., 2016; Merz et al., 2015, 2017; Treyvaud et al., 2016). Cognitive growth is greater if parent responsiveness is consistently high, as opposed to consistently low or inconsistent from high to low (Landry et al., 2001). It is important to note that the mother's and father's responsiveness each contributes uniquely to their child's cognitive functioning (Malmberg et al., 2016).

The quality of parent–child interactions is also associated with children's academic achievement, which is a measure of educational performance rather than ability. In a meta-analysis of 308 studies conducted from 1974 to 2015, responsive parenting, behavior control (in which parents set high, positive expectations for children's behavior), and an authoritative parenting style (in which parents display high warmth and high levels of expectations) all related to better academic achievement as measured by children's performance on standardized achievement measures or grade point average (Pinquart, 2016). Parents' harsh behavioral and psychological control and authoritarian parenting (in which parents display low warmth and high, rigid, harsh expectations) related to lower academic achievement. Also related to lower academic achievement was permissive parenting, in which there is warmth but little parental monitoring or involvement.

Executive function (EF), another aspect of cognitive development, encompasses a set of critical abilities such as working memory, impulse control, planning, and flexible thinking (Bernier et al., 2012). Although EF continues to develop through adolescence and into early adulthood, dimensions of EF can be assessed in toddlers. EF may be one of the aspects most impacted by the quality of parenting (Bernier et al., 2012). Using a range of measures of parenting quality (e.g., rating scales, Q-sorts, behavioral observation), variable longitudinal intervals (e.g., 12 months to 5 years), and assorted dimensions of EF, higher quality parenting has repeatedly related to children's higher EF (C. Blair et al., 2014). Mothers' sensitivity to their 12-month-old toddlers and support of their toddlers' autonomy in a teaching task at 15 months predicted early dimensions of EF (e.g., working memory, set shifting) at 26 months, even after controlling for toddlers' general cognitive ability (Bernier et al., 2010). Children who were more securely attached to their mothers at 12 to 24 months demonstrated better functioning on dimensions such as working memory, planning, selective attention, and categorizing 4 to 5 years later, upon entry into kindergarten (Bernier et al., 2015). The link between parent responsiveness and child executive function may be bidirectional. In a large ethnically diverse sample (71% Hispanic/Latinx, 28% African American, 1% European American) of children 3 to 5 years of age, parents' warmth, acceptance, sensitivity, and scaffolding (nonintrusive guidance and support of skills) predicted children's EF 6 months later (Merz et al., 2017). Within the same period, children's impulse control predicted positive changes in parents' responsiveness. Quality of parenting may exert different levels of influence on various dimensions of cognitive functioning. However, overall, parenting that is warm and nurturing, addresses children's emotional and behavioral needs, and encourages developmentally appropriate autonomy plays a role in the growth of children's ability to think flexibly, to control impulses, and to succeed at academic tasks.

Emotion and Behavior Regulation

Emotion regulation is a core ability that underlies an individual's capacity to cope with challenging or adverse experiences and to enjoy positive experiences (Calkins & Leerkes, 2004). When children are able to regulate their emotions, they are more likely to succeed in social situations, with peers and in school. *Behavior regulation* is a related construct that also affects children's ability to manage challenging situations, get along with peers, and maintain social expectations and rules (Batum & Yagmurlu, 2007). Behavior regulation is frequently operationalized as children's level of problem behaviors (e.g., conduct problems) or ability to follow rules. The development of emotion and behavior regulation is a critical task of early childhood. In a comprehensive meta-analysis, self-regulation in early and middle childhood predicted a host of positive outcomes across developmental domains, suggesting that regulation is a key attribute of positive developmental cascades (Robson et al., 2020). From a clinical perspective, therefore, understanding how the parent–child relationship supports the growth of self-regulation can provide insights for intervention.

As discussed in Chapter 1 of this volume, in early infancy, parents play a primary role in helping children to regulate emotion and behavior, as well as biological functions such as sleep cycles and feeding. Throughout the 1st years of life, the process becomes less dyadic and more internal to the child (Bernier et al., 2010). From an attachment theory perspective, the history of interactions between parent and child will influence a child's ability to achieve self-regulation. In fact, high-quality parenting and positive parent–child interactions have demonstrated consistent associations with children's ability to self-regulate (Buttitta et al., 2019; Groh et al., 2017; Pallini et al., 2018; Sroufe, 2005; von Suchodoletz et al., 2011). Specifically, parent sensitivity based on Ainsworth's (1969) definition as well as the broader construct of responsiveness relate to children's capacity to regulate emotion and behavior, with greater parental warmth and contingent and appropriate responding predicting children's ability to control impulsiveness, willingly comply with directions, and manage affect (Buttitta et al., 2019; Spinrad et al., 2012; von Suchodoletz et al., 2011). Similarly, an authoritative parenting style (parenting that includes moderate/high demandingness and high warmth) relates to better behavior regulation in children. This relationship has been found among samples of Black, European American, and Hispanic/Latinx families (Coley et al., 2014; LeCuyer & Swanson, 2017; Querido et al., 2002). However, the relationship between authoritarian (harsh, rigid) styles and child regulation may differ across cultures. A study of Hispanic/Latinx, Black, and European American families with children in Head Start found that parents' harsh discipline related to children's aggression only among European American families (Stacks et al., 2009). The association is not a straightforward one, as social determinants influence the ways in which parents interact with their children (Bluestone & Tamis-LeMonda, 1999). Among Black families, for example, parents may implement more demanding strategies with the goal of protecting their children from dangers related to systemic racism (Iruka, 2009; Pezzella et al., 2016).

More research is needed, particularly among families from marginalized racial and ethnic backgrounds, to understand the complex interaction of various social determinants, responsive parenting, and child outcomes. A limited attempt has been made to tease apart the dimensions of responsive parenting that play differing roles in children's development of regulation. In an investigation of the connections among fathers' parenting sensitivity, reflective functioning (the ability to think about a child's mental states), and children's emotion regulation, fathers' reflective functioning did not predict children's emotion regulation but parenting behavior—warmth, engagement, scaffolding—did (Buttitta et al., 2019). This finding highlights the importance of actual parenting behavior over mental states to promote children's well-being. Similar associations are found between attachment quality and children's emotion and behavior regulation, with secure attachment to caregivers predicting fewer externalizing behaviors—and to a lesser extent, fewer internalizing symptoms in children—even when predicting across years of development (Groh et al., 2017).

Appetite Regulation, Responsive Parenting, and Responsive Feeding Practices

In the past several decades, both the incidence and the prevalence of obesity in children have climbed precipitously. From 1975 to 2016, the number of children worldwide who met definitions for overweight or obesity (e.g., body mass index > 85th percentile for age and gender) increased 10-fold (NCD Risk-Factor Collaboration, 2017). As of 2013–2014, it was estimated that approximately one in three U.S. children between the ages of 6 and 11 years met definitions for overweight or obesity (Skinner et al., 2016). Obesity disproportionately affects children from marginalized and underprivileged backgrounds, contributing to increasing health disparities (Ogden et al., 2014). For instance, children from the most financially distressed neighborhoods experience rates of obesity up to twice that of children from affluent backgrounds (Shih et al., 2013). Obesity contributes to individuals' risk for serious and chronic negative health outcomes such as asthma, hypertension, heart disease, Type 2 diabetes, and cancer (Barlow & the Expert Committee, 2007). Further, children with obesity are more likely to experience dangerous complications from illness. Investigations during the coronavirus disease 2019 pandemic found that children with obesity who contracted the disease were more likely to require hospitalization and ventilator support and were more likely to suffer long-term effects (Nogueira-de-Almeida et al., 2020).

From a theoretical perspective, the parent–child relationship can reduce obesity risk through two primary pathways: (a) responsive parenting that fosters child self-regulation, including appetite regulation; and (b) effective parenting that supports healthy management of child behavior. In infancy, parent and child individual characteristics (e.g., temperament, psychopathology) contribute to dyadic interactions (e.g., responsiveness), which influence attachment security and parents' responsiveness in feeding (e.g., responding to child cues of hunger and satiety; Bergmeier et al., 2020). This cascade is likely to lead to children's better self-regulation generally and appetite regulation specifically, which subsequently decreases obesity risk (Saltzman et al., 2018). Increasing evidence connects responsive parenting and secure attachment with lower obesity risk in childhood (Anderson & Keim, 2016; Pinquart, 2014). In a meta-analytic review, attachment quality was significantly related to obesity in adulthood, with secure attachment related to lower adult obesity risk, suggesting a long-term relationship between the quality of the parent–child relationship and obesity risk (Diener et al., 2016). Further, authoritative parenting styles—with both high warmth and high expectations—are related to lower obesity risk, whereas authoritarian and permissive styles relate to greater risk (Kakinami et al., 2015; Loncar et al., 2021; Olvera & Power, 2010; Shloim et al., 2015). In longitudinal studies, parenting styles were a better predictor of child body mass index than specific parent feeding practices, emphasizing the importance of fostering a strong parent–child relationship reduce risk (Shloim et al., 2015).

Peer Relationships

In considering the potential positive cascade from early parent–child interactions to children's future relationships, the developmental literature and attachment theory propose that responsive parenting leads children to develop (a) better emotion and behavior regulation, which in turn relates to better social competence and peer relations; and (b) internal working models of relationships as safe, close, and satisfying, which leads to positive interactions in new relationships. Two meta-analytic reviews supported the potential cascade, finding significant, positive associations between attachment security and peer relationships, such that children with secure attachments to caregivers in early childhood demonstrated better social competence and peer relations in later childhood (Groh et al., 2017; Pallini et al., 2014). In exploring the second potential stream of the cascade, parenting in early childhood also predicts adolescents' internal working models of attachment, with responsive parenting predicting representations of secure attachment (T. G. O'Connor et al., 2019).

RESPONSIVE PARENTING BUFFERS AGAINST ADVERSE EXPERIENCES

In the past 30 years, appreciation has grown for the impact of early life experiences on functioning not only into later childhood but also through adolescence and across the life span. Although mental health providers have long appreciated this connection, since the early 1990s three particular changes have reinforced and clarified our understanding:

- Advances in brain imaging technologies have allowed for the identification of differences in the structure and function of neurological systems related to early childhood experiences.
- Growth of the science of genomics has provided evidence for epigenetic mechanisms that link early experiences with long-term and intergenerational functioning.
- Expansion of the scope of investigation has included the impact of early experiences not only on socioemotional and behavioral health but also on physical well-being and longevity.

In parallel to these advances, investigators have increasingly focused on uncovering the complex associations among individual, family, and system characteristics in an attempt to better identify risk and protective factors within developmental cascades. One of the repeated and robust findings across a range of child outcomes is the protective effects of responsive parenting against early adverse experiences (see Table 2.1).

TABLE 2.1. Protective Effects of Responsive Parenting and Healthy Parent–Child Interaction Against Adverse Experiences

Parenting/Parent–child protective factor	Risk factor	Child outcomes	Findings	Study
Parent attuned mind-mindedness	Infant difficult disposition; Parent power-assertive control	Disruptive behavior problems	• Fathers' mind-mindedness of their children prevented a negative developmental cascade from infant difficult disposition to parent power-assertive control to child conduct problems. • Children whose fathers had low mind-mindedness were more likely to experience the negative cascade.	An & Kochanska (2020)
Responsive parenting (i.e., maternal positive affect, positive engagement, emotion labeling, responsiveness to child emotions & behaviors, scaffolding)	Maternal PTSD	Disruptive behavior problems; Stress reactivity	• Responsive parenting protected children from the impact of maternal PTSD sx: – When maternal responsiveness was high, PTSD sx did not influence children's disruptive behavior and stress reactivity. – When maternal responsiveness was low, higher PTSD sx predicted higher child symptoms.	Greene et al. (2020)
Responsive parenting (i.e., sensitivity to child cues, support for child autonomy, affection/enjoyment)	Maternal power-assertive control	Disruptive behavior problems	• Parent responsiveness protected against the negative cascade from maternal power-assertive control to children's unresponsive/defiant behavior to conduct problems. • Children with highly responsive mothers did not experience the negative trajectory.	Kim & Kochanska (2015)
Secure attachment	Maternal depression	Systemic inflammation	• Secure attachment protected children of depressed mothers from higher levels of salivary indicators of inflammation.	Measelle & Ablow (2018)

Supportive parenting (i.e., encouragement, involvement, effective communication)	Family poverty	Connectivity in neural networks related to executive functioning and emotion regulation	• Supportive parenting in childhood protected young adults from the impact of poverty on connectivity among neural networks related to cognitive and emotion regulation. • More years living in poverty was associated with less connectivity for young adults who had parents with low supportiveness, but not for those with supportive parents.	Brody et al. (2019)
Participation in a parenting intervention designed to foster supportive parenting	Family poverty	Brain volume of regions associated with stress reactivity, memory, and emotion regulation	• Parents' participation in a parenting intervention when children were 11 years old protected against the impact of poverty on child brain development as measured at age 25 years. • Among children whose parents did not participate in supportive parenting intervention, years in poverty predicted smaller brain volume in amygdalar and hippocampal regions. • Poverty did not predict brain volume for individuals whose parents participated in the parenting intervention.	Brody, Gray, et al. (2017)
Responsive parenting (e.g., child-centered interactions)	Early childhood adversity (e.g., neglect, exposure to DV, parent substance abuse, inadequate housing)	Telomere length (genetic marker of chronic stress; longer = lower stress)	• Parental responsiveness buffered children from the impact of adversity on telomere length. • High parental responsiveness was associated with longer telomeres for children at high risk but not for children with low risk.	Asok et al. (2013)

Note. DV = domestic violence; PTSD = posttraumatic stress disorder; sx = symptoms.

Socioemotional and Behavioral Outcomes

When examining children's socioemotional and behavioral functioning, such as quality of mental health, substance use, and peer relationship quality, responsive parenting appears to buffer against the impact of several types of adversity. Among a sample of financially stressed mothers and their young children, a negative developmental cascade linked parents' power-assertive control (e.g., forceful, physical control) at 30 months to children's unresponsive and adversarial behaviors at 33 months and subsequently to mothers' reports of children's conduct problems at 40 months (S. Kim & Kochanska, 2015). In other words, parents' use of higher levels of forceful control led to increases in observed levels of child adversarial behaviors, which led to more conduct problems by the time the children were 3½ years of age. However, this developmental cascade occurred for children whose mothers had low or average levels of responsiveness. Children whose mothers were highly responsive did not experience the cascade effect. Highly responsive parenting provided protections against the negative effects initiated by use of excessive control.

Another dimension of parenting relevant to responsiveness is *mind-mindedness,* which reflects parents' ability to consider their children's emotional, behavioral, and physical perspectives. Mind-mindedness has been related to parent sensitivity and attachment (J. E. Miller et al., 2019); thus, it may also have the potential to buffer against the impact of power-assertive control on child conduct problems. In a study of children with difficult dispositions in infancy, the children whose fathers had few expressions of mind-mindedness were more likely to experience a negative cascade that led from the infant's difficult disposition to the parent's power-assertive control to the child's level of conduct problems (An & Kochanska, 2020). However, children who had difficult dispositions and fathers with appropriate mind-mindedness were protected from experiencing the negative developmental cascade.

As observed in the case of Luna and Marc, parent psychopathology can have a detrimental impact on both parenting ability and children's mental health, particularly as related to child emotion and behavior regulation (S. H. Goodman et al., 2011; Greene et al., 2020; J. E. McCabe, 2014). Yet the children of parents who maintain responsive and effective interactions do not experience the level of negative impact of their parents' psychopathology. For instance, warm, responsive parenting protected children against the influence of their parents' depression on their internalizing symptoms, peer relations, and conduct problems (Boyd & Waanders, 2013; Brennan et al., 2003; Compas et al., 2010; Leckman-Westin et al., 2009). Among mothers experiencing symptoms of PTSD, responsive parenting that included positive emotion, labeling of child's emotional expressions, responsiveness to child's emotions and behaviors, warm engagement, and scaffolding protected children from the influence of the mother's symptoms on the child's experiences of stress and levels of disruptive behavior (Greene et al., 2020). Children with fathers with alcoholism were less likely to demonstrate disruptive behaviors when they had secure attachments with their mothers (Edwards et al., 2006).

Close caregiving relationships promote positive developmental cascades from childhood into adulthood as well (T. M. Jones et al., 2016). In a sample of 808 individuals followed over approximately 23 years, children who experienced closer family relationships and less conflict at 10 to 12 years of age reported fewer symptoms of anxiety and depression and lower risk for substance abuse in early adolescence (13–14 years), experienced closer romantic relationships at 24 to 27 years of age, and had greater overall positive functioning at 30 to 33 years of age.

Still focusing on children's socioemotional and behavioral outcomes, the parent–child relationship has a protective effect against not only individual and dyadic risk factors but also environmental risk factors such as poverty. Children living in impoverished environments are more likely to experience internalizing symptoms and conduct problem behaviors (Letourneau et al., 2013). However, parenting is an important factor that mediates that link (Baker & Brooks-Gunn, 2020). An investigation of outcomes of parent–child interventions that increased responsive parenting among families from low-income backgrounds found that children experienced fewer mental health problems and fewer conduct problems subsequent to the intervention (Brody et al., 2004; Morris et al., 2017). Specifically, children who participated with their parents demonstrated fewer risky sexual and substance use behaviors and were more likely to accept their parents' influence (Brody et al., 2004).

In summary, responsive and effective parenting buffers children from the negative impact of some types of adverse experiences on socioemotional and behavioral outcomes, such as the development of conduct problems and experiences of stress and anxiety. The buffering effect has been observed against risk factors related to parent characteristics such as the use of negative control and psychopathology, and against environmental risks such as poverty.

Neurobiological and Genetic Outcomes

Responsive parenting has also been associated with neurobiological and genetic outcomes. As described in the following sections, high-quality parenting acts as a buffer against the impact of some adverse experiences on brain development and cellular aging.

Brain Development

Poverty is an environmental risk factor with the potential to have a pervasive and lasting impact not only on children's socioemotional and behavioral outcomes but also on neurodevelopment (S. B. Johnson et al., 2016; P. Kim et al., 2013). As with the work related to behavioral outcomes, however, it appears that responsive and effective parenting is a mechanism through which the risk associated with poverty may be ameliorated (Brody, Gray, et al., 2017; Perry et al., 2019). Researchers conducted a 12- to 14-year follow-up of children whose families had participated in a seven-session parenting intervention when their children were 11 years old. Findings revealed that high levels of supportive parenting buffered children from the impact of poverty on brain development. That is, the more years that individuals had lived in poverty, the more likely they were to demonstrate decreased hippocampal and amygdalar volume (areas of the brain associated with memory, stress reactivity, emotion regulation) and decreased executive and emotion-regulation neural-network activity. However, individuals who had experienced high levels of supportive parenting did not show the negative effects on either brain structure or neural network function (Brody, Gray, et al., 2017; Brody et al., 2019). This work is relatively recent, and replication is needed; yet the potential for positive change in the face of ongoing adversity is deeply compelling. For the cost of a brief parenting intervention, children from severely impoverished backgrounds experienced protective effects that will remain throughout their lives.

Cellular Aging

The impact of parenting on children's physiological stress response has primarily been examined by evaluating the activity of children's hypothalamic–pituitary–adrenocortical (HPA) axis, which is one of the two major stress response systems (Gunnar & Quevedo, 2007). Although a number of investigations of HPA axis activity have demonstrated that parenting quality influences children's concurrent physiological response to stress, a review of the literature from 1970 through 2017 did not find a relationship between parenting and later HPA axis activity (Hackman et al., 2018). Other domains (e.g., genetic studies) may provide perspectives on the lasting influence of stress and adversity on children's physiology and the potential buffering role of parenting in that relationship.

Telomeres are sequences of nucleotides at the end of the chromosome that protect the DNA from damage during replication. With ongoing cell replication, telomeres grow shorter, until the cell is no longer able to divide; thus, telomere length has been considered a measure of cell aging and increased disease risk (National Human Genome Research Institute, n.d.; K. K. Ridout et al., 2018). Only in the past decade has adversity in early childhood been investigated as a potential contributor to reduced telomere length; however, the number of investigations has rapidly increased (Drury et al., 2012; S. J. Ridout et al., 2015; Shalev et al., 2013). A review of existing studies through 2016 found a significant, moderately sized relationship between adversity and telomere length, with more severe adversity related to shorter telomeres (K. K. Ridout et al., 2018). The implication for children experiencing early adversity is increased risk for disease and early biological aging. To date, two studies on telomere length suggest that attachment and parenting quality may protect against the physiological impact of adversity (Asok et al., 2013; Dagan et al., 2018). The first study included two samples of young children ($M = 4.9$ years, $SD = 0.59$), one group considered by child welfare services to be at high risk for maltreatment and the other at low risk (Asok et al., 2013). Parent responsiveness, measured through observation of parent–child interactions, included warm, engaged, child-centered parent behavior. Children of high-risk status had significantly shorter telomeres than children of low-risk status, even when controlling for family income and minority status. However, among children in the high-risk group, parent responsiveness related to telomere length such that greater responsiveness related to longer telomeres. Consistent with this protective effect, the second study explored the link between early adversity, attachment representations, and telomere length in young adults (Dagan et al., 2018). Number of adverse experiences in childhood related to shorter telomere length for individuals with insecure-dismissing representations but not for those with secure attachment representations.

GENDER AND SEXUALITY MINORITY PARENTS AND CHILDREN

Children and youth who identify as a gender or sexuality minority or who have parents who identify as being within the lesbian, gay, bisexual, transgender, queer/questioning, and others (LGBTQ+) community are at particular risk for experiencing stigma, discrimination, isolation, and victimization (P. C. McCabe et al., 2013; McGuire et al., 2010; Myers et al., 2020). A review of the current research on victimization in the school setting found that LGBTQ+ identification was related to a range of types of youth victimization, including specific gender-based and homophobic-based bullying, violent and sexual victimization, theft, and general bullying (Myers et al., 2020). Transgender identification was most strongly associated with victimization. The relationship between identifying as part of a sexuality minority group and victimization was not weaker in more recent studies (i.e., it does not appear that stigma against LGBTQ+ youth is lessening in the school setting). Children and youth whose parents identify as LGBTQ+ are also more likely to be exposed to stigmatization, peer rejection, and discrimination, regardless of children's identification (Trub et al., 2017; van Gelderen et al., 2013).

The threat or experience of victimization, rejection, and other stressors related to identifying as part of a sexuality or gender minority group places children at higher risk for experiencing negative socioemotional and physical health outcomes. In samples of children with same-sex parents, homophobic stigmatization has been related to child psychological functioning, self-esteem, level of behavior problems, and life satisfaction (Bos et al., 2008; Bos & van Balen, 2008; van Gelderen et al., 2013). Youth who identify as LGBTQ+ have significantly higher rates of depression (Pearson & Wilkinson, 2013) and nonsuicidal self-injury (NSSI; R. T. Liu et al., 2019) than heterosexual and/or cisgender peers, with lifetime prevalence rates of NSSI for sexual minority individuals at 24.68% and for gender minority individuals at 46.61% compared with 14.67% for heterosexual and/or cisgender individuals. The rates of NSSI have not dropped over time. Suicidal thoughts and behavior are also more prevalent among sexual and gender minority youth (Hatchel et al., 2021).

Parent–Child Relationship: A Protective Factor for Sexuality Minority Children and Youth

Although elevated risk for children and youth who are LGBTQ+ or children with LGBTQ+ parents has been documented, more recently efforts have turned to uncovering protective factors within the family system that might buffer some of the internal (e.g., internalized homophobia) and external (e.g., discrimination, victimization) risks associated with sexuality and gender minority status. Supportive parenting and healthy attachment have both been implicated as protective factors. Children of same-sex parents are as likely as children of heterosexual parents to have positive and securely attached relationships with their caregivers (Fedewa et al., 2015; McConnachie et al., 2020). In a study of adoptive gay, lesbian, and heterosexual parents, gay fathers displayed more responsiveness to their children than heterosexual parents (Golombok et al., 2014). Such responsiveness may help to counter homophobic attitudes and discrimination. Among a sample of adolescents with lesbian parents, compatibility with their parents reduced the negative impact of stigmatization on life satisfaction (van Gelderen et al., 2013).

Youth who identify as LGBTQ+ may not experience relationships with their parents that are as positive as that of heterosexual and/or cisgender adolescents (Pearson & Wilkinson, 2013). However, parent support remains related to child and adolescent well-being. In a large representative sample of children in Grades 7 to 12, same-sex attracted youth reported less closeness with their parents than other-sex attracted youth (Pearson & Wilkinson, 2013). However, youth who experienced more closeness, support, and involvement from their parents experienced fewer depressive symptoms. Similarly, in an ethnically diverse group of adolescents who identified as LGBTQ+ (56% Black/African American, 16% Multiracial, 13% Latinx, and 13% White), attachment to parents related to later level of mental health symptoms, with stronger attachment related to fewer symptoms (Starks et al., 2015). Quality of attachment to parents was indirectly associated with quality of later relationships through both adolescents' mental health and the quality of peer relationships such that stronger parent attachment predicted stronger peer attachment and better mental health, which were associated with more satisfaction with later romantic relationships. Finally, parental acceptance also acts as a buffer against negative mental health outcomes for sexuality minority youth such that same-sex attraction and gender nonconformity do not predict distress and social anxiety for youth who experience high levels of parental acceptance (van Beusekom et al., 2015).

Internal working models of attachment may also play a role in moderating the impact of discrimination. For adults in same-sex relationships, experiences of discrimination led to higher levels of internalized homophobia, which were associated with negative attitudes toward children of same-sex parents. However, these associations were not significant for individuals with more healthy attachment models. In a sample of transgender individuals, internalized transphobia was associated with lower life satisfaction only for those who reported high attachment anxiety (Cronin et al., 2019).

The research on parent–child relationships among youth who identify as LGBTQ+ and children with LGBTQ+ parents has limitations, such as a focus on questionnaire and survey data over interview or behavioral observation measures to assess relationship quality. Existing studies suggest that LGBTQ+ youth face risks to the parent–child relationship but that the quality of the relationship still plays an important role in individuals' well-being. For children experiencing discrimination, rejection, and victimization because of their or their parents' sexuality or gender minority status, interventions to strengthen the parent–child relationship may be particularly relevant to prevent negative socioemotional and behavioral outcomes.

CLINICAL IMPLICATIONS OF THE DEVELOPMENTAL LITERATURE

Parent–Child Interventions: Promotors of Positive Developmental Cascades

Responsive and effective parenting clearly plays a core role in children's development, with the power to set in motion a cascade of positive effects across time and developmental domains. Parenting interventions that increase responsive parenting and improve the parent–child relationship therefore have the potential to serve as initiators of positive developmental cascades. These cascades not only impact children's functioning over time but also foster gains within parents, broader family systems, and potentially within communities (Doty et al., 2017; Gonzalez & Jones, 2016; Landry et al., 2006; Purewal Boparai et al., 2018).

To illustrate cascades that may be stimulated by effective intervention, consider two evidence-based parent–child treatment programs. The first intervention, Parent–Child Interaction Therapy (PCIT), is an attachment and behaviorally based transdiagnostic intervention for families with children from ages 2 to 7 developed to increase responsive parenting, strengthen the parent–child relationship, and reduce child disruptive behaviors (Eyberg & Funderburk, 2011; Niec, 2018a). The second intervention, the Strong African American Families program (SAAF), is a parent–child intervention for families with preadolescent children. This program is designed to increase protective factors such as nurturing and involved parenting, to reduce youth engagement in health-risk behaviors (e.g., substance use, sexual promiscuity), and to build children's resilience in response to racism and discrimination (Brody et al., 2004).

Outcome studies of PCIT and SAAF support positive cascade effects for parents, children, and communities. Figures 2.2 and 2.3 depict tested and hypothesized outcomes for each intervention. Parents who participate in PCIT demonstrate significant increases in their responsive and effective parenting and their ability to regulate their emotions (Lieneman et al., 2020; Niec et al., 2016; Rothenberg et al., 2019; Schuhmann et al., 1998). Physically abusive parents who complete PCIT demonstrate fewer toxic parent–child interactions and significantly reduced recidivism rates (Chaffin et al., 2004). Subsequent to improvements in responsive and effective parenting, children who participate in PCIT exhibit increases in emotion regulation and decreases in externalizing (e.g., defiance, aggression) and internalizing (e.g., anxiety, withdrawal)

FIGURE 2.2. Potential Positive Developmental Cascade Initiated by Parent–Child Interaction Therapy (PCIT)

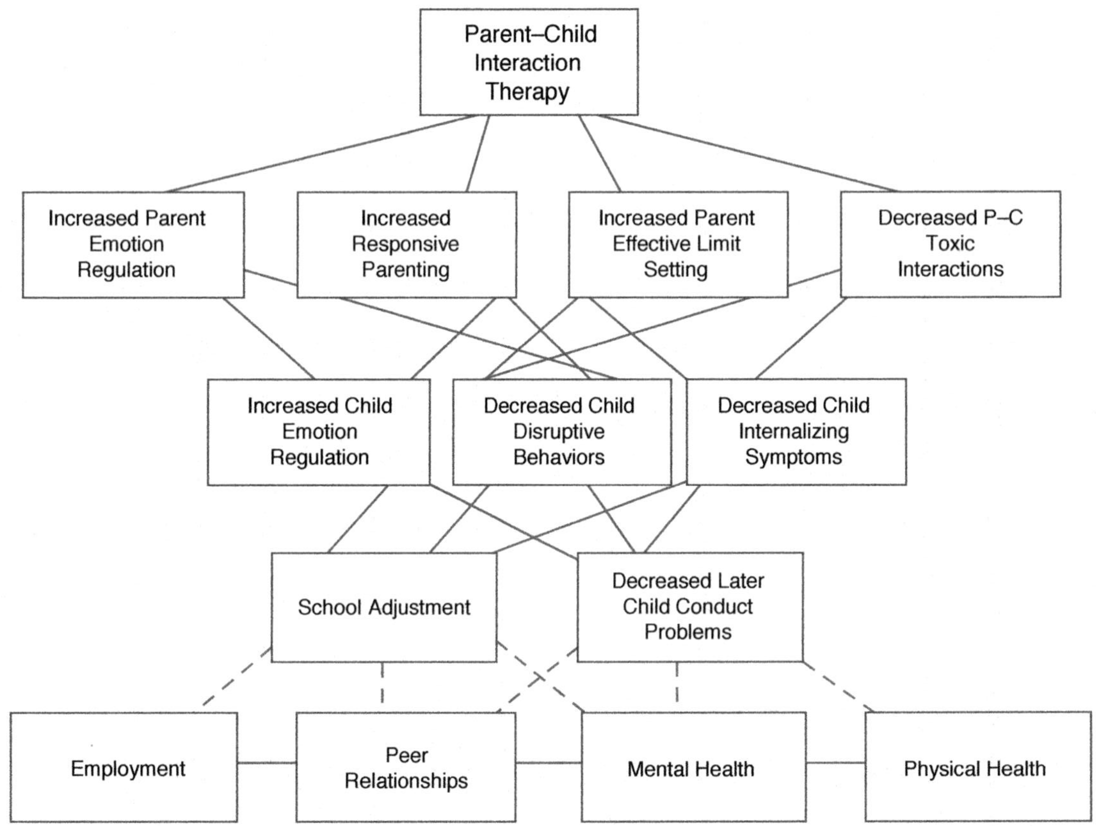

Note. Dashed lines represent theoretically based outcomes not yet tested. See Chaffin et al. (2004), Funderburk et al. (1998), Hood and Eyberg (2003), Lieneman et al. (2020), Niec et al. (2016), Rothenberg et al. (2019), Schuhmann et al. (1998), and Zimmer-Gembeck et al. (2019). P–C = Parent–Child.

FIGURE 2.3. Potential Positive Developmental Cascade Initiated by the Strong African American Families Program (SAAF)

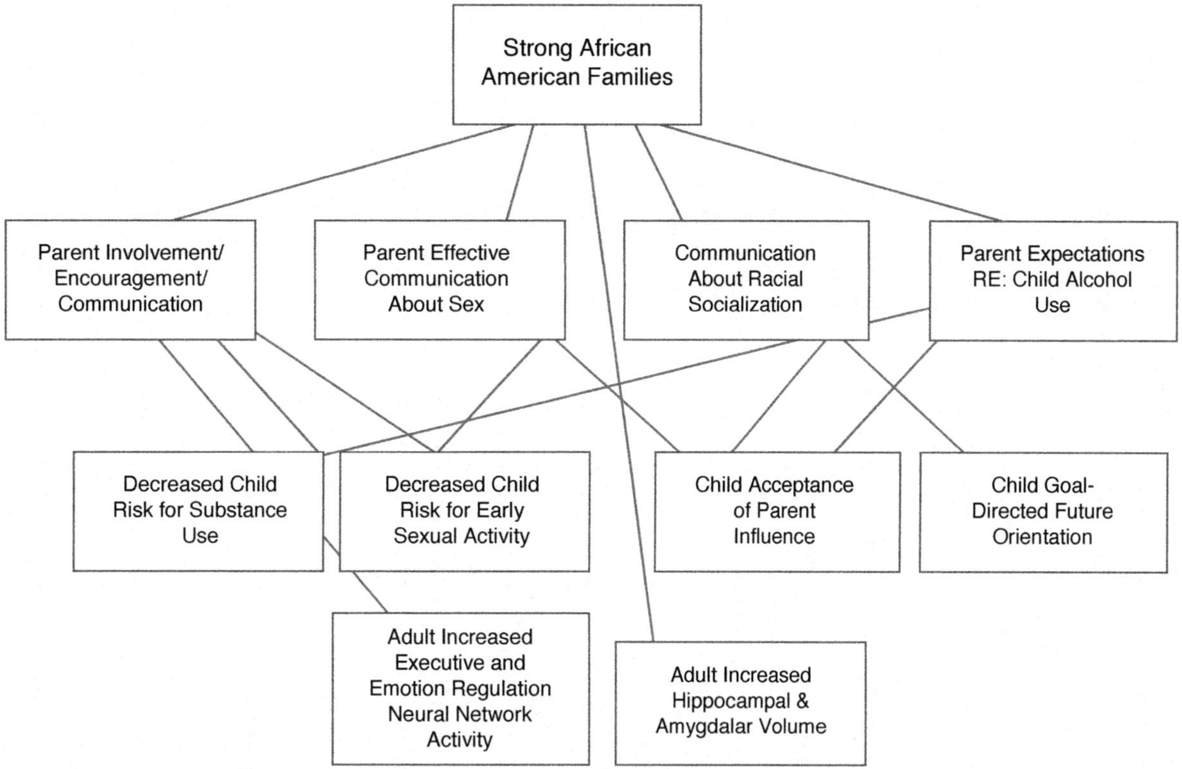

Note. Based on information from Brody and colleagues (Brody et al., 2004; Brody, Gray, et al., 2017; Brody et al., 2019).

symptoms (Lieneman et al., 2020; Niec et al., 2016; Schuhmann et al., 1998). Cascading across developmental domains and across time, children also demonstrate improvements in school functioning (Funderburk et al., 1998), and 4 to 6 years later they exhibit less risk for conduct problems (Hood & Eyberg, 2003). Subsequent outcomes for parents include an increased sense of parenting efficacy and decreased stress (Niec et al., 2016; Schuhmann et al., 1998). On the bases of theoretical models, these positive changes in school, family, and individual functioning are likely to be associated with additional positive outcomes such as later mental health, fewer health risk behaviors, and positive peer relationships.

The SAAF intervention differs from PCIT in that it targets children later in childhood, was developed particularly for Black/African American families living in rural and impoverished environments, and focuses on increasing parent supportiveness generally and on health risk behaviors specifically. Families who participate in SAAF also demonstrate meaningful and long-term positive changes associated with the intervention and with increased supportive parenting (Brody et al., 2004; Brody, Gray, et al., 2017; Brody, Yu, et al., 2017; Brody et al., 2019). Parents who completed SAAF became more involved with their children and demonstrated more supportiveness and more direct communication about risky sexual behavior, expectations about alcohol use, and adaptive coping with racial discrimination (Brody et al., 2004). Children who participated with their parents demonstrated fewer risky sexual and substance use behaviors and were more likely to accept their parents' influence. As discussed earlier, follow-up of these children as young adults (12–14 years later, at participants' age 25 years) found better outcomes in regard to brain structure and function in the context of environmental risk factors related to poverty (Brody, Gray, et al., 2017; Brody et al., 2019). The mechanisms linking supportive parenting to better neural development in the face of environmental risk have not yet been tested among participants of SAAF, but the positive developmental cascade initiated by the parenting intervention is one that will have lifelong impact on individuals' functioning.

SUMMARY

The parent–child relationship and responsive parenting represent key initiating factors for children's healthy development, influencing well-being across domains (e.g., socioemotional, behavioral) and across developmental stages (e.g., infancy through adolescence and young adulthood). Responsive parenting has the potential to promote positive developmental cascades, even in the presence of serious risk factors occurring at the individual (e.g., parent psychopathology), family (e.g., domestic violence), and systemic (e.g., poverty, discrimination) levels. Child outcomes that are influenced by responsive parenting include cognitive, emotional, behavioral, interpersonal, and physiological domains. Parenting may impact these domains concurrently and over time. In cases where child or family risk is high, parent–child interventions have the potential to initiate positive developmental cascades by fostering responsive and effective parenting. Reducing the negative impact of chronic and pervasive stressors on children's development can alter an individual's lifelong trajectory.

Key Takeaways

1. Parenting quality has both direct and indirect effects on children's healthy development.
2. Developmental cascades can be initiated by one or a set of conditions and may impact child functioning across developmental stages and domains.
3. Responsive and effective parenting impacts children's cognitive, socio-emotional, and neurobiological functioning in ways that have lifelong positive consequences.
4. System-level risk factors such as pervasive poverty and systemic discrimination are unlikely to be resolved soon; however, increasing responsive parenting and strengthening the parent–child relationship can buffer against some of the negative impact of such adverse experiences on children's well-being.
5. Effective parent–child interventions have the potential to initiate positive developmental cascades, with implications for parent, child, and family functioning.

Clinical Growth Questions

1. How can an understanding of the links between parent–child interactions and healthy child development help me to form a strength-based conceptualization of families who are experiencing many risk factors?
2. At what point in the developmental cascade do I typically intervene with parents and children? How might I intervene earlier to prevent negative outcomes from becoming pervasive?
3. What are some common risk factors faced by families with whom I work, and how might strengthening parenting quality help to buffer children against the adverse effects of those risks?
4. In what ways do I currently support the parent–child relationships of families with sexuality or gender minority parents or youth? Are there ways I can better address the risks faced by LGBTQ+ families?
5. Considering the type of parent–child interventions I currently implement, what might a positive developmental cascade look like for a family?

3

Risk and Disruption in the Parent–Child Relationship

The biology of toxic stress tells us that relational health, or the ability to form and maintain safe, stable, and nurturing relationships is the antidote to significant child adversity.

—GARNER AND SAUL (2018)

On a hot summer evening, a police officer discovered 3-year-old Rose walking barefoot and alone down a busy street. Rose told the officer she was going to her auntie's house because "Daddy hurt Mommy." Upon investigation, the bodies of Rose's parents were found in their home. Her father had killed his wife and then himself.

Rose had no history of involvement with child protective services, nor had law enforcement or any formal support system been involved with her parents. However, interviews with Rose and her aunt revealed that Rose had likely witnessed violence against her mother intermittently for much of her life.

The court placed Rose into the care of her maternal aunt and uncle, caregivers she knew well. By the time the family could be seen for an evaluation, nearly 6 months had passed. Her aunt and uncle reported that Rose was experiencing significant emotional and behavioral issues. She was unable to tolerate separation from her caregivers, especially her aunt, crying when her aunt left her sight, even just to go into another room in the house. She became observably distressed at the occurrence of loud noises (e.g., vacuum cleaner, loud car engine) and would run to escape the noise when possible or plead for it to go away if not. Nightmares disrupted her sleep three to five

https://doi.org/10.1037/0000304-003
Strengthening the Parent–Child Relationship in Therapy: Laying the Foundation for Healthy Development, by L. N. Niec

times a week, and she could not return to sleep without her aunt or uncle in the room. Although she appeared to have a positive relationship with her uncle and to feel safe with him (e.g., turning to him for help, for comfort when frightened, or for play), she would often startle if he stood too quickly or laughed loudly. When asked to discontinue a preferred activity or transition to a new setting (e.g., go with caregivers to the grocery store), Rose displayed a rapid escalation of her anger and frustration. She expressed her anger in destructive tantrums, during which she would shriek curse words, throw chairs, and flail her arms at others' faces to scratch at them. Rose's aunt and uncle, who were dealing with their own grief over the murder and suicide of their family members, expressed deep concern for Rose but also uncertainty about how to help her.

After a comprehensive assessment, Rose was diagnosed with posttraumatic stress disorder. The family was referred to a parent–child intervention as a first step to provide Rose with a safe, stable environment; to increase her caregivers' understanding of the impact of exposure to violence on children's physiological, emotional, and behavioral functioning; and to increase their abilities to provide Rose with responsive and effective parenting.

Experiences of abuse, neglect, and exposure to violence can cause disruptions in the parent–child relationship and have short- and long-term consequences for children's functioning. This chapter begins with a taxonomy of stress responses and a framework of development that provides a model for the complex influences of a child's environment and biology on long-term behaviors and health. Then I discuss three key sources of toxic stress that strain or disrupt the parent–child relationship and have been shown to contribute to negative developmental cascades. A closing discussion of the clinical implications of the developmental literature sets the stage for the next section of the book, which considers effective assessment and intervention strategies through which clinicians can reduce risk and build healthy parent–child relationships.

IDENTIFYING TOXIC STRESS

The experience of stressful events in early childhood is not necessarily detrimental. When children have adequate relational support, the experience of temporary mild to moderate stressors can be valuable, allowing children to develop a range of healthy coping skills and to build their confidence in the ability to manage challenges. Whether a stress experience is categorized as something beneficial or damaging depends in part on the characteristics of the event but more so on the individual's existing relational support and physiological responses to the event (National Scientific Council on the Developing Child, 2005/2014). *Positive stress* causes a brief and relatively mild increase in the body's stress response (e.g., elevated heart rate). Events that might evoke positive stress in childhood include being introduced to a new peer group, undergoing a routine medical or dental procedure, and approaching a large unfamiliar dog (Table 3.1).

TABLE 3.1. Taxonomy of Stress Responses

Type of stress	Examples of potential stressors	Available relational support	Physiological stress response	Physiological recovery
Positive	First day of school Visit to the dentist Performing in a play	Adequate	Brief increases in heart rate and stress-related hormones	Yes
Tolerable	Death of a loved one Car accident Parent divorce	Adequate	More severe and longer elevations	Yes, over time
Toxic	Chronic child maltreatment Severe economic hardship Exposure to violence	Inadequate	Lasting elevations: Some aspects of the stress-response system may not return to baseline functioning	May have lasting impact on stress-response, brain structure and function, and other biological systems

Note. Based on information from the National Scientific Council on the Developing Child (2005/2014).

In the case of positive stress, children have the relational support—particularly responsive caregiver support—to cope with the event, and the physiological response quickly abates. *Tolerable stress*, on the other hand, causes a more extreme activation of the physiological stress response, which may require a longer period to return to baseline function. Stress that is categorized as tolerable is still within a child's range of coping, when supported by existing caregiving relationships. Experiences that might cause a tolerable stress response include a car accident, the loss of a loved one, or an acute environmental loss (e.g., house fire).

Different from positive and tolerable stress, a *toxic stress* response overwhelms a child's coping mechanisms and may cause a severe and lasting physiological reaction. If the experience of toxic stress is chronic (e.g., ongoing child abuse), then the body's stress response systems may remain activated and in fact may become the new baseline. This elevated baseline suggests that children experience a heightened level of arousal, even in times of low threat; therefore, future events may provoke emotional, behavioral, and physiological responses more quickly and at levels that appear excessive compared with the responses of other children (National Scientific Council on the Developing Child, 2005/2014; Shonkoff et al., 2012; Shonkoff & Richmond, 2009). Imagine, for example, children carrying cups of hot water that represent the level of activation of their stress response systems. For children who have not experienced toxic stress, the cups contain small amounts of hot water poured in by minor stressors such as falling on the playground, fighting with a friend, or receiving a vaccination. Those stressors pass swiftly, the hot water cools down, and the cup never (or rarely) overflows. In contrast, children who have experienced events such as exposure to violence or chronic physical abuse may be carrying cups already half filled with hot water, even if the stressors have been removed. The same minor stressors their peers experience with little physiological, emotional, and behavioral distress may cause the hot water to spill over and burn them. This constant activation of the body's stress systems may also lead to strain on developing organs and to changes in the structure and function of the brain (C. Blair & Raver, 2016; Callaghan & Tottenham, 2016; Shonkoff et al., 2012).

PLASTICITY THROUGHOUT DEVELOPMENT

For centuries, philosophers, naturalists, and developmental scientists have debated whether human development is influenced more strongly by innate characteristics with us from birth—identified in the 19th century as *genetic composition*—or by the environment. Decades of twin studies have focused on specifying the proportions of the contributions of genotype and environmental factors, such as family structure and dynamics, on a range of outcomes from intelligence to conduct problems to personality traits and physical health. Until relatively recently, the contribution of genotype was seen as largely immutable: DNA sequences were believed to define the genetic contribution to our functioning. Theories gradually evolved that allowed for an interaction between genetics and the environment: Diathesis–stress theories of disease risk, for example, proposed that the combined influence of inherited genetic vulnerability and environmental stressors could lead to disorders such as schizophrenia (Rosenthal, 1963); yet, the mechanisms of the proposed gene-stress interaction remained unknown.

Only in the past few decades have we begun to identify genetic mechanisms that link early stress experiences with changes in the developmental process; that is, through the influence of early experiences—particularly early parent–child interactions—on the regulation of gene activity, there is a subsequent impact on the structure and function of biological systems (Kundakovic & Champagne, 2015; Figure 3.1).

Animal models have provided evidence that early maternal caregiving influences genetic expression in offspring through epigenetic changes that either activate or silence certain genes (Weaver et al., 2004, 2006). In studies of laboratory rodents, differences in mothers' nurturing of their offspring (low or high maternal grooming of pups) have been associated with differences in gene expression related to brain development. Separation from mothers—and, in biparental species, separation from fathers—lead to stress behaviors in the offspring (e.g., exaggerated stress responses, anxious behaviors, disruptions in playful behaviors), which in some cases subsequently impacted the expression of particular genes related to the hypothalamic–pituitary–adrenal axis and

FIGURE 3.1. From Toxic Stress to Brain Structure and Function: The Epigenetic Link

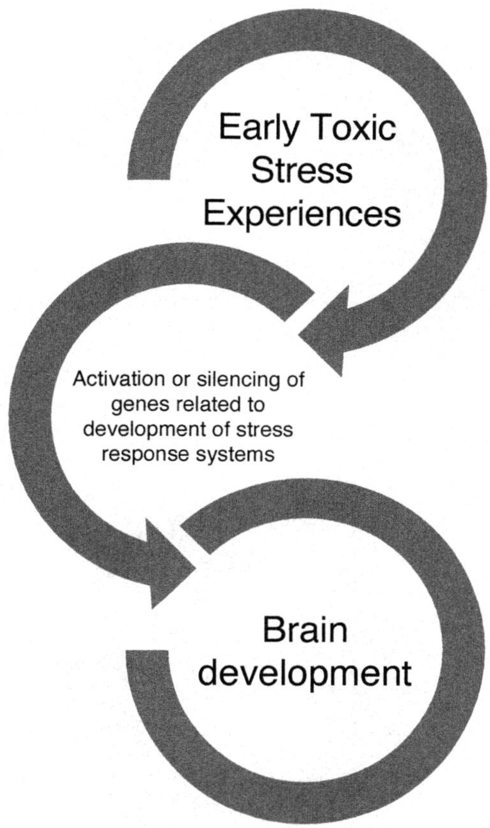

in others related to neurobiological changes (Callaghan & Tottenham, 2016; Kundakovic & Champagne, 2015; Shonkoff et al., 2012).

The ecobiodevelopmental (EBD) model offers a framework derived from diathesis–stress theory that encompasses the complex gene–environment interactions that influence the developmental process (Figure 3.2; Shonkoff et al., 2012).

The EBD model conceptualizes a child's environment or *ecology* as inclusive of social, emotional, and physical characteristics (e.g., parenting quality, nutritional access, physical safety), whereas biology includes genetic and epigenetic characteristics and processes. The EBD model is enhanced by the integration of ecological systems theory, which is included in Figure 3.2 (Bronfenbrenner, 2005). Bronfenbrenner's (2005) model expands the conceptualization of ecology, which is necessary if we are to identify the relevant factors that may promote resilience or increase risk through epigenetic processes. The ecological systems framework distinguishes four levels within which a child functions: microsystems, mesosystems, exosystems, and macrosystems. At the microsystem level, the child interacts with others (e.g., parents, teachers, peers)

FIGURE 3.2. Integration of the Ecobiodevelopmental Model and Ecological Systems Theory

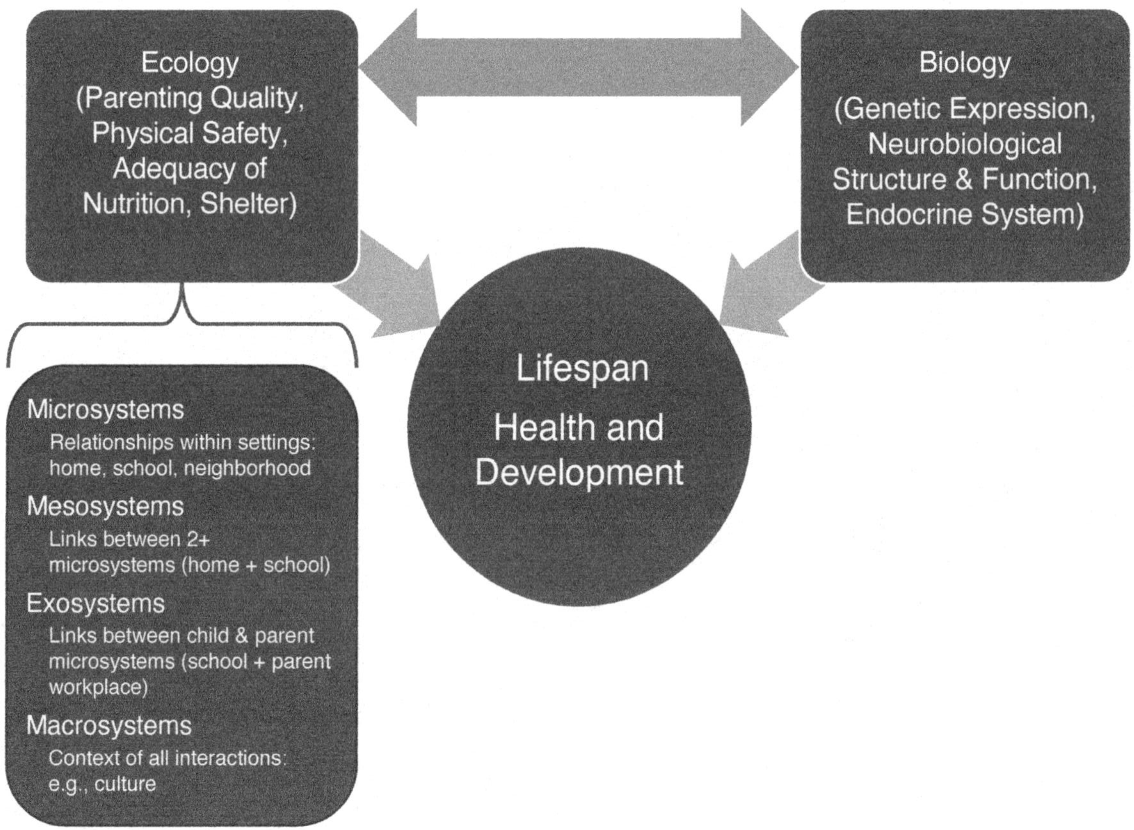

Note. See Shonkoff et al. (2012) and Bronfenbrenner (1992/2005).

within the context of various physical settings (e.g., home, school, neighborhood). Mesosystems and exosystems represent the processes that affect the child when various microsystems interact. For example, the mesosystem includes the influence of interactions between home and school on a child: What kind of communications occur between parent and teacher? How do parents' harsh discipline practices impact child functioning at school? Similarly, exosystems also include processes between microsystems, with at least one microsystem that does not include the child; for example, interactions between home and the parent's workplace would be part of the exosystem. At this level of ecology, we can ask questions such as the following: How does parent stress in the workplace relate to their capacity to provide responsive parenting? How do government policy decisions affect a child's ability to receive needed mental health services? Finally, at the macrosystem level, we consider the impact of culture (e.g., geographic, ethnic/racial, religious) and history (e.g., historical traumas) on the child through the influence on lower levels of systems.

The EBD model proposes that the characteristics of a child's ecology act upon epigenetic and neurodevelopmental processes and that each subsequently contributes to long-term cognitive, socioemotional, behavioral, and physical health. In other words, genotype is not fixed but may change in response to environmental pressures at different, sensitive points in development. This plasticity implies that adverse experiences in childhood may increase vulnerability for certain negative outcomes, particularly at critical developmental periods. However, it also allows for the possibility that negative influences may be reversed.

Before a discussion of the impact of specific stressors on development, it is important to note limitations to the existing literature on the impact of toxic stress. First, although animal models of the impact of toxic stress on genetic expression provide clues to relationships that may exist in humans, they cannot simply be superimposed on our understanding of child development. Further, because it is not possible to conduct controlled experimental studies of early adversity on human gene expression, we cannot assume causality. Correlational studies, such as those linking harsh parenting to increased child stress response, do not allow us to conclude that one factor or set of factors has caused another. Instead, for instance, factors that influence both parenting and children's stress responses may be at work.

Second, although animal studies have repeatedly demonstrated a link between postnatal parent–offspring interactions and epigenetic processes, the way in which those processes influence the subsequent development and functioning of biological systems is not well understood (John & Rougeulle, 2018). Similarly, in human studies, although exposure to toxic stress (e.g., child maltreatment) relates to epigenetic changes, those changes in gene expression do not consistently account for socioemotional outcomes (e.g., depression; Bustamante et al., 2018). Thus, the implication of many epigenetic changes on long-term child well-being is not clear.

A third limitation has to do with problems related to the identification of experiences of adversity. Different stressors (e.g., physical abuse, neglect, exposure to community violence) can lead to different outcomes in terms of emotional and behavioral responses and, evidence suggests, in terms of biological responses (McLaughlin et al., 2015). Therefore, they should not be grouped in one generic category of "adverse childhood experiences" if we hope to develop a better understanding of developmental pathways to dysfunction and resilience. Finally, researchers' inconsistent findings regarding the reactivity of human stress response systems subsequent to early adversity do not always demonstrate a long-term effect (Hackman et al., 2018; McLaughlin et al., 2015; Wesarg et al., 2020); thus, we must look to explain the inconsistencies. We must resist oversimplifying the associations between children's experiences of stress and adult physical and mental health, instead searching for appropriate targets for effective intervention.

CHILD MALTREATMENT

According to the Centers for Disease Control and Prevention (2020), in 2018 one in seven children in the United States had experienced some form of maltreatment within the past year. This percentage is significantly higher in the population of children presenting for mental health treatment. *Child maltreatment*—which includes physical abuse, neglect, psychological/emotional abuse, and sexual abuse—is defined differently across cultures and depending on the perspective from which it is being examined (e.g., legal, sociological, or psychological). The experience of pathogenic parenting and conflict in the parent–child relationship underlie the construct of maltreatment; sexual abuse by an unrelated perpetrator is the potential exception.

In the attachment literature, the rupture in the parent–child relationship in the context of child maltreatment is reflected by an increased risk for insecure attachments (Cassidy & Shaver, 2016). Children who have experienced abuse are more likely to display insecure attachment patterns, particularly disorganized patterns (Cyr et al., 2010). In the 30-year Minnesota study examining child development from birth to adulthood, children's disorganized attachment was predicted by caregiving that was physically abusive, intrusive, and psychologically unavailable but not by infant difficult temperament or early neurodevelopmental concerns (Sroufe, 2005). Children with insecure attachment patterns, particularly disorganized attachment patterns, are more likely to exhibit deficits in behavior regulation (e.g., conduct problems; R. P. Fearon et al., 2010) and emotion regulation (Sroufe, 2005). The association of insecure attachment with externalizing problems is robust and stronger than the association with internalizing symptoms (Groh et al., 2012).

Although the broad category of maltreatment encompasses a range of caregiver behaviors on a continuum of severity, types of maltreatment are intercorrelated and children commonly experience more than one type (Cecil et al., 2017). Children exhibit a range of responses to maltreatment that span developmental domains (Gardner et al., 2019; Weissman et al., 2019). Severity is one factor that predicts the level of sequelae an individual experiences. Severity of maltreatment in childhood can impact the reactivity of physiological stress response systems—both heart rate and cortisol response—in adults (Ouellet-Morin et al., 2019). More chronic maltreatment is associated with greater risk for deliberate self-harm among adolescents (Hu et al., 2017) and more serious socioemotional and behavioral symptoms in young adulthood (Jonson-Reid et al., 2012). The experience of multiple types of maltreatment is also related to significant symptoms (Cecil et al., 2017). Among two samples of children followed for 15 years from ages 5 to 20 years, individuals who had experienced maltreatment in early childhood were more likely to report externalizing (e.g., antisocial personality) and internalizing (e.g., depression) disorders, more likely to experience economic instability, and more likely to experience poorer health as young adults than individuals who had not been maltreated (Lansford et al., 2021). In a 2-year longitudinal study of 365 children from low-income backgrounds, the number of maltreatment types a child had experienced predicted the level of peer aggression and conduct problems they exhibited but not their levels of morning cortisol (a measure of physiological stress response). Subsequently, conduct problems were the most consistent predictor of later risk factors, and the level of conduct problems accounted for the relationship between child maltreatment and later peer aggression (DePasquale et al., 2019). The association between maltreatment and childhood conduct problems is one of the most robust findings in the literature (Cicchetti & Handley, 2019; Debowska et al., 2017; Rosen et al., 2018). As a key factor in the negative developmental cascades initiated by child maltreatment, conduct problems are a particularly relevant target for early intervention in the context of the parent–child relationship.

EXPOSURE TO VIOLENCE

In the United States, two of the most likely forms of violence to which children are exposed as witnesses are intimate partner violence (IPV) and community violence (e.g., violent crime). The National Survey of Children's Exposure to Violence, a comprehensive, nationally representative survey, found that one in 15 children witnessed violence between parents or between a parent and their partner within the past year (Hamby et al., 2011). One in four children (26%) witnessed some form of family violence in their lifetime (Hamby et al., 2011). Within the same nationally representative sample, rates of exposure to community violence were also disturbingly frequent: Nearly one in five children (19.2%) witnessed physical assault in the community, 5.3% witnessed a shooting, and 0.5% (one in 200 children) witnessed a murder in the past year (Finkelhor et al., 2009). Among the oldest age group (children 14–17 years of age), 42.2% had witnessed assault, 10.2% witnessed a shooting, and 1.3% witnessed a murder. Close to half of the entire child sample (46.3%) had themselves been assaulted within the past year. These statistics are especially disturbing considering that violent crime rates are even higher among socio-economically disadvantaged neighborhoods (R. Peterson & Krivo, 2010).

It is well established that exposure to violence generally, and to IPV specifically, has a detrimental impact on children's functioning. Studies that examined the impact of IPV on children over time found that, overall, children such as Rose who are exposed to IPV are more likely to experience more mental health symptoms, including both externalizing symptoms (e.g., conduct problems) and internalizing symptoms (e.g., anxiety, withdrawal; Jouriles & McDonald, 2015; Vu et al., 2016). In a review of 74 longitudinal studies through 2015, the overall relationship between IPV and child symptom level was small but significant. Evidence suggests that the negative influence of IPV may increase over time, as studies that had a greater time span between measurement of IPV and measurement of child externalizing and internalizing symptoms (even up to 10 years) found stronger effects, although these may be confounded in part by experiences of ongoing IPV (Vu et al., 2016). Children who have been exposed to IPV are also more likely to demonstrate deficits in executive functioning (Gustafsson et al., 2015), social and academic problems (Kitzmann et al., 2003), and delays in language development (Conway et al., 2021).

In addition to direct effects on child functioning, such as child maltreatment, IPV places the parent–child relationship at risk, impacting parents' ability to provide responsive and effective care. Mothers with a history of trauma and PTSD symptoms, for example, are more likely to be rated highly for child abuse potential (Cross et al., 2018). Mothers who have experienced IPV specifically are less likely to demonstrate responsive parenting, whereas the quality of parenting accounts for the link between IPV and children's executive functioning (Gustafsson et al., 2015). Research on exposure to IPV and children's attachment is relatively sparse. However, in a synthesis of existing longitudinal studies that examined the relationship between IPV and later attachment quality ($k = 15$), a weak but significant relationship was found, showing that children who have witnessed IPV between their caregivers are more likely to be insecurely attached (Noonan & Pilkington, 2020).

Exposure to community violence impacts children in many ways that are similar to exposure to IPV. Witnessing community violence is related to experiencing more PTSD symptoms and more externalizing behaviors (Fowler et al., 2009). Among a sample of high-risk adolescent boys living in impoverished urban neighborhoods, witnessing community violence predicted more symptoms of depression, more aggression, and more attention problems (Elsaesser, 2018). Maternal support and involvement did not reduce the impact of witnessing community violence on adolescents, although it did reduce the impact of nonviolent stressors (Gaylord-Harden et al., 2018). Maternal support and involvement in the study were measured with only six-item and 12-item self-report scales that may not have captured the essential aspects of responsive parenting. However, there is another explanation for the lack of association: In the case of traumatic experiences related to violence, responsive parenting may be needed earlier, prior to adolescence, to provide protection from negative outcomes. Community violence is also a stronger predictor of externalizing symptoms in adolescents than in younger children (Fowler et al., 2009), an additional risk that may be partially because adolescents have more years of possible violence exposure. Additional support for the importance of engaging protective factors—particularly positive parenting quality—earlier can be found within the resilience literature. Among preschoolers who had been exposed to IPV, higher parenting quality was associated with children's better emotion regulation and social competence, which subsequently related to fewer conduct problems (Howell et al., 2010).

When intervention does not occur early, the potential exists for exposure to violence to drive negative developmental cascades across time (Borofsky et al., 2013). In a community sample of boys and girls ages 10 to 14 years, exposure to community violence was associated with more externalizing and internalizing symptoms. The initial level of symptoms accounted for the relationship between community violence and children's engagement with school 2½ years later. Engagement in school subsequently accounted for the relationship between community violence exposure and later grade point average. In other words, children who were exposed to more community violence were at greater risk for externalizing and internalizing symptoms, which put them at risk for poorer school engagement and subsequently a lower grade point average. These relationships remained significant even when controlling for family income, race, and gender. Although in this investigation the cascade was not tested further out, the implications of the triad of risk factors (i.e., conduct problems, disengagement from school, and poor grade point average) have been linked with later challenges such as antisocial behavior, detention, and poor employment. Such a cascade is further complicated by more recent evidence that exposure to violence is related to acceleration of cellular aging, changes in brain development, and cognitive ability (O. Butler et al., 2018). After taking into account the effects of families' socioeconomic status (SES), exposure to community violence was associated with children's lower IQ and smaller gray matter volume in areas related to executive function and integration of emotion and cognition. A synthesis of the literature on the impact of early adversity on biological aging processes also found that exposure to violence in childhood was associated with accelerated cellular aging and changes in brain structure (Colich et al., 2020).

THE PERVASIVE IMPACT OF POVERTY

Although poverty is operationalized by the U.S. government based solely on income and household size (income of $26,500 or less for a family of four in 2021), this complex and multidimensional construct relates to the availability of material, educational, and social resources (Yoshikawa et al., 2012). Children living in households near or below the poverty line—approximately one in seven children in the United States (Parolin et al., 2021)—experience serious and pervasive disparities in many areas of daily life relative to their more affluent peers. For instance, children from low-income backgrounds are more likely to live in unsafe neighborhoods, be exposed to violence, attend schools with inadequate facilities, experience food insecurity, be exposed to toxins, experience unsafe water sources, and have less access to quality health care (Evans, 2004; A. A. Lee et al., 2020; Sanetti, 2017).

It is well established that children who live in impoverished environments suffer negative effects on multiple domains of development. They are more likely to exhibit lower academic achievement and poorer attention and impulse control than their nondisadvantaged peers (Baker & Brooks-Gunn, 2020; Yoshikawa et al., 2012), to experience internalizing symptoms (e.g., depression; Letourneau et al., 2013), to demonstrate poorer behavior regulation (Sturge-Apple et al., 2017), and to experience more conduct problems (Baker & Brooks-Gunn, 2020; Yoshikawa et al., 2012). The mechanisms responsible for these negative outcomes are not yet entirely clear. However, many of the risk factors associated with family poverty are likely to play a role, and the impact may be cumulative (Funk et al., 2012; S. Kim & Kochanska, 2021; Yoshikawa et al., 2012). For example, children living in poverty are at greater risk for experiencing toxic stress: They are 5 times more likely than children from higher socioeconomic backgrounds to suffer abuse or neglect (Centers for Disease Control and Prevention, 2020) and are more likely to be exposed to community violence, both of which can contribute to changes in biological regulation systems and to deficits in brain development (Figure 3.3). Fewer educational opportunities, poorer nutrition, and less access to health care also impact development among impoverished children.

FIGURE 3.3. Social Determinants Linked to Poverty Increase Children's Risk for Exposure to Maltreatment and Violence

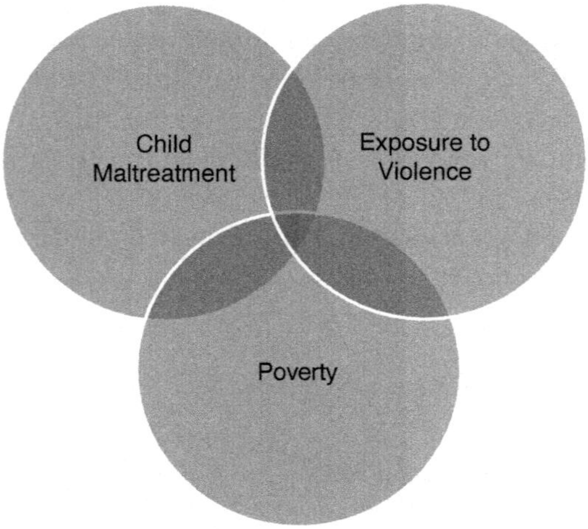

Note. Children living in poverty are 5 times more likely to experience child abuse and neglect, are more likely to live in neighborhoods experiencing high rates of violent crime, and are more likely to witness intimate partner violence than children from affluent neighborhoods.

Developmental theory and current research demonstrate that parenting and the parent–child relationship remain important in the cascade from poverty-related stressors to child functioning. Previous investigations have largely focused on the ways in which parenting mediates that link (Baker & Brooks-Gunn, 2020). Responsive, available, and predictable parenting is threatened by the environmental stressors associated with poverty. For instance, a parent who works long hours for low wages, worries about being able to provide sufficient food for her family, has no reliable day care for her children, and lives in an unsafe neighborhood is challenged to provide responsive parenting. The parent–child relationship may be further strained by a parent's own experiences of trauma, a history of pathogenic care, or mental health symptoms. Among a sample of 216 mothers experiencing socioeconomic adversity (parent low income, low education, single parenthood, food insecurity), with or without prenatal cocaine use, a developmental cascade across 7 years linked prenatal substance use to socioeconomic adversity. Mothers' socioeconomic adversity subsequently predicted that lower parenting sensitivity and lower sensitivity predicted children's poorer rule-following at 2 years of age. Rule-following at 2 years subsequently predicted teachers' reports of child conduct problems at ages 7 to 8 years (Ettekal et al., 2020). In the same sample, a second pathway to childhood conduct problems was initiated by mothers' depression through infancy and toddlerhood. In other words, socioeconomic adversity, prenatal substance use, and parent psychopathology each contributed to children's conduct problems, with the impact of socioeconomic adversity mediated through its effect on parenting sensitivity.

In a community sample of infants and their parents followed over 8 years (children ages 7 months to 8 years), an alternate cascade to conduct problems was identified, including child temperament and parent harsh discipline. Results showed that only families experiencing economic hardship also experienced the negative developmental cascade that progressed from children's difficult temperament (proneness to anger, inability to delay gratification) at ages 2 to 3 years to parents' observed use of harsh discipline at 4½ years of age and mothers' reports of children's conduct problems at 8 years of age (S. Kim & Kochanska, 2021).

It is important to note that measures of SES/income do not always predict worse outcomes. A recent meta-analysis of the effects of early life adversity on symptoms of major depression in adulthood found that experiences of child abuse but not family poverty increased the likelihood of depression (LeMoult et al., 2020). Among a low-income, stressed sample of mothers and children, no relation was found between families' SES and children's inflammatory load score, a composite measure of physiological stress response (Measelle & Ablow, 2018). Similarly, no relationship was found between family income and father–child or mother–child attachment in a general community sample (Bureau et al., 2017).

Two elements may help to explain the inconsistent findings regarding the association between economic adversity and child well-being. First, measures of

SES are only a proxy for assessing the level of burden on a family caused by low resources. SES may not always be sufficient to capture the extent of a family's risk or protective factors. For example, a family with an average income may have excessive medical bills that tap their resources and make their housing and food security unstable. In contrast, a parent with a small income may receive familial or neighborhood support to provide care for her children and safe housing. Second, as discussed in Chapter 2 of this volume, responsive parenting provides a buffer against some of the negative influences of economic hardship. Among families with high-quality parenting and strong, positive parent–child relationships, SES has demonstrated less influence on child functioning (Brody et al., 2004; Morris et al., 2017).

In sum, poverty is associated with a staggering list of risk factors that can contribute to negative developmental cascades. Many of the environmental risks reflect large systemic issues that will not soon be resolved. If our goal is to slow the negative cascade and reduce harm, we must identify factors that are malleable and that have demonstrated the ability to buffer children against adversity. The parent–child relationship has a clear place among those factors and, as shown in Chapter 2 of this volume, can contribute significantly to the reduction of risk.

CLINICAL IMPLICATIONS OF THE DEVELOPMENTAL LITERATURE

When clinicians understand the factors that challenge a parent–child relationship, they may target the therapeutic intervention to reduce or buffer against the harm caused by those challenges. However, it is important to avoid assuming that a family has experienced harm merely because of the existence of risk factors. The following sections describe the importance of developing a comprehensive and strength-based conceptualization of a parent–child dyad when considering the existence of systemic factors related to risk.

Understanding a Family's Resources

Socioeconomic status is related to parenting challenges and puts children at risk for negative developmental outcomes. However, SES itself does not always predict important aspects of family functioning. Instead, functioning is better understood in the context of the collection of stressors associated with economic hardship. Thus, in a clinical setting, it is important to assess a child's ecology from a multisystems perspective that includes risk and protective factors in the individual parent and child, the parenting relationship, and the community (e.g., neighborhood, school, church). Using the language of ecological systems theory, it is also valuable to consider the child's meso- and exosystems: That is, how does one microsystem (e.g., the parent–partner relationship) influence another (e.g., parent–child relationship), and how do those interactions support or threaten parenting quality? The Cultural Formulation Interviews are a set of questionnaires and interview questions that guide therapists to develop an integrated understanding of clients' systems, maintaining a focus on a family's lived experience (Aggarwal & Lewis-Fernández, 2015/2020). The Cultural Formulation Interviews may be helpful in the development of a comprehensive conceptualization of a family's material, social, and relational resources, and the identification of key targets for intervention.

Prevention When Treatment Is Not Indicated

Whether children experience an event as toxic stress depends on several factors, some related to the event (e.g., severity, duration) and others related to children's individual and relational coping resources. Not every child who has experienced maltreatment or been exposed to community violence will experience dysfunction and require a treatment intervention. However, even if a child is not exhibiting significant dysfunction immediately or soon after stressful events, early experiences of violence can tax the parent–child relationship and a parent's ability to provide responsive care, which may contribute to future problems. Some evidence suggests that children experience more negative effects of violence exposure over time. Thus, when treatment is not warranted, a prevention approach that fosters parenting quality and connects parents and children to supportive resources may reduce the potential for future dysfunction.

The Concept of ACEs

The term *adverse childhood experiences* (ACEs) became a buzzword after the now-landmark study found a correlation between adults' retrospective reports of childhood experiences of social and environmental stressors (e.g., abuse, parent substance use, parent incarceration, exposure to violence) and adults' current health status (Felitti et al., 1998). The data were collected with a survey mailed to potential participants, adults who were members of a Kaiser-Permanente health plan in San Diego from August 1995 to March 1996. The survey included 17 questions about seven types of adversity exposure (physical, psychological, sexual abuse, caregiver substance abuse, mental illness, incarceration, caregiver victim of IPV). Findings suggested that the more adversity individuals experienced in childhood, the more likely they were to experience emotional, behavioral, and physical health problems such as depression, alcoholism, heart disease, chronic lung disease, and cancer. The study, which included data from approximately 9,500 individuals, drew attention to the connection between early life experiences and the occurrence of later health risk behaviors and physiological diseases.

Since that time, the use of the term *adverse childhood experiences* has drastically increased within the scientific literature, among clinical providers, and in the general population. In particular, some initiatives press physicians and other providers to screen for ACEs routinely using the survey from the original study or the shorter 10-item version. A quick internet search pulls up dozens of websites where one can "take the ACE quiz" and "get your ACE score." The intention to increase awareness of the many factors that can impact individual health and well-being is a good one, especially when targeting the various professions that work closely with children. However, significant problems come with using a scope that is too narrow, relying on the framework of the original survey, and focusing on risk factors out of context of the actual strength of their associations with long-term problems and the existence of protective factors.

What Can Measures of ACEs Do?

The measurement of ACEs through the surveys developed by Felitti et al. (1998), and similar instruments, is useful and appropriate for assessing the prevalence of some types of early life experiences within populations of adults. The surveys were developed for epidemiological work—to examine the occurrence of adversity within a large population (Kelly-Irving & Delpierre, 2019). They are most appropriate for research and for identifying needs at a community level.

Within a clinical setting, assessing families for the existence of stressors such as child maltreatment, exposure to violence, and poverty—as well as parental psychopathology and history of trauma, among other factors—is an essential part of the assessment process, when the capacity exists to provide support and resources related to those stressors. In such a setting, the assessment should extend beyond the ACEs surveys, which return yes/no answers to a limited number of questions about adversity, to gather an understanding about the frequency, duration, and severity of experiences that may be related to toxic stress responses.

Inappropriate Uses of Survey Measures of ACEs

The ACE-related questions used in the original study, and now widely disseminated, were not developed for clinical purposes (Felitti et al., 1998). They are not meant to assist in the diagnosis of adults or children with any psychological or physical disorder (Kelly-Irving & Delpierre, 2019). In fact, they were developed for population-wide assessment and not intended for the individual screening of adults or children for mental health problems. Because they were not meant for use as screening tools, they have not been evaluated for the type of psychometric properties necessary in a good screening measure (e.g., sensitivity and specificity). Properties such as sensitivity and specificity reveal how accurately a measure can identify whether a person does or does not have a specific problem (Shreffler & Huecker, 2021). Screening with ACEs surveys cannot identify any specific mental or physical disorder, as *adverse childhood experiences* is a generic term for many types of events that may (or may not) be associated with many types of health outcomes in an individual.

An assessment of individuals' experiences of early life adversity in a supportive, clinical setting is useful and important, particularly when the assessment includes the ability to (a) conduct a follow-up assessment as to the meaning of the experiences to that individual and their current psychological and health status and (b) provide intervention resources when needed. Routine assessment of ACEs in a school, church, or other nonclinical setting is unlikely to be helpful. Instead, this assessment is potentially harmful if effective intervention resources are unavailable or when it becomes another way to label individuals as damaged (Kelly-Irving & Delpierre, 2019).

Adversity Is Not Destiny

At the beginning of a workshop on reactive attachment disorder (RAD), I asked the audience of day care providers and preschool teachers the percentage of children in their classrooms that they thought might meet the criteria for a diagnosis of RAD. The responses ranged from 50% to 100%, when the actual prevalence of RAD in maltreated samples has been estimated at around 5% (Bruce et al., 2019) and in distressed samples at between 1% and 2% (Minnis et al., 2013); the prevalence in the general population is presumed to be significantly lower. Underlying the wildly inflated answers I received was a deep misunderstanding about the nature of attachment and a reflection of our society's tendency to overpathologize individuals who may have experienced adversity (Bonanno, 2004). Watch almost any movie that depicts adult survivors of child abuse and you will see the societal narrative that abuse either leaves individuals scarred, doomed to experience serious mental illnesses, and reenact unhealthy relationships, or destined to become perpetrators of violence themselves (Niec et al., 2008). That narrative is missing the understanding that although early adversity can increase risk for many problems, the relationship between early adversity and later difficulties is typically small to moderate, depending on the specific type of adversity and on the outcomes measured. Also missing is a lack of appreciation for the plasticity of neurodevelopment and the resilience exhibited by many children. In fact, a review of studies examining outcomes for individuals who have experienced traumatic events reveals that resilience, not dysfunction, is the most common response to trauma (Galatzer-Levy et al., 2018). Most children who experience adversity do not suffer from serious, chronic consequences. A recent meta-analysis synthesizing the factors that best promote children's resilience after exposure to violence (including child abuse, IPV, and community violence) highlighted that (a) family factors such as parental responsiveness and effective parenting play a significant role in supporting children's resilience; (b) other relational factors such as peer and school staff support contribute to positive outcomes; (c) self-regulation, which is impacted by the parent–child relationship, is the strongest child-specific predictor of resilience; and (d) the factors related to resilience are highly consistent across all three types of adversity, suggesting that they are fundamental to successful development in the face of early life stressors (Yule et al., 2019).

SUMMARY

Our understanding of the ways in which stress experiences impact development starting from the molecular level is continuing to increase, yet we have a lot still to learn. Although we have a clearer grasp of the potential physiological mechanisms through which adversity relates to long-term outcomes, many findings have not been replicated or have been observed only in animal models. A well-established fact, exposure to violence, maltreatment, and the stressors related to poverty can lead to negative developmental cascades that have a pervasive influence on many domains of emotional, behavioral, and cognitive functioning. However, we are also continuing to learn where the most likely opportunities for change occur throughout the developmental process. More plasticity exists in the genetic influence and in neurodevelopment than once was thought, and with relational support—particularly parenting support—children exhibit significant resilience. Even while investigating the detrimental effects of toxic stress, we must recall that the experience of early adversity is only a risk factor and is not equivalent to disease or dysfunction.

Key Takeaways

1. The experience of stress, when it is temporary and within a child's relational and personal coping resources, is not detrimental; rather, it is a valuable opportunity for children to practice and enhance their coping skills.
2. Toxic stress involves the prolonged and severe elevation of a child's biological stress response. In the case of chronic stressors, such as ongoing physical abuse, the biological stress response may establish a new, elevated baseline. Ongoing activation of the stress response is related to wear on organs and regulation systems and may be one mechanism responsible for increasing risk for health problems such as cardiovascular disease.
3. The EBD model provides a structure to explain how a child's ecology may influence genetic expression over time and how both ecology and biology then influence short- and long-term developmental outcomes.
4. Child maltreatment, exposure to violence, and poverty are prevalent sources of toxic stress that can have a significant negative impact on children's cognitive, socioemotional, behavioral, and physical functioning.
5. The quality of parent–child interactions has been implicated as a protective or risk factor in three sources of toxic stress: child maltreatment, exposure to violence, and poverty. Negative developmental cascades driven by each of these sources of adversity include the quality of parent–child interactions.

Clinical Growth Questions

1. In my conceptualization of threats to a child's functioning, do I discriminate between positive, tolerable, and toxic stress responses? Do I help parents to discriminate between these different experiences?

2. How might I help parents to leverage positive stress to build a child's coping resources?
3. How do I assess a family's existing resources (e.g., material, social, relational) to determine the types of risks they may be experiencing?
4. Do I make assumptions about a child's functioning or a parent's capacity for improvement based on their early experiences of adversity?
5. What are three ways in which I could actively counter the common belief among colleagues, child care professionals, and parents that "adversity is destiny"?

II

REPAIRING AND STRENGTHENING THE PARENT–CHILD RELATIONSHIP IN THERAPY

4

Determining Treatment Targets and Monitoring Progress

The Importance of Assessment

Donna, a single working mother with two daughters ages 5 years and 3 years, presented at the behavioral health clinic reporting that her older child, Danielle, was "out of control." Donna reported that Danielle was often unmanageable at home, did not follow directions, ran out of the house without letting her mother know, and got into dangerous items (e.g., played with matches). The conflict between mother and child had escalated, and Donna reported feeling ineffective and exhausted. Danielle displayed no behavior problems at school and had no cognitive delays.

As part of the intake process prior to determining the treatment approach, the therapist conducted an assessment of the parent–child relationship that included a standardized behavioral observation. Donna was asked to interact with her older daughter in three different play scenarios, each 5 minutes long. In the first scenario, Donna was directed to follow her daughter's lead in the play. During this child-led play time, Donna and her daughter played comfortably together with the toys in the room. Donna's interactions with her child were playful, warm, and child-centered, and both parent and child appeared to enjoy the interaction. In the second scenario, Donna was directed to set the rules for the play. During this parent-led play time, Donna began by providing clear but restrictive rules for the interaction. At first, her daughter complied, although reluctantly. When Donna attempted to implement additional rules, her daughter immediately became defiant, shouting "No," whining, and pushing toys off the table. This defiance continued into the third scenario, in which

https://doi.org/10.1037/0000304-004
Strengthening the Parent–Child Relationship in Therapy: Laying the Foundation for Healthy Development, by L. N. Niec

Donna was asked to have Danielle clean up the toys. Donna, remaining calm, repeated her direction to clean up the toys approximately 60 times over a 5-minute period, at times attempting to reason with her daughter or threatening her with consequences that were impossible to implement (e.g., "If you don't pick up the toys, we'll stay here all day"). Throughout the remainder of the observation period, both child and parent were regulated but visibly tense and frustrated. Ultimately, Donna was unable to obtain her daughter's compliance or to implement effective consequences.

WHY CONDUCT A PRETREATMENT ASSESSMENT?

The assessment just described provided a great deal of meaningful information about the strengths and weaknesses of the parent–child dyad in a short time. For example, it was clear that mother and child felt warmth toward each other and could enjoy being together. Also evident was Donna's ability to maintain a calm demeanor even while experiencing significant frustration with her child. The observation further provided information about some of the keys to the parent–child conflict and specific areas of parenting with which Donna struggled. Although Donna remained emotionally regulated, she did not have the ability to follow through on her directions or to implement a developmentally appropriate consequence for misbehavior. Danielle, on the other hand, had developed a pattern of responding to her mother's requests that allowed her to effectively evade tasks she did not want to complete. Her high levels of defiance were already aggravating the parent–child conflict, and although they had not yet generalized to school, they had the potential to impact her functioning at home, at school, and with peers.

With the information gained from the assessment of Donna and Danielle's relationship, it was possible not only to identify an appropriate treatment approach but also to tailor that approach to target the specific needs of mother and child. Despite the exhaustion and frustration that Donna expressed in the interview, the behavior observation made it possible to identify her strengths as well in order to use them to facilitate change.

In addition to the important information gained during the assessment prior to treatment, as in this case, some assessment tools can also be used throughout treatment to evaluate a family's progress, inform a therapist if the intervention is working, and provide an objective indication that a family is ready to graduate from treatment.

WHAT TO INCLUDE IN AN ASSESSMENT TO MAKE IT USEFUL AND VALID

Before embarking on the evaluation of the parent–child relationship, it is crucial to consider the components that make an assessment process a good one. First, a quality assessment allows the therapist to answer the questions necessary to select and implement the appropriate treatment. Measures and techniques should therefore capture the dimensions of the parent–child relationship relevant to the family's presenting problem. For example, is there concern about parental sensitivity and emotional availability? About the effectiveness or developmental appropriateness of limit setting? About the child's or parent's emotion regulation? Once a therapist has identified the most relevant dimensions to be assessed, a strong assessment procedure will include multiple information-gathering methods (e.g., interview, questionnaire, observation) and multiple sources of information (e.g., parent, therapist, teacher; De Los Reyes et al., 2015; Whitcomb, 2017). The multimethod approach to assessment helps to escape the pitfalls inherent in any one type or source of information. For instance, within a child welfare population in which families are mandated to treatment, parents may be motivated to minimize their conflicts with their children and therefore may underreport problems during interviews and on parent-report questionnaires. Using assessment techniques other than parent-report will help therapists to develop a more complete understanding of the family. Finally, assessment tools must have adequate psychometric properties; they should be reliable and valid within the population with which the therapist intends to use them. In other words, the measures should capture the constructs they claim to measure and do so in a way that is consistent.

In sum, without a valid assessment process, even if we have an effective intervention to offer a family, we are playing darts in the darkness. We might have great technique, but we are still unlikely to hit the target.

Assessment Tools

Despite agreement among most clinicians that the parent–child relationship has a foundational influence on a child's development, surprisingly few measures exist that are designed to help clinicians to develop an understanding of the relationships of the parents and children with whom they work. Many existing tools were designed primarily for research or are too time-consuming or expensive to use regularly in practice (Hill et al., 2008). Others do not have solid psychometric properties. Although each of the following measures has advantages and drawbacks, all were selected to provide a range of assessment methods (parent-report, behavior observation, therapist report) that are feasible and appropriate for clinical use and that tap a variety of important dimensions of parent–child interactions (Table 4.1).

Parent-Report Questionnaires

In the assessment of parenting and the parent–child relationship, parents are typically the primary source of information. This makes sense clinically, as parents are the experts on their relationships with their young children, and understanding the parents' perspectives on the strengths and vulnerabilities within the relationship is essential to developing a strong therapeutic alliance. Certain parent-report questionnaires tap various aspects of the parent–child

TABLE 4.1. Parent-Child Relationship Measures

Measure	Type	Cost Start-up fee? Per-use fee?	Time to administer	Child ages	Used with caregivers other than mothers	Domains assessed
PSI	Parent-report questionnaire	Start-up: Yes Per use: Yes	FF = 20m	2y–12y	Yes	Parent stress in relation to parenting, child behavior, and parent-child interactions
CRBI	Parent-report questionnaire	Start-up: No Per use: No	10m	2y–10y	Yes	Children's positive and negative behaviors as related to the parent-child relationship
CPRS	Parent-report questionnaire	Start-up: No Per use: No	5m	3y–12y	Yes	Conflict and Closeness in the parent-child relationship
PRQ	Parent-report questionnaire	Start-up: Yes Per use: Yes	PRQ-P = 15m PRQ-CA = 20m	2y–5y 6y–18y	Yes	Attachment, Discipline Practices, Involvement, Parenting Confidence, and Relational Frustration. Communication and Satisfaction with School only on PRQ-CA
DPICS-IV	Observation measure	Start-up: Yes Per use: No	FF = 20m SF = 5m	2y–7y	Yes	Parent child-centeredness, quality and effectiveness of limit-setting, and child responsiveness to direction
KIPS	Observation measure	Start-up: Yes[a] Per use: Yes	20m	2y–5y, 11mo	Rarely	Parent child-centeredness, quality of limit-setting, and scaffolding
EAS	Observation measure	Start-up: Yes[a] Per use: No	20m or longer	0–14y	Yes	Parent and child emotional sensitivity and responsiveness
PIRGAS	Global rating	Start-up: Yes Per use: No	10m or longer + clinical interview	0–3y	Rarely	Overall assessment of behavioral, affective, and psychological functioning of the parent-child relationship

Note. PSI = Parenting Stress Index; FF = full form; SF = short form; m = minutes; y = years; CRBI = Child-Relationship Behavior Inventory; CPRS = Child-Parent Relationship Scale; PRQ = Parenting Relationship Questionnaire; P = preschool form; CA = child and adolescent form; DPICS-IV = Dyadic Parent-child Interaction Coding System-Fourth Edition; KIPS = Keys to Interactive Parenting Scale; mo = months; EAS = Emotional Availability Scales; PIRGAS = Parent-Infant Relationship Global Assessment Scale.
[a]An additional fee is charged for annual recertification in the use of the measure.

relationship. Advantages of these tools include their wide availability, ease and speed of administration, ease of scoring, and reasonable psychometric properties. Generally, existing parent-report measures of the parent–child relationship are not intended for—and do not have the psychometric soundness to be used for—diagnosing individual children. However, they can provide information about specific areas where a parent–child dyad is experiencing distress or dysfunction. The four measures that follow capture different dimensions of the parent–child relationship and have demonstrated utility within a clinical setting.

Parenting Stress Index, Fourth Edition

Description. The Parenting Stress Index, Fourth Edition (PSI-IV), is an established, standardized parent-report questionnaire focused on 12 domains of stress and dysfunction in the parent–child relationship of parents with children from 1 to 12 years of age (Abidin, 2012). Two forms are available: a long form with 120 items and a short form with 36 items. Child domains assessed on the long form of the measure include Distractibility/Hyperactivity, Adaptability, Reinforces Parent, Demandingness, Mood, and Acceptability (Abidin, 2012). Parent domains include Competence, Isolation, Attachment, Health, Role Restriction, and Spouse/Parenting Partner Relationship. Parents are directed to consider how much they agree with each item and to respond on a 5-point scale from *strongly agree* to *strongly disagree*. The measure requires approximately a fifth-grade reading ability. The short form of the measure (PSI-SF) comprises three subscales: Parental Distress, Parent–Child Dysfunctional Interaction, and Difficult Child.

Parenting stress is associated with a number of constructs relevant to the parent–child relationship and to treatment success. For instance, parents' elevated stress has been related to punitive discipline and abusive parenting (Haskett et al., 2003; Pinderhughes et al., 2000). Scores on the PSI have also been associated with the number of family risk factors, an increased risk for developing insecure attachment, and lower parenting efficacy (Laganière et al., 2003; Raikes & Thompson, 2005). In a sample of children with sexualized behavior problems, caregivers' scores on the PSI-SF were elevated (Silovsky & Niec, 2002). The PSI has been used frequently as an outcome measure for parent–child interventions and demonstrates sensitivity to changes in treatment. Parents who completed the evidence-based parent–child intervention parent–child interaction therapy (PCIT) demonstrated significant and meaningful reductions in their stress as measured by the PSI-SF (Niec et al., 2016; Schuhmann et al., 1998).

The PSI has adequate psychometric properties to use as a screening measure for possible distress and dysfunction, to assist in the development of treatment plans, and to assess treatment progress. For the most recent edition of the PSI (fourth edition), norms were updated to include fathers (previously only mothers had been included in the normative sample) and to reflect the demographic composition of the United States based on the 2007 census (Abidin, 2012). Clinical cutoff scores have been established to help determine a range of stress levels that can be considered to be meaningfully above average and of concern. Age-based norms allow for comparison of a parent's stress to the stress of parents with children of a similar age. The PSI and PSI-SF scales demonstrate adequate to good internal consistency ($\alpha = .70–.95$; Abidin, 2012). The measure has been used with families from a wide range of racial, ethnic, geographical, and socioeconomic backgrounds (Aracena et al., 2016; Barroso et al., 2016; S. J. Lee et al., 2016; Waisbren et al., 2004). One disadvantage of the PSI and PSI-SF is the cost of administration, at more than $4.50 per client form for the PSI-SF.

What questions can the PSI/PSI-SF help to answer? Many parents presenting with their young children for psychological treatment report elevations in their stress levels. Often, such stress can be quickly identified with a clinical interview. However, the PSI is useful in assessing the specific source of the stress. Further, the PSI provides a way to quantify the level of a parent's stress so that it can be measured at different time points throughout treatment to determine whether the intervention is addressing the problem and to provide important information about the outcome of treatment.

Child-Relationship Behavior Inventory

Description. The Child-Relationship Behavior Inventory (CRBI) was developed to assess children's positive and negative responses within the parent–child relationship (Briegel, 2014a, 2014b; Briegel et al., 2018). It is composed of two scales—the Child Relationship Development Questionnaire and the Child Relationship Checklist—that can be used jointly or independently. The CRBI was developed for dyads with children 2 to 10 years of age. It includes a total of 28 items to which parents respond in two ways: First, parents use a Likert scale from 0 (*never*) to 7 (*always*) to specify the frequency with which their child displays each behavior. Second, parents indicate whether they perceive the behavior to be a problem (yes or no). Items on the Child Relationship Development Questionnaire include child behaviors indicative of a positive parent–child relationship (e.g., My child "shares with me," "praises or compliments me"), whereas the Child Relationship Checklist includes behaviors that suggest a distressed parent–child relationship (e.g., My child "nags me," "threatens me").

Validity studies with community samples in the United States and Germany support the psychometric properties of the CRBI. Internal consistency is adequate to good for each of the individual scales, ranging from $\alpha = .78$ to .89 for mothers and fathers (Briegel et al., 2018). As is often seen on parent-report measures of children's functioning, mothers' and fathers' ratings on the CRBI scales are only moderately associated, indicating that parents have different perceptions of their relationships with their children. Mothers report more negative behaviors and more positive behaviors related to their relationships with their children than fathers report. This finding demonstrates the importance of independently assessing each caregiver's relationship with their child. In studies comparing children with disruptive behaviors and those who are typically functioning, both of the CRBI scales reveal significant differences. Parents of children with elevated scores on a measure of behavior problems (Eyberg Child Behavior Inventory; Eyberg & Pincus, 1999) described fewer positive and more negative behaviors in the parent–child relationship (Briegel et al., 2018). The CRBI has been used successfully to track treatment progress throughout the course of parent–child interventions (Briegel et al., 2018). The measure is currently available at no cost and can be accessed by contacting the developer.

What questions can the CRBI help to answer? The CRBI does not yet have clinical cutoff scores and therefore cannot be used to classify a parent–child relationship as typically functioning or distressed. However, the CRBI has shown good sensitivity to treatment change and is appropriate for use to monitor progress throughout treatment. Further, because it is freely accessible and easy to administer, the CRBI is a feasible measure for use in many agency and private practice settings. A particular strength of the CRBI is its inclusion of scales of both positive and negative aspects of the parent–child relationship rather than only negative aspects. Only a small association has been found between the positive and negative scales, suggesting that the existence of problems in the parent–child relationship does not mean the absence of strengths (Briegel et al., 2018). Understanding the strengths within a parent–child relationship is as important as identifying the pathology and has implications for treatment success and the maintenance of treatment gains.

Child–Parent Relationship Scale

Description. The Child–Parent Relationship Scale (CPRS) is a 15-item measure developed to assess parents' perceptions of conflict and closeness in their relationships with their children 3 to 12 years of age (Pianta, 1992). Parents are directed to consider their current relationship with a specific child and to respond on a 5-point Likert-type scale from 1 (*definitely does not apply*) to 5 (*definitely applies*). Based on constructs consistent with attachment theory, conflict on the CPRS is conceptualized as the amount and type of negativity parents feel in their relationships with their children (e.g., "My child and I always seem to be struggling with each other," "My child remains angry or is resistant after being disciplined"). Closeness includes parents' perceptions of the levels of caring, warmth, and positive communication in their relationships with their children (e.g., "When I praise my child, he/she beams with pride," "If upset, my child will seek comfort from me"). As discussed in Chapters 2 and 3 of this volume, conflict and closeness in the parent–child relationship are associated with children's functioning in important domains such as behavior regulation, social competence, and school adjustment.

Parents' scores on the CPRS have been associated with relevant constructs of child and family functioning. Mother–child conflict and closeness on the CPRS both predicted increases in children's disruptive behaviors, with greater conflict and less closeness relating to more conduct problems (E. E. O'Connor et al., 2014). Further, across samples of families from Asian, Black, multiracial, and White ethnic backgrounds, children with high levels of conduct problems were more likely to demonstrate lower quality parent–child relationships (Gutman, 2019). Among a sample of stepfamilies, stepfathers who reported more frequently engaging in behaviors meant to develop a positive relationship with their stepchildren (e.g., seeking to spend time with them) experienced less conflict in the parent–child relationship (Ganong et al., 2019). Both scales of the CPRS have demonstrated validity for use with African American families (Burchinal et al., 2008) and with low-income fathers living outside the home (Dyer et al., 2017). The CPRS has also been used as a measure of treatment outcome (Maupin et al., 2017). Internal consistency of the Conflict and Closeness Scales range from adequate to excellent (Driscoll & Pianta, 2011; Ganong et al., 2019; Gutman, 2019). The CPRS can be accessed from the developer and used for no charge.

What questions can the CPRS help to answer? Similar to the CRBI, the CPRS does not have clinical cutoff scores and should not be used to categorize the parent–child relationship as functional or distressed. However, the measure is quickly and inexpensively administered and demonstrates adequate psychometric properties to be useful as a means to track changes in the parents' perceptions of the relationship during treatment. In particular, it may be a good measure to estimate parents' perception of the level of conflict in their relationship with their child.

Parenting Relationship Questionnaire

Description. The Parenting Relationship Questionnaire (PRQ) is a parent-report measure developed for clinical and research purposes to capture aspects of the parent–child relationship associated with important developmental domains (Kamphaus & Reynolds, 2006; Rubinic & Schwickrath, 2010). Two versions of the questionnaire are available for different child age groups (preschool form = 2–5 years, 45 items; child and adolescent form = 6–18 years, 71 items). The subscales on both forms of the PRQ are Attachment (e.g., "When upset, my child comes to me for comfort"); Discipline Practices, which assesses parents' consistency in implementing consequences for children's misbehavior; Involvement (e.g., "I teach my child how to play new games"); Parenting Confidence (e.g., "I am confident in my parenting ability"); and overall Relational Frustration (e.g., "I lose my temper with my child"). The two scales Communication and Satisfaction with School are found only on the child and adolescent form. Items tap parents' thoughts, beliefs, and feelings about each relationship domain. Parents respond to items on a 4-point Likert-type scale from 1 (*never*) to 4 (*always*).

Parents' perceptions of relationship quality as rated by the PRQ showed moderate associations with parenting stress in the standardization sample and a sample of military-dependent parents (Kamphaus & Reynolds, 2006; Lowe et al., 2012). Consistent with other measures, on the PRQ mothers and fathers demonstrate different perceptions of relationship quality with their children, with mothers reporting higher quality than fathers (Ferreira et al., 2016)

However, PRQ ratings of relationship quality with both fathers and mothers have been associated with children's prosocial behavior, with healthier relationships predicting more positive child behavior (Ferreira et al., 2016). The PRQ has helped to demonstrate the importance of parent–child relationship quality in the link between family stress (e.g., work-related stress and conflict) and children's internalizing and externalizing behaviors (Vieira et al., 2016). That is, work-related family stress in mothers and fathers was associated with lower parent–child relationship quality, which was subsequently linked to children's emotional and behavioral symptoms. The PRQ has been used with populations of parents of children with developmental disabilities and pervasive developmental disorders such as autism spectrum disorder (Lewallen & Neece, 2015; Schiltz et al., 2018; Wilkes-Gillan et al., 2017).

The normative sample of the PRQ included more than 4,000 respondents from across the United States with a distribution generally representative of the national composition in terms of race and ethnicity, geographical region, and mothers' education level (Rubinic & Schwickrath, 2010). Based on the standardization studies, internal consistency of the subscales is good ($\alpha = .82–.87$; Kamphaus & Reynolds, 2006). Test–retest reliability has also been shown to be adequate ($r = .72–.89$) over a delay of 33 to 35 days (Rubinic & Schwickrath, 2010). The PRQ is a published measure and has a cost for the start-up kit and subsequent client forms.

What questions can the PRQ help to answer? The PRQ is longer than many other measures of parent–child relationship quality (45 and 71 items) and therefore takes longer to administer than some measures. It may therefore be more useful as a pretreatment assessment tool to develop hypotheses about areas of struggle in the parent–child relationship than as an ongoing monitor of progress. Because the PRQ is sensitive to differences in perceptions across parents, it may also help to illuminate areas where caregivers within a family system have different needs for intervention.

Behavior Observation Measures

Although parent-report questionnaires have an important place in the assessment of the parent–child relationship, they come with disadvantages. In fact, what parents report about their parenting behavior is often unrelated or only weakly related to what they actually do (Comfort & Gordon, 2006; Lovejoy et al., 1999). The use of a behavior observation measure can contribute important information that is not available from parent report alone. For more than 2 decades, the American Academy of Child and Adolescent Psychiatry has described clinical observation as a critical aspect of a diagnostic assessment of young children's functioning (J. M. Thomas et al., 1997).

Standardized behavior observation measures use structured scenarios and/or coding systems to allow therapists to view and rate actual interactions between parents and their children. Some behavioral observation measures are designed to be administered in a clinic setting and create interaction situations that are similar to situations in which parents and children engage in daily life (e.g., free play time, cleaning up toys). Other observation measures provide a way for therapists to evaluate parent–child interactions in natural settings such as the home. Both types of measures use direct observation of behavior and thus, circumvent some of the subjective biases that exist in parent-report measures. Actual observation of parent–child interactions is a better predictor of long-term outcomes than parent or teacher report (Aspland & Gardner, 2003; Patterson & Forgatch, 1995).

Dyadic Parent–Child Interaction Coding System–Fourth Edition

Description. The Dyadic Parent–Child Interaction Coding System–Fourth Edition (DPICS-IV), is both a coding system and a standardized set of scenarios developed to assess a range of aspects of the parent–child relationships for children 2 to 7 years of age (Eyberg, Nelson, et al., 2014). The DPICS tools allow therapists to quantify important qualitative dimensions of the relationship—especially those associated with abusive parenting and child disruptive behaviors—such as parents' ability to be child-centered; to provide effective, developmentally appropriate direction; and to implement safe, effective limits. The full-length version of the DPICS-IV observations includes three parent–child interaction situations—child-led play, parent-led play, and toy clean-up—that each requires parents to implement a different degree of direction and control with their children. As illustrated by Donna and Danielle's case, the three scenarios, which pull for distinct types of interactions from parents and children, can illuminate important strengths and weaknesses in a parent–child dyad. The full version of the DPICS scenarios is useful for assessment prior to and after treatment and takes 20 minutes to administer.

Shorter versions of the DPICS-IV, which include only one scenario and take 5 minutes to administer, were developed for use during treatment. The single-scenario versions of the DPICS-IV allow therapists to specifically focus either on parents' abilities to be child-centered in their interactions with their children or on parents' abilities to give effective, developmentally appropriate directions and consequences.

The DPICS scenarios are meant to be coded by clinicians using the standardized DPICS-IV coding system. Two systems exist: one for research (Eyberg, Nelson, et al., 2014) and one specifically developed to be feasible for use in clinical settings (Eyberg, Chase, et al., 2014). The systems are entirely compatible; the research version has codes that are not necessary in most clinical settings. The clinical coding system assesses nine categories of parent behaviors and three categories of children's responses to parent requests. For each category, observers (e.g., therapists) rate the number of times a parent or child displays the behaviors during the observed period. Parent categories include nurturing skills consistent with child-centered play therapy (Landreth, 2002), such as providing a narrative of a child's actions (Behavior Descriptions; e.g., "I see you're drawing a kitty") and paraphrasing a child's verbalizations (Reflections; e.g., Child: "I found a pink one!" Parent: "You did find a pink one!"). Positive parenting categories also include social reinforcement such as praises that specify the child's prosocial behaviors (Labeled Praises; e.g., "Great job picking up the toys") and those that are positive but do not specify a behavior (Unlabeled Praises; e.g., "Great job"). Directive parent categories include limit-setting (Direct Commands, Indirect Commands), negativity (Negative Talk), and questions. General statements are captured with the broad category Neutral Talk. Child categories are coded in response to parents' use of directives (Compliance, Non-compliance, No Opportunity for Compliance).

The categories of the DPICS relate to other important indicators of child and family functioning. (Nelson & Olsen, 2018). For instance, parents' interactions with their children on the DPICS have been associated with parenting stress and with children's prosocial behaviors (Niec et al., 2016; Pemberton et al., 2013). The DPICS also demonstrates good sensitivity to changes that occur throughout treatment (Niec et al., 2016; Schuhmann et al., 1998). Physically abusive parents who completed a parent–child treatment program demonstrated more child-centered interactions and fewer negative physical and verbal interactions as assessed with the DPICS (Chaffin et al., 2004). Parents who had children with disruptive behavior disorders and completed either an individual format or a group format of a parenting program demonstrated more child-centered relationships (Niec et al., 2016; Schuhmann et al., 1998). In the treatment of children with autism spectrum disorder, the DPICS has been used to assess changes in communication and parent–child relationship quality (Ginn et al., 2017).

The DPICS observation scenarios and coding system are sensitive to differences in parenting styles across cultures (K. M. McCabe et al., 2013) and have been used successfully among various cultures within the United States (Danko et al., 2016; K. M. McCabe et al., 2013; Niec et al., 2016) and globally (Abrahamse et al., 2016; Akcinar & Baydar, 2014; Bjørseth & Wichstrøm, 2016; Briegel et al., 2015; Chen & Fortson, 2015).

More than 4 decades of use provide support for the psychometric soundness of the DPICS (S. M. Eyberg, Nelson, et al., 2014). Unfortunately, normative data do not include a representative sample of the U.S. population. Although a number of studies including parents from the general community and from clinical populations provide some comparative information, the primary value of the DPICS is its ability to reliably capture important dimensions of the parent–child relationship and its sensitivity to treatment change. Interrater reliability of the parent and child categories ranges from adequate to excellent, with kappa coefficients from .54 (S. M. Eyberg, Nelson, et al., 2014) to 1.00 (Shanley & Niec, 2010). Parent–child interactions during the DPICS scenarios are meant to capture typical behavior patterns. Evidence finds that changes to the DPICS instructions alter parents' behaviors; therefore, as for other standardized measures, it is important to administer the DPICS using the precise instructions provided in the manual (Niec, Shanley, et al., 2015). This finding also raises questions about observation measures that lack a standardized administration protocol. Training materials for the DPICS-IV including the clinical manual with definitions of categories and extensive examples and a clinical workbook with coding exercises are available through PCIT International (https://www.pcit.org). A cost is associated with the initial training, but subsequent uses of the measure are free. Live and online training is available nationally and internationally through PCIT International–certified trainers.

What questions can the DPICS-IV answer? The DPICS is particularly useful in evaluating (a) the level of child-centeredness in parents' interactions with their children; (b) parents' ability to use safe, effective limit-setting; and (c) children's responsiveness to parents' direction. The measure can be used prior to treatment to test hypotheses about areas of parent–child conflict and parenting effectiveness and to develop treatment plans. The measure is also used appropriately as an evaluation of treatment outcome. The single scenarios of the DPICS can be used weekly during parent–child interventions to assess parents' skill acquisition, guide treatment direction, and determine when graduation from treatment is appropriate. An interesting advantage of the standardized DPICS scenarios is that they can be coded with different systems, such as those described next, to capture wide-reaching aspects of the parent–child relationship.

Keys to Interactive Parenting Scale

Description. Similar to the DPICS-IV, the Keys to Interactive Parenting Scale (KIPS) was developed to assess actual parent–child interactions during a period of behavior observation (Comfort & Gordon, 2006). The measure is appropriate for parent–child dyads with children aged 2 years to 5 years 11 months. Different from the DPICS-IV, the KIPS is a coding system only and does not include a standardized interaction scenario. Instead, the KIPS has been used to code parents' interactions during parent–child free play over a 20-minute period, during a 15-minute free play/5-minute clean-up situation, and during the three standardized DPICS scenarios (Comfort & Gordon, 2006; Lanier et al., 2016). Administered within a home, community, or clinic setting, the KIPS requires that children are provided with age-appropriate toys, and parents are instructed to play as they typically would (Comfort & Gordon, 2006). During observation of the parent–child interaction, raters score 12 parent behaviors on a scale from 1 to 5, with higher scores reflecting higher quality. A total score is obtained by calculating the average rating for all 12 items. Parent behaviors include those related to child-centered interactions (e.g., sensitivity of responses, supports emotions, open to child's agenda, adapts strategies to child, physical interaction), limit-setting (e.g., limits & consequences, supportive directions, reasonable expectations), and developmental scaffolding (e.g., promotes exploration and creativity, involvement in child's activities, encouragement, language experiences). No child categories are included on the KIPS.

Ratings of parenting interactions on the KIPS relate to other measures of observed parenting behavior (Comfort et al., 2011). The KIPS has been used to assess outcomes of parenting programs (McFarlane et al., 2017; Shapiro et al., 2014), with a population of mothers in the child protective services system as a result of intimate partner violence (Lanier et al., 2016), and with dyads with children with developmental disabilities (Shapiro et al., 2014).

In development studies, the KIPS demonstrated good internal consistency in a primarily White sample ($\alpha = .89$; Comfort & Gordon, 2006) as well as in samples of African American ($\alpha = .95$) and Latinx ($\alpha = .96$) families (Comfort et al., 2011). Interrater reliability was reported to be adequate, although the developers used a liberal definition of agreement, counting two coders as having "agreed" so long as they both rated the item within 1 point of one another on the 5-point rating scale (Comfort et al., 2006). This approach creates a 52% chance that raters would agree even if they responded arbitrarily. A subsequent study that reported interrater reliability, taking into account the possibility of agreeing by chance, found agreement between raters to be low ($\kappa = .47$; Lanier et al., 2016), whereas other studies did not report any information on interrater reliability (McFarlane et al., 2017; Shapiro et al., 2014). These findings suggest it may be challenging for therapists to be trained to code the KIPS in a meaningful way. No representative norms are available for the KIPS, although the development studies report the total mean scores for several populations of parents (e.g., recovering mothers, fathers with children in Head Start; Comfort & Gordon, 2006) and for samples of African American and Latinx families (Comfort et al., 2011). Training for the KIPS, which includes didactic materials and example videos to code, is available online through the developer (http://www.comfortconsults.com). To use the KIPS, there is a cost for initial training, for yearly recertification, and for each use of the measure.

What questions can the KIPS answer? The KIPS provides global impressions of 12 important parenting behaviors. In particular, the KIPS can provide information about parents' use of certain types of scaffolding behaviors with their children (e.g., promotes exploration and creativity, language experiences) that other observation tools feasible for use in clinical settings do not include. Because the KIPS items can be coded from the parent–child interactions within different samples of behaviors, one approach may be to use a standardized behavior scenario such as the ones offered by the full version of the DPICS, which would allow for the coding of both the DPICS-IV and the KIPS dimensions not captured by the DPICS. As with other measures lacking normative data, the KIPS cannot be used to confirm a diagnosis or to place a parent–child dyad into a category of risk, but it has been used to assess treatment outcomes in parent–child interventions.

Emotional Availability Scales

Description. The Emotional Availability Scales (EAS) coding system captures parents' and children's responsiveness (with a focus on emotional responsiveness) to one another in dyads with children 0 to 14 years of age (Bagner et al., 2012; Biringen et al., 2014). Parent categories coded by the system are sensitivity, structuring, nonintrusiveness, and nonhostility. Infant/child categories are the child's involvement of the adult and responsiveness to the adult. Each category is rated across seven subscales, with the sum of the scores creating a total scale score. A global score of the interaction can also be coded from 1 to 7. Two versions of the EAS exist, one appropriate for rating parent interactions with infants/young children and the other for school-age children (Biringen et al., 2014). The scales have been used to assess the parent–child interactions in dyads who are refugees, with physically abusive parents, with adopted children, with children in foster care, and with children with developmental disabilities such as Down syndrome and intellectual disabilities (R. Thomas & Zimmer-Gembeck, 2011; Van Den Dries et al., 2012; van Ee et al., 2012; van IJzendoorn et al., 2007; Venuti et al., 2008). The scale has been used with father–child dyads (Atzaba-Poria et al., 2010). Authors van IJzendoorn et al. (2007) suggested that the EAS may not be appropriate for use in dyads of children with autism, as the ways in which children with autism spectrum disorder involve their parents in their play may have a different relationship to their attachment patterns.

For one to reliably code the EAS, parent–child interactions should be no shorter than 20 minutes and preferably at least 30 minutes (Biringen, 2005). However, there is no standardized interaction developed for the EAS; rather, it can be used to code parent–child interactions in varied situations such as during free play, in parent-directed play, or after a parent–child separation and reunion (Biringen et al., 2014). The scales have been used successfully to code interactions during the DPICS scenarios (Kohlhoff et al., 2021; Timmer et al., 2012).

A large base of research provides information on the psychometrics of the EAS (see Biringen et al., 2014, for a review). Overall, the reliability and validity of the EAS have been acceptable. Interrater reliability of the scales (interclass correlation coefficients) for codes of mother–child interactions has been reported from .76 to .96 (Biringen et al., 2014). The scales have also demonstrated reasonable stability over time. The EAS has been used to evaluate treatment change in parent–child interventions, including clinic-based and home-visiting programs, and demonstrates good sensitivity to treatment (Kohlhoff et al., 2021; Nicolson et al., 2013; Olds et al., 2002). One outcome study evaluating the impact of a parent–child treatment program on parents' use of child-centered skills (coded via DPICS) and emotional sensitivity (coded via EAS) found that not all parents who increased their child-centered interactions also increased their sensitivity (Biringen et al., 2014; R. Thomas & Zimmer-Gembeck, 2011). This finding suggests that the two measures tap different important aspects of the parent–child relationship. Depending on the target of change for treatment, either or both measures may be useful.

Like many other observation measures of the parent–child relationship, the EAS does not have normative data available based on a representative sample with the United States. One challenge with developing norms for the EAS is the fact that the coding system is used across many different interaction scenarios. Any norms would be relevant only for the specific scenario through which the EAS was coded. Further, some caution in interpretation is warranted when using the EAS with families from different socioeconomic backgrounds, as the scales have been found to relate to socioeconomic status, although they did not relate to parent psychopathology (De Falco et al., 2014). A strength of the EAS is that it has been used successfully across various cultures within the United States (e.g., Robinson et al., 1993; Shivers, 2008; Timmer et al., 2012) and globally (e.g., van IJzendoorn et al., 2007; Venuti et al., 2008; Wünsche & Brisch, 2010; Ziv et al., 2000). Training for the EAS is available through the developer (http://www.emotionalavailability.com). The EAS has fees for initial training and annual recertification but not for each use.

What questions can the EAS answer? The EAS provides a valid way to assess important aspects of parent sensitivity as well as emotional reciprocity in the parent–child relationship. Because the scales are more reliable when coded from longer (20 minutes or more) samples of parent–child interaction (Biringen, 2005), they are likely to be most useful as a tool for pretreatment and posttreatment assessments. The EAS may also be used in combination with coding systems that provide details about other important parent–child interactions such as limit setting and contingent reinforcement. Particularly if there are concerns about a parent's responsiveness to a child, the EAS could be a useful part of the assessment process.

Therapist-Rated Global Scales

Therapists' global ratings of the parent–child relationship are an additional source of information to help track progress and outcomes in treatment. Unfortunately, there is a lack of psychometrically sound global measures. However, the Parent–Infant Relationship Global Assessment Scale (PIRGAS) has demonstrated adequate support for use in clinical settings.

Parent–Infant Relationship Global Assessment Scale

Description. The PIRGAS is a global scale that provides an overall assessment of functioning in the parent–child relationship (Zero to Three, 2005). Through a clinical interview of the parents and observations of parent–child interactions, the PIRGAS is coded on a continuous scale from 0 to 100 with nine anchor points (e.g., 100–91 = *well adapted*, 10–0 = *dangerously impaired*). Three dimensions of the parent–child relationship are considered in the rating: behavioral quality of the interaction, affective tone, and psychological involvement. A rating of 91 or higher signifies a conflict-free relationship characterized primarily by mutual positive affect, whereas a rating of 10 or lower signifies pervasive, rigid, and dangerous interaction patterns that put the child at risk of harm.

PIRGAS scores have demonstrated significant associations with measures of children's current and future functioning. For example, the PIRGAS of 53 mother–child dyads with 20-month toddlers predicted the toddlers' internalizing symptoms and compliance to mothers 4 months later (Aoki et al., 2002). The PIRGAS has demonstrated reasonable interrater reliability, although not all studies have reported on reliability (Paris et al., 2015) and the scale has shown sensitivity to treatment (Paris et al., 2015). It has been used to assess the parent–child relationships of mothers with histories of trauma and substance abuse, of infants in the child welfare system, and of children receiving day treatment services (Albers et al., 2020; Chinitz et al., 2017; Paris et al., 2015). The PIRGAS has been used with samples within the United States and Europe (Albers et al., 2020; Hatzinikolaou et al., 2016). A description of the PIRGAS anchor points and the rating process can be found in the Diagnostic Classification of Mental Health and Developmental Disorders of Infancy and Early Childhood–Revised (Zero to Three, 2005; https://www.zerotothree.org). The PIRGAS has an initial start-up cost.

What questions can the PIRGAS answer? The PIRGAS is a relatively quick and straightforward global rating system and thus can be used as part of almost any assessment of the parent–child relationship for children from 0 to 3 years of age. The therapist's overall rating of the quality of the parent–child relationship contributes information unique from that obtained from parents or children (Albers et al., 2020). Because it is a global rating, the PIRGAS does not offer insight into the specific areas of strength and weakness in the relationship. However, it is a useful tool for describing the level of dysfunction and for tracking treatment outcome.

SUMMARY

During early childhood, the parent–child relationship has the potential to either complicate or protect against many socioemotional and behavioral difficulties and disorders. Conversely, problems of early childhood can strain the parent–child relationship. A thorough assessment, therefore, provides clinicians with valuable information to develop a conceptualization of the presenting problem—including an understanding of the parent–child system rather than the child or parent in isolation—and to identify, implement, and monitor appropriate treatment strategies. Despite the importance of a good-quality assessment, few measures of the parent–child relationship are feasible for use in a clinical setting and have sound psychometric properties. Selecting assessment tools that (a) capture the dimensions of the parent–child relationship relevant to the problem, (b) include the parent's perceptions as well as a standardized observation of actual parent–child interaction, and (c) have acceptable reliability and validity is key to creating an appropriate and effective treatment plan.

Key Takeaways

1. Quality assessment of the parent–child relationship is essential to effective treatment because it helps to identify key targets for intervention, monitor treatment progress, and determine when treatment is complete.
2. Assessment of the parent–child relationship is stronger when it includes standardized tools from the perspectives of the parent, therapist, and direct behavior observation.

3. Assessment of the strengths in a parent–child relationship is as important as assessment of the vulnerabilities and deficits.

4. Not all assessment tools marketed to therapists have good psychometric qualities. It is important to be familiar with the psychometrics of the tools chosen for any assessment.

5. When selecting a tool to assess the parent–child relationship, ask yourself the following: (a) How will the information gained from the measure increase my understanding of the parent–child dyad? (b) How will the measure influence my treatment approach? (c) Has the measure been used effectively for the same purpose I intend to use it?

Clinical Growth Questions

1. Are there ways I can make better use of the assessment information I currently collect?

2. How might I integrate a multimethod, multisource pretreatment assessment into my agency or practice?

3. Do I assess a family's strengths prior to treatment? Can I better use those strengths to facilitate change?

4. How can I better assess families' progress during treatment in order to determine whether the treatment is bringing about positive change?

5. What new assessment tool or technique would I like to learn within the next year?

5

Fostering Responsive Parenting

If a community values its children, it must cherish their parents.

—JOHN BOWLBY (BOWLBY & WORLD HEALTH ORGANIZATION, 1952)

I had run to the grocery store only to grab something for dinner, but the after-work crowd filled the place until it was a challenge just to get down an aisle. Customers shoved carts around one another, jockeying for the shortest cashier line. Hungry children whined at their tired parents, many of whom were staring at their mobile phones. In the long line ahead of me, a father waited with a full cart of groceries and his son of about 6 years. The child stood with one hand on the cart, shifting from foot to foot and darting a brown-eyed gaze toward a group of older children who were serving themselves slushies by the counter beyond the cashier. Slowly, the line moved forward. The boy sighed. Just as it appeared he might give up waiting and dart off to join the other children, his father ruffled the boy's hair.

"Hey, buddy, thanks for helping me pick out dinner. Macaroni and cheese was a good idea!"

The child grinned and looked up at his dad. "Can I squeeze the cheese into the bowl? When we get home?"

"Sure. I'd love it. We can cook together."

The child tapped his foot restlessly and rocked back and forth. "I'm hungry."

"You're feeling hungry. I know. It's time for dinner. We'll eat when we get home."

https://doi.org/10.1037/0000304-005
Strengthening the Parent–Child Relationship in Therapy: Laying the Foundation for Healthy Development, by L. N. Niec

The boy's gaze went back to the slushie counter, where the older kids were now drinking, a look of longing crossed his face. "Can I get a slushie?"

"Not today, buddy."

"Please? Just a small one?"

"You'd really like a small slushie."

"Yeah!"

"I understand. They're good. I like them too."

"So can we?"

Father repeated, still calmly: "Not today."

The child's eyes grew tearful, and he slumped dramatically against the side of the cart. "Ohhh!"

"I know, bud. It's disappointing not to get something you really like. Another time we'll have a slushie. Can you put that box of cereal on the belt? I can't reach it."

Slowly, pouting, the boy put the box on the belt.

"Thanks, bud. You're a big help. I can hardly wait to make our macaroni and cheese."

The child nodded, gave a little sniffle, and then, beginning to smile a little, he continued to put items from the cart onto the belt. His father smiled and ruffled the child's hair again. "Thanks."

From an attachment theory perspective, parental sensitivity is a key component of parenting that influences children's functioning across time and domains. As already discussed, *sensitivity* is one important but narrow aspect of parenting defined specifically in the context of attachment to refer to a caregiver's ability to read, interpret, and respond to a child's cues (Ainsworth, 1969). *Responsiveness* is a broader term that refers to multiple dimensions of parenting behaviors beyond attachment-specific interactions (Caplan et al., 2019; Mesman & Emmen, 2013; Sroufe, 2005). In the brief interactions between the father and son just described, the parent demonstrated a number of behaviors that can be considered responsive: support of the child's prosocial/helping behaviors (responsiveness to behavior), empathy for his hunger (responsiveness to physical/emotional needs), validation of his disappointment (responsiveness to emotion, emotion labeling), redirection to prevent prohibited behavior (scaffolding), and physical affection (warmth). Further, this father was positively engaged and attuned. He modeled patience and emotion regulation, even when his son became fussy, providing the message that the experience of negative emotion is not in itself something that must be avoided or is in some way unsafe. From the behaviors they each displayed, the parent appeared to be attentive to and respectful of his child's emotional experiences, and the child appeared to be receptive to his parent's involvement and support.

Most parents who present for treatment do not at first show as many of the positive interactions with their young children as this father. In Chapter 2 of this volume, I discussed the pervasive positive influences that warm, responsive, and child-centered parenting has on multiple domains of child development.

These associations have been supported within the developmental literature and the treatment outcome research. Not only does responsive parenting have a direct effect on children's health and well-being (e.g., Eshel et al., 2006), it also acts as a buffer against adverse experiences (e.g., Brody, Gray, et al., 2017; Clark et al., 2019; Greene et al., 2020). Thus, responsive parenting is a fundamental target for treatment. This chapter (a) offers useful ways to operationalize "responsive parenting" in order to identify, target, and track these important parenting behaviors for treatment; (b) discusses factors that increase parents' risk for poor responsiveness; and (c) considers the bidirectional influence of parents' and children's behaviors on the quality of their relationships.

RESPONSIVE PARENTING INCLUDES FATHERS TOO

Before moving on to describe the behaviors that compose responsive parenting, it is important to recall the importance of the father–child relationship. The early attachment research consistently neglected the role of fathers' parenting in children's development, and although increasing effort has been made to include fathers in development and intervention research, they are still significantly underrepresented (Davison et al., 2017; Fabiano & Caserta, 2018; Parent et al., 2017). Fathers have been so excluded within the literature that many studies explicitly define responsive "parenting" as interactions between "mother and child" and/or do not consider fathers as participants (e.g., Bailey et al., 2017; Eshel et al., 2006; Hill et al., 2008; Landry et al., 2006; Ravindran et al., 2019). In Chapter 8, I discuss in more depth the contribution of fathers to children's development and strategies to increase fathers' engagement in the treatment process. Here, it is essential to keep in mind that both mothers and fathers influence their children's well-being and that the behaviors that make up responsive parenting are important for each of the key caregivers in a child's life.

OPERATIONALIZING RESPONSIVE PARENTING

Ainsworth, who developed some of the first observational measures of infant attachment and maternal sensitivity, conceptualized "sensitivity" as a set of behaviors that occurred within the parent–infant interaction, particularly in the context of the infant's distress (Ainsworth et al., 1974). As mentioned in Chapter 1, sensitivity referred to a mother's (not a father's) ability to recognize her infant's cues, to decipher their meaning, and to respond to them appropriately (Ainsworth et al., 1978). Researchers have since developed dozens of measures to assess parent sensitivity and responsiveness (Mesman & Emmen, 2013). Although the existence of so many different approaches to assessment suggests a lack of consensus about the meaning of the construct, it also demonstrates that many types of behaviors can be conceptualized as a part of responsive parenting.

In the next sections, I discuss seven core dimensions of responsive parenting from the developmental literature that are relevant to clinical intervention: responsiveness to child behaviors, responsiveness to child physical/emotional needs, warmth/affection, emotion labeling, engagement/attunement, parental positive affect, and scaffolding (Table 5.1). These dimensions have been associated with child and family functioning and reliably assessed in clinical and home settings.

Prompt, Contingent, and Appropriate Child-Centeredness

Across all types of parenting behaviors, to be considered responsive, the behaviors must be delivered by the parent in a *prompt, contingent,* and *appropriate* manner subsequent to the child's behavior or cue (Bornstein et al., 2008; Keller et al., 1999; Landry et al., 2006). In other words, thinking of the father–son example presented earlier, when a child communicates a need or expresses an emotion (e.g., growing tearful after being told he could not have a treat), the parent reacts quickly in response to the child's communication and in a developmentally appropriate manner (e.g., validating the child's disappointment).

Responsive behaviors are also generally described as child-centered. To behave in a child-centered way is to interact with children in a manner that is consistent with their needs, interests, and goals, or in other words, to follow

TABLE 5.1. Key Components of Responsive Parenting

Parent behavior	Examples
Responsiveness to child behavior	Following the child's lead; child-centered descriptions of child behavior; social reinforcement of positive behavior
Responsiveness to child physical/ emotional needs	Validating child's emotional experiences; providing comfort and support in times of distress; meeting child's physical needs
Warmth/affection	Nonintrusive, appropriate physical (e.g., hugs) and emotional expressions (e.g., "I love you") of warmth
Emotion labeling	Identifying and reflecting emotions implicit or explicit in child's behavior (e.g., "It looks like you're feeling angry right now," "It's frustrating when that happens," "Your big smile tells me you're happy")
Engagement or attunement	Verbal and nonverbal, behavioral and affective involvement in the interaction; interpreting child's cues without distortion; maintaining interaction even when child's behavior is challenging (e.g., whining, defying parent)
Parental positive affect	Congruent verbal and nonverbal communication of joy/pleasure (e.g., smiles, laughter, expression of positive emotion)
Scaffolding	Verbally elaborating on child's experiences; child-centered comments to help maintain child interest; structuring environment to support child's positive behavior

the child's lead. Child-centered interactions may look different depending on the context (e.g., play vs. a joint task) and the child's initiating behavior (e.g., interacting with toys vs. indicating a need for help). To be part of responsive parenting, the behaviors described next should be child-centered and performed in a way that is prompt, contingent, and appropriate.

Responsiveness to Child Behaviors

For a parent to be responsive to a child's behaviors requires that the parent be attuned to the behavior and follow the child's lead (Bailey et al., 2017; Pauli-Pott et al., 2018). Responsiveness to behaviors can include describing or commenting in a neutral way on the child's actions, offering encouragement or providing social reinforcement (e.g., positive attention, praise; Greene et al., 2020; Hill et al., 2008). In a play situation, a parent who is responsive to the child's behavior allows the child to choose the activity, follows along with that activity, and supports the activity verbally and behaviorally. Social reinforcement of children's prosocial behaviors might include, for example, a parent thanking his daughter for sharing a toy, telling her he enjoys her creative thinking, or giving her a high-five for persevering with a difficult task. In the case of the father and son at the grocery store, the father observed his son's positive behaviors and provided social reinforcement. The father's responsiveness to his son supported the child's ability to stay near to his father even in the face of a distracting and desired object across the store.

Responsiveness to Child Physical/Emotional Needs

Like responsiveness to behavior, responsiveness to a child's physical and emotional needs first requires parents to be attuned to their children's expressions. In addition, parents must interpret their children's expressions accurately (Biringen & Easterbrooks, 2012; Eshel et al., 2006). Depending on the child's age and developmental level, interpretation may involve understanding verbal and nonverbal behavior (Dunst & Kassow, 2008). Responsiveness to physical and emotional needs also depends on the context and the child's signals. For example, it might include a parent feeding her hungry child, providing comfort when a child is sick, helping a child to reach the water fountain, or offering support when a child is in distress.

Parent responsiveness that includes responsiveness to physical and emotional needs is associated with better child health and well-being (e.g., Eshel et al., 2006). When examined apart from other aspects of responsiveness, parent responsiveness to children's distress has been related to the development of children's empathy and prosocial behaviors (Davidov & Grusec, 2006). Responsiveness to physical and emotional needs is a parent skill that can be strengthened through therapeutic intervention. Parenting interventions delivered in high-income and low-income countries have demonstrated effectiveness in building parents' responsiveness to their children's physical and emotional needs (e.g., Eshel et al., 2006; Yousafzai et al., 2015).

Warmth/Affection

Parental warmth is a construct that crosses theoretical approaches and has been recognized for decades as a key aspect of positive parenting (Baumrind, 1971; Biringen et al., 2014; Maccoby & Martin, 1983). As a part of parenting responsiveness, *warmth* refers to a parent's expressions of fondness, nurturance, affection, and appreciation for the child (Baumrind, 1971; MacDonald, 1992). Like other affective constructs, warmth may be expressed verbally (e.g., "I love playing with you," "That's my sweetheart") or nonverbally (e.g., a pat on the back, affectionately ruffling a child's hair). As mentioned in Chapters 1 and 2 of this volume, Baumrind (1971) identified warmth as one of two primary dimensions that describe a parent's overall style of interaction with their child; the other dimension is parent demandingness. Parents who are highly demanding of their children but express little warmth (i.e., authoritarian style) are more likely to have children with conduct problems such as defiance and aggression (Thompson et al., 2003). Low warmth has also been associated with potential for abusive parent–child interactions (Rodriguez, 2010). In one of the few studies to attempt to disentangle the influences of different aspects of parent responsiveness on child functioning, maternal warmth but not responsiveness to children's distress was related to regulation of positive affect in 6- to 8-year-old boys and girls; in boys, maternal warmth was also related to acceptance by peers (Davidov & Grusec, 2006).

Warmth that is responsive is appropriate and not intrusive (Hill et al., 2008). A parent may be intrusive when they are excessively effusive or ignore the child's cues for physical space. For example, Ms. T and her 6-year-old son Marcus were participating in a standardized observation of their interactions during an intake assessment prior to starting treatment. During the child-led component of the observation, verbal and nonverbal behaviors of both parent and child demonstrated that the relationship was positive in many ways and that they enjoyed interacting with each other. As the play continued, however, Ms. T became loud and wildly enthusiastic, shouting out cheerful encouragement as her son played (e.g., "WOW! You're doing GREAT!") and leaning farther and farther into his space. In response, Marcus slowly began to physically withdraw from his mother, sliding his chair away to win himself room until he was clinging to the very edge of the table. One of the treatment goals became helping Ms. T to recognize her son's cues when he expressed a need for calmer responses from her and for her to regulate her expressions of warmth to be less intrusive.

Emotion Labeling: Why "Big" Emotions Should Be Named

Attachment theory posits that parental sensitivity and responsiveness play an important part in the development of children's understanding of emotions and emotion regulation. By expressing empathy through labeling children's observed emotion, parents (a) validate children's internal experiences, (b) help children begin to name their experiences, (c) foster children's abilities to connect their physical and affective states to identify their emotions (e.g., When I'm sad, I cry, my chest feels tight, and my stomach hurts), and (d) communicate acceptance of children's emotion.

Many parents, and adults generally, feel an often well-intentioned inclination to try to convince children not to experience their emotions—particularly negative emotions—or they communicate to children that their emotions are somehow improper, wrong, or unsafe. Take the following examples of a parent with her 5-year-old child who has just thrown down his crayon and ripped up his drawing:

Example: Parent Criticizing Child

CHILD: This is too hard. I can't draw!

PARENT: Don't tear up your drawing! That's not nice.

CHILD: It's ugly! I can't do anything!

PARENT: Why are you so upset? You can do another one.

Example: Parent Dismissing Child's Experience

CHILD: This is too hard. I can't draw!

PARENT: Oh, it's a good drawing. It's great!

CHILD: It's ugly! I can't do anything!

PARENT: That's not true! Let's try again.

CHILD: [*pushes the rest of the crayons off the table*] It's stupid! Everybody is better than me.

In the first example, the parent explicitly dismisses the child's emotional experience and communicates that his emotion and behavior are unacceptable. The tone is harsh, and the behavior is not responsive. In the second example, although the parent displays more warmth, she still dismisses the child's emotional experience. By trying to convince the child that his picture is "great," the parent communicates a message that *your experience is not valid. You don't have the right to feel this way.* Dismissiveness of a child's emotions in this manner sends the message that negative emotions are unsafe to be expressed

(Ravindran et al., 2019). Instead, a responsive interaction with emotion labeling might look like this:

Example: Parent Validating Child's Experience

CHILD: This is too hard. I can't draw!

PARENT: That was really hard for you.

CHILD: Yeah! I wanted it to be a horse, but I messed it up.

PARENT: You feel like you messed it up. That sounds frustrating.

CHILD: [*sits back in his chair more calmly*] I don't know if I can ever do it right.

PARENT: Sometimes it feels like you can never make it like you want it to be. I wonder if it just takes more practice. Maybe we could work on it together.

In this third example, the parent demonstrates responsiveness with her use of emotion labeling. When the child's experience is acknowledged, he no longer needs to escalate his behavior in order to feel heard. His mother's responses help him to feel understood. No longer having to argue his case, so to speak (i.e., *Believe me, I am frustrated and disappointed!*), the child is then able to move the next step to seek a coping strategy to regulate his emotion and manage his frustration. In addition, labeling the emotion directly rather than using general terms such as "big feelings" or "big emotions" helps children to identify what it is they are experiencing and to build a vocabulary to verbalize those experiences. Naming emotions communicates to children that even negatively valenced affect such as anger and sadness is acceptable and safe to experience and to share.

Engagement or Attunement

Engagement or *attunement* refers to a parent's involvement in the interaction with their child—the ability to accurately read the child's cues and to adjust their interactions with the child to maintain a positive connection (Bailey et al., 2017; Biringen et al., 2014; Hill et al., 2008). An engaged parent remains involved in the interaction even when the situation becomes challenging (e.g., child grows fussy or defiant; Hill et al., 2008). Verbal and nonverbal demonstrations of engagement include the parent remaining in proximity to the child, making eye contact, participating in the child's activities, and remaining attuned to the child's expressions. Poor engagement can manifest in a parent's lack of involvement. He or she may tune out the child, engage in a competing activity (e.g., checking mobile device), avoid eye contact, or show other nonverbal signs of inattentiveness. Poor engagement can also manifest as hostility and intrusiveness, displayed by parents who overcontrol their children's activities, express anger or resentment toward their children during interactions, and interpret their children's cues based on their own needs. Consider the following examples of parent–child interactions in a behavioral health clinic waiting room.

Example: Poorly Engaged Parent

CHILD: Look, Mom, the LEGOs are out today!

PARENT: [*pulling smartphone out of her bag*] Mmhmm.

CHILD: Maybe there's enough to make the dinosaur this time.

PARENT: [*sitting in a chair across the room from the toy area*] Yep.

CHILD: [*glancing over at mother, his positive affect fades, and he loses interest in the toys*] I'm hungry.

PARENT: You can't be hungry. You ate all my French fries at lunch.

Example: Engaged Parent

CHILD: Look, Mom, the LEGOs are out today!

PARENT: [*nodding and smiling at the child*] They are out.

CHILD: Maybe there's enough to make the dinosaur this time.

PARENT: [*sitting next to the child in the toy area*] Could be. There's a lot of them.

CHILD: [*growing more interested in the toys*] I'm gonna make the T-rex. Like the one on the box.

PARENT: Sounds like fun. I'm here to help if you need it.

In the first example, the parent displayed poor engagement with her child, not merely because she failed to join in the play but also because she failed to get involved with the child himself (e.g., lack of eye contact, failure to respond to a request for reaction). In addition, the parent dismissed her son's expression of physical needs as invalid based on her own experience. On the other hand, the parent in the second example demonstrated engagement and attunement with the child in terms of his activities and his affect. The parent's positive engagement with the child kept his attention and interest on the play.

Similar to other aspects of parent responsiveness, engagement/attunement has generally been examined as part of the broader construct rather than as a separate factor. In that context, engagement/attunement is related to important child outcomes, including attachment security, social and cognitive development, child behavioral regulation and physiological stress responses, and physical well-being (e.g., Eshel et al., 2006; Greene et al., 2020; Hill et al., 2008; Martinez-Torteya et al., 2014). Maternal attunement specifically has demonstrated a more consistent relationship with child attachment patterns than two other aspects of responsiveness: parent positivity and accessibility (Bailey et al., 2017). Infants of mothers who were more attuned at 12 months were more likely to demonstrate secure attachment patterns at 15 months and at 2 years (Bailey et al., 2017).

Parental Positive Affect

Parents display their emotional experiences with their children verbally (e.g., expressions of enjoyment, pleasure) and nonverbally (e.g., smiling, laughter, positive touches such as hugs). Therapists may observe parental affect directly during parent–child interactions (e.g., in the waiting room, in the home, during standardized parent–child observations) or may elicit affect with specific questions during a clinical interview. Understanding the tone of the emotions a parent expresses toward their child provides important information about the parent–child relationship and can facilitate the development of the treatment plan.

Parental positive affect was not a component of the original maternal sensitivity scales developed by Ainsworth (1969), as parents' affect was seen as a separate construct from their responsiveness. That is, some parents might enjoy interacting with their children without being responsive. Imagine, for example, the father who enjoys teasing his young son even when the teasing clearly causes the child discomfort, or the mother who laughs as she tickles her infant although the infant recoils and grimaces at the prodding. Other parents may be responsive without experiencing enjoyment. For example, think of the mother who promptly and adequately addresses her child's needs while displaying depressed affect, or the father who cares for his child with an angry manner. For this reason, many scales that integrate parental positive affect into the concept of responsive parenting also consider the child's response and the context of the interaction within the rating (Biringen et al., 2014; Hill et al., 2008; Mesman & Emmen, 2013).

When observing and assessing parental positive affect, therapists should consider the *intensity* of the expression directed toward the child, the *pervasiveness* of the expression across the interaction, and whether the parent's expressions are *congruent* (i.e., verbal and nonverbal communications match; Biringen et al., 2014; Hill et al., 2008). An example of optimal parental positive affect is seen in parents who express pleasure in their interactions with appropriate intensity—for instance, displaying animation and enthusiasm rather than either flatness or excessive, overstimulating emotion. Their positive affect with their children is pervasive (i.e., spans different situations such as play, feeding, joint tasks), even when they may also sometimes experience situational frustration or anger. And their expressions of positive affect are congruent across verbal and nonverbal communication channels; for example, a mother smiles when she tells her child she loves him, or a father pats his daughter on the back while telling her he is having fun playing with her.

As would be expected, parental positive affect is related to other aspects of parenting responsiveness, but it also appears to contribute independently to domains of child functioning such as cooperation with parental requests and language development (Landry et al., 2006). Parental positive affect can be increased through interventions focused on the parent–child interaction (e.g., Chaffin et al., 2004; Landry et al., 2006). For example, mothers and fathers with a substantiated history of physically abusive behavior toward their children displayed fewer verbal and physical negative interactions with their children after participating in the parent–child intervention parent–child interaction therapy, which fosters parent responsiveness (Chaffin et al., 2004). Mothers who participated in a 10-session home visiting program that was focused explicitly on improving responsiveness demonstrated more emotional support, including expression of positive affect (Landry et al., 2006). As a component of responsive parenting that is amenable to change and demonstrates significant associations with child development, parental positive affect is a component of responsive parenting to be considered in the clinical setting.

Scaffolding

Vygotsky (1978) described the concept of *scaffolding*, in which adults provide children with support and guidance to facilitate the growth of their abilities from one developmental level to the next. The process of scaffolding does not intrude on the child's learning by providing answers or completing a presented task for the child. Instead, an adult who provides scaffolding might offer clues, ask questions, or elaborate on the child's observations to the extent it is needed in order to foster the child's progress. In the context of responsive parenting, scaffolding has been conceptualized similarly and has included parent behaviors such as verbally elaborating on the child's expressions, using child-centered descriptions or questions to help maintain the child's interest in their chosen activity, and structuring the environment to support positive behavior (Caplan et al., 2019; Greene et al., 2020; Hill et al., 2008; Landry et al., 2006).

In the example of the father and son at the grocery store, the father used emotion labeling and validation in combination with scaffolding to support his child's positive behavior. With his description ("It's disappointing not to get something you really like. Another time we'll have a slushie. Can you put that box of cereal on the belt?"), the parent remained child-centered yet helped to foster the child's ability to regulate his own behavior by shifting attention away from the prohibited activity.

As with other dimensions of responsive parenting, scaffolding is often evaluated as part of the broader construct of responsiveness rather than examined for its separate influences (e.g., Hill et al., 2008). Responsive parenting that includes appropriate scaffolding predicts the development of greater behavioral regulation in preschoolers (Pauli-Pott et al., 2018) and the well-being of children of mothers with symptoms of posttraumatic stress disorder (PTSD; Greene et al., 2020). Mothers who displayed more responsive parenting with scaffolding in their interactions with their infants were less likely to use harsh, punitive, and physical discipline strategies (O'Dor et al., 2017). In a study of the influences of different aspects of responsive parenting (e.g., verbal scaffolding) on children's development, mothers' use of verbal scaffolding was associated with children's development in three domains: level of cooperation, positive affect tone, and growth in word use (Landry et al., 2006). Mothers who participated in an intervention designed to foster their responsive parenting demonstrated a greater ability to provide supportive scaffolding for their infants relative to a group of mothers who received feedback only on their infants' developmental levels (Landry et al., 2006).

When Responsiveness Is Lacking: Identifying Risk in Parents

The parent–child relationship does not develop in isolation but within a rich and complex context of intrapersonal, interpersonal, cultural, and societal variables. Some important elements that influence the parent–child relationship and parenting have been found in the environment (e.g., family income, economic stress; Davis et al., 2020; García et al., 2014), the family structure (e.g., single vs. partnered parents; Martinez-Torteya et al., 2014), and the individual parent and child characteristics (e.g., parent psychopathology, child temperament; Muzik et al., 2017). A number of these factors have been identified as risks for lower parenting responsiveness (e.g., Asok et al., 2013; Epkins & Harper, 2016; García et al., 2014). Clinicians who are aware of these risk factors can develop a more comprehensive conceptualization of the pressures that may be influencing the relationships of the parents and children who present for treatment. Two domains of parent risk are presented next for particular consideration because they are commonly encountered within clinical populations and they can be addressed within the therapeutic setting.

Parent Psychopathology

Parent psychopathology, such as mood and anxiety disorders, can tap parenting resources and add strain to the parent–child relationship. Although a great majority of parents experience psychological symptoms or distress, many do not report them to their providers (Beardslee, 2019; England & Sim, 2009). Reluctance to report on their own symptoms may be particularly true for parents from ethnic minority backgrounds (e.g., Chaudron et al., 2005). Given the relationship between parent mental health symptoms, parenting, and child mental health, clinicians should routinely inquire about parents' mental health history and consider the role of distress in their parenting abilities and in the parent–child relationship.

Because depression is prevalent, a wealth of research has been conducted on the specific impact of depression on parenting and on children's functioning (for reviews, see S. H. Goodman et al., 2011; Lovejoy et al., 2000). Many of the children who enter the mental health system have parents who are experiencing depression (Beardslee, 2019; Tompson et al., 2015). Those parents struggling with depressive symptoms are more likely to demonstrate harsh and intrusive parenting styles and are less likely to be responsive in interactions with their children (Forehand et al., 2012; Lovejoy et al., 2000). High levels of depressive symptoms are also related to less parental warmth, more hostility and rejection, less effective communication, and less child-centeredness (Epkins & Harper, 2016; Henry et al., 2018). Such deficits in parenting responsiveness have been subsequently related to less adaptive coping strategies in children (Hardy et al., 1993; Henry et al., 2018; Jaffe et al., 2010). In a sample of 583 Spanish-dominant Latinx families, parents with more severe depressive symptoms also provided less warmth and emotional responsiveness to their children. Further, parent emotional responsiveness was the link between parents' depression and children's social competence deficits (Valdez et al., 2013).

Significant overlap exists in the presentations of parents who experience depression and anxiety. However, researchers have made attempts to separate the influences of each type of symptoms on parenting and children's development. In a study of 153 mothers with experiences of maltreatment during their own childhoods, symptoms of depression—but not PTSD—were associated with lower parental responsiveness and more hostility (Martinez-Torteya et al., 2014). Similarly, when examining the unique influences of parent depression and anxiety on parenting responsiveness in both mothers and fathers, researchers found that symptoms of depression in either parent were associated with more hostile, rejecting, and neglectful parent–child interactions. The association between parents' depression and their nonresponsive parenting remained significant even when controlling for the influence of anxiety, family socioeconomic status, parents' participation in treatment, and their children's symptoms of depression and anxiety (Epkins & Harper, 2016).

Parent History of Trauma

Strong evidence supports the negative impact of parents' trauma-related symptoms on children's functioning (Lambert et al., 2014; Leen-Feldner et al., 2013). Like depression, a history of trauma is also a common risk factor within the population of parents presenting for mental health treatment with their children. Similar to other types of psychopathology, the primary mechanism through which parents' trauma history is likely to impact children is through issues in parenting and strains in the parent–child relationship (van Ee et al., 2016). Parenting has been conceptualized as the primary intermediary factor between trauma and child functioning across trauma types—for example, a parent childhood history of abuse, intimate partner violence, and military deployment-related trauma (Gewirtz et al., 2011; Letourneau et al., 2007; Martinez-Torteya et al., 2014). Two systematic reviews of the impact of parents' trauma histories on parenting found deficits in a number of important domains, including the parent–child relationship, parent emotional availability, and parenting warmth and sensitivity (Christie et al., 2019; van Ee et al., 2016).

Responsive Parenting Is a Protective Factor

It is critical to remember that not all parents who have experienced trauma or who suffer from depression and anxiety demonstrate deficits in their parenting, and not all children whose parents struggle with some form of psychopathology suffer ill effects. In other words, protective factors exist that support resilience in parents and in children (Brody, Gray, et al., 2017; Greene et al., 2020; J. Snyder et al., 2016). Responsive parenting specifically has demonstrated the ability to buffer children from the adverse impact of early stress experiences such as mothers' trauma-related symptoms (Asok et al., 2013; Greene et al., 2020). That is, when mothers interact with their children in ways that are highly responsive to child behaviors and emotions and positively engage with their children, when they express positive affect, use scaffolding, and use emotion labeling, their trauma symptoms no longer predict high stress-related symptoms and disruptive behaviors in their children (Greene et al., 2020). Through responsive parenting, these children are more likely to develop adaptive coping strategies and good emotion regulation that helps them to cope with stressors related to a parent's psychopathology (Greene et al., 2020; Henry et al., 2018). The protective influences of responsive parenting in the case of parent mental health symptoms once again emphasizes the importance of responsiveness as part of a family case conceptualization and treatment plan.

Parents and Children Influence Each Other

The characteristics of any relationship are influenced by the interactions that are initiated and maintained by each member. Although early research on parent–child attachment focused primarily on the influence of parents' behaviors on children's relationship patterns, more recent developmental theories consider the parent–child relationship to be dynamic and bidirectional (e.g., Belsky, 1984; Granic & Patterson, 2006; Patterson, 1982, 2002; Sameroff, 2009). Increasing research supports transactional approaches to parent–child behaviors. That is, parents and children influence each other's actions, and each contributes to the overall status of the relationship.

How do bidirectional effects manifest between parents and children? Much of the research has focused on the mutual influence of parent and child behaviors or characteristics over a significant time span (months to years) to examine changes across a period of development (e.g., Cherry et al., 2019; Merz et al., 2017; Tiberio et al., 2016). For example, in a study of 534 families whose children attended Head Start (71% Hispanic/Latinx, 28% African American, 1% European American), parenting responsiveness predicted children's ability to delay gratification (i.e., effortful control) demonstrated 6½ months later (Merz et al., 2017). In parallel, children's ability to delay gratification predicted parents' responsiveness 6½ months later. In other words, parents who were positively engaged, were warm, and provided scaffolding during their parent–child interactions supported the development of an important aspect of behavior regulation in their 3- to 5-year-old children, and the demonstration of better behavior regulation in children fostered parents' warm, responsive behaviors (Merz et al., 2017). It may be easy to forget or dismiss the role that children play in influencing their parents' actions, until one imagines differences that would be likely when responding to a child who is generally able to control their own behaviors compared with a child who consistently oversteps limits. In the face of repeated child misbehavior, the latter parent is more likely to try to exert control. Similar reciprocal patterns were found in a study exploring parent responsiveness and children's effortful control in families of children from the approximate ages of 3 to 13 years (Tiberio et al., 2016).

Fewer studies have examined the mutual influences of parent and child behaviors in moment-to-moment interactions (Del Vecchio & Rhoades, 2010; Lunkenheimer et al., 2017; Ravindran et al., 2019). By examining immediate sequences of parent and child behaviors during challenging tasks (e.g., cleaning up toys, waiting for a snack, completing a difficult activity), it is possible to determine whether a specific behavior by parent or child makes it more or less likely that the partner will respond in a specific manner. This type of microanalysis allows for the testing of developmental theories such as Patterson's coercion theory, a transactional model of the development of parent–child conflict and child disruptive behaviors (Patterson, 1982, 2002; Figure 5.1).

Coercion theory posits that during parent–child interactions in which the parent attempts to exert control over the child (e.g., gain compliance to a request), both players influence the behavior of the other in two parallel cycles. In one cycle, parents' use of increasingly harsh discipline (e.g., from a request to threats to yelling to corporal punishment) results in intermittent child compliance, which reinforces parents for their use of coercive strategies. In the second cycle, children's escalation of defiance (e.g., ignoring parent to whining to tantrums) results in parents' intermittent relinquishment of the request, which reinforces children for their disruptive behaviors. Coercion theory helps to explain the mutual escalation of parent–child conflict often seen when parents' responsiveness to their children is low and limit-setting is inconsistent and when children's behavior regulation is poor.

Investigation of moment-to-moment parent–child interactions has revealed a mutual influence on behaviors consistent with coercion theory (Del Vecchio & Rhoades, 2010; Ravindran et al., 2019). Mothers of 2- to 4-year-olds were asked to encourage their children to complete three tasks as independently as possible (clean up toys, wait while parent talks on phone, play quietly alone) in the context of other preferred and prohibited objects (e.g., candy jar, desk items). Examined sequences included mothers' use of discipline (appropriate, overreactive, lax) and children's negative affectivity and misbehavior (Del Vecchio &

FIGURE 5.1. Parallel Escalating Cycles Reinforcing Parent Coercion and Child Disruptive Behavior

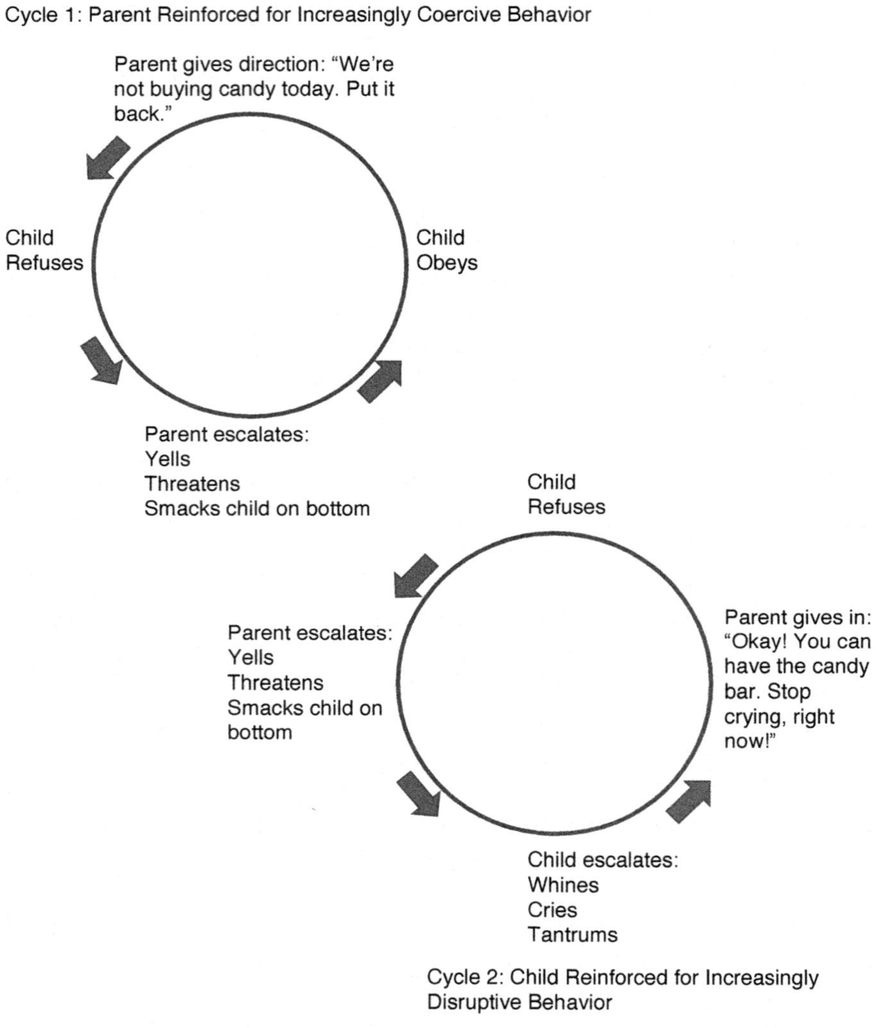

Note. Data from Patterson (1982, 2002).

Rhoades, 2010). As proposed by Patterson (2002), when mothers responded to child misbehavior with overreactive discipline (e.g., anger, yelling), children were more likely to display negative affect (e.g., whining, crying). At the same time, a child's display of negative affect was more likely to be followed by a mother's response of lax discipline (e.g., coaxing, pleading, ignoring the misbehavior; Del Vecchio & Rhoades, 2010). In a similar study, mothers and their 2½- to 3-year-olds interacted in a delay task in which children were required to wait for a visible snack while parents completed paperwork (Ravindran et al., 2019). Again, consistent with coercion theory, mothers and toddlers each influenced the escalation of parent–child conflict in the situation. When mothers acted in ways that were negative and nonresponsive, children were more likely to increase their disruptive behaviors and displays of negative emotion. When children increased their aversive responses, mothers were more likely to follow with an increase of their nonresponsive, harsh interactions (Ravindran et al., 2019). Mothers' supportive behaviors were not associated with children's aversive responses.

Looking closely at these parent–child microinteractions is particularly useful from a clinical point of view. As a therapist, understanding the moment-to-moment influences that lead, for example, to escalating parent–child conflict, better cooperation or greater parenting warmth allows for the assessment and identification of strengths or deficits in those contexts. Further, when the mutual influences on the parent–child relationship are understood (e.g., children are more likely to respond with negative emotion when mothers are harsh; when children respond with negative emotion, mothers are more likely to be inconsistent), interventions that specifically address those influences can be selected, stopping negative cycles of interaction and promoting positive ones.

The Role of the Therapist in Fostering Parent Responsiveness

The role of the therapist in child psychotherapy has alternately been conceptualized as that of a teacher/coach (e.g., cognitive behavior therapy), a reparative parent (psychodynamic therapy), and a source of unconditional support (child-centered play therapy). The assumption of each of these orientations is that, as in adult psychotherapy, the therapist–child relationship itself serves as a primary mechanism of change (Shirk & Russell, 1996). For young children, however, such an assumption can lack developmental sensitivity. In the case of problems that are caused or maintained by deficits in the parent–child relationship, in fact, the therapist–child relationship is not the relationship of key importance in treatment. The overall goal of the therapist is to strengthen the parent–child relationship—with a focus on the specific parent characteristics/behaviors (e.g., lack of warmth, difficulty identifying and interpreting child cues, overreactive discipline) and child characteristics/behaviors (attention deficits, conduct problems, internalizing symptoms) that are related to the specific issue. In interactions with the child, the therapist models healthy, responsive behaviors but does not seek to overshadow the parent.

Case Example: Parent–Child Interaction in a Unification Case

Mr. M, the father of 3-year-old Bri, had been in and out of his daughter's life since her birth, having no consistent contact with her and no ongoing relationship. When her biological mother, the custodial parent, died of a drug overdose, the court considered a permanency plan that would place Bri with Mr. M. However, Mr. M was first mandated to participate in a parent–child intervention with his daughter. At the start of treatment, Mr. M expressed feeling completely uncertain about how to interact with a 3-year-old and doubt about whether his daughter would like him. Assessment of the parent–child interactions revealed that Mr. M had an authoritarian parenting style and displayed little responsiveness. He was highly demanding, set excessive limits that were not developmentally appropriate, demonstrated little warmth or emotional validation, and had difficulty recognizing or interpreting his child's behavioral and emotional cues (e.g., differentiating tired behavior from defiant behavior). Bri exhibited high levels of anxiety and disruptive behaviors that tended to escalate when in the presence of Mr. M. A repeated sequence of parent–child interactions observed in the assessment occurred when Bri displayed mild misbehavior (e.g., refusing to put on her shoes), to which Mr. M responded with a harsh, controlling tone. In response to her father's harsh tone, Bri's negative affect escalated (e.g., crying, flopping onto the floor), after which Mr. M expressed frustration, feelings of ineffectiveness, and certainty that his daughter would never like him.

With Mr. M's active collaboration, the therapist developed a treatment plan that focused on strengthening the parent–child relationship and increasing the father's ability to provide responsive care for his child. The specific focus was on helping Mr. M to (a) attune to his daughter's behavioral and emotional cues in order to provide prompt, contingent, and appropriate responses; (b) increase his child-centeredness (responsiveness to behaviors and to physical/emotional needs, emotion labeling, expressions of warmth, positive affect, and scaffolding); and (c) provide his daughter with developmentally sensitive limits.

Mr. M participated in 23 sessions of the evidence-based intervention parent–child interaction therapy. During parent–child interactions, the therapist actively coached Mr. M to observe his daughter's behaviors and to respond in child-centered ways. In the initial sessions, Mr. M reported doubt about his ability to make changes in his parenting skill. However, he committed to following the treatment recommendations for four sessions, with a review of progress at that time. By the fourth coaching session, Mr. M was demonstrating an increased ability to interpret and distinguish his daughter's signals (e.g., anxiety vs. defiance) and to actively engage with her with child-centered interactions. Upon review, he decided to continue the program. A turning point in the treatment came when Mr. M was spontaneously interacting with responsiveness to Bri's play and his daughter turned to him with a smile and threw her arms around him in a hug. Mr. M reported that he had not expected to enjoy being with his child or her to enjoy being with him. As Mr. M continued to practice his new parenting skills—increasing his warmth and responsiveness—Bri's anxiety and her disruptive behaviors steadily declined. During play interactions, child and parent often expressed shared positive affect. During more challenging interactions (e.g., transitions, mealtimes), Mr. M was able to remain child-centered while setting appropriate, healthy limits. At one session, he proudly reported that during a family visit his mother praised him for being calm and sensitive with his daughter.

Mr. M completed treatment after 23 sessions. Standardized observation of his interactions with his daughter (Dyadic Parent–Child Interaction Coding System–Fourth Edition; see Chapter 4, this volume), self-reported ratings of the stress in the parent–child relationship (Parenting Stress Index, Fourth Edition; see Chapter 4, this volume), and the therapist's global rating (Parent–Infant Relationship Global Assessment Scale; see Chapter 4, this volume) revealed that Mr. M felt more confidence and less stress related to his role as a parent and that his interactions with his daughter were more child-centered and developmentally responsive. Mr. M continued to receive therapeutic support through the unification process, which proceeded successfully.

SUMMARY

Responsive parenting includes a range of parenting behaviors that cross theoretical approaches and demonstrate different associations with children's physical, emotional, and behavioral health. Overall, parenting that includes the key components of responsiveness (e.g., prompt, contingent, and appropriate responsiveness to child behavioral, emotional, and physical needs; emotion labeling; engagement/attunement; scaffolding) is associated with more positive child outcomes. Given the significant impact of parent responsiveness on children's functioning, it is critical to assess for strengths and weaknesses in responsiveness and to include responsiveness in the conceptualization of the parent–child relationship. Two findings about responsiveness make it of particular importance in treatment: (a) responsive parenting has been shown to protect children against the negative impact of risk factors such as maternal PTSD, and (b) responsiveness in parents is a malleable ability that can be increased through evidence-based therapeutic intervention.

In sum, parent responsiveness is a core aspect of the parent–child relationship and child functioning that therapists have the potential to foster and strengthen. When forming a conceptualization of the parent–child relationship and developing a treatment plan, it is crucial to recall that the interactions between parents and children are bidirectional. As parent responsiveness influences the child, the child's behavior influences the parent, and both sets of influences should be considered in any intervention.

Key Takeaways

1. Responsive parenting is a broad concept that includes multiple dimensions, such as responsiveness to a child's behavioral, physical, and emotional needs; warmth; emotion labeling; engagement/attunement; parental positive affect; and scaffolding.

2. To be responsive, any parent behavior must be delivered in a way that is prompt, contingent, and appropriate, subsequent to the child's expression or behavior.

3. More responsiveness in parenting has been associated with numerous important developmental outcomes for children (e.g., language development, social skills, emotion and behavior regulation).

4. Responsiveness is not just for mothers. It is important for fathers and other significant caregivers in children's lives (e.g., extended kin, stepparents, foster parents) to be responsive in their parenting.
5. Risk factors such as parent psychopathology can damage parent responsiveness; however, higher responsiveness is a protective factor that can buffer children against the negative impact of some types of adverse experiences.
6. Responsiveness is malleable. That is, through clinical interventions, parents can learn to be more responsive.
7. The interactions between parents and children are bidirectional. Not only do parents influence children, but child behaviors influence parent behaviors and may play a role in the escalation or reduction of parent–child conflict.
8. Therapists can play an important role in the development of parent responsiveness. We must keep in mind that the relationships that are most important to children's functioning are the long-term relationships they have with their caregivers.

Clinical Growth Questions

1. What dimensions of responsive parenting do I currently consider when developing a treatment plan for families? What dimensions might I add to more comprehensively address issues of responsiveness?
2. Do I routinely screen for common intrapersonal, familial, and environmental risk factors that may strain the parent–child relationship and reduce responsiveness?
3. How do I integrate the bidirectional influences of parent–child behavior into case conceptualizations and treatment plans?
4. How might I foster responsiveness in each of the key caregivers in children's lives (e.g., mothers, fathers, stepparents, foster parents, grandparents)?
5. Do the interventions I implement build parenting responsiveness?
6. What are some of my personal strengths as a therapist when working to strengthen the parent–child relationship? Are there areas in the assessment or treatment or the parent–child relationship in which I would like to grow?

6

When Negative Emotion Is a Positive Experience

Healthy Limit-Setting in the Parent–Child Relationship

When working with parents of young children, teaching them child-directed strategies without also teaching them how to set healthy limits is like sending someone off in a rowboat with only one oar.

"I've been working with them for 8 weeks, and these parents are still struggling to manage their child's behaviors. I'm hesitant to teach them limit-setting, though. What if they do it incorrectly?"

The question came from a young clinician. He had been working with Mr. and Ms. B and their 5½-year-old biological daughter, Audrey. While the parents continued to experience conflict in their relationships with their daughter, the therapist struggled with his own sense of confidence and his misconceptions about what limit-setting means and how it can be taught.

When Mr. and Ms. B first entered the clinic for an intake assessment, they appeared exhausted and frustrated. Their daughter, Audrey, had "taken over the family," they said. She had been a challenging child since infancy, always restless, difficult to keep on a schedule, and often fussy and difficult to soothe. As Audrey reached toddlerhood and became mobile, her restless behavior transformed into high levels of activity. Her parents described her as always on the move, running through the apartment, jumping on furniture, knocking over her siblings, and breaking toys with her rough play. In the past year, Audrey had drawn flowers with an indelible marker all over the wall of her bedroom, thrown her sister's gloves out the car window and onto the highway,

https://doi.org/10.1037/0000304-006
Strengthening the Parent–Child Relationship in Therapy: Laying the Foundation for Healthy Development, by L. N. Niec

and cut off the cat's whiskers with her mother's sewing shears. Ms. B grew tearful describing her daily struggles with Audrey, which started early in the morning when she tried to get her daughter ready for school and ended in the evening only after long arguments and yelling about bedtime.

Mr. B declared that his daughter needed a good smack or two, like his dad would have given him. Ms. B quickly interrupted her husband and said she did not believe in spanking. When the therapist inquired further about the parents' use of corporal punishment, Mr. B acknowledged spanking Audrey on the bottom with an open palm at times when she did something dangerous (e.g., bolting across the street alone) or when she blatantly defied him, which he stated seemed to increase on a daily basis. Audrey's older brother and sister had never acted "so badly," Ms. B reported. She reported that she had tried using time-out with Audrey but that recently a friend told her time-out was like child abuse, and she didn't know what to do. Both parents expressed feeling that they had tried every strategy to manage Audrey's behavior and "nothing worked." They reported that in the face of Audrey's problem behaviors, they typically either gave up and let Audrey have her way, just to end the conflict, or sent Audrey to her room for long periods (an hour or more), where she had toys and video games (so everyone could "have a break"). Mr. and Ms. B reported that they were "at the end of their rope."

Six months previous, Audrey had received a psychological evaluation after her kindergarten teacher reported that she was routinely disrupting the classroom with her inability to stay in her seat, refusal to follow simple directions, and aggressive play. Audrey had been given a diagnosis of attention-deficit/hyperactivity disorder (ADHD) and oppositional defiant disorder. Mr. and Ms. B had come to the clinic upon the recommendation of the psychologist.

After speaking with Mr. and Ms. B, the intake therapist recognized a number of risks to Audrey's healthy development and the parent–child relationship: (a) Audrey's challenging temperament and the symptoms associated with ADHD, (b) Mr. and Ms. B's high levels of distress and sense of helplessness, and (c) the coercive cycle occurring between parents and child that was exacerbated by the parents' use of inconsistent consequences and little support for Audrey's appropriate and prosocial behaviors. These factors together, as well as Mr. B's inclination to escalate to harsh, power-assertive discipline, made it likely that without intervention, the cycle would continue to escalate, causing Audrey's behaviors to grow more severe and the parent–child conflict to intensify. The intake therapist referred the family to begin an evidence-based parent–child intervention with a focus on increasing responsive and effective parenting.

For eight sessions, the family worked on strategies to increase warmth and responsiveness in their interactions with Audrey. Over the past 2 years, conflict had been escalating in the parent–child relationship. It had reached such a point that at the start of treatment, Mr. and Ms. B were unable to identify even small positive behaviors of Audrey's. Through their practice of responsive parenting techniques during live play sessions with their daughter and in brief play interactions at home, both Mr. and Ms. B increased the level of their mutual positive engagement with Audrey. At the same time, many of Audrey's negative, attention-seeking behaviors (e.g., shouting parents' names over and over, pushing every toy off the table one by one) decreased. Yet overall, Audrey's oppositional behaviors remained at a clinically significant level. The therapist, confronted by his own uncertainty, found himself at an impasse.

HOW TO PROCEED?

To gain a clearer sense of the family's strengths and challenges, the therapist and I reviewed recordings of the treatment sessions during which Mr. and Ms. B interacted with Audrey using their new responsive interaction skills. Observing the parent–child interactions during play, we saw evidence that Audrey enjoyed spending time with her parents and that their time together contained fewer conflicts than at the start of treatment. Audrey actively sought her parents' attention, and when they provided that attention, with a focus on her prosocial behaviors (e.g., taking turns, sharing, calm play), the prosocial behaviors increased. However, Audrey continued to balk at developmentally appropriate requests from parents (e.g., refusing to put on her shoes, arguing nightly for a later bedtime). As Audrey became increasingly oppositional, Mr. and Ms. B grew frustrated and became increasingly ineffective (e.g., repeating directions multiple times, raising their voices or threatening consequences that were inappropriate and that they were unlikely to carry through). In other words, the coercive cycle continued to accelerate.

From observations of the therapy sessions, it was evident that Mr. and Ms. B were engaged in treatment and that they were working to implement the strategies their therapist offered to them. It was also clear that the family would benefit when Mr. and Ms. B were able to implement appropriate and effective limit-setting strategies to manage Audrey's oppositional behaviors. Supervision then turned to discussing the types of limit-setting strategies that were evidence-based for children Audrey's age with diagnoses of ADHD and oppositional defiant disorder. At that point, the therapist disclosed his own lack of knowledge about what effective limit-setting might look like for this family. Limit-setting for young children was a specific area that had been addressed only generally in his training, and his own research online had provided him with much conflicting information. His concerns about teaching limit-setting thus had to do with his lack of knowledge and low confidence rather than about the family's challenges. An immediate goal of supervision became to scaffold the therapist's learning and to directly guide his interactions with the family to best meet their needs.

Parents seeking mental health treatment for their young children frequently express high stress and a low sense of self-efficacy in their parent–child interactions. One of the most common reasons parents reach out for treatment is to find help managing their children's disruptive behaviors (Kimonis et al., 2014). In other cases, parents may be mandated by the child welfare system to participate in treatment because of pathogenic parenting such as child abuse. In still other cases, parents come to the attention of treatment providers because of factors such as parent psychopathology, which put them at risk for problems in the parent–child relationship. Across all of these different presenting problems, a common need is for parents to understand and be able to implement safe, effective, and developmentally appropriate strategies to manage the challenging behaviors of childhood.

In previous chapters in this volume, I described some of the decades of research on parenting styles, which support a robust association between authoritative parenting—in which parental responsiveness and expectations are balanced—and positive developmental outcomes (e.g., Pinquart & Kauser, 2018). Theoretical and empirical literatures show that children do better across many developmental domains when they are given consistent limits. However, as therapists, we may sometimes be challenged by a lack of knowledge of effective limit-setting strategies. We may also be challenged by parents', children's, and our own affect when we begin to address this essential aspect of the parent–child relationship. It may sometimes be tempting to avoid the discussion about limit-setting with parents and even more tempting to avoid teaching parents to implement safe, effective limit-setting strategies. In this chapter, I define healthy limit-setting and review developmentally appropriate, empirically supported limit-setting strategies for children from preschool to early childhood. I then discuss one of the most effective, and recently controversial, limit-setting procedures for young children—time-out—with an examination of the procedure from an attachment perspective. Finally, I offer ways to speak with parents about the importance of healthy limit-setting, to work with the challenges presented by authoritarian and permissive/anxious parents, and to consider a therapist's own anxiety about implementing effective limit-setting. A number of handouts are provided that may be helpful to support and guide parents through the development of limit-setting skills.

WHAT IS LIMIT-SETTING?

In the past several years, many misconceptions have spread among parents, clinicians, and policymakers regarding the meaning of limit-setting and its impact on children. Therefore, it is important to start with a definition. *Limit-setting*, which is synonymous with *discipline*, refers to parent interactions with a child that are meant to teach societal or safety rules and expectations for behavior. Limit-setting teaches children to increase appropriate behaviors (e.g., complying with parent or teacher directions) and to decrease behaviors that are not acceptable (e.g., hurting others, destroying toys). The key term is "teach." Children are not born knowing social rules for behavior or understanding their parents' expectations. Appropriate limit-setting helps children to learn and to internalize the rules that are necessary to function safely and adaptively in society. Further, appropriate limits, with their contingent consequences, help children learn to self-soothe and self-regulate; that is, they foster emotional, behavioral, and attentional regulation (Dadds & Tully, 2019). A parent who sets appropriate limits is acting consistent with the parameters of a secure parent–child attachment.

Limit-setting is often mistakenly equated solely with negative consequences for child misbehavior; however, limit-setting is a construct that encompasses many different types of parenting behaviors. During the toddler and early childhood years, parent–child conflict is common and normative as children begin to develop more mobility and autonomy and begin to strive toward their own goals. Some estimates suggest that parents of young children may engage in conflict (e.g., working toward opposing goals) with them from 3½ to 15 times per hour, or more (Dix, 1991; Klimes-Dougan & Kopp, 1999). Many of those engagements offer opportunities for parents to support children's autonomy. For instance, the 2½-year-old who wants to work at putting on her shoes without help can be provided scaffolding and encouragement. On the other hand, the 3-year-old who hits her siblings or defies a parent's instruction to step away from the stove may require limit-setting that includes a negative consequence. Limit-setting includes strategies that foster children's prosocial behaviors as well as negative consequences (Di Bartolo & Braun, 2017). As described next, positive and nonconfrontational strategies should be used with greater frequency than negative consequences, yet both are necessary.

WHAT IS APPROPRIATE LIMIT-SETTING FOR YOUNG CHILDREN?

Certain core characteristics can help therapists and parents to identify appropriate and healthy limit-setting strategies (Table 6.1). The first characteristic of appropriate limit-setting is *developmental sensitivity*. That is, any limit-setting strategy must be responsive to a child's level of cognitive, behavioral, and emotional functioning. A common error, for example, is when subsequent to a child's misbehavior (e.g., Audrey's drawing on the walls) parents demand that their child explain why they acted as they did. Requiring a young child to explain why is an inappropriate request for two primary reasons: (a) preschool-aged children often act impulsively in the moment without premeditated motivations, and (b) children in this age range are not yet able to reflect upon complex internal motives and express them. Demanding a motivation from a young child can be confusing and frustrating for parents and children alike, and may lead to the escalation of parents' anger if they believe their children are defying them by refusing to give a coherent reply. Thus, developmental sensitivity is a foundational requirement of the limit-setting process. A second characteristic of appropriate limit-setting is that it is conducted in the context of responsive parenting and a positive parent–child relationship. Within a warm,

TABLE 6.1. How to Evaluate Limit-Setting Strategies for Young Children: A Handout for Parents

Appropriate limit-setting is . . .	Questions to ask
sensitive to a child's age and abilities.	Is my child physically and cognitively capable of completing the requested behavior?
used in the context of a warm and supportive parent–child relationship.	Am I already paying warm and enthusiastic attention (e.g., praise) to my child's positive behaviors? Am I responsive to my child's needs at other times?
effective at reducing problem behaviors, halting the escalation of anger and aggression between parents and children, and fostering alternate positive behaviors.	When I use this strategy, does the problem behavior get less frequent? Does it give me a way to stay calm and consistent with my child, even if I'm feeling frustrated?
supportive of a healthy parent–child relationship and secure attachment.	Does it give me a way to show my child that even when I am unhappy with their behavior and I set clear limits they are still safe with me?
able to build a child's ability to calm themselves and make good choices about their behaviors.	Does the strategy allow my child to make choices about their behaviors? Does it allow my child to start building the ability to regulate their emotion and behavior by letting them calm themselves?
fair, predictable, and consistent; not used as an outlet for parent anger.	Is the strategy always the same and predictable for me and my child? Is it a reasonable limit/consequence for the targeted misbehavior?
consistent with a family's and society's values about what is right.	Is the strategy something I can use to help my child behave more positively within our family, culture, and society?

supportive parent–child relationship, children are more likely to accept parents' expectations (Kochanska & Thompson, 1997; Laible & Thompson, 2000). Whether or not children comply, however, they are more likely to view their parents' limit-setting favorably when positive affect exists in the relationship (Berlin et al., 2009; Gershoff, 2002). The importance of the context within which limit-setting is implemented is a core reason why some of the most effective parent–child interventions focus first on building a strong, positive parent–child relationship prior to teaching limit-setting strategies (Kaehler et al., 2016; Kaminski et al., 2008; Niec, 2018a).

Five additional characteristics of appropriate limit-setting for young children have been proposed based on a consideration of the primary developmental theories: attachment, ecological/family systems, self-regulation, and social learning (Dadds & Tully, 2019). To be considered appropriate, a limit-setting strategy must do the following:

- reduce the targeted problem behavior, halt the escalation of the coercive cycle between parents and children, and foster positive alternate behaviors;
- support a healthy parent–child relationship and secure attachment;

- build a child's ability to self-regulate (i.e., behavioral, emotional, and attentional regulation);
- be implemented in a way that is fair and predictable, not in response to parent anger or a desire to "make the child pay" for misbehavior; and
- fit within the family's and society's values about what is right.

Using these five characteristics as a guide, a set of limit-setting strategies appropriate for preschool to early-school-age children is proposed next. See Figure 6.1 for a summary of these strategies that may also be helpful as a handout for parents. The pyramid reflects the relative frequency with which the strategies should be used and some of the behaviors for which they are most appropriate. In other words, the strategies best for frequent use are those that promote children's positive behaviors (e.g., praise for prosocial behavior), foster children's developmentally appropriate autonomy (e.g., choices), and reinforce clear expectations for behavior (e.g., rule setting). Less frequent strategies are those that include negative consequences or are confrontational. Figure 6.1 offers more detailed descriptions.

Supporting Positive Behavior

Responsive strategies are a core part of appropriate limit-setting. With responsive strategies, parents help to build a child's foundational ability to self-regulate. Yet parents with children who exhibit conduct problems often inadvertently ignore their children's positive behaviors and provide excessive attention to negative behaviors (Patterson, 1982, 2002). Consider the parents who are sitting in the clinic waiting room while their children are playing quietly. What are those parents often doing—interacting positively with their children, or ignoring them while immersed in their smartphones? When are parents most likely to turn to their children? Often attention goes to the child only when something disrupts the quiet: a tussle over a toy, a child whining about the length of the wait. At that moment of negative behavior, a parent makes eye contact and responds; yet they have just missed the opportunity to promote all their child's previous, lovely prosocial behavior. Parents, such as Mr. and Ms. B, who feel ineffective and frustrated often no longer notice when their children engage in positive behaviors. Upon entering treatment with me, many parents have said things such as, "He never listens to me," "Nothing I do makes a difference in her behavior," and "The only time there's any quiet in the house is when he's asleep!" Before moving to more directive or confrontational limit-setting strategies, then, it is important for parents to understand the power of their attention in altering their young children's behaviors. Investigation of the components of parenting interventions that build children's positive behaviors found that interventions that include parents' positive reinforcement generally and praise specifically have higher effects than interventions that do not include teaching praise (Leijten et al., 2019). Drawing from the dimensions of responsiveness discussed in the previous chapter of this volume, consider warm and genuine praise for prosocial behaviors, parental

FIGURE 6.1. Strategies to Promote Children's Prosocial Behavior

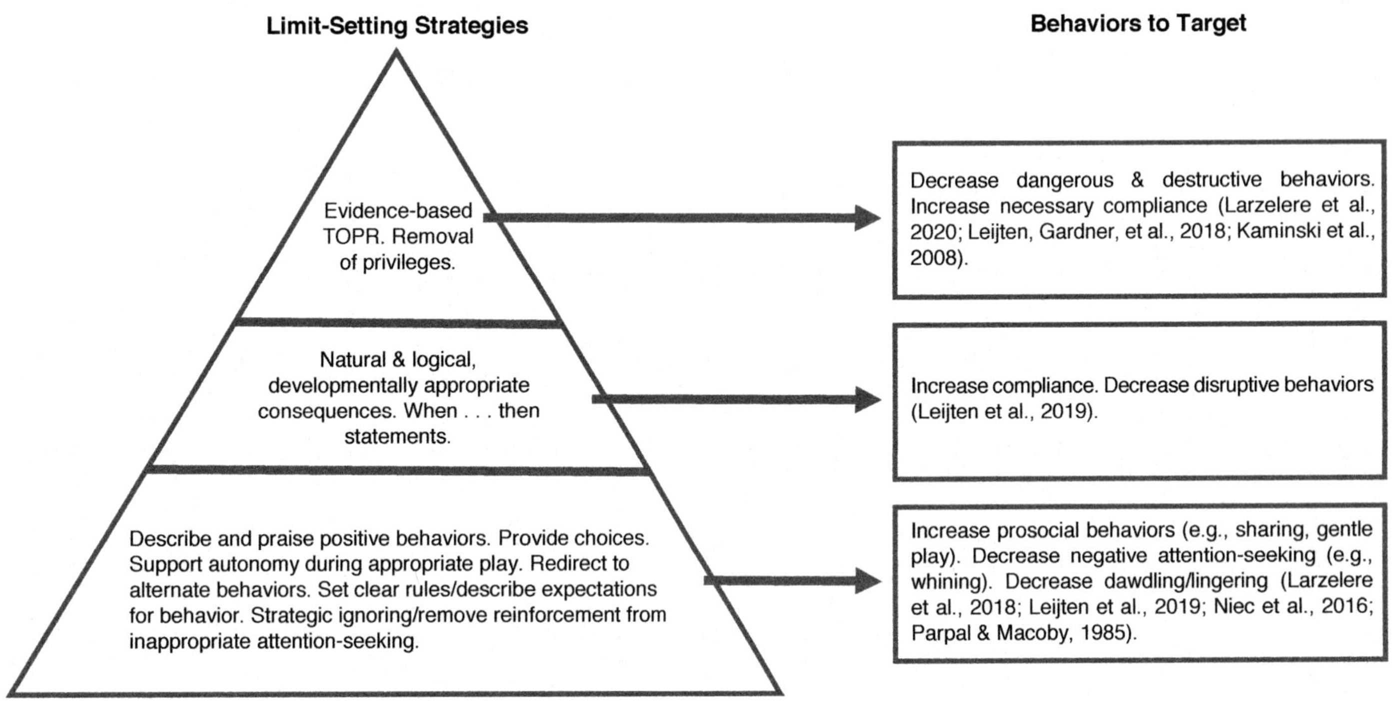

Note. Promote children's positive behaviors by starting with strategies at the base of the pyramid. TOPR = time-out from positive reinforcement.

positive affect, engagement in shared prosocial behavior, and scaffolding as strategies that promote children's ability to comply with parental and social expectations.

Setting Clear Expectations/Conditional Statements

A central aspect of limit-setting is to specify for children what the limits are (Exhibit 6.1). A common refrain I've heard from parents presenting for treatment is, "Oh, he knows better!" Yet a disconnect often exists between the expectations a parent believes their child understands and the expectations parents have actually set. It is unfair to implement consequences for a child's behavior if the expectations for that behavior have not been communicated in a way the child can understand. As part of fostering a safe and healthy parent–child relationship, then, parents must mindfully and deliberately establish the expectations for their children in different settings (e.g., home, church, playground) and at different times (e.g., hurrying out to complete a quick errand vs. spending an afternoon at the park). When working with parents of young children, even before moving to other limit-setting strategies, it can be important to assist them in (a) identifying some of the essential expectations they hold for their children's behaviors, (b) considering times and places their expectations might vary, and (c) communicating those expectations effectively to their children (see Exhibit 6.1 for a handout for parents).

This conversation helps a therapist to better understand a family's culture and the types of child behaviors that are important to them. It may also lead to a discussion about what expectations are developmentally sensitive for the child's age and level of functioning. Conditional statements—sometimes referred to as "If–Then" or "When–Then" statements—are a helpful way for parents to communicate their expectations in a particular setting, for example, "When you hold my hand, then we can go outside" or "If you sit calmly in the cart, then you can help me to pick out dessert."

Providing Choices

For individuals to function adaptively in most Western cultures requires both a respect for rules and an ability to advocate for oneself (Di Bartolo & Braun, 2017). Thus, developmental tasks of childhood include building the capacities for both self-regulation and self-assertion. These two tasks are supported when parents provide age-appropriate opportunities for autonomy to children. In fact, limit-setting is more effective when provided in the context of a parent–child relationship that promotes children's autonomy in safe and developmentally appropriate ways. For instance, it is not an option for children to refuse to put on clothes for school; however, they can be allowed to choose between outfits. Compromising with children about their options or reasoning with them about their behavior has been shown to be a sufficient and effective form of limit-setting for children without clinical levels of disruptive behaviors

EXHIBIT 6.1

Setting Clear Expectations for Children's Behavior: A Handout for Parents

Every family has different expectations for how children should behave in different settings. As your therapist, I would like to understand the expectations you have for your child that are the most important to you. This will help me to get a better understanding of your family and it will help us to work together to increase your child's positive behaviors. Please answer the questions below as honestly as possible. We will discuss them at your next session.

My child is ___________ years old.

1. In daily interactions with my child, I expect that they will (e.g., talk to me and other adults respectfully; stand up for themselves, even if it means talking back to me; do everything I tell them to do; be polite most of the time, etc.)

   ____
   ____
   ____
   ____
   ____

2. Places and times when I have more or different expectations for my child's behavior include (e.g., church, school, with grandparents or other elders)

   ____
   ____
   ____
   ____
   ____

3. When we are in the different situations listed above, I expect

   ____
   ____
   ____
   ____
   ____

4. The ways in which I communicate my expectations to my child include (e.g., telling them how I want them to behavior just before we enter the situation; correcting them when they misbehave so they don't do it again; they just know what I expect)

   ____
   ____
   ____
   ____
   ____

(Larzelere et al., 2018). On the other hand, children who are oppositional require a combination of strategies such as choices/compromising and strategies from farther up the pyramid, such as time-out. It is particularly important then for parents to seek opportunities to provide choices when possible. When parents provide children with a sense of autonomy and self-agency during developmentally appropriate times (e.g., during play), children are more likely to comply with parent requests during more challenging tasks, such as cleaning up (Parpal & Maccoby, 1985).

Strategic Ignoring

Strategic ignoring is also at the base of the pyramid as a strategy that can be used frequently. It is a powerful, effective, and nonconfrontational limit-setting technique that, with therapist support, parents can learn to use correctly (Eyberg & Funderburk, 2011). Some important rules make strategic ignoring effective. When parents follow the rules, it is an excellent technique for changing minor annoying or disruptive child behaviors. However, if parents do not follow the rules, then the targeted behavior can grow worse. Effective strategic ignoring has five rules:

1. The primary function of the targeted behavior must be a child's **inappropriate attention-seeking**—in other words, those small behaviors that "push a parent's buttons" (e.g., whining, repeatedly asking for a treat after being told no, making fart noises). The behavior should not be something destructive or aggressive (e.g., breaking toys) and must not be reinforcing on its own (e.g., playing video games when told to stop).
2. The parent must **remove all their attention from the target behavior** (e.g., no smiling, no scowling, no talking about it).
3. Once the parent begins to ignore the behavior, they must **continue to ignore it until it stops**. Giving attention to the behavior at any point in the process teaches the child that if they keep up with the annoying/disruptive behavior (e.g., be louder for longer), then it will be effective at drawing parents' attention. In other words, the attention the parents give at that point will reinforce and strengthen the misbehavior.
4. Parents must understand that when they begin strategic ignoring, **the behavior will briefly grow worse** as their child tests the new contingency (e.g., this behavior worked before; will it work again?). The brief increase in the behavior means that the technique is working and that parents must stick with it. When parents are consistent with their strategic ignoring, their child will soon reduce or discontinue the behavior.
5. Parents **ignore the behavior, not the child**. That is, while removing all attention from the targeted behavior (e.g., farting noises), parents should identify the positive behaviors their child is exhibiting to which they can attend in the moment (e.g., sitting calmly, keeping their hands to themselves). This helps children to learn the types of behaviors that draw the

parents' positive attention. It is important to note that if the annoying behavior is related to whining or repetition of a demand from the child (e.g., "I want French fries!"), it is always important for a parent first to respond with validation and a straightforward answer before moving to ignoring.

Example: Validating the Emotion and Ignoring the Attention-Seeking Behavior

CHILD: Can I get French fries?

PARENT: Not today, sweetie.

CHILD: I want French fries!

PARENT: You really like French fries. We'll get them another time, but not today.

CHILD: French fries! I want French fries!

PARENT: [*calm and neutral tone*] I'm looking forward to eating hamburgers tonight. Yum. Thanks for keeping your seat-belt on. We're almost home. Hamburger time!

When the annoying behavior no longer elicits attention from the parent, and the child receives attention for prosocial behaviors, the annoying behavior will stop or be greatly reduced.

Natural and Logical Consequences

Natural and logical consequences move one step up the pyramid of limit-setting strategies because they involve negative consequences for problem behaviors. *Natural consequences* occur without parent intervention as a direct result of child behavior. For example, if a child leaves toys outside on a stormy day, they may blow away or be ruined by rain. *Logical consequences,* on the other hand, are consequences implemented by parents yet are still directly and immediately connected to the misbehavior. For example, if a child breaks his sibling's crayons, he may be required to give her his crayons. Natural and logical consequences are both closely tied to a child's behavior and therefore can offer powerful teaching moments. Because of the low level of parent intervention required and the close connection between behavior and consequences, these moments may help children to develop a better understanding of the relationship between their actions and outcomes. A number of evidence-based parent–child interventions include teaching caregivers how to implement natural and logical consequences (Eyberg & Funderburk, 2011; Sanders & Turner, 2019; Webster-Stratton, 2016). In a meta-analysis that examined 26 components of parenting interventions (e.g., teaching parents problem solving, providing knowledge about children's development, teaching parents positive reinforcement/praise), teaching natural and logical consequences was one of three components (along with positive reinforcement generally and labeled praises specifically) associated with stronger effect sizes in the reduction of child behavior problems (Leijten et al., 2019). That is, when the treatment included natural and logical consequences, children had better outcomes (e.g., fewer externalizing behaviors) than for treatments that did not include those strategies.

Removal of Privileges

Removal of privileges is one of the limit-setting strategies at the top of the pyramid. For children on the older side of our age range (e.g., 4–8 years), implementing a response cost for misbehavior (e.g., removing a token or a preferred activity) can be an effective strategy to reduce conduct problems (Conyers et al., 2004). To be effective and appropriate, however, the response cost should

- be implemented immediately contingent to the misbehavior or as close to it in time as possible (i.e., for young children, it is not a useful strategy to remove privileges at home for a behavior that occurred at school),
- be linked to a clear and specific misbehavior,
- involve a consistent cost (i.e., the privilege removed should be specified before the misbehavior occurs and should not be arbitrary or escalating),
- include a brief removal with clear parameters (e.g., go to bed 15 minutes early, lose 20 minutes of screen time), and
- involve a preferred leisure activity (e.g., losing time playing video games) and never a physical or emotional need (e.g., going to bed without supper, losing special time with dad).

As with any consequence, it should be made clear to children beforehand—at a time when parents and children are calm and unhurried—which behaviors will result in the privilege removal.

Time-Out From Positive Reinforcement

Like removal of privileges, *time-out* sits at the top of the limit-setting pyramid as a strategy to use with disruptive behaviors that have not improved with the use of other strategies, are dangerous or destructive, or require quick compliance. Because of confusion about what time-out means and what the procedure involves, some developmental scientists and clinicians have returned to identifying time-out by its original, more descriptive label: *time out from positive reinforcement* (TOPR; Dadds & Tully, 2019). This name refers to the facts that time-out is meant to be implemented in a parenting environment that is responsive and rich with positive reinforcement and that the procedure involves a brief period of removal from that positively reinforcing environment. I continue the convention of referring to TOPR here as a small step toward fostering a more accurate understanding of the technique.

More than 50 years of research supports the effectiveness of TOPR in reducing young children's problem behaviors and increasing compliance (Corralejo et al., 2018; Everett et al., 2010; Larzelere et al., 2020; Leijten, Gardner, Melendez-Torres, et al., 2018). A recent meta-analysis included studies of TOPR conducted from 1979 to 2018, reviewing only investigations with a rigorous design that allowed for attributions of causality; in other words, conclusions could be made with relative confidence that TOPR was a cause of children's behavior change (Larzelere et al., 2020). Based on this body of work, the overall effect of TOPR to improve children's behaviors was large, Cohen's $d = 1.67$. (An effect size of Hedges's g or Cohen's $d \geq 0.80$ is considered a large effect; ≥ 0.50 is a medium effect; ≥ 0.20 is a small effect; Cohen, 1988.) To put the effectiveness of TOPR into perspective, across intervention types the overall effect of psychotherapy on children's functioning has been found to be small ($g = .39$; Pilling et al., 2020) and the effect of child-centered play therapy specifically is also small ($d = 0.47$; Lin & Bratton, 2015).

In addition to the studies that have specifically examined the impact of TOPR on child functioning, most evidence-based parenting interventions (e.g., Incredible Years, Parent–Child Interaction Therapy, Parent Management Training–Oregon, Triple P) include the use of TOPR as a part of the intervention (Chamberlain et al., 2016; Eyberg & Funderburk, 2011; Sanders, 2008; Webster-Stratton, 2016). Parenting interventions that teach parents how to use TOPR demonstrate greater positive outcomes for children than parenting interventions that do not teach TOPR (Kaminski et al., 2008).

What Makes TOPR Effective?

As is true for other limit-setting techniques, to be optimally effective TOPR must be implemented correctly—that is, with fidelity to the evidence-based procedure. Eight components of the TOPR procedure that have been identified as important are described next (Brodd & Niec, 2021; Corralejo et al., 2018; Drayton et al., 2014; Drayton et al., 2017; Everett et al., 2010; Riley et al., 2017). Thinking of Audrey's case, the family's therapist expressed concern that Mr. and Ms. B would implement limit-setting strategies incorrectly. In fact, we know that without training, parents are unlikely to use all the evidence-based steps of TOPR and instead do many things that make TOPR ineffective. However, the outcome research of parenting interventions that include TOPR demonstrates that parents are able to implement limit-setting appropriately and effectively with therapeutic support. Recall that prior to implementing any new limit-setting strategy, children should be made aware of how the procedure will go and what behaviors will lead to that consequence. Effective TOPR procedures include the following (Figure 6.2):

1. After being given a direction (e.g., "Please hold my hand while we cross the street"), **children are given only one warning** in a calm, neutral manner before TOPR is implemented. (e.g., "If you don't do what I told you to do, you'll have to go to time-out"). When commands and warnings are repeated, children are less likely to comply.
2. **TOPR location is safe and boring.** The location may be an adult-sized, daily-use chair (avoid cute, small "time-out" chairs that make time-out fun

FIGURE 6.2. Primary Components of an Evidence-Based Time-Out From Positive Reinforcement

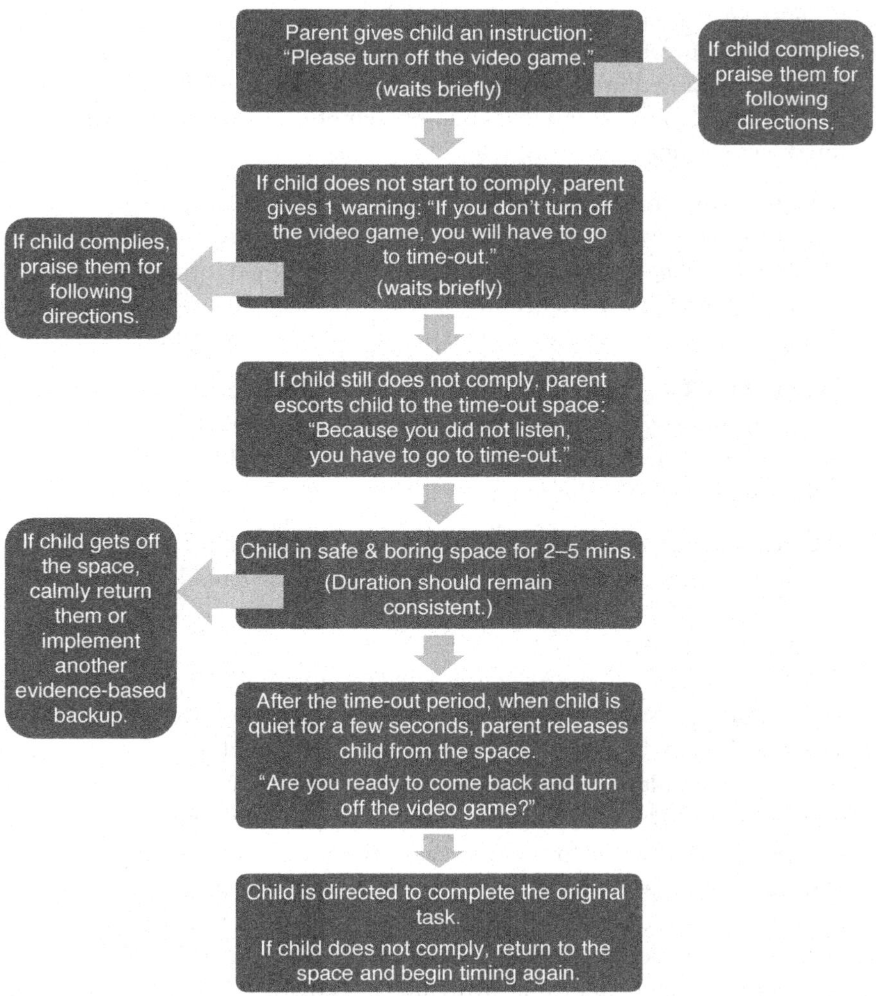

Note. Data from Brodd and Niec (2021), Corralejo et al. (2018), Drayton et al. (2017), Everett et al. (2010), and Eyberg and Funderburk (2011).

or special) or an empty space on the floor. It should not be in a location with entertainment (e.g., television or radio on, lots of activity around).

3. **During TOPR, children have no access to entertaining activities,** and parents and others do not engage with them.
4. **Duration of the TOPR is brief (5 minutes or less).** Determining the length of a time-out based on children's ages or the type of misbehavior does not have empirical support.
5. **TOPR ends when the child is calm/quiet for a brief period (a few seconds).** To date, the research finds no additional benefit or harm in requiring a child to be calm briefly prior to leaving the time-out. However, behavioral principles suggest that requiring a quick period of quiet prior to ending the time-out prevents a child from superstitious learning—that is, mistakenly believing that being loud during the time-out caused them to be let out. Outcome studies of parent–child interventions, such as parent–child interaction therapy, that require a brief period of calm prior to release from time-out have found that children's emotion and behavior regulation increases (Lieneman et al., 2020).
6. **Parents, not children, end the TOPR** (Everett et al., 2007). If a child leaves the space without permission, a backup procedure is used to promote the child's ability to stay in the space, such as calmly returning the child to the chair, providing a brief (e.g., 1 minute) exclusionary time in a safe and boring room, or removing a privilege (e.g., 10 minutes earlier to bed).
7. **When TOPR is ended, the child must complete the original task** (e.g., putting away the toys). If the TOPR was for breaking a "don't" rule (e.g., no hitting), then upon leaving the TOPR, the child is reminded of the rule (e.g., remember, the rule is no hitting).
8. **TOPR is used consistently** for breaking rules or failing to comply with expectations that have been clearly described to the child.

The Safety of TOPR

When used according to the evidence-based recommendations and in concert with the characteristics of appropriate limit-setting, TOPR is not only a highly effective technique but also a safe one, with the potential to foster children's ability to self-regulate and to promote a healthy parent–child relationship (Dadds & Tully, 2019). TOPR is recommended as an appropriate limit-setting technique by the Centers for Disease Control and Prevention (2019) and the American Academy of Pediatrics (2018). Longitudinal evidence shows that children whose parents use TOPR experience no long-term ill effects, including no effects on their behavioral functioning, on their emotional functioning, and on the parent–child relationship (Knight et al., 2020).

It is important to note that parent–child interventions that include TOPR have been identified as appropriate for children with a history of pathogenic parenting and trauma. Specifically, the evidence-based intervention parent–child interaction therapy, which includes a TOPR based on the scientific recommendations, has been identified as a best-practice intervention in cases of child physical abuse (Kauffman Best Practices Project, 2004). The National Child Traumatic Stress Network (2019) has also named PCIT as appropriate for cases in which children have experienced complex, interpersonal trauma. A study of PCIT implemented in community mental health settings found that trauma symptoms decreased among children whose families completed PCIT (Pearl et al., 2012).

It is to the detriment of many families and young children that critics who base their claims on no scientifically sound evidence have been given wide platforms to disseminate inaccurate information (e.g., Siegel & Bryson, 2014a, 2014b). When this misinformation continues to be disseminated by well-meaning therapists, health care providers, and policymakers, children pay the price. After considering TOPR from multiple theoretical perspectives (e.g., attachment, ecological/family systems, social learning theories) and from the extensive base of empirical support, a recent review described the situation in this way:

> the adoption of policies that prohibit the use of TOPR with children may be ill-considered and deny access of children in need to an effective evidence-based procedure. Given the wealth of evidence showing that TOPR is a positive perturbation in child mental health, and the absence of evidence showing it is harmful after five decades of research, clinical, and common usage, claims that it is harmful should be considered extraordinary, and thus require an extraordinary level of evidence to back them up. (Dadds & Tully, 2019, p. 805)

A more recent and extensive review went even further, concluding that "there is no evidence at all" to suggest that TOPR is a harmful procedure (Larzelere et al., 2020, p. 24).

WHY NEGATIVE EMOTION CAN BE A POSITIVE EXPERIENCE

Part of the criticism of TOPR seems to stem from a more encompassing social perception recently observed among some mental health clinicians, health care providers, and occasionally parents—that is, the perception that children should be prevented from experiencing any type of negative emotion. "I can't even talk about putting a child in time-out," a young therapist recently blurted during a workshop. "It's traumatic." This misunderstanding of children's developmental needs has been perpetuated by some parenting interventions that reject any form of limit-setting that includes negative consequences. These parenting interventions have been styled as "exclusively positive parenting" or "strong positive parenting" (Holden et al., 2017). Yet, the implication that implementing a negative consequence for child misbehavior is equivalent to negative parenting is misleading and irresponsible. It signals a message that is counter to developmental theories and years of research on discipline strategies

(Dadds & Tully, 2019; Kaminski et al., 2008; Larzelere et al., 2020; Leijten et al., 2019). Similarly, the idea that a child should not be allowed to experience and express anger, hurt, anxiety, or frustration is inconsistent with an understanding of development. From a theoretical perspective, young children benefit from the experience of low levels of frustration with their caregivers, which allows them to learn to self-regulate and to begin to develop autonomy (Winnicott, 1971). From an empirical perspective, as discussed in Chapter 3 of this volume, the concept of negative emotion as a negative experience is counter to the research on childhood stressors: Experiences that provoke temporary stress responses and occur within a supportive parent–child relationship are considered valuable and positive experiences (Garner & Saul, 2018).

In sum, negative emotion is not an inherently negative experience. Rather, when children experience temporary, mild to moderate negative emotion, it helps them to develop their ability to regulate their emotions and behavior and to learn to use healthy coping mechanisms. Effective limit-setting strategies, including highly effective consequences such as TOPR, provide children with necessary opportunities and safe scaffolding to facilitate healthy development.

Other Positive Lessons Learned Through TOPR: An Attachment Perspective

Children who are seen within outpatient mental health care settings are more likely than children in the general population to have a history of experiencing unpredictable, inconsistent, and unsafe limit-setting. Thus, as described earlier, when parents begin to implement consistent limits and consequences, children may experience and express a range of emotions. They may cry, wail, or call their parent names. They may at first refuse to stay on the TOPR space. A few children will urinate on the TOPR space. Part of the behaviors that occur during the initial use of TOPR is about learning the new limits. Children are scientists seeking to understand their world. When parents change their responses to child misbehaviors, children will explore the new possibilities. They will be investigating to find out, "What happens if I do X?"

Once again, remember that children should always be introduced to the new limit-setting technique and new expectations *before* it is implemented, during a neutral time when parents and children are calm. However, most children will still need to test the new situation for themselves. During this testing, a few children may sob, become highly upset, angry, disappointed, or frustrated. Why can this be considered an important and positive experience, then? To answer that question, we must consider the messages a child receives from an evidence-based TOPR procedure. Two foundational messages relevant to parent–child attachment security are embedded in this experience: You will be safe. Our relationship remains strong.

You Will Be Safe

Throughout the TOPR procedure, parents learn, with therapist support, to regulate their own emotion and to follow through in a consistent, predictable manner—saying the same things and doing the same things throughout the procedure (e.g., Eyberg & Funderburk, 2011). In those moments, children learn a lesson they may not have had the opportunity to learn before: "No matter how upset I am, no matter how much I cry, scream, kick, or shout curse words, I will be safe. No one will yell at me or hit me. My parents will remain regulated."

This is a powerful lesson about limit-setting. In these moments, when parents demonstrate the ability to accept their child's emotions and to maintain appropriate limits for child behavior, children can begin to develop a new internal working model of the parent–child relationship. The new model includes the information that limits are safe and predictable and that expressing negative emotion is not dangerous. In that safe and contained context, children are more likely to begin to regulate their own emotion and to develop autonomy in developmentally appropriate ways. This type of lesson, therefore, has the potential to promote a positive developmental cascade, as it strengthens the parent–child relationship and enhances children's self-regulation.

Our Relationship Remains Strong

A second foundational message embedded in the TOPR procedure also supports the parent–child relationship. As described in Chapter 1, secure attachment develops through repeated parent–child interactions in which the child experiences a frustration, a need, or a brief separation, which is then followed by the parent's response and/or a reunion. An evidence-based TOPR procedure is not arbitrary or prolonged. It occurs in response to a specific behavior, and the way in which it ends is always the same. Thus, the message communicated to the child is that a particular behavior is not acceptable but that the parent remains present and the relationship remains strong (Dadds & Tully, 2019).

Where Parents Often Need Help With TOPR

Parents' ability to access accurate information about the use of TOPR has been deeply compromised. First, the available information has been influenced by the critics of TOPR who have made wild and unsubstantiated, yet highly visible, claims about TOPR as a discipline strategy (Larzelere et al., 2020; Society of Clinical Child and Adolescent Psychology, 2014). Second, hundreds—perhaps thousands—of websites offer recommendations about how to implement TOPR, but much of this information is inaccurate. An analysis of the information that most frequently comes up in an online search on time-out revealed that 68.5% of the recommendations had little to no empirical support or were explicitly counter to research-based recommendations (Corralejo et al., 2018). In another analysis, none of the reviewed webpages included accurate information about all of the components of TOPR (Drayton et al., 2014). Accurate information is essential; it empowers parents to use limit-setting strategies with fidelity and effectiveness. Parents who have a better understanding of behavior principles as they relate to child behavior are more likely to find TOPR to be an acceptable limit-setting strategy and to use TOPR with fidelity to evidence-based recommendations (Brodd & Niec, 2021). Further, when parents use TOPR with greater fidelity, they are more likely to perceive the procedure as effective (Riley et al., 2017). In other words, accurate information about TOPR helps parents to accept the procedure, to implement it correctly, and to experience its effectiveness.

As clinicians, we are obligated to provide families with accurate, science-based information about effective limit-setting. This responsibility requires that we ourselves understand what the science says about TOPR. It is also helpful to be aware of the common mistakes parents make or misunderstandings they have about TOPR so that we might provide support that targets the problems. The following issues have been identified in the literature or are those that parents have shared with me over years.

Limit-Setting in Anger

As is the case for any limit-setting strategy, TOPR should be implemented by parents in a confident and calm manner. Any discipline technique implemented in uncontrolled anger (e.g., yelling at or belittling child, using physical force) communicates harmful messages (e.g., "You can't do anything right," "I'm sick of dealing with you"). In addition, parents' emotional dysregulation provides a poor model for children to learn how to manage their own emotions. When a parent becomes emotionally escalated or overreactive, it is more likely that the child will escalate as well (Del Vecchio & Rhoades, 2010; Patterson, 1982). Although such strategies may reduce misbehavior in the short term, a child's information processing may be impacted by the activation of the stress response, causing emotion-related material to be encoded more readily (e.g., *Mom is scary*) but nonstressor-related material to be less likely to be encoded (e.g., *The rule is not to break toys*; Vogel & Schwabe, 2016). As discussed in Chapter 3, children who have experienced early adversity may be particularly at risk for hyperarousal of their physiological stress response. Thus, any limit-setting technique implemented with anger is likely to help a child internalize only the parents' lack of control or threatening demeanor, not the societal/family rule (e.g., It's not okay to destroy property).

The evidence-based TOPR procedure specifically helps parents maintain their regulation during what can often be emotionally laden moments. Because TOPR helps parents to know exactly what to say and do, it removes the need to create a new consequence in a heated moment. Because it is effective, TOPR can reduce parents' stress and frustration. TOPR allows parents to remain calm, predictable, and consistent for their children.

TOPR Is Too Long

In a survey of nearly 300 mothers and fathers (47% fathers), almost 70% of respondents used a length for time-out that was not based on scientific support (e.g., it was too long, of inconsistent length, or changed depending on the misbehavior; Brodd & Niec, 2021). As in the case of Audrey, it is not uncommon for parents to use TOPR as a means of discontinuing the parent–child conflict rather than as a limit-setting strategy and teaching moment. This intention may lead parents to send their children to their room or other location for extended periods, without providing any follow-up. Time-out then becomes an unpredictable and unfair consequence that is unlikely to lead to learning. Another common piece of misinformation is the recommendation for TOPR length to be based on child age (e.g., 1 or 2 minutes per year). In most cases, that duration is longer than necessary to be effective. Investigation of the length of TOPR needed to reduce aggression, destruction, and noncompliance in young children found that a duration of 4 minutes was more effective than 10 seconds or 1 minute (Hobbs et al., 1978). However, there was no difference in the effectiveness when TOPR was increased. No differences were found across time-out durations of 5, 10, and 20 minutes within a sample of children on an in-patient hospital unit (McGuffin, 1991). Likewise, no differences were found across durations of 5 and 10 minutes or a 15-minute duration with the opportunity to decrease time for sitting quietly (Fabiano et al., 2004). Based on these findings, the evidence-based recommendation is to use the shortest time necessary to see positive effects on children's behaviors, a period between 2 and 4 minutes. The shortest effective time-out not only reduces problem behaviors but also is more feasible for parents to implement. Note that when the length of the time-out is inconsistent (e.g., time-out starts longer and then is shortened), misbehavior can significantly increase (White et al., 1972). In other words, a brief (less than 5 minutes) TOPR is sufficient to reduce young children's aggressive and destructive behaviors and to increase compliance. However, to maintain the effectiveness of the procedure, the length of TOPR should not change depending on children's misbehavior.

Use of a TOPR Space With Entertaining Activities

The TOPR space should always be safe and boring. If a child has access to toys, siblings, computers, or other screen devices, then it is not a removal from reinforcement and is unlikely to decrease the child's misbehavior (Corralejo et al., 2018; Drayton et al., 2017). Parents may need therapists' help in determining the best location for a TOPR space in their home. For families living in a small environment (e.g., studio apartment or mobile home), the space may be simply an unoccupied corner of the room or a small hallway. If families have a two-floor home, it can be helpful to identify a TOPR space on each floor to reduce the distance a child must travel to reach the space.

TOPR Is an Escape From Compliance

The term *escape from compliance* refers to a TOPR procedure in which children complete their time on the space but need not comply with the parent's original request (e.g., "Please put away the video game"). Based on behavior principles, if TOPR is a way to avoid completing a parent's requested task, then children are likely to go to time-out more frequently (Everett et al., 2007). In one survey of 55 mothers, 100% reported that their children were not required to comply with the original request after completion of the time-out (Drayton et al., 2017).

A national survey of mothers and fathers, on the other hand, found that 69% of parents ($N = 297$) required their children to complete the original command before continuing with other activities (Brodd & Niec, 2021). The national survey results are encouraging; they suggest that requiring child compliance is an acceptable and feasible aspect of TOPR for most parents. When parents understand behavioral principles and the reason for requiring child compliance after TOPR, they are more likely to follow through.

Parents Talk/Explain During TOPR

Providing a child with the reason for their time-out before or after the procedure does not impact its effectiveness (Corralejo et al., 2018). In fact, it may help parents to provide a succinct and clear rationale for the child's behavior before the procedure (e.g., "Because you hit your brother, you are going to time-out"). However, talking with children *during* the TOPR period is counter to the intention, which is to provide children with a brief removal from reinforcement. Giving attention to children while they are in the time-out space may increase the time it takes a child to self-regulate and is likely to decrease the effectiveness of TOPR in reducing misbehavior. Further, if parents continue to engage with their children during the time-out period, parents and children both lose that time to regulate their own emotion and behavior. Therapists can provide active support or in vivo coaching to help parents to remove all attention from children during the TOPR period (Eyberg & Funderburk, 2011).

WHAT IF WE DON'T TEACH PARENTS LIMIT-SETTING?

Avoiding the challenge of helping parents to manage their children's disruptive behaviors does not make those behaviors go away. When children exhibit clinical levels of conduct problems at a young age, the behaviors are likely to remain stable or grow significantly worse (Kimonis et al., 2014; Moffitt et al., 2002; Patterson, 1982, 2002). Even if children exhibit only typical misbehavior, parents still need effective limit-setting strategies to teach and support them (Passini et al., 2014). What happens, then, if parents do not have those strategies and clinicians do not provide them? For parents who have already manifested problematic parenting—through abuse, for example—a high likelihood exists that they will reabuse their children if they are not taught effective limit-setting strategies (Chaffin et al., 2004). Further, without the ability to effectively manage their children's behaviors, parents who are dealing with risk factors such as their own mental health issues, financial hardship, and marital conflict have a higher likelihood that the coercive cycle in the parent–child relationship will escalate.

If therapists do not help parents to implement healthy limit-setting, the potential damage then lies in two domains: the escalation of parents' harsh discipline and the negative outcomes for children. Parents' sense of self-efficacy has been implicated in children's display of conduct problems and in the use of problematic discipline (T. L. Jones & Prinz, 2005; Roskam et al., 2015). Parents, such as Mr. and Ms. B, who feel ineffective and helpless in their ability to manage their children's behaviors are more likely to turn to harsh, coercive, and potentially abusive behavior control strategies (Beckerman et al., 2017; T. L. Jones & Prinz, 2005). Patterson's (1982, 2002) coercion theory demonstrated that when parents are unable to bring about change in their children's behaviors with one level of limit-setting (e.g., giving the child an instruction), they are more likely to increase to a level of greater negative control (e.g., yelling, threatening). Thus, when therapists avoid teaching effective limit-setting, we increase the risk that parents will choose problematic discipline strategies.

The second domain of damage lies in the negative outcomes for children. Research shows that for children with clinically significant conduct problems, increasing responsive parenting is insufficient to reduce problem behavior to within normal limits (Danko et al., 2016; Eisenstadt et al., 1993; Leijten, Melendez-Torres, et al., 2018). As discussed in Chapter 3, early childhood conduct problems promote a negative developmental cascade that has serious, pervasive, and potentially lifelong effects (Masten & Cicchetti, 2010). Without effective limit-setting, children are more likely to have problems adjusting to the expectations for behavior at school and may have problems with peer interactions, which can then lead to problems such as disengagement from school, association with deviant peers, and escalating problem behavior. Safe, effective limit-setting is necessary. Children deserve safe and effective limits to foster their healthy development. When therapists neglect to teach parents appropriate limit-setting, we set up families for failure and leave children vulnerable to increasingly coercive interactions.

TALKING WITH PARENTS ABOUT LIMITS

First, Addressing Our Own Anxiety About Implementing Limits

Before we can work effectively with children and families, we need to check our own ability to sit with children's negative affect. Children are healthier in nearly every developmental domain when they have consistent and predictable limits. Yet, for children with conduct problems or children for whom limit-setting has previously been arbitrary or unsafe, they are likely to experience frustration, anger, disappointment, or anxiety when parents begin to set consistent limits. The only way in which we can support parents—and children—in regulating their emotions during the limit-setting process is if we remain calm, confident, and present in the moment. If we have trouble dealing with children's negative emotion, we must address it as part of our development as therapists. We can explore for ourselves questions such as, What makes it difficult for me to sit with a child's expression of negative emotion? What emotions do I experience? What are the thoughts I have related to those moments? How can I cope effectively with my emotions so that I can be present as a therapist? These questions are a start to our exploring how we can enhance our work with families. I return to this topic in more depth in Chapter 9.

Discussing Limit-Setting and TOPR

Parents in community mental health settings who bring their children for services may present with a lack of knowledge about safe and effective limit-setting and little or no experience implementing it. Therapists therefore have a valuable opportunity to introduce parents to new ways of interacting with their children that can decrease parent stress, increase children's healthy functioning, and enhance the parent–child relationship.

How therapists speak with parents about limit-setting generally and TOPR specifically can play a significant role in whether parents understand and buy into the treatment process. It is important to listen to a parent's questions and to answer them within a frame that fits with the family's values and expressed concerns. For some parents—those who are more permissive—the discussion of limit-setting and TOPR may be anxiety provoking. They may express concerns about the impact of consequences on their relationships with their children. For parents who are authoritarian, the concept of TOPR may seem too permissive, as if children are being allowed to escape a "real" consequence. The following section provides examples of concerns that parents may express and some points to begin responding to them. These points can be part of a larger conversation that occurs in the context of a family's strengths and challenges and that is sensitive to the family culture.

Helping Anxious/Permissive Parents Implement Consistent Limits

"I don't have any problems at home. I don't mind that kind of [defiant] behavior."

- *By setting consistent limits for him, you're teaching him self-regulation skills that he needs at school and with friends. Skills he needs to get along with others.*
- *When you give him limits that are appropriate for his age, you are setting him up for successful behavior as he gets older.*

"I'm afraid she'll hate me if I tell her *no*."

- *Just like adults, children can feel frustrated or angry when they're asked to do something they don't want to do, but that's okay. She'll learn that it is safe for her to have those feelings.*

- *Setting appropriate limits doesn't damage the parent–child relationship; it shows her that you will be consistent. On the other hand, being unpredictable about expectations can cause the relationship to feel unsafe and increases conflict.*
- *She'll learn that when you tell her "no" it's important for her to listen.*

"Time-out will just make him angry, and I didn't sign up for that."

- *He might feel angry at first, but with your follow-through, he will learn that [breaking toys] is not okay.*
- *Soon you will both feel less stressed because he will understand the rule and will follow it.*
- *Remember that time-out is at the top of the pyramid. It's one of many techniques you can use to help him learn positive behavior. When you use time-out in a balanced way—and continue using your responsive strategies—he will be able to accept it more easily.*
- *By following through with an appropriate consequence like time-out, you will no longer have to nag at him throughout the day. You'll be able to enjoy being with each other.*

"It's not fair to put her into time-out."

- *Remember, an important step in the time-out process is that you always give her one warning. That way, she has the chance to decide whether to follow your directions or go to time-out.*
- *Time-out is always safe, boring, and not too long.*

"Isn't time-out like child abuse?"

- *Time-out is not abusive. It is safe and boring. It gives children and parents a brief time apart to calm themselves.*
- *With time-out, she will learn to follow your directions without you having to yell or threaten.*
- *Through the time-out process, children learn that no matter how upset they become, no matter what they say or do in the time-out space, they will be safe and you will remain calm.*
- *Children need sensitive limits so that they can feel safe. When limits are consistent, predictable, and developmentally sensitive, children feel less anxious.*

Helping Authoritarian Parents Implement Safe Limits

"Children should respect their parents. I'm not going to take that kind of behavior."

- *Time-out shows him that you are the one in control of your behavior, not him.*
- *He's learning that he can't push your buttons.*
- *When you use responsive strategies, you model respect and he'll learn it from you.*
- *When you set appropriate limits that are consistent and safe, she'll learn to follow your rules.*

"Time-out doesn't work. I've tried it."

- *Lots of procedures are called "time-out." What I'll help you to use is a very specific set of steps that is different from what you've done in the past.* [Understanding the types of limit-setting techniques parents have tried before—including a detailed understanding of what they've used as a "time-out"—is necessary for this conversation.]
- *When you're consistent, then you'll no longer have these struggles over misbehaviors because he'll know what you expect.*

"He should just do what I say without my having to explain it."

- *Children don't understand the rules unless we first make our expectations clear in a way they can understand. When we notice and praise them for following our rules, they'll begin to know what behaviors earn our approval. Then, when we consistently implement appropriate consequences for rule breaking, children begin to understand what the limits are.*
- *Think of what it's like to start a new job in a new setting. It takes time to learn what all the expectations are in that new situation.*

SUMMARY

A healthy parent–child relationship includes both responsive and effective parenting. Children need safe and consistent limits to develop their ability to self-regulate. Parents need effective ways of managing the challenging behaviors of childhood. Limit-setting should include a range of evidence-based strategies that are implemented in the context of a positive parent–child relationship. These strategies include reinforcement for prosocial behaviors and negative consequences to reduce problem behaviors.

A robustly effective and appropriate limit-setting strategy for young children is time-out from positive reinforcement. Unfortunately, among parenting websites and in the popular media, misinformation about TOPR is more common than accurate information. Four pieces of knowledge for therapists and parents are essential. First, 50 years of support demonstrate that TOPR is a highly effective strategy to reduce child aggression and increase compliance (Larzelere et al., 2020). Second, TOPR is a safe and developmentally sensitive limit-setting technique: No evidence exists that the TOPR procedure is harmful for children or damages the parent–child relationship (Dadds & Tully, 2019; Knight et al., 2020; Larzelere et al., 2020). Third, parenting interventions that include teaching parents how to use TOPR are more effective than parenting interventions that do not teach parents TOPR (Kaminski et al., 2008). Some of these interventions have been identified as effective and appropriate for children who have experienced complex trauma (Chaffin et al., 2004; National Child Traumatic Stress Network, 2019). Finally, TOPR includes specific components that make it safe and effective.

Key Takeaways

1. Effective limit-setting is a foundational aspect of a healthy parent–child relationship.
2. Limit-setting includes a range of parent–child interactions aimed to teach children necessary expectations for behavior. Limit-setting promotes children's prosocial behaviors and decreases inappropriate behaviors.
3. Appropriate limit-setting is implemented in the context of a positive parent–child relationship.
4. Time-out from positive reinforcement is a highly effective limit-setting strategy with 50 years of research supporting its safe use for children from 2 to 8 years old.
5. No evidence suggests that the evidence-based TOPR procedure threatens the parent–child attachment. To the contrary, TOPR provides an opportunity for children with a history of problematic or inconsistent discipline to learn that limit-setting is a safe and predictable experience.
6. Parents benefit from the active support of therapists to help them to understand TOPR and to implement the procedure correctly.
7. In the popular media and online, parents are more likely to find inaccurate rather than accurate recommendations regarding TOPR. Therapists are ethically obligated to provide parents with scientifically accurate information about effective limit-setting, including TOPR.

Clinical Growth Questions

1. In what ways do I currently support the core needs of parents to learn both responsive parent–child interaction skills and healthy limit-setting strategies?

2. In what ways could I expand parents' understanding of appropriate limit-setting, and why it is important?
3. How can I help parents to implement the "pyramid" of strategies, focusing on reinforcement of prosocial behaviors as the foundation to all other limit-setting strategies?
4. Do I have a clear understanding of how to implement a time-out procedure according to scientifically supported recommendations?
5. Are there ways in which my own discomfort with children's expressions of negative emotion impedes my ability to provide parents with the skills they need to manage their children's behaviors? What steps can I take to enhance my own emotion regulation in my work with families?
6. What are my primary strengths in my work with families who need to learn safe and effective limit-setting strategies?

7

Relationship-Based Interventions for Parents and Young Children

I was wrapping up a workshop on parent–child interventions for community therapists when one of the participants—a therapist with many years of experience in community mental health—said, "I'm so excited to learn how to use a new intervention, because the more evidence-based tools you have as a clinician the more likely you will be able to meet the needs of the families you serve."

I was deeply struck by the openness of such an experienced clinician. Not only was she receptive to reaching outside her comfort zone to learn new treatment strategies, but she was also open to understanding families and the parent–child relationship from different theoretical perspectives. Over the decades during which I have trained clinicians, I have been lucky to work with many such open, creative, and insightful individuals. It is no easy thing to try a new approach to treatment. Therapists in community settings must often manage bulging caseloads, long waitlists, and ongoing crises. In such challenging settings, mindfulness and courage are required to counter the very human biases that can lead us to perceive different problems in similar ways or in the ways that are most familiar (and comfortable) to us.

This chapter reviews four widely disseminated parent–child treatment models: child–parent psychotherapy, child–parent relationship therapy, circle of security, and parent–child interaction therapy. For each intervention, I provide an overview of the theoretical foundation, describe the primary therapeutic strategies, and review the research base (see Table 7.1). Although the

https://doi.org/10.1037/0000304-007
Strengthening the Parent–Child Relationship in Therapy: Laying the Foundation for Healthy Development, by L. N. Niec

TABLE 7.1. Comparison of Parent–Child Interventions for Young Children

Model	Child age	Child present in session	Tx length/ format/setting	Primary targets of change	Secondary targets of change	Treatment effect sizes	Evidence of effectiveness for fathers	Evidence for telehealth delivery
CPP	0–5 yr with hx of child abuse or IPV	Yes	≈50 sessions (12 months)/ weekly, individual, 1-hr/clinic or home	Physical and psychological safety of child and parent; quality of caregiving; parent distorted representations of the child and parent–child relationship	Child attachment security	Child PTSD Sx $d = 0.63$ Child depression $d = 0.39$ Maternal PTSD Sx $d = 0.44$ Maternal depression $d = 0.43$	No data	None to date
CPRT	3–8 yr	No	10 sessions/ weekly, group, 2-hr/clinic	Parent responsive-ness; parent developmental expectations; parent–child relationship	Child disruptive behavior	Child disrupt behaviors $g = 0.55$	Landreth & Lobaugh (1998; incarcerated sample $n = 16$)	Hicks & Baggerly (2017)

COS	0–5 yr	No	20 sessions/ weekly, group, 90-min/clinic/ adaptations for individual	Child attachment security; parent reflective functioning; parent self-efficacy	Parent depression	Child attachment security $g = 0.65$ Maternal sensitivity $g = 0.60$ Maternal depression $g = 0.53$ Maternal self-efficacy $g = 0.98$	No data	None to date
PCIT	2–7 yr	Yes	≈16 sessions/ weekly, individual, 1-hr/clinic/ adaptations for group, home, and telehealth	Quality of caregiving; parent–child relationship; child disruptive behavior; parent self-efficacy; parent stress	Child and parent emotion regulation; parent reflective functioning; parent depression	Parent responsive care $d = 1.15$ Child disrupt behaviors $d = 1.65$ Parent emotion function $d = 1.11$ Parent reflective function $d = 0.32$	Effective Brestan et al. (1997); Eyberg et al. (1995); Eyberg & Robinson (1982); Hood & Eyberg (2003); Niec et al. (2016); Schuhmann et al. (1998)	Comer et al. (2015, 2017); Kohlhoff et al. (2021)

Note. Child–Parent Psychotherapy (CPP) effect sizes from Washington State Institute for Public Policy (2019). Child–Parent Relationship Therapy (CPRT) effect size from Allen (2020; child disruptive behaviors). Circle of security (COS) effect sizes from meta-analysis (Yaholkoski et al., 2016). Parent–Child Interaction Therapy (PCIT) effect sizes for child disruptive behavior from meta-analysis (Ward et al., 2016). Effect sizes for observed parent responsive care and parent emotional functioning (stress, self-efficacy, locus of control) meta-analysis by Thomas and Zimmer-Gembeck (2007). Effect size for parent reflective function Zimmer-Gembeck et al. (2019). Interpretation of Hedges's g and Cohen's d: .20–.50 = small effect; .50–.80 = medium effect; .80+ = large effect. Tx = treatment; yr = year; hx = history; IPV = interpersonal violence; hr = hour; PTSD = posttraumatic stress disorder; sx = symptoms; min = minute.

four programs originate from different theoretical perspectives and conceptualize challenges to the parent–child relationship in somewhat different ways, they share a focus on the repair or reinforcement of the parent–child relationship. Thus, they offer multiple pathways to reach similar goals. Other volumes have discussed in-depth interventions that particularly address the needs of infants (e.g., H. Steele & Steele, 2018); consequently, this discussion centers on parent–child interventions that extend to children of preschool or early school-age, up to 8 years. Certain evidence-based behavior parent training interventions specifically address child behavior problems. These interventions (e.g., the Incredible Years and Triple-P programs) were not included in this discussion, as they do not focus on the development of the parent–child relationship (e.g., Julian et al., 2017; Leijten, Gardner, Landau, et al., 2018; Sanders et al., 2014). Interventions developed primarily for older children were also not included (e.g., Alternatives for Families-Cognitive Behavior Therapy; Kolko et al., 2012).

The interventions discussed in this chapter have disparate levels of research support. They have all been included because they are frequently implemented within community mental health settings. However, therapists should be aware that the implementation of a program within an agency is not a guarantee that it has been evaluated with rigorous research or has demonstrated positive outcomes. In the discussion of intervention effectiveness, I give particular attention to the methods used for evaluation (e.g., pre- to posttreatment designs, quasi-experimental designs, and randomized controlled trials [RCTs]). Unlike case studies or pre–post assessment designs, an RCT allows investigators to be more confident that positive changes in parent–child functioning are due to the treatment model rather than to other factors unrelated to treatment. Random assignment and a control group comparison are two components that increase a study's rigor and have been defined as necessary for identifying an intervention as efficacious (Chambless & Ollendick, 2001; Gold, 2015). Other important components to increase study rigor include

- an active comparison group rather than a no-treatment control, allowing us, for example, to answer the question of whether one treatment model is more effective than another treatment model and not just whether receiving a particular treatment model is better than receiving no treatment;
- a sufficient sample size in the study (e.g., more than 25 families per treatment condition); and
- a multimethod assessment of outcomes (e.g., parent report, therapist evaluation, and actual, observed behavior) rather than only parent report.

EVALUATING AND SELECTING AN INTERVENTION

Not all parent–child interventions may be appropriate for all families. It may be particularly challenging to select a feasible and effective intervention for families who have been unresponsive to previous treatments (Shafi et al., 2019).

Finding a match between a family's needs and belief system and the treatment approach may increase engagement and reduce treatment attrition. Because not all parent–child interventions have demonstrated the ability to improve parent and child functioning, it is also essential to understand the extent of the research base supporting the model. As discussed in Chapter 4 of this volume, the first critical step in selecting an appropriate intervention is to conduct a valid and relevant assessment of the family. The second step is to consider several foundational questions regarding the available interventions:

1. Is the intervention designed to be implemented with the target child's age?
2. What is the strength of the scientific evidence that the intervention will effectively address the family's presenting problem?
3. What are the primary mechanisms of change in the intervention, and are they appropriate or feasible for implementation with the family?
4. Is the primary approach of the intervention to build parent knowledge and insight or to change parenting behavior? If the focus is on building knowledge and insight, how will that knowledge lead to changes in the parent–child relationship?
5. How are changes measured, and how does one know when the treatment has been successful?

Answering these questions at the start of treatment can facilitate the selection of an appropriate, effective, and feasible intervention for each family.

CHILD–PARENT PSYCHOTHERAPY

Theoretical Foundation and Model Overview

Child–parent psychotherapy (CPP) was developed for parents with children from birth to 5 years of age who have experienced traumatic events such as child abuse or witnessing intimate partner violence (Lieberman et al., 2015). The model was derived from the psychoanalytic intervention infant parent psychotherapy (Fraiberg, 1980) but is informed by developmental psychopathology, attachment theory, and trauma theory in order to address threats to the parent–child relationship that may be exacerbated because of the family's exposure to violence (Lieberman et al., 2015; Toth et al., 2018). The primary goals of the CPP model are to (a) foster a safe physical and psychological environment for parents and children, (b) increase responsive parenting, (c) increase parents' ability to balance their children's needs with their own, and (d) identify and correct distorted representations that parents hold of children and children hold of parents (Toth et al., 2018).

CPP is delivered in an individual format through weekly 1-hour sessions. Although the intervention progresses at the pace of the parent–child dyad, treatment typically lasts 10 months to 1 year (Toth et al., 2018). CPP is manualized to support fidelity; however, the format of the intervention has a high level of flexibility. For example, individual parent sessions may be added to the weekly parent–child sessions to support the caregiver in coping with her own trauma history. Although the research on CPP has been conducted with mothers, the model is described as appropriate for other caregivers and extended kin (e.g., foster parents, grandparents; Toth et al., 2018).

CPP begins with the foundational phase, a period of assessment of the parent–child relationship and engagement of parents in the intervention. Assessment focuses on developing an understanding of the risk and protective factors in the family's physical environment and in the parent–child relationship. Information is gathered regarding the child's and the parent's exposure to trauma, and the therapist begins to learn about the family's cultural beliefs and how they influence parenting. Unlike some attachment-based interventions, CPP does not specifically measure children's attachment to caregivers or use the attachment categories (Toth et al., 2018); rather, a broader perspective is taken on the parent–child relationship that includes a number of domains related to children's development and the impact of trauma such as children's sensorimotor organization, biological rhythms, and aggression/fearfulness (Lieberman & Van Horn, 2005).

Subsequent to the foundational phase, therapists guide parents during play interactions with their children, helping parents to identify and respond with sensitivity to their children's communications. Arising from a psychodynamic perspective, one of the key tasks of CPP is to explore caregivers' internal representations (named *schema* in the social cognition literature), which develop through repeated interactions with others (Westen, 1991). Internal representations of the self, others, and relationships are primarily implicit and provide a script about what to expect from human interactions. Children and adults who have experienced abuse are more likely to have internal representations of relationships as unsafe and conflict as dangerous and to attach negative affect to perceptions of the self and others (Freedenfeld et al., 1995; Lawson, Speidel, et al., 2020; Waldinger et al., 2001). Although such internal scripts may be adaptive in the abusive situation—helping a child to predict outcomes in an unsafe environment—they can prevent individuals from accurately interpreting new environments and healthy forms of interaction. Through therapist observations, guidance, and modeling of the parent–child play, CPP seeks to correct distorted representations related to the dyad's trauma history and to teach parents new interaction strategies (Lieberman & Van Horn, 2008). The primary mechanism of change in the CPP model is the learning and rehearsing of new, responsive parenting interactions (Toth et al., 2018). The therapist's sensitive observations to the parent and modeling of appropriate responsiveness to the child are meant to provide a "corrective emotional experience" for parents and children in order to reduce the negative impact of the trauma experiences. In the final phase of CPP, the focus shifts to celebrating a family's positive changes, processing the meanings for the family of saying goodbye to the therapist, and planning for the future.

Efficacy and Maintenance of Treatment Gains

CPP has approximately 30 years of research behind it, including five RCTs conducted by the developer and by independent researcher teams (Cicchetti et al., 2006; Lieberman et al., 1991, 2005; Toth et al., 2002, 2006). Three of those controlled trials examined the efficacy of CPP compared with another intervention (e.g., psychoeducation, home visiting, case management with individual therapy), and two compared the outcomes with those of a group who received no treatment. Relative to children in dyads who did not receive treatment, children in dyads who received CPP were more likely to be securely attached (Toth et al., 2006) and to display less anger and a better partnership in interactions with their mothers (Lieberman et al., 1991), whereas mothers were more likely to demonstrate empathy in their interactions with their infants (Lieberman et al., 1991). In a study of maltreated preschoolers, children who received CPP demonstrated more positive internal representations of their mothers and of the parent–child relationship after treatment than children who received a psychoeducational home visiting program (Toth et al., 2002). On the other hand, when compared with the outcomes of a psychoeducational parenting intervention, maltreated infants whose family participated in CPP did not demonstrate a significant difference in attachment security; rather, both interventions demonstrated large and significant improvement from baseline to posttreatment (Cicchetti et al., 2006). In a meta-analytic review of 17 programs designed to reduce the impact of trauma in children, CPP was described as showing preliminary positive effects in need of further investigation (Mavranezouli et al., 2020).

More recent studies have begun to examine the effectiveness of CPP when delivered within the community. One effectiveness study with no control condition found that mothers and children who participated in CPP experienced fewer posttraumatic stress symptoms at the end of treatment. The amount of parent improvement was associated with the expertise of their therapist (Hagan et al., 2017).

Follow-up studies of CPP have been conducted at 6 months, 1 year, and 6 years after the treatment (Cicchetti et al., 2011; Guild et al., 2017; Lieberman et al., 2006). In the only follow-up study of CPP that examined treatment outcomes beyond 1 year, children who participated in CPP with their depressed mothers between 2 and 3 years of age did not have significantly better teacher-reported peer relations at 9 years of age than the children of depressed mothers who had not received treatment (Guild et al., 2017). In the same study, children's attachment status at postintervention mediated the relationship between the treatment group and later peer relations such that secure attachment was related to better peer relations regardless of whether the family received CPP (Guild et al., 2017).

Effectiveness With Fathers

Although CPP has been described as appropriate for a range of caregivers, the five controlled trials of the treatment model to date included only mothers

(Cicchetti et al., 2006; Lieberman et al., 1991, 2005; Toth et al., 2002, 2006). No data have been reported on the effectiveness of CPP with male caregivers.

Evidence for Telehealth Delivery

To date, there is no evaluation of CPP delivered in a telehealth format.

Cultural Responsiveness

Because family beliefs about emotional expression and regulation can be so deeply influenced by culture, the work that CPP therapists do with parents to develop an understanding of their beliefs and perceptions and to intervene in a culturally responsive manner is critical (Toth et al., 2018). It is a strength that the controlled outcome studies of CPP have included culturally and ethnically diverse samples (e.g., Lieberman et al., 1991, 2005). The participants in the initial controlled trial were Spanish-speaking mothers who had recently immigrated to the United States from Mexico or Central America (Lieberman et al., 1991). These dyads demonstrated positive outcomes relative to the dyads who did not receive treatment. In an RCT comparing CPP with case management plus community treatment, the ethnic composition of the sample included families who identified themselves as from Latinx, African American/Black, Asian, and multiethnic backgrounds, with only 9.3% of families identifying as White (Lieberman et al., 2005). Families who completed CPP reported that their children had fewer posttraumatic symptoms and fewer overall behavior problems (internalizing and externalizing) compared with families who completed community treatment (Lieberman et al., 2005).

Two of the five controlled studies that included an ethnically diverse sample provided no information regarding the racial/ethnic background of the participating families except to describe them as of "minority race/ethnicity" (Cicchetti et al., 2006; Toth et al., 2002). No conclusions can be drawn, therefore, about the relative efficacy of the intervention across racial or ethnic groups. As with previous studies, the final controlled study, which did describe the specific ethnic composition of the sample, did not provide data across groups to allow for comparison or consideration of factors that might impact the outcomes for families of different cultures (Toth et al., 2006).

Dissemination Model and Therapist Training Requirements

CPP is disseminated by endorsed CPP trainers (see the website https://www.childparentpsychotherapy.com). The training to become competent in CPP includes multiple, intensive learning components over 18 months or longer (Toth et al., 2018; https://childparentpsychotherapy.com/providers/training/lc). To begin training, therapists must be licensed mental health professionals at the master's or doctoral level. Graduate students are unable to participate in CPP training until they enter a predoctoral internship, postdoctoral fellowship, or a master's-level social work position. Over the 18 months, therapists attend three separate in-person workshops (3 days, 2 days, 2 days). Between the workshops, therapists receive remote consultation on their cases from certified CPP trainers. Training formats include didactics, discussion, and active learning. Reflective supervision is an essential component of CPP training as a means to help therapists consider how (a) parents' and children's histories and internal representations influence their interactions and how they might be restructured, (b) the therapist's own experiences and representations impact their relationships with parents throughout the treatment process, and (c) vicarious trauma through ongoing exposure to the trauma narratives of families influences their own well-being and their ability to provide a safe space for their clients. The CPP training process includes measures of therapist competence and model fidelity.

CHILD–PARENT RELATIONSHIP THERAPY

Theoretical Foundation and Model Overview

Child–parent relationship therapy (CPRT) is a 10-session group intervention based on techniques from child-centered play therapy and drawing from attachment theory (Landreth & Bratton, 2006). The model was adapted from filial therapy—a treatment that typically continues for 1 year or more—to provide a more feasible and potentially more cost-effective intervention format (Lindo et al., 2016). CPRT was designed to be implemented in a group format with families with children from 3 years to 8 years of age who are exhibiting behavioral, emotional, or attachment issues. Consistent with attachment theory, CPRT is based on the position that caregivers have significant influence on their children's development and well-being; thus, the focus of treatment should be to foster a parent's capacity to be the agent of change for the child. The primary program goal is to increase parent responsiveness and thereby improve children's emotional and behavioral functioning (Lindo et al., 2016).

CPRT is considered an appropriate intervention for any caregivers who are important in a child's life (e.g., biological parents, foster parents, extended kin). Identified caregivers attend group sessions without their children present. No standardized assessment of parent and child functioning is included in the treatment; rather, the first three sessions of the group focus on providing psychoeducation to parents regarding the importance of responsive parenting and introducing the participants to the child-centered skills. By the 3rd week of the program, parents are assigned to play with their children using the new skills for 30 minutes one time during the week. Parents are instructed to video-record the play practice and to bring it to the following meeting. In Weeks 4 through 10, two of the six to eight parents in the group become the focus of each session. The entire group reviews the parent–child videos and provides feedback and encouragement about the interaction and each parent's skill use. The primary mechanisms of change during these sessions include video feedback, role-play, and therapist demonstrations of skills. During Weeks 4 through 8, the group discusses strategies for limit setting in addition to the video review. In Week 10, parents review their and their children's successes and consider steps for the future.

Efficacy and Maintenance of Treatment Gains

Although an extensive number of studies have been conducted using CPRT, the research is plagued by significant methodological weaknesses that limit the ability to draw conclusions about its effectiveness. In a review of 18 controlled studies of CPRT from 1995 to 2014 (Lindo et al., 2016), 100% were conducted by the developers of the model and none by independent research teams; 16 of the 18 studies compared CPRT with no treatment, and all of the studies had small to extremely small sample sizes (11 studies had 15 or fewer participants per condition; six studies had 25 or fewer per condition, and one study had more than 25 per condition). Compared with parents who received no treatment, parents who completed CPRT have demonstrated more observed empathy with their children (Bratton & Landreth, 1995) and less parenting stress (Carnes-Holt & Bratton, 2014) and have reported fewer internalizing symptoms in their children (Ceballos & Bratton, 2010). A more recent study, also including the model developers, compared the outcomes of CPRT with an active control—systematic training for effective parenting—for a sample of immigrant Latinx mothers (Ceballos et al., 2019). The sample size again was very small (10 participants or fewer per condition), making findings difficult to interpret or generalize.

A single meta-analysis has been conducted of studies that focus on the CPRT model (Allen, 2020). The recent review explored one outcome: children's levels of disruptive behavior. Across 23 studies, there was a moderate effect size for changes in children's disruptive behaviors (Table 7.1). However, in comparing the CPRT effect size with the overall effect size for other psychosocial interventions for child disruptive behavior (Epstein et al., 2015), CPRT appeared to be less effective. Further, Allen (2020) noted methodological weaknesses such as small sample size, controlled trials with low ratings for rigor, and samples of children with subclinical levels of behavior problems prior to treatment. These flaws in research design may lead to artificially higher effect sizes and make conclusions about efficacy uncertain. Studies of CPRT have not yet included long-term follow-up of treatment outcomes.

Effectiveness With Fathers

The majority of outcome studies of CPRT have included only female caregivers, or if male caregivers were included, outcomes were not reported separately. One exception is a study of incarcerated fathers in which 16 men in a medium-security detention facility received an early version of CPRT (Landreth & Lobaugh, 1998). Compared with fathers who received no treatment, fathers who completed CPRT reported more acceptance of their children, less parenting stress, and fewer child behavior problems. No observation measures or independent ratings of fathers' functioning were included (Landreth & Lobaugh, 1998), and the findings have not been replicated.

Evidence for Telehealth Delivery

To date, one study has examined the feasibility and acceptability of delivering CPRT in a telehealth format (Hicks & Baggerly, 2017). Of 31 parents who met the inclusion criteria for the study, 22 began the treatment process, and 8 mothers completed the program (treatment attrition rate = 64%). No information was collected on children's or parents' behavioral and emotional functioning prior to treatment; thus, risk status of the sample was unknown. One quantitative outcome measure—parents' report of acceptance of their children—showed gains from pre- to posttreatment for the eight families. Although parents reported appreciating the accessibility of the online format, the high attrition rate (exceeding many in-person parenting interventions; Niec et al., 2016) suggests that barriers to treatment engagement remain (Hicks & Baggerly, 2017). Based on this finding, it is not yet possible to consider CPRT an effective online intervention.

Cultural Responsiveness

A strength of the studies examining CPRT is that they have included ethnically and racially diverse samples (e.g., Ceballos & Bratton, 2010; Ceballos et al., 2019; Glover & Landreth, 2000; Landreth & Lobaugh, 1998). No comparison data are yet available to answer questions about differences in acceptability, attrition, or treatment outcomes across families of various cultural or racial/ethnic backgrounds.

Dissemination Model and Therapist Training Requirements

The certification process for CPRT is maintained by the original developers (https://cpt.unt.edu/child-parent-relationship-therapy-certification). To be eligible for certification in the CPRT 10-session model, providers must be licensed mental health professionals and must first complete a certification in child-centered play therapy. Subsequent to obtaining the play therapy certification, CPRT training includes 24 hours of didactic through an approved university course or community-based workshop provided by an endorsed trainer. After successfully completing the didactic, therapists must complete two CPRT groups under supervision, pass a certification exam, and complete a self-evaluation paper.

CIRCLE OF SECURITY

Theoretical Foundation and Model Overview

Circle of security (COS) is an intervention developed for parents with children from infancy to 5 years of age (Powell et al., 2014). Attachment and object relations theories underlie the content of the treatment, which was originally developed to be implemented in a session-limited (20-week) group format

(Marvin et al., 2002). The primary goal of COS is to foster parent–child attachment security by increasing parents' sensitive responding in the context of children's distress and exploration and improving parents' abilities to reflect upon how their own histories influence their caregiving (Woodhouse et al., 2018).

The COS 20-week protocol, which is distinguished from adaptations of COS with the name circle of security–intensive (COS-I), includes an assessment phase and three treatment phases. The overall goal of the assessment phase is to develop an understanding of the parent–child relationship. Parents are interviewed using the COS Interview (Powell et al., 2014), which focuses on assessing parents' internal representations (i.e., schema) of their children, themselves, and the parent–child relationship. Parents and children also complete three behavior observation measures: the Strange Situation procedure (SSP; Ainsworth et al., 1978) to assess children's attachment security, a shared reading activity during which parents are asked to read to their children, and a clean-up task in which parents are directed to have their children put away toys. The assessment information is meant to be used to identify the core conflict in parent–child interactions (labeled the "linchpin struggle") that impacts the child's ability to develop a healthy attachment (Woodhouse et al., 2018).

Using the information from the assessment, therapists develop an individual treatment plan for the parent. This allows for tailoring of the intervention to each dyad's needs, even in the context of group treatment. The group treatment in Phase 1 begins with psychoeducation about the importance of attachment and children's attachment-related behaviors. A graphic depiction of young children's behaviors as related to their exploration of the environment in the presence of a safe caregiver (secure base behaviors) and comfort-seeking during times of distress is used as a teaching tool. After the initial psychoeducation, parents in the COS-I group take turns being the focus of the session. Children are not present for any treatment session; rather, group members watch video clips of their own and the other members' interactions with their children from the assessment. With therapist support, parents describe what was happening in the moment and learn to reflect on the possible attachment-related needs being exhibited by their children. This reflective process, named *seeing and guessing*, is offered to each caregiver for three sessions. Through the process, parents learn responsive parenting concepts such as scaffolding, engagement/attunement, enjoyment, and emotion labeling (see Chapter 5, this volume).

During the second phase of treatment, parents receive psychoeducation about the concept of internal representations, which are implicit schema or scripts about self, others, and relationships. Internal representations develop over time through an individual's relationship/attachment history and can influence present and future relationships (Westen, 1991). Parents are encouraged to reflect on their own perceptions and expectations of relationships and how those expectations impact their behaviors toward their children, allowing them to either meet or neglect their children's attachment needs. Negative or distorted representations of the relationship are identified, and therapists facilitate parents' identification of specific interactions with their children that activate those representations and prevent parents from responding in a manner that addresses their children's needs.

Example: Parent Internal Representations/Schema Influences Perceptions of Child

PARENT INTERNAL REPRESENTATION/SCHEMA:	Other people only stay close to me because they want something from me. People are mostly selfish and treat me like I'm a doormat.
CHILD BEHAVIOR:	[*running to parent to seek emotional and physical reassurance when distressed*]
PARENT SCHEMA OF CHILD:	He needs too much from me. He doesn't love me; he's just being manipulative.
PARENT EMOTIONAL/ BEHAVIORAL RESPONSE:	[*pushes child away in annoyance*]

The premise of the COS-I intervention is that by developing parents' insights into their own internal representations and the way those representations impact their responses to their children, parents then have the opportunity to consider responses that are more likely to foster their children's secure attachment. Developing those insights is the focus of the second phase. In the third phase of the intervention (starting in Week 15), parents and children are again video recorded in a modified SSP. Clips from the interaction are reviewed in the final weeks of the intervention, with a focus on identifying parents' new strengths and ongoing challenges. The final week of the intervention (Week 20) is a celebratory graduation session.

Efficacy and Maintenance of Treatment Gains

Examination of the efficacy of the COS intervention is still in the early stages, and findings to date are mixed (Ramsauer et al., 2020; Yaholkoski et al., 2016). The primary support for the COS-I intervention comes from studies with pre–post treatment designs and no control groups. In the most recent of those studies, outcomes were examined from the archival data of 83 parent–child dyads (90% female caregivers) who had completed the COS-I intervention in an Australian community mental health clinic over a 6-year period (Huber et al., 2015). A strength of the study was that it included both parent-report (COS-interview) and behavior observations (e.g., SSP) to assess treatment outcomes. At the completion of treatment, only parents who started with a very low ability to consider their children's mental states (sometimes called *reflective functioning*) demonstrated improvements in their reflective functioning. Parents overall exhibited more positive representations of their children and the parent–child relationship. Despite the improvements in parents' representations, however, children's attachment classification did not change (i.e., children classified as insecurely attached were not more likely to be securely attached; Huber et al., 2015).

To date, one RCT of COS-I has been completed. In that study, the COS-I intervention was compared with treatment-as-usual (TAU; eclectic psychological services) in a sample of German mothers experiencing postpartum depression and their 4- to 9-month-old infants. Findings revealed that COS-I had no benefit over TAU (Ramsauer et al., 2020). That is, infants whose mothers participated in the COS-I intervention were no more likely to be securely attached than infants whose mothers participated in TAU and were no less likely to demonstrate disorganized attachment (Ramsauer et al., 2020). Both treatment conditions were related to improvements in maternal sensitivity at completion, and mothers who participated in COS-I showed no more improvement than mothers who participated in TAU.

No long-term follow-up of the impact of the COS-I intervention has yet been conducted. A small study explored the outcomes of a hybrid of two versions of the COS model—COS-I and COS-Parent (COS-P; see the description that follows)—provided in either group or individual format 1 year following treatment completion (Huber et al., 2021). Of the 36 families who completed treatment, 17 families completed the follow-up assessment. From pretreatment to 1-year follow-up, mothers reported improvements in their reflective functioning, supportive parenting, and sense of competence and self-efficacy. No behavioral measures were included, and no measures of child functioning were reported. More research is necessary to determine whether the COS-I intervention is related to positive changes that are maintained over time.

Adaptations

The COS model has been adapted into several different formats for delivery in alternative settings (e.g., home, day care) and by providers with different levels of training (e.g., lay health workers, licensed therapists; Cassidy et al., 2017; Cooper et al., 2017; Maupin et al., 2017). Two adaptations have been evaluated with a controlled design: COS-P and COS-4-session Home Visiting (COS4HV). COS-P is an eight- to 10-session prevention model designed to be provided by interventionists without formal mental health credentials (Cassidy et al., 2017). The intervention includes psychoeducation and review of standardized video clips rather than parent review of the videos of themselves and the other group families. No individualized assessment is conducted in the COS-P model. A controlled trial compared the outcomes for 164 mothers and their 3- to 5-year-old children enrolled in Head Start who received COS-P with those who received no treatment. Primary outcome variables demonstrated no improvement for children who completed COS-P relative to children who received no treatment. That is, there were no improvements in attachment status, externalizing behavioral symptoms, or internalizing behavioral symptoms. Similarly, mothers did not improve their sensitive responding to their children in distress (Cassidy et al., 2017).

In an examination of a four-session home visitation model of COS, 220 irritable infants and their mothers were assigned to either the COS4HV intervention or a home-based psychoeducation intervention. Similar to the outcomes for COS-P, the COS4HV demonstrated no treatment effect such that children in the COS4HV group experienced no improvement in attachment status (Cassidy et al., 2011).

Intervention Effectiveness With Fathers

As with many parent–child interventions, fathers and other male caregivers have been largely excluded from investigations of the efficacy of COS. Most of the pre–post treatment studies have not involved fathers, and those few studies that have (e.g., 6% male caregivers, Hoffman et al., 2006; 10% male caregivers, Huber et al., 2015) conducted no separate analyses of the data by caregiver gender, making it impossible to assess how outcomes differ for mothers and fathers or whether certain variables (e.g., readiness for change, perception of child behavior problems) might moderate caregiver outcomes. No fathers were included in any of the controlled trials of COS-I, COS-P, and COS4HV (Cassidy et al., 2011, 2017; Ramsauer et al., 2020).

Intervention Effectiveness via Telehealth Delivery

COS-I has not yet been evaluated for delivery through telehealth.

Cultural Responsiveness

COS includes a reflective framework that is designed to support and respect parents' differing belief systems (https://www.circleofsecurityinternational.com/circle-of-security-model/is-cosp-culturally-responsive/). Currently, the intervention has been implemented in multiple countries (e.g., Australia, Germany, Iran, United States). However, research to date has not explored differences in outcomes for families from ethnically or racially diverse backgrounds. The recent RCT of COS-I, conducted in Germany, included a sample that was 99% White (Ramsauer et al., 2020). Samples from other studies include a greater composition of families from ethnically diverse backgrounds or from marginalized communities; however, samples have been largely composed of White participants (e.g., Hoffman et al., 2006; Huber et al., 2015). More research is needed to better understand the influence of culture on treatment response for the COS model.

Dissemination Model and Therapist Training Requirements

Training and certification for COS is provided through Circle of Security International (https://www.circleofsecurityinternational.com). Licensed mental health professionals who wish to become certified COS providers of the COS-I model must complete a multistage training process with one of the 14 trainers who contract with the COS organization. The initial stage of training includes a 10-day workshop that covers the COS assessment and treatment planning. Participants learn to administer and interpret the SSP and the COS Interview (Woodhouse et al., 2018). To continue from the workshop to the consultation component of the training and to reach eligibility for certification, therapists must pass an exam that requires them to develop a treatment plan for two parent–child dyads based on video clips of their interactions. After passing the exam, therapists must receive consultation on two 20-week COS-I groups or on 50 hours of individual treatment over a minimum period of 1 year (https://www.circleofsecurityinternational.com/circle-of-security-model/cosp-vs-cos-intensive/; Woodhouse et al., 2018). Consultation includes discussion and extensive review of therapists' video-recorded treatment sessions.

PARENT–CHILD INTERACTION THERAPY

Theoretical Foundation and Model Overview

PCIT is an attachment- and behaviorally-based transdiagnostic intervention for parents and their 2- to 7-year-old children (Eyberg & Funderburk, 2011; Niec, 2018a). By strengthening the parent–child relationship and building responsive parenting skills, PCIT provides a foundation that fosters children's healthy functioning across a range of behavioral and emotional domains (Niec, 2018b). The PCIT model includes three phases: assessment, child-directed interaction (CDI), and parent-directed interaction (PDI). During the assessment phase, which requires one to two sessions, therapists gather sufficient information to develop a working conceptualization of the parent–child conflict, determine whether the intervention is appropriate for the presenting problems, and identify parent and child strengths to build upon during treatment. The assessment phase includes four components: (a) a clinical interview focusing on child developmental history, family/caregiving history, and the presenting problems; (b) parent-report measures of child functioning that include a focus on disruptive behaviors (e.g., Eyberg Child Behavior Inventory) as well as a broad screening measure of externalizing symptoms (e.g., defiant behavior, aggression, conduct problems) and internalizing symptoms (e.g., anxiety, depression), such as the Strengths and Difficulties Questionnaire (R. Goodman, 1997) or the Behavioral Assessment System for Children (Reynolds & Kamphaus, 2015); (c) a self-report measure of parent stress/pathology, such as the Parenting Stress Index–Short Form (Abidin, 1995) or Brief Symptom Inventory-18 (Derogatis & Savitz, 2000); and (d) a direct, standardized observation of the parent–child relationship (Dyadic Parent–Child Interaction Coding System–Fourth Edition [DPICS-IV]; see Chapter 4, this volume).

Treatment Phases

Equipped with the information from the assessment, the therapist introduces the family to the first treatment phase of PCIT—the CDI. The primary goal of

CDI is to increase parent responsiveness, including the use of child-centered play therapy skills and nonconfrontational strategies to manage children's challenging behaviors. Therapists introduce parents to the skills and the rationale for using them in one session called a "teach session." The child-centered skills include descriptions of the child's behavior, reflections of their verbalizations, imitation of children's appropriate behavior, genuine and contingent praise, and engagement and enjoyment of the interaction (Eyberg & Funderburk, 2011). Parents learn to avoid interactions that are leading (e.g., asking questions), coercive, or critical.

Subsequent to the CDI teach session are the CDI coach sessions. During the coach sessions, which are 1-hour weekly sessions, therapists provide live, immediate feedback to parents (coaching) while parents play with their children. The in vivo coaching is delivered to parents through a bug-in-the-ear device while the therapist observes from another room. Coaching, which is the primary mechanism of change in PCIT, uses behavioral principles to allow parents to practice new interaction patterns with their children through play—a natural medium of communication for young children—and in other real-life situations.

The quality of the parent–child attachment is developed over time, across numerous moment-to-moment interactions between children and their caregivers. During those interactions, children learn what to expect from their caregivers during times of distress, when in need of comfort, and what to expect in response to their own emotional and behavioral expressions. If problematic or toxic interactions have led to an unhealthy relationship, then changing those interactions (e.g., changing parents' responsiveness) is one key way to strengthen the relationship. Parents and children learn a new, healthier pattern of interacting. In coaching, therapists use a wide range of strategies to build parents' skills. Positive reinforcement and modeling, for example, increase parents' abilities to be child-centered in their interactions (Shanley & Niec, 2010). Process comments—coaching statements that connect the parents' child-centered behaviors to the child's behaviors—help parents to understand the importance of responsive parenting and build parents' sense of self-efficacy (Barnett et al., 2014; Niec et al., 2019). Child observations—pointing out children's behaviors and emotions in the moment—help parents to develop more accurate representations of their children. Overall, therapeutic in vivo coaching has been shown to build parents' responsiveness to their children and to decrease negative and coercive interactions (M. L. Barnett et al., 2014; M. L. Barnett et al., 2015; Shanley & Niec, 2010).

Example: Therapist Coaching

CHILD: [*Arranging the blocks*] I'm making a cake!

PARENT: Oh, a cake!

THERAPIST:	Great reflection. [*Praise*]
CHILD:	Strawberry is my favorite.
PARENT:	[*Playing silently*]
THERAPIST:	Thanks for telling me what you like. [*Modeling*]
PARENT:	Thanks for telling me what you like.
THERAPIST:	Great job with that praise. When you let him know you enjoy his sharing his feelings, he'll share more often. [*Praise, Process Comment*]
CHILD:	[*Continuing to play enthusiastically, casts a smile at parent*]
THERAPIST:	Did you see that smile? He really enjoys being with you. [*Child Observation*]
PARENT:	[*Returns the child's smile*] It's fun to play together, buddy.

An overarching and essential position of PCIT is that caregivers deserve to be empowered to provide safe, nurturing, and effective parenting for their children. Therefore, the focus of the intervention is on the parent–child relationship rather than the therapist–child relationship; parents are the primary agents of change for their children. Skill acquisition that begins in session with coaching is continued at home in 5-minute therapeutic play sessions between parents and children. Brief daily practice helps parents to move their new skills from the clinic into everyday interactions with their children. The 5-minute time keeps the practice feasible for parents to maintain a high level of therapeutic skill use and is sufficient to bring about change in both parents' and children's behaviors (Eyberg & Funderburk, 2011).

Throughout treatment, therapists "meet parents where they are." That is, parents move from the CDI phase of treatment to the PDI phase at the pace they need in order to develop their child-centered skills. Parent skill development and the parent–child interaction are assessed at the beginning of each weekly coaching session using a 5-minute standardized behavioral observation of parent–child play (DPICS-IV; see Chapter 4, this volume, for more details).

Once parents reach the skill criteria that support warm, child-centered interactions, they participate in the PDI teach session. The primary goal of the PDI phase is for parents to acquire developmentally appropriate and effective limit-setting skills to help them to manage challenging child behaviors and to build children's healthy functioning. Like the CDI teach session, the teach session in PDI provides parents with an exposure to the strategies and the rationale behind them, but parents' acquisition of the strategies takes place during the PDI coach sessions with therapeutic in vivo feedback during parent–child interaction.

Graduation From Treatment

A family's graduation from PCIT is based on the achievement of four important goals: parents demonstrate the ability to use child-centered interactions and to provide safe, effective limits for their children; they report that their children's disruptive behaviors are typical compared with others of the same age; and parents express confidence in their ability to manage challenging child behaviors in multiple settings (e.g., home, public). In other words, successful treatment completion includes positive outcomes for parents and children, in terms of both parent perception and actual observed behavior change.

Efficacy and Maintenance of Treatment Gains

The research on PCIT spans more than 40 years and includes dozens of single-group design studies as well as approximately a dozen controlled trials conducted by the developer of the intervention, Dr. Sheila Eyberg, and independent research teams. Parents who complete PCIT demonstrate significant and meaningful increases in responsive parenting and decreases in negative interactions with their children, whereas children demonstrate reductions in disruptive behaviors (Niec et al., 2016; Schuhmann et al., 1998; R. Thomas et al., 2017; R. Thomas & Zimmer-Gembeck, 2007). The effect sizes of the intervention for male and female caregivers and for child behavioral functioning are large to very large (see Table 7.1; R. Thomas et al., 2017; R. Thomas & Zimmer-Gembeck, 2007; Ward et al., 2016).

PCIT has been used extensively with children who have experienced traumatic events, and it has been identified as a best practice intervention for families in which physical abuse has occurred (Chaffin et al., 2004, 2011; Kauffman Best Practices Project, 2004; Timmer et al., 2005). PCIT reduces toxic patterns of interaction between parents and children (Chaffin et al., 2004); it improves emotion regulation in both parents and children, fostering a healthier and safer parenting environment (Lieneman et al., 2020; Rothenberg et al., 2019; Zimmer-Gembeck et al., 2019); and it reduces both externalizing (e.g., aggression, defiance) and internalizing symptoms in children (e.g., anxiety and withdrawal; Niec et al., 2016; Schuhmann et al., 1998; R. Thomas et al., 2017). Parents who complete PCIT also demonstrate an improvement in reflective functioning (Zimmer-Gembeck et al., 2019). Follow-up studies find that, on average, children maintain positive behavior gains 6 months, 1 year, 2 years, and as far as 4 to 6 years after treatment (Eyberg et al., 2001; Hood & Eyberg, 2003; Niec et al., 2016; Nixon et al., 2004).

Effectiveness With Fathers

The efficacy of PCIT with fathers has been examined independently from that of mothers in multiple studies (Brestan et al., 1997; Eyberg et al., 1995; Eyberg & Robinson, 1982; Hood & Eyberg, 2003; Niec et al., 2016; Schuhmann et al., 1998). Although fathers often enter parenting interventions feeling less ready to make changes in their own behaviors and perceiving less of a need for treatment (Niec, Barnett, et al., 2015), overall, fathers who complete PCIT demonstrate similar positive outcomes to those of mothers (R. Thomas & Zimmer-Gembeck, 2007). In a study comparing individual and group formats of PCIT, fathers demonstrated large, significant changes in their use of child-centered skills regardless of which treatment format they completed (Niec et al., 2016).

Evidence for Telehealth Delivery

Restrictions on in-person contact during the COVID-19 pandemic forced therapists all over the world to translate their mental health services into a telehealth format. PCIT is one of the few parent–child interventions that had been evaluated in a virtual delivery format prior to the pandemic (Comer et al., 2017; Kohlhoff et al., 2021). PCIT lends itself readily to a virtual delivery, in part because in vivo coaching is the primary mechanism of change. That is, in standard PCIT, therapists intervene through the bug in the ear and are already one step removed from the parent–child interaction. Coaching from the other side of a computer screen is not so different from coaching on the other side of a two-way mirror. Of course, challenges exist in coaching in an environment where the therapist has much less control (e.g., family home; Gurwitch et al., 2020); however, one balancing advantage is that, even more than during in-person PCIT, during telehealth delivery therapists have the opportunity to observe and coach parents in relevant real-life interactions with their children.

Initial investigations of internet-delivered PCIT (I-PCIT) include an RCT that compared I-PCIT with standard in-clinic PCIT (Comer et al., 2017) and a qualitative study of treatment acceptability (Kohlhoff et al., 2021). In the controlled trial, the number of sessions for families to reach the positive parenting skills criteria did not differ for I-PCIT or in-person PCIT. Parents in both treatment formats reported a reduction in child behavior problems and in their perception of the burden of child behaviors, with no differences across conditions. Treatment satisfaction was high for both groups and did not differ by treatment format. In a rural Australian sample of parents who completed I-PCIT, qualitative interviews revealed that parents felt the treatment successfully reduced their children's behavioral issues, increased their children's ability to regulate emotion, and improved their self-esteem. Parents also reported that after I-PCIT the parent–child relationship was warmer and closer and their own confidence as parents was improved (Kohlhoff et al., 2021).

Therapists have also reported satisfaction with the internet delivery of PCIT. In a survey of 223 PCIT therapists in the community, 82% reported moving from in-person to telehealth formats during the pandemic (M. L. Barnett et al., 2021). Those therapists reported that PCIT delivered via a telehealth format was not substantially different from PCIT delivered in person and that they appreciated the increased accessibility for families. Therapists also reported that implementing PCIT within families' homes provided enhanced opportunities to help parents to generalize their new interaction skills. Challenges related to the internet delivery of PCIT were primarily related to technological difficulties (e.g., availability of internet access) and managing environmental distractions (e.g., siblings, pets). A vast majority (more than 80%) of therapists who were implementing PCIT via telehealth during the pandemic reported hoping to continue to use the telehealth delivery after the lifting of contact restrictions (M. L. Barnett et al., 2021).

Adaptations

Many adaptations have been developed from the original PCIT model with differing levels of empirical support for their effectiveness (Niec, 2018a). Some of the adaptations that have been most rigorously examined include group PCIT, teacher–child interaction training, and PCIT-Home (Abrahamse et al., 2016; Fernandez et al., 2015; Galanter et al., 2012; Garbacz et al., 2014; Lyon et al., 2009; Niec et al., 2005, 2016). PCIT has been provided effectively to parents in an individual and a group format. It has demonstrated positive outcomes when implemented in the clinic, school, and home settings. Increasing evidence supports the use of PCIT not only for children with externalizing problems but also for children who are experiencing internalizing problems such as anxiety and depression (Carpenter et al., 2014; Catchpole et al., 2019; Comer et al., 2012; Lenze et al., 2011; Pincus et al., 2008). Ongoing investigation is evaluating the use of PCIT to reduce health-risk behaviors such as those related to childhood obesity (Domoff & Niec, 2018; Niec et al., 2022). Several of the existing adaptations require further evaluation prior to broad dissemination.

Cultural Responsiveness

PCIT has demonstrated a high level of transportability across cultures (Abrahamse et al., 2018). It has been successfully transported to approximately 20 countries. Outside of the United States, RCTs have been conducted in Australia, China, the Netherlands, and Norway, with significant positive outcomes for parents and children across cultures (Abrahamse et al., 2016; Bjørseth & Wichstrøm, 2016; Leung et al., 2009, 2015, 2017; Nixon et al., 2004; R. Thomas & Zimmer-Gembeck, 2011). Pre-post and case studies have also been conducted in Japan and Taiwan (Chen & Fortson, 2015; Hosogane et al., 2018). Within the United States, some initial work has examined outcomes for families from marginalized communities. For example, a small, controlled trial of PCIT in Puerto Rico found that families who completed PCIT demonstrated significantly fewer child externalizing behavior problems and lower parenting stress relative to families who had not completed treatment (Matos et al., 2009). Positive changes were maintained at a 3½-month follow-up.

Many investigations of PCIT have contained samples of families from a diverse range of ethnic and racial backgrounds; however, efforts to explore differences in outcomes across cultures within the United States or to explore moderators of treatment response for families from different backgrounds remain preliminary. In a study of treatment attrition in an urban community sample, families from marginalized ethnic backgrounds (Black/African American, Hispanic/Latinx, Asian American) were no more likely to drop out of treatment than White families (Danko et al., 2016). On the other hand, a small study ($N = 18$) of financially stressed African American/Black families found an attrition rate of 56% (Fernandez et al., 2011). One well-controlled clinical trial with a sample of Mexican American families compared the outcomes of standard PCIT with a cultural adaption of the treatment, Guiando a Niños Activos (GANA; K. M. McCabe et al., 2005), and to TAU (K. McCabe et al., 2012; K. McCabe & Yeh, 2009). Subsequent to treatment, families who completed standard PCIT and GANA demonstrated greater positive changes in child behavioral symptoms and parent stress than the families receiving TAU (eclectic, community-based psychotherapy). No differences existed in outcomes for the families who completed standard PCIT and those who completed the culturally adapted version. Positive changes for children and parents were maintained 6 to 24 months after treatment completion. Overall, Mexican American families who completed PCIT demonstrated similar effect sizes to the effects seen in non-Hispanic/Latinx White families who complete PCIT (K. McCabe et al., 2012). A recent meta-analysis that investigated differences in outcomes between families who completed standard PCIT and those who completed cultural adaptations such as GANA found smaller effects when PCIT was modified from the standard protocol (R. Thomas et al., 2017).

Certain aspects inherent in the PCIT model make it a flexible and culturally responsive intervention, and they may help to explain why treatment outcomes have been similar (a) across countries that have very different parenting styles (e.g., China vs. Netherlands vs. United States) and (b) within the United States when the standard model is compared with a culturally tailored adaptation (Niec, 2018c). First, PCIT welcomes and encourages all caregivers who are important in a child's life (e.g., biological, adoptive parents, stepparents, foster parents, extended kin, adult siblings, nannies) to participate in treatment, which makes it responsive to cultural differences in caregiving and the identification of who important caregivers are. Second, the primary agent of change for the child is the parent, not the therapist, which empowers families and demonstrates respect for their beliefs and resiliency. Finally, coaching is a highly flexible mechanism of change that can target a family's specific needs, honoring the ways in which culture and individual differences interact to influence the strengths and vulnerabilities in the parent–child relationship.

Dissemination and Training Requirements

The training and certifying organization of PCIT is PCIT International, an organization founded by the developer of the treatment model (http://www.pcit.org). PCIT is disseminated internationally using a train-the-trainer model through which individuals who are trained to be therapists by a certified, experienced trainer may receive support and additional consultation to become trainers themselves. The dissemination model includes three levels of trainers: global trainers, who train nationally and internationally and who play a role in the leadership of the organization and ongoing evaluation of the treatment; regional trainers, who train within a geographical region (within the United States, typically a state) and who also often play a leadership role in the organization; and within-agency trainers, who train therapists using a co-therapy model within their agency and who are often key advocates for evidence-based implementation in their communities.

The process to become a certified PCIT therapist is similar to the processes of other parent–child interventions described here. To participate in training, therapists must be licensed mental health professionals at the master's or doctoral level or may be graduate students who are in a mental health field, in their third year of training, and under the supervision of a PCIT trainer. The first stage of PCIT training requires a 40-hour initial workshop offered in person or live online, which provides therapists with a background on the foundational theories of PCIT and the PCIT research base, and heavily emphasizes the active practice of the assessment and treatment skills of each of the model's phases. Subsequent to the initial workshop, therapists may begin to see PCIT cases under the bimonthly consultation of their trainer. Consultation includes the trainer's review of recorded therapy sessions or live observation of the trainee's cases and in-depth feedback and discussion with trainees. Treatment fidelity is embedded in the intervention, with fidelity checklists for each session included in the protocol manual. Trainers monitor fidelity; however, therapists are encouraged to review and assess their own fidelity. Consultation lasts a minimum of 1 year, during which a list of competencies must be achieved and two PCIT cases successfully graduated prior to being eligible for certification.

SUMMARY

Evidence exists to indicate that, overall, parent–child interventions targeting parents and their preschool- to early school-aged children have a positive effect on parents' responsiveness, children's behavioral functioning, and the parent–child relationship, with some evidence for an impact on children's attachment security. CPP has several well-controlled studies that demonstrated positive outcomes for children who have experienced traumatic events and their mothers. The CPP model is intensive and requires family's long-term commitment (about 50 weekly sessions). More follow-up studies are required to determine if changes seen immediately and 1 year after completing the intervention are maintained or influence later domains of child development. No investigations currently evaluate fathers' responses to the CPP model and whether or how families might benefit from fathers' participation.

PCIT also has well-controlled studies that demonstrate positive outcomes for children with a range of behavioral and emotional symptoms and families in which children have been physically abused. Effect sizes reported in meta-analyses demonstrate that PCIT has large to very large positive effects on parents' responsive parenting, children's behavioral functioning, and parenting stress. Parents who complete PCIT also demonstrate higher emotion regulation and reflective functioning. PCIT is effective for mothers and fathers. Long-term follow-up finds positive gains maintained up to 4 to 6 years after treatment.

Not all parent–child interventions have strong support for their efficacy. Notably, CPRT has little evidence to suggest that it has better outcomes than TAU, as positive changes have mainly been demonstrated when comparing families who completed CPRT to families who received no treatment. COS also has insufficient support for its effectiveness. Multiple studies of COS have found a lack of significant outcomes, and to date there are no follow-up investigations of the maintenance of treatment gains beyond the end of the intervention. Nothing is currently known about the response of fathers to the COS model or its adaptability to telehealth delivery.

A universal weakness of the reviewed interventions is insufficient research on the responses of families from marginalized ethnic and racial backgrounds. To select an appropriate intervention for a particular family, therapists should consider questions about topics such as the intended age range of the intervention, the modality and mechanisms of change, and the evidence for effectiveness in addressing the family's presenting problems.

Key Takeaways

1. Multiple parent–child interventions exist that target the relationships of caregivers with their preschool- and early school-age children.
2. Asking foundational questions about an intervention prior to implementation will help to match a family's goals with an appropriate and effective treatment model.
3. Not all widely disseminated intervention models have strong support for their efficacy. Specifically, CPRT and COS have significant gaps in the research supporting their efficacy, and in multiple situations, positive change of the primary outcome variables has not been found.
4. Even some widely disseminated parent–child interventions have failed to investigate how the model works for fathers or other male caregivers.
5. Therapist training in evidence-based parent–child interventions typically includes three core components: the initial workshop, ongoing consultation, and trainers' review of therapists' sessions (live or video-recorded).

Clinical Growth Questions

1. How do I currently select an intervention to use with a family? How much of the decision is determined by my comfort level and how much is

determined by the needs of the client? Are there questions I could ask myself to ensure a better fit between a family's goals and the treatment model?

2. What is one new way I can obtain up-to-date information about the interventions I use in my clinical work?
3. What is one new intervention strategy or treatment model in which I would like to develop competence within the next 6 months, the next year, and the next 4 years?

Additional Resources for More Information About Evidence-Based Parent–Child Interventions

- https://www.cebc4cw.org/
- https://effectivechildtherapy.org/
- https://www.nctsn.org/treatments-and-practices/trauma-treatments

III

OVERCOMING BARRIERS TO SUCCESS

8

Engaging Fathers

Building a Positive Father–Child Relationship

"I don't understand why they dropped out of treatment. They seemed invested." These distressed words came from a novice therapist during the supervision of one of her family cases. She had seen the family—two biological parents (Mr. and Ms. W) and their 3-year-old son—for two initial sessions subsequent to Ms. W's call requesting services to help her and her husband manage their child's tantrums and increasing defiance. During the intake sessions, the therapist conducted a clinical interview and a behavioral observation of parent–child interactions. Both parents completed rating scales to measure their own stress and their child's behavioral and emotional functioning. During the assessment, the therapist recognized several meaningful strengths in the parent–child relationships, including engagement and warmth between mother and child and shared positive affect between father and child. Strains in both relationships appeared related to inconsistent discipline strategies between mother and father, with mother using primarily permissive discipline strategies (e.g., ignoring misbehavior, pleading for child compliance) and father using primarily rigid, authoritarian strategies. Ms. W reported high levels of parenting stress and clinical levels of child disruptive behavior, whereas Mr. W reported stress levels within the typical range and only slightly elevated child disruptive behavior. After the assessment, the therapist provided the family with feedback about the findings and offered recommendations regarding treatment, which would include both parents and the child. The following week, the family did not show for their appointment. On a follow-up call from the

https://doi.org/10.1037/0000304-008
Strengthening the Parent–Child Relationship in Therapy: Laying the Foundation for Healthy Development, by L. N. Niec

therapist, Ms. W reported that she and her husband had discussed the matter and they no longer felt the need to pursue services.

WHAT HAPPENED?

The therapist reported that from the intake phone call to the assessment feedback session the parents had seemed interested and invested in reducing their child's problem behaviors and building stronger parent–child relationships. Both parents appeared to participate openly in the assessment process. During the feedback session, Ms. W had expressed enthusiasm about the prospect of treatment. Mr. W had appeared quiet but not defensive or resistant. To gain a clearer understanding of why the family might have decided to forgo treatment, the therapist and I watched the recording of the assessment and feedback sessions. In observing the interactions of Mr. and Ms. W and the therapist, clues to the situation became apparent:

- Mr. W rarely spoke spontaneously; instead, he sat quietly with a neutral facial expression. His responses were most often in the form of nods or brief verbalizations in apparent agreement with his wife's comments.
- Ms. W was gregarious and forthcoming. Frequently, she spoke both for herself and her husband. Her expressions were animated, ranging from clear distress regarding her child's behavior to earnest descriptions of her attempts to manage him and questions about options for treatment.
- Although the therapist started the session facing both parents across a table and addressing both parents equally, as Ms. W answered questions quickly and demonstrated emotional engagement in the conversation, the therapist turned increasingly to Ms. W. The therapist then directed interview questions consistently to Ms. W first.
- When Ms. W appeared to answer for both parents, the therapist did not always seek Mr. W's independent input. When she did ask Mr. W for his perceptions, she more often used closed-ended, leading questions that pressed Mr. W simply to confirm his wife's responses (e.g., "Is that true for you too?" "Have you had similar experiences with your son?").
- By the end of the session, the therapist had turned directly toward Ms. W, and verbal and nonverbal communications were almost exclusively aimed toward her. Mr. W stopped contributing to the conversation.

VALUING FATHERS

Although in this case we cannot know exactly why the family decided not to pursue treatment, upon review it became clear that from the first contact—a phone call with Ms. W—to the wrap-up of the assessment feedback session we had not placed equal value on Mr. W's perceptions of his child's behavior, his attitudes toward parenting, and his motivation for treatment. Based on his self-reported ratings of parenting stress, he was not experiencing distress about his child's behavior and did not report seeing as many conduct problems as had Ms. W. During interactions with the therapist, Mr. W never presented as defensive or dismissive of treatment; however, the "family's" enthusiasm came from Ms. W and not from her husband. The possibility exists that Mr. W did not see sufficient reason to expend family resources on treatment and may have convinced Ms. W of the same; perhaps he felt uncomfortable seeking help in a mental health setting, or perhaps he believed that the treatment options offered were not relevant to him. Although we cannot know for certain, we do know that each parent came to the session with different perspectives and expectations, which we did not fully assess.

Fathers have historically been neglected in the research on parent–child relationships and in the clinical setting. Despite repeated calls from the literature for therapists to better connect with fathers and to include them in empirical investigation and in the treatment process, systemic biases about the roles of mothers and fathers perpetuate the overburdening of female caregivers and the marginalization of male caregivers (Fabiano & Caserta, 2018; Panter-Brick et al., 2014; Tully et al., 2018). This chapter (a) provides an overview of the evidence that connects fathers' parenting to child development and to the processes and outcomes of parent–child interventions, (b) considers barriers to fathers' access to and engagement in treatment, and (c) offers clinical strategies for building an inclusive treatment environment for all caregivers.

THE FATHER–CHILD RELATIONSHIP AND CHILD DEVELOPMENT

Fathers play a significant role in their children's development. Although the literature is far less extensive relative to studies of mothers, it is well established that fathers' parenting and the father–child relationship impact children's well-being from infancy into adolescence and young adulthood (Du Rocher Schudlich et al., 2019; Grossman et al., 2019; Lamb & Lewis, 1976/2010; Lucassen et al., 2011; Rasing et al., 2020; Scourfield et al., 2016; Zhang et al., 2020). Fathers' parenting has been linked to children's expressive and receptive language skills (Pancsofar et al., 2010; Pancsofar & Vernon-Feagans, 2006), literacy (Chacko et al., 2018; Nuttall et al., 2019), and academic achievement (Gordon, 2016; McBride et al., 2005; McWayne et al., 2013; Tamis-LeMonda et al., 2004). Their parenting has also been linked to health-related behavior such as children's eating patterns (Litchford et al., 2020) as well as to behavioral and emotional adjustment (Amato & Gilbreth, 1999; Buttitta et al., 2019; Leidy et al., 2013; Rasing et al., 2020; Zhang et al., 2020) and peer relations (Lux & Walper, 2019).

Children form relationships with their fathers with comparable patterns of secure and insecure attachments as they form with their mothers, and those attachments appear to play similar roles in influencing children's later functioning, although they may influence different areas of development (Bretherton, 2010; Lamb & Lewis, 2010). For instance, among preschoolers, father–child insecurity has been more strongly associated with child conduct problems than mother–child insecurity (Bureau et al., 2017). Also, as is true for mothers, the quality of the paternal–child relationship is influenced by fathers' responsiveness and amount of involvement with their children (G. L. Brown et al., 2007, 2012; Buttitta et al., 2019). Fathers' responsiveness varies across individuals and is influenced by intrapersonal and contextual factors (Lamb & Lewis, 2010). Fathers who describe warm, secure relationships with their own parents are more likely to be responsive and involved with their children than fathers who describe negative relationships in their childhood (Bretherton et al., 2006; Shannon et al., 2006). Fathers experiencing more conflict with their partners demonstrate less parenting sensitivity (Du Rocher Schudlich et al., 2019). As is similar for mothers, fathers who are experiencing psychopathology such as depression or poor emotion regulation are more likely to exhibit negative parenting styles and less likely to demonstrate responsive parenting (Cheung & Theule, 2019; van Eldik et al., 2019; Wilson & Durbin, 2010; Zhang et al., 2020). In turn, these paternal risk factors are related to increased behavioral and emotional risk in their children (Rasing et al., 2020; Zhang et al., 2020).

FATHERS NEED TREATMENT—TREATMENT NEEDS FATHERS

The impact of fathering and the father–child relationship on children's growth and well-being is in itself a compelling reason to include fathers in the treatment process. However, it is certainly not the only reason. Since around 1970, the amount of time that fathers engage with their children has tripled (Parker & Livingston, 2019). As fathers spend more time parenting, they report a need for effective support. Among a group of community fathers with children 2 to 9 years of age, 72% rated parenting as "extremely demanding" and 22% rated parenting as "very stressful and depressing" (Frank, Keown, Dittman, & Sanders, 2015). Fathers who present for treatment often report high rates of stress (Niec et al., 2016). It is not only paternal distress that may draw fathers into treatment, however. In fact, as a group, men tend not to be active help-seekers (Triemstra et al., 2017); rather, fathers express an interest in learning about parenting issues. Fathers have indicated that building a positive relationship with their children and increasing their children's confidence and self-esteem are the two most important topics to include in parenting interventions (Frank, Keown, & Sanders, 2015). Fathers also express an interest in program content that addresses concerns specific to their parenting interactions and not just concerns related to mother–child interactions (Lechowicz et al., 2019). In other words, fathers play a significant role in children's development, have a need for parenting support, and express investment in helping their children to flourish. Access to and engagement in effective treatment, therefore, is clearly important. The following questions are answered in the next sections: Do interventions strengthen fathers' involvement with their children, their parenting skills, and the father–child relationship? Does father participation affect the outcomes of treatment for coparents and children?

For more than 4 decades, clinicians and researchers have been calling for a more inclusive approach to the study of parenting and parenting interventions (e.g., Budd & O'Brien, 1982; Fabiano & Caserta, 2018; Lamb, 1975; Parent et al., 2017). As in the developmental literature, progress has been relatively slow. Two of the greatest limitations to our understanding of the impact of treatment on fathers and the impact of fathers on treatment are (a) the relatively few programs that include fathers and (b) the fact that even among programs in which fathers are included, most studies have not examined outcomes for fathers and mothers separately or evaluated the impact of coparent participation (Panter-Brick et al., 2014). With these limitations in mind, it is still possible to be optimistic regarding treatment outcomes. A meta-analysis of 26 studies evaluating the effectiveness of parenting interventions found that interventions in which fathers participated demonstrated greater improvements in children's behaviors and parenting (Lundahl et al., 2008), suggesting that father participation is related to greater positive change. A more recent study found similar positive outcomes (Bagner, 2013). Among families who participated in a parent–child intervention for their children with disruptive behaviors and developmental delays, single mothers were more likely than two-parent families to discontinue treatment prematurely, and two-parent families who completed treatment demonstrated greater improvements in their children's reported and observed disruptive behaviors than single mothers who completed treatment (Bagner, 2013). Other studies have found positive outcomes for fathers and father–child interactions similar to the outcomes for mothers, even when the relative outcomes for coparent families versus single-parent families have not been investigated. In an evaluation of a parenting program that included father-preferred content, fathers who received treatment reported greater improvements in child disruptive behaviors and parenting skills than fathers who had not received treatment (Frank, Keown, & Sanders, 2015). Mothers and fathers both reported satisfaction with the program. In a controlled trial of a group format of parent–child interaction therapy, both fathers and mothers reported significant reductions in their stress and their children's behavior problems whether they completed group or individual parent–child interaction therapy. Further, observed parent–child interactions revealed that subsequent to treatment, fathers and mothers both interacted with their children in more child-centered and responsive ways (Niec et al., 2016).

Better understanding about the interaction between paternal engagement in parent–child interventions and the treatment outcomes for children and parents will help clinicians to better support fathers. Despite the continuing gaps in the literature, four things are evident: (a) fathers influence their children's functioning directly and indirectly, (b) the father–child relationship tends to be a better predictor of child outcomes than fathers' individual traits,

(c) fathers express a need for parenting support and a desire for positive relationships with their children, and (d) effective parenting interventions make a difference in fathers' interactions with their children and in children's well-being.

COPARENTING

The associations among paternal parenting, the father–child relationship, and children's outcomes are complex and bidirectional. As for mothers, fathers influence their coparents and their children, and children and coparents influence fathers (X. Ding et al., 2020; Du Rocher Schudlich et al., 2019). That is, fathers' parenting occurs within family systems and not in isolation. This can be true even if parents are not sharing a residence and are not partners. An increasing amount of work supports the connection between the extent to which caregivers share the parenting role and support one another in that role (*positive coparenting*) or undermine one another (*negative coparenting*) and children's developmental outcomes (McHale & Lindahl, 2011). In fact, coparenting may be a stronger predictor of children's and parents' well-being than the relationship quality of the caregiver couple (Frosch et al., 2000). Thus, an approach to treatment that considers the father–child system and not the parent or child in isolation is more likely to address the multiple factors affecting child and family functioning. Coparenting interventions go another step further, focusing not just on the parent–child relationship and individual parenting but also on the caregivers' relationship and the extent to which they cooperate as parents (Pruett et al., 2017b). Initial findings from interventions that focus on coparenting suggest that they may have a positive impact on fathers' parenting involvement (Pilkington et al., 2019) as well as on outcomes for parents and children, reducing parent stress and problematic parent–child interactions, improving child behavior, and supporting couple satisfaction (Frank, Keown, & Sanders, 2015; Pruett et al., 2017a). However, the strength of the effects so far is small to moderate, and the quality of the data tends to be low (Pilkington et al., 2019). For example, with few exceptions, the work to date has measured parent reports of change but not actual observed behavior change in parents or children, and not all interventions have demonstrated positive changes in child behavior or couple satisfaction (Pruett et al., 2017a). From a developmental and practical perspective, addressing parents as a team has advantages for children and for caregivers, yet so far it is not apparent that interventions created specifically to focus on coparenting are robustly effective in improving the parent–child relationship or changing parent and child behavior. Although it is clear that the quality of coparenting effects children's functioning, an alternative intervention strategy may be to select existing intervention models that have already demonstrated large and reliable positive effects on the father–child relationship (e.g., parent–child interaction therapy) and to tailor those models by increasing the relevance to fathers and the attention to coparenting in order to address the parent system and begin reducing barriers to fathers' participation.

BARRIERS TO FATHERS' PARTICIPATION

Obstacles to fathers' participation in parenting interventions arise from multiple sources at multiple system levels, including the individual parent, the family, the clinician, the agency, and the culture (Fabiano & Caserta, 2018; Frank, Keown, Dittman, & Sanders, 2015; Tully et al., 2018). Exploration of these obstacles has come primarily from surveys and focus groups of fathers in the community, fathers who have participated in parent–child interventions, and clinicians who work with families (Davison et al., 2017; Frank, Keown, Dittman, & Sanders, 2015; Glynn & Dale, 2015; Tully et al., 2018). Identifying the obstacles is a necessary first step toward increasing paternal access and engagement in treatment.

Paternal Attitudes and Understanding

A number of barriers to fathers' access and participation in mental health interventions have to do with individual parental attitudes toward parenting and help-seeking. Those attitudes are influenced, in turn, by societal judgments about the roles of men, particularly those related to conventional Western gender roles. Fathers often feel they are unimportant as a parent (Cosson & Graham, 2012) or that caregiving is a maternal role (Tully et al., 2018). Their feeling of exclusion from the parenting team is compounded by a reluctance to seek psychological support, either for themselves or for their children (Triemstra et al., 2017). In one survey, more than 50% of the clinicians who responded ($N = 210$) said that among all the families they served, only 5% of fathers initiated contact for services (Tully et al., 2018). Finally, fathers often lack knowledge of the existing options for support (e.g., What is a parenting intervention, and how would I access an effective one?). In a study of 161 fathers in the community, only 13% reported having any knowledge of even one of the eight existing parenting programs in their area (Frank, Keown, Dittman, & Sanders, 2015). When fathers feel unimportant, are reluctant to ask for help, and lack knowledge of the existing services for parents, they are unlikely to access support to strengthen their relationships with their children.

Family Attitudes and Resources

Limited family resources—time, money, transportation, reliable childcare—present a barrier not just to fathers but to many caregivers, impeding their ability to access services. However, clinicians have reported that these barriers play a particularly significant role in reducing paternal involvement (Tully et al., 2018); therefore, any effort to increase access and involvement should include a consideration of ways to address the family's level of resources. In addition to tangible resources, family attitudes can also be a barrier. For example, mothers' beliefs about the importance of fathers in children's lives can impact the level of fathers' involvement with their children and in the treatment process (Glynn & Dale, 2015; Piotrowska et al., 2017). Mothers (or other coparenting caregivers) may act as gatekeepers who can discourage or facilitate fathers' involvement.

Clinician and Program Attitudes

The clinician's attitude toward the role of fathers has emerged repeatedly as an important factor in engaging and retaining fathers in treatment (Frank, Keown, Dittman, & Sanders, 2015; Glynn & Dale, 2015; Pfitzner et al., 2017). Clinicians have rated their ability to communicate the value of fathers as one of the key aspects of fostering fathers' participation (Glynn & Dale, 2015; Tully et al., 2018). However, as in the case example at the start of this chapter, it is easy to be inadvertently drawn to interactions with the most engaged caregiver, which may mean giving fathers the message that their input is unnecessary or not valued. Clinicians may also assume that fathers are incapable of participating, and therefore clinicians may interact with the family in ways that confirm their belief (e.g., contacting only mothers, scheduling sessions only according to mothers' schedules). In fact, service providers have reported having little confidence in fathers' skills or involvement (Ewart-Boyle et al., 2015). Approaching fathers with this deficit model of parenting creates an unwelcoming space and makes it more difficult to engage them (Lechowicz et al., 2019; Panter-Brick et al., 2014). Clinicians' participation in training specifically to build sensitivity and competence in working with fathers has been related to higher clinician confidence and reported skill use (Tully et al., 2018). At the program and agency level, when no deliberate efforts are made to consider how to engage fathers, policies around recruitment, scheduling, and retention are likely to target mothers rather than coparents or fathers. Creating a father-inclusive agency that places importance on recruiting all key caregivers in a family can support the efforts of individual clinicians and improve father attendance (Lechowicz et al., 2019).

READINESS FOR CHANGE: MEETING FATHERS WHERE THEY ARE

All therapists have worked with—or will at some point in their practice—parents who are not yet prepared to make changes in the way they interact with their children. *Readiness for change* is a multidimensional construct that includes the importance a parent places on change, their sense of efficacy in their ability to make change, their defensiveness about the need to change, and their perception that change is something they are ready to undertake (Niec, Barnett, et al., 2015). A lack of readiness for change may signal a range of different issues. Some parents do not yet perceive problems in their relationships with their children; other parents view change in themselves as unnecessary because they see the problem as seated within the child; still others might wish things to be different but feel change is not possible.

The idea that individuals come to treatment with different levels of readiness for change grew largely from the work of DiClemente and Prochaska (1998) on the transtheoretical model of intentional human behavior change (TTM). The TTM proposes that the process of changing a behavior occurs gradually and in five stages: During the *precontemplation* stage, parents do not identify a problem within themselves or with the parent–child relationship and have no intention of changing. During the *contemplation* stage, parents express ambivalence about change but consider its potential value (e.g., "Maybe sometime in the future I'll try something different"). The *preparation* stage is when parents are likely to take initial steps to make changes (e.g., seeking information about treatment options). During the *action* stage, parents are engaged in making changes in their parenting (e.g., participating actively in treatment), and the *maintenance* stage is when parents work to consolidate their changes and avoid returning to previous patterns of interaction (Niec, Barnett, et al., 2015; Prochaska et al., 2002).

The implication of the TTM for psychotherapeutic intervention is that clients—even those who present voluntarily for treatment—are not necessarily in the action stage and therefore are not necessarily ready to make changes in their behavior. The clinician's goal is to meet clients where they are in the change process and to help them move toward the action stage using motivational enhancement strategies (W. R. Miller & Rollnick, 2002). The concept of readiness for change is particularly important in the context of fathers' parenting for two reasons. First, investigations of parents' readiness for change at the start of treatment show that it can impact treatment participation, retention, and family outcomes (Andrade et al., 2015; Chaffin et al., 2009; Spoth et al., 1995). Parents with greater readiness demonstrate more positive outcomes after treatment for parents and children (Spoth et al., 1995), whereas parents who perceive less need for treatment attend fewer treatment sessions (Andrade et al., 2015). Second, fathers and mothers often do not present for treatment at the same stage in their readiness for change. In a study of 120 fathers and mothers who voluntarily sought mental health services for their children's disruptive behaviors, fathers endorsed less readiness than mothers on all key dimensions of the construct (Niec, Barnett, et al., 2015). Fathers were more likely to rate themselves in the precontemplation stage (having no investment in change) and were less likely to rate themselves in the contemplation and action stages (considering change and seeking to make change) than mothers. Further, fathers reported that treatment was less important to them, they felt less able to make changes, they were more defensive about the need for treatment, and they felt less ready to invest in making any change in their parenting compared with mothers (Niec, Barnett, et al., 2015; see Figure 8.1).

FIGURE 8.1. Mothers' and Fathers' Self-Reported Readiness for Change

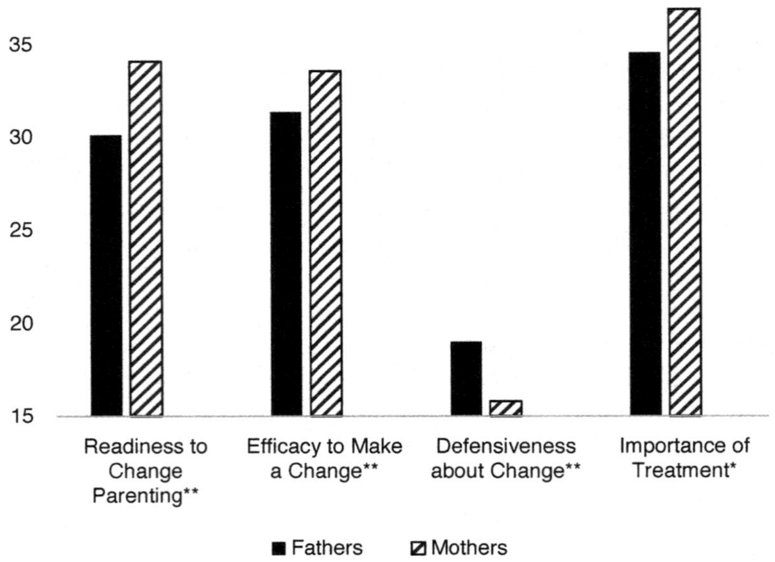

Note. Based on information from Niec et al. (2015). *$p = .01$. **$p = .001$.

In other words, mothers and fathers were likely to enter treatment at different stages of change, with fathers being less invested, willing, and ready to change than mothers. If therapists approach treatment for the parental system based on mothers' readiness, then fathers may feel left behind and will be less likely to engage actively in the treatment process or to remain in treatment if they do engage.

FLIPPING THE SCRIPT: CLINICAL STRATEGIES TO ENGAGE FATHERS

Engagement of fathers (and other caregivers) in parent–child treatment is a process that has been conceptualized in multiple phases (Moran et al., 2004; Pfitzner et al., 2017; Piotrowska et al., 2017; see Figure 8.2).

In the first phase, a program must reach out to fathers, connect with them in the community, and bring them into an initial session. The second phase involves retaining fathers in treatment so that they attend regularly; therefore, they and their children have the potential to experience changes. In the third phase, the engagement process includes fostering fathers' active participation and adherence to treatment recommendations (e.g., home practice of new skills) to acquire and maintain positive gains. To address issues related to each of the phases of engagement, the following compilation of clinical strategies has been extracted from the literature and from years of clinical work with caregivers in community settings. Reflected at the core of each strategy is a need to "flip the script" that remains embedded in many public health policies,

FIGURE 8.2. Caregiver Engagement Process

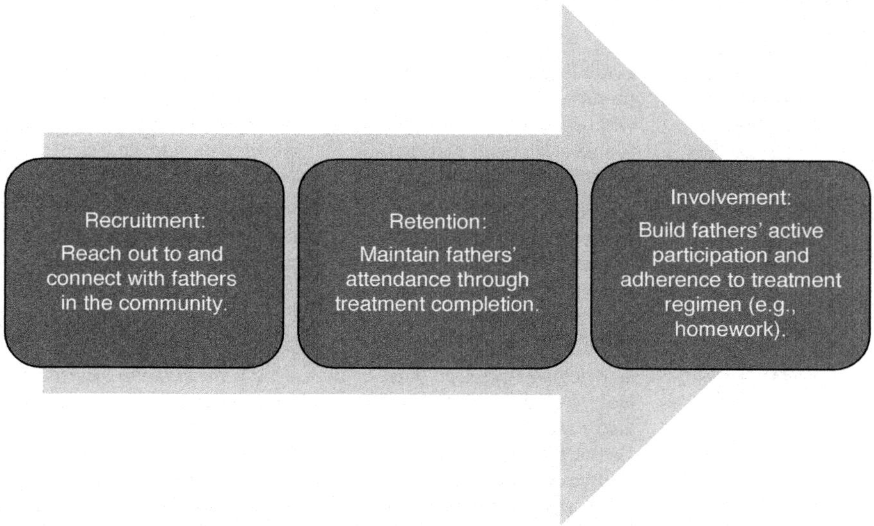

Note. Based on information from Moran et al. (2004), Pfitzner et al. (2017), and Piotrowska et al. (2017).

agency approaches to parents, researcher attitudes, and therapist training—that is, the marginalization of fathers' roles in parenting and the minimizing of the importance of the father–child relationship (Cabrera et al., 2018; Fabiano & Caserta, 2018; Panter-Brick et al., 2014; Table 8.1).

Promote Parenting Interventions to Reach Fathers

As noted earlier in this chapter, many fathers are unaware of programs that exist in their own communities to provide them support. Disseminating information about programs through sources and with messages that are acceptable to fathers is the first step to increasing involvement. Choosing trusted, familiar sources—and those that have less association with the stigma of help-seeking—is important. For example, sending information about treatment programs through the schools is considered one effective point of dissemination (Pfitzner et al., 2017). Other community-based sources, such as sports events, churches, primary care clinics, or even workplace settings, may also be valuable, as many parents report preferring personal "word-of-mouth" sources of information (Pfitzner et al., 2017; Pruett et al., 2017a). In choosing dissemination points, one should consider where fathers are likely to be found.

In addition to the source of the information about treatment programs, the way that the program is described is important; that is, what message is being given to parents? From a clinician or agency perspective, the key message often lies in offering a solution to a problem (e.g., This program will help you with your parenting struggles), but fathers may be less likely to respond to

TABLE 8.1. Flipping the Script: Strategies to Promote Fathers' Participation in Parent-Child Interventions

Strategy	How to do it?	Why do it?
Promote parenting interventions to reach fathers.	Provide information about treatment services in locations where fathers are often found (e.g., work settings, sports leagues, churches).	Fathers are often unaware of parent-child treatment services—what they are and where they can be found.
Include fathers from the first contact.	Regardless of which parent makes the first contact, request to speak with the other parent, either on the same call or in a separately scheduled call.	Communicate to fathers from the first moment that their participation is important.
Assume fathers will participate.	Use inclusive language (e.g., Not: "Will your partner also participate?" Instead: "What time works for you and your partner to come in?"). Make appointments for both parents.	Just by inviting fathers/partners to be a part of treatment, the participation rate will increase. Fathers need to understand they are important and valued in order to invest resources in the process.
Be aware of nonverbal messages.	Be mindful of eye contact and body language with each caregiver. Deliberately turn to each caregiver and provide nonverbal as well as verbal indicators of attention.	When one caregiver is more talkative than the other, it is common to give them more frequent verbal and nonverbal attention. Neglecting the quieter parent gives the message "You're not important" and may lead to treatment dropout.
Be sensitive to father-specific concerns.	Ask each parent for their goals for their child and themselves. Listen for differences and value father's and mother's goals.	Helping each parent to understand how treatment will help them to reach their goals for their children and themselves will increase treatment retention.
Educate parents about their differing perceptions.	Explain that different perceptions about a child's behavior and functioning are common because each parent has a different relationship with their child. Value all perceptions.	Each parent's perceptions are important to help therapists to develop a comprehensive understanding of the child and family. Valuing the differences between parents supports the development of a healthy parent-parent alliance.
Don't assume caregivers enter treatment with the same expectations.	During the assessment and throughout treatment, actively seek input from each parent regarding their understanding of the process. Assess the readiness for change of each parent independently. Address each parent in treatment depending on their stage of change.	Parents often enter treatment at different points of readiness to make change in their parenting and with different levels of investment in treatment. Addressing each parent where they are will increase their engagement and retention, which will improve outcomes for the family.

TABLE 8.1. Flipping the Script: Strategies to Promote Fathers' Participation in Parent–Child Interventions (*Continued*)

Strategy	How to do it?	Why do it?
Consider alternate delivery formats.	Explore formats that are most acceptable to fathers in the community. Consider offering group or telehealth formats.	Reducing barriers to accessing parent–child interventions can increase father participation.
Recognize fathers' needs for support.	Don't wait for parents to ask for information: Provide parents with a list of resources for personal support. Normalize the process of asking for help for all caregivers.	Male caregivers are less likely to ask for help and support, even when they need it. Making the information available reduces barriers to accessing care.
Expect home practice from all parents.	Give each parent separate handouts/homework sheets. Ask each parent where and when they will do their practice. In the following week, ask the quieter parent to report on their practice first.	Reinforcing all parents for their practice increases the chance they will continue it and communicates that their interactions with their child are equally important.
Communicate with all parents.	Reach out to each parent individually to communicate about changes in schedule or treatment information.	It lets each parent know they are valued in the therapeutic process. It avoids giving one parent the power of "gatekeeper."

messages that imply they do not know how to parent or cannot manage their children (Frank, Keown, Dittman, & Sanders, 2015). Avoid using a deficit model in promotional materials (Lechowicz et al., 2019). Instead, a strength-based approach that describes programs as focusing on children, building children's well-being and resilience, and providing support for the tough job of parenting may be more acceptable and effective in reaching fathers.

Include Fathers From the First Contact

Increasing fathers' participation in treatment begins at the moment of first contact with the family. Clinicians report that mothers are far more likely to initiate contact seeking services for their family (Tully et al., 2018). However, that is the ideal point at which clinicians and agencies can begin to demonstrate the importance of all key caregivers in the process. In the initial screening phone call(s), ask for the names of each of the child's primary caregivers and their relationship to the child. Provide brief and basic information about the contribution of all caregivers to the child's functioning and the value of each caregiver's involvement in the treatment process. Personal invitations to fathers to engage in services are valuable (Pruett et al., 2017a). Speak with each caregiver during the initial or follow-up screening call and include them in scheduling the first session.

Assume Fathers Will Participate

Clinician attitudes regarding fathers' noninvolvement in services can become a self-fulfilling prophecy. Repeated societal messages communicate that fathers are not welcome or are unimportant in the child-rearing domain; therefore, in the clinical setting it is important to deliberately counter those messages. Assume that fathers will participate rather than assuming they will not. For instance, rather than asking *whether* a father or other coparent will attend treatment, use language that assumes participation: "What is a good day for you and your partner to come in?" or "Let me tell you a little about what the session will include for you and your partner." or "I look forward to meeting you and [your child's father]." Reach out to fathers even if a coparent reports that he is not interested in services. A father's initial lack of interest may be due to a lack of understanding of his importance to the process, or a coparent may make assumptions about his interest without investing in trying to engage him. Coparents can be influential gatekeepers to services, so connect directly to fathers rather than relying on the partner to communicate information. Further, beware of language that is only mother-focused and excludes fathers. At the first face-to-face contact, actively reinforce the attendance of all caregivers and provide additional information about the importance of all caregivers in the treatment process.

Be Aware of Nonverbal Messages

Especially in the initial assessment and treatment sessions, focus on building rapport with each caregiver individually. Be aware of verbal and nonverbal signals that may inadvertently communicate that one parent is more valued than another. When one caregiver is more active in the conversation than another—a common situation—it can be easy, even for experienced therapists, to unintentionally shift attention to the more engaged person. To avoid that trap, speak directly to the quieter parent first. Ask open-ended questions of each caregiver. Avoid allowing one caregiver to speak for the others.

Be Sensitive to Father-Specific Concerns

Although there is significant overlap in fathers' and mothers' concerns for their children (e.g., building the parent–child relationship, enhancing children's well-being), fathers may also have concerns about parenting that are different, just as their patterns of interaction with their children can differ (Piskernik & Ahnert, 2019). Some fathers, for example, feel they specifically need more focus on how to regulate their negative emotional responses to their children and on how to express physical affection (Frank, Keown, & Sanders, 2015). The style of parent–therapist communication for fathers and mothers may also differ. Exploration of fathers' and mothers' communication during a group parenting intervention found that fathers used humor more often than mothers, whereas mothers were more likely to share personal stories (Frank, Keown, Dittman, & Sanders, 2015). Awareness of these differences can help therapists to develop rapport with fathers and to maintain the relevance of the treatment. In sum, carefully assess fathers' and mothers' treatment goals for themselves and their children, and be aware of how those goals differ. Throughout treatment, make time to connect each caregiver's goals to the intervention strategies.

Educate Parents About Differences in Their Perceptions

Parents rarely agree on the intensity of their children's behavior problems or the quality of their relationships with their children (Calzada et al., 2004; Christensen et al., 1992). Differences are common because of the differences in parents' perceptions of their children and because of differences in the ways in which they interact. Although common, such disagreement can lead to parent conflict (De Los Reyes et al., 2015; Fabiano & Caserta, 2018). As in the case example earlier in this chapter, disagreement may also create a barrier to treatment attendance. From the beginning of the intake process, normalize differences in parents' perceptions of their children and emphasize the value of each parent's perspective. Point out that each parent may see not only different challenges but also different strengths in their child and that understanding all caregivers' perspectives will foster the therapist's understanding of the child's functioning.

Don't Assume Caregivers Come to Treatment With the Same Expectations

Fathers and mothers typically approach treatment with different expectations. In particular, parents differ in how much they value treatment, how willing they are to change, and how effective they believe they would be at attempting to change (Cunningham et al., 2008; Niec, Barnett, et al., 2015). Allow each caregiver to share their attitudes toward treatment for themselves and their child. Note differences that may influence their willingness to participate. Find commonalities across parents' perceptions, needs, and goals. When developing a treatment plan, if parents are not starting at the same point of readiness for change, plan strategies to enhance the motivation of the less-ready parent. Motivation enhancing strategies are effective at increasing treatment retention (Chaffin et al., 2009). However, if left unaddressed, unmotivated parents are likely to discontinue treatment.

Consider Alternate Delivery Formats

Individual barriers to treatment engagement such as fathers' concerns about the stigma of help-seeking and resource-related obstacles such as lack of time and reliable transportation may be addressed with service delivery formats other than traditional in-clinic or in-home therapy. Increasing support demonstrates the effectiveness of interventions delivered via telehealth (Barak et al., 2008; Comer et al., 2017) and suggests that innovative delivery settings such as children's sports leagues are also feasible (Fabiano & Caserta, 2018). Fathers have reported an interest in out-of-clinic services such as internet-based programs (Frank, Keown, Dittman, & Sanders, 2015; Lechowicz et al., 2019). Since the widespread shutdown of face-to-face mental health services during the COVID-19 pandemic, many community mental health agencies have developed the capacity to provide services outside of the traditional in-person format. These new services have opened up the possibility of reaching out to fathers in new ways.

Recognize and Address Fathers' Needs for Support

Overall, men are less likely than women to seek help for themselves (Galdas et al., 2005; Narendorf et al., 2018). Therapists should be sensitive to the fact that fathers may sometimes need additional support in relation to health, mental health, or educational concerns even if they do not actively seek it (Panter-Brick et al., 2014). Select strategies to reduce the stigma of help-seeking. For example, therapists can normalize the need for support as a parent, identify themselves as a resource for support, and provide all caregivers with a list of general health and education resources that include referrals appropriate for mothers and fathers.

Expect Home Practice From All Caregivers

To change parenting styles and strengthen the parent–child relationship for all caregivers, it is essential that all caregivers practice the skills they are developing through treatment. When families are assigned home practice of skills or other activities to build knowledge and abilities, provide each caregiver with their own worksheets to track their work. In session, discuss each caregiver's assignment completion individually to reinforce the importance of each parent's practice.

Communicate Individually With All Parents

Another way that therapists can communicate a father's importance to the treatment process is by maintaining direct communication with him. For instance, if a change occurs in the treatment schedule or other reasons arise to contact families outside of treatment, connect with each caregiver individually. Similarly, if one parent misses a session, resist the temptation to pass along information only through the attending parent. Instead, contact the absent parent directly to prevent miscommunication, emphasize the value of each caregiver's attendance, and ensure everyone knows the date of the next session.

SUMMARY

Fathers play a unique and important role in their children's development. Fathers' parenting and the father–child relationship influence children's literacy, academic achievement, social development, and emotional and behavioral health. Given the importance of fathers in their children's lives, it is important for them to have access to effective parenting and parent–child relationship interventions. Fathers' active participation in the treatment process enhances child and family outcomes. Despite the clear significance of fathers' involvement in their children's treatment, and even after 4 decades of calling for more father involvement, the paternal participation rate remains disturbingly low. This low rate results from factors that occur at various levels (e.g., parent, clinician, program, agency), and many of these factors can be readily addressed with strategies designed to create a more inclusive environment for fathers.

Key Takeaways

1. Fathers influence their children's well-being across developmental domains.
2. The father–child relationship can be either a protective factor or a risk factor for children against the impact of adverse experiences.
3. Fathers need access to good-quality parenting interventions, but barriers at the personal, family, and organizational levels continue to reduce fathers' involvement.
4. Clinicians play a significant role in the recruitment, retention, and involvement of fathers in the treatment process.
5. Numerous strategies can be implemented that increase fathers' engagement at the process at every stage.

Clinical Growth Questions

1. How do I connect with fathers and help them to feel welcome in the clinical setting?
2. Do I communicate to all caregivers their unique value to their children's development and to the treatment process?
3. What new strategies can I implement at each of the stages of engagement—recruitment, retention, and involvement—to build fathers' participation?
4. What policies within my agency support father involvement? Are there any policies that act as obstacles to the participation of fathers in treatment?

9

Difficult Cases, Therapist Burnout, and the Importance of Self-Care

"She's out of control! Doesn't listen to anything we say. She still talks back to me and her father all the time. I thought you said this new thing would stop it." "We've been through all this before. It's not working. It never works. Aren't you therapists supposed to help?" These were the words of a mother and father during the second session of one of my first cases as a graduate student. Both caregivers were angry and demanding. I still remember their anger, and the pressure I felt to immediately fling solutions at their family's problems. Although I do not remember exactly how I responded, I am certain that in the moment my anxiety created a barrier to my ability to provide effective treatment.

During my early years of clinical training, I was lucky to receive strong and supportive supervision that helped me to develop the skills to manage challenging cases. I can look back now knowing how to ally with parents who are experiencing high levels of emotion and how to help parents move toward readiness for change. Even with experience and knowledge, however, working therapeutically with parents offers unique challenges. Working with parents and their children together presents additional complexities. Parent–child intervention techniques, such as the therapist modeling that takes place in child parent psychotherapy and the in vivo coaching that is core to parent–child interaction therapy, require clinicians to be active and engaged with families at a more intense level than required by many other treatment models. The relationship between the therapist and parent must be collaborative to be

https://doi.org/10.1037/0000304-009
Strengthening the Parent–Child Relationship in Therapy: Laying the Foundation for Healthy Development, by L. N. Niec

effective. Yet many parents seeking treatment believe that the problem lies within their children and thus the focus of treatment should be the child. As a result, clinicians who work with parent–child dyads may find themselves dealing with parents' reluctance, resistance, or anger. When working with families, therapists are also likely to encounter stories of conflict and intergenerational trauma that take a toll on their mental health and well-being. System factors such as large caseloads and sparse administrative or supervisory support may further complicate therapeutic work. All of these factors can contribute to therapists' own frustration and anxiety, impeding the ability to serve families, impacting well-being, and sometimes leading to burnout.

This chapter starts with a description of challenges common to work with parent–child dyads and the ways in which those challenges can impact therapists. I then explore the experience of therapist burnout and review interventions that have been proposed to support the health and functioning of mental health professionals. Finally, I offer personal and professional self-care techniques, including strategies for approaching parents in ways to reduce therapist anxiety and empower families.

CHALLENGES OF WORKING WITH PARENT–CHILD DYADS

The following subsections present challenges that therapists face routinely when working with parents and children. It is valuable to reflect on the ways in which these challenges may impact the therapist–parent relationship and to consider the therapeutic skills necessary to manage them.

Multistressed Families

Early in training, while learning about discrete psychological issues and treatment models that address specific disorders, a therapist may imagine working with parents who present with a clearly identified problem and the motivation and resources to address it. It only takes a short time in practice, however, to realize that families are often struggling to manage a host of environmental, interpersonal, and individual stressors in addition to mental health issues (e.g., financial hardship, systemic racism, intergenerational or parental conflict, histories of trauma). Those stressors often interact with one another to influence individuals' functioning. Overwhelmed parents may feel reluctant to take on the demands of treatment or resigned to living in a constant state of distress. A therapist working in community mental health once said to me, "Many parents I see have lived with conflict, stress, and the impact of trauma for so long—all their lives—they can't imagine things being different."

Helping families to envision a more hopeful future while negotiating their many levels of need adds complexity to the implementation of parent–child interventions. Among two samples of therapists trained in parent–child interaction therapy (one within the United States and one in the Netherlands), therapists reported that managing the needs of multistressed families was a barrier to implementing the intervention with fidelity (Christian et al., 2014; Niec et al., 2018). Therapists face the challenge of prioritizing families' presenting problems in a way that meets the most urgent needs and facilitates positive change. Sometimes that means distinguishing between identified needs (e.g., safety of parent and child) and perceived crises (e.g., phone call from a Head Start teacher). Therapists must also deal with the personal challenges such cases can provoke. Facing a family's stories of repeated loss and ongoing stress may engender a sense of futility within therapists. In some cases, the need to make a difference in the face of so much adversity may be expressed through a therapist's overinvolvement with the family, intense emotional engagement, or overidentification with the family's struggles (Simionato & Simpson, 2018). In other cases, a therapist's sense of helplessness may manifest in disengagement from the family, keeping them at a distance or making it difficult for the therapist to express empathy (Madsen, 1999; Simionato & Simpson, 2018).

Parents Who Are Reluctant

As discussed in Chapter 8 of this volume, adults enter therapy with differing levels of commitment and readiness to work toward change. This is true whether they are seeking services for themselves or for their children. Any therapist may experience frustration or regret if, despite therapeutic strategies to support self-efficacy and enhance motivation, they find a client unwilling or unable to move toward growth. Yet individual adults possess the agency to make decisions for themselves about whether to engage in the therapeutic process. Part of maintaining healthy professional boundaries and respecting each individual's self-determination involves keeping the responsibility for change in the hands of the client. When working with parents and children, however, a unique layer of pressure weighs on therapists. Young children do not have the developmental capacity or the power to bring about deliberate changes in their environment. To make meaningful and lasting changes in a child's developmental trajectory, it is necessary to work collaboratively with parents. This work creates a dynamic in which therapists may experience a sense of urgency to successfully engage parents in treatment. Therapists may be pulled to engage in power struggles, or even inadvertently to shame parents for their lack of involvement. Skills in motivational enhancement techniques will help therapists to build a collaborative approach to problem solving and foster parents' readiness to take action for themselves and their children (Miller & Rollnick, 2002).

Parents Who Want Their Child "Fixed"

Therapists regularly encounter a specific type of reluctance in parent–child work: the parent who believes the focus of treatment should be their child. This belief can stem from misperceptions about therapy, child development, and the parent–child relationship. In some cases, parents believe that the problems they experience within the parent–child system exist solely within their child rather than within the relationship. In other cases, parents have a misunderstanding of the treatment process and believe that psychotherapy is meant to address individual issues rather than systemic ones. For still others, placing the focus on their child may serve to externalize the problem, reducing a sense of personal blame or avoiding the stigma of having a child who is experiencing emotional and behavioral issues. Social convention continues to view parents—especially mothers—as fully responsible for their children's struggles. It is important to understand which of these types of misperceptions influences a parent in order to address them.

Parents Who Are Angry

Working through a session with an angry parent is not an easy thing. Even experienced therapists can find their physiological stress responses activated by a parent who is yelling or cursing about the lack of progress or a recent parent–child conflict. In contrast, it is easier to bring a young child into the treatment room and leave the parent behind. Therapists may sometimes be tempted to avoid dealing with the challenges of parent–child work. Yet the work with the parent and child is where and how positive change occurs. Without working with a parent, the young child's environment will remain the same, and lasting changes are unlikely to happen. The effects of parent anger in the context of psychotherapy have rarely been explored; however, studies within health care settings find that when patients express anger, it is associated with negative changes in the patient–provider relationship. Patients in a hospital setting who expressed anger experienced a deterioration in the support they perceived from their provider, and at 1-month follow-up, they reported a significant decay of the patient–provider relationship (Gerhart et al., 2015). Confidence and competence in managing parents' anger are both essential in effective parent–child therapeutic work.

Family History of Trauma and Conflict

A vast percentage of parents and children who present for services within community mental health settings have survived adverse experiences, including some form of traumatic events. In a study of 505 adults receiving services at a community mental health center, 91% reported experiencing at least one traumatic life event (Cusack et al., 2004). Working with parents and young children together often means working with the influence of at least two generations of trauma on parenting and the parent–child relationship. Depending on the communities within which therapists work, they may routinely be exposed to stories of child abuse and intimate partner violence, sexual assault, neighborhood violence, or torture.

The nature of the work with survivors of trauma places therapists at increased risk for experiencing *vicarious trauma* (VT) and *secondary traumatic stress/compassion fatigue* (STS), two related but separate constructs (Jenkins & Baird, 2002; Robinson-Keilig, 2014). VT is associated with a shift in therapists' schema of the world and others, such that therapists feel more vulnerable and view others as potentially untrustworthy and dangerous (Pearlman & Mac Ian, 1995). Through repeated exposure to stories about human cruelty, a therapist's basic sense of the world as safe and others as basically good becomes disrupted, increasing cynicism and hopelessness. STS, also referred to as *compassion fatigue*, is different from VT in that it includes the experience of symptoms similar to posttraumatic stress disorder, such as reexperiencing the survivor's traumatic event, avoidance of places/situations that bring the event to mind, and hyperarousal (Figley, 1995). STS is conceptualized as having a swift onset of symptoms, whereas the cognitive shifts associated with VT are considered to develop over time (Jenkins & Baird, 2002). A review of the qualitative literature on the experiences of therapists working with trauma survivors identified five common themes that encompass both VT and STS (McNeillie & Rose, 2021). Therapists reported (a) altered perceptions of the world, self, and others; (b) intense and often hurtful emotional experiences; (c) physiological experiences such as exhaustion and somatic complaints; (d) cognitive experiences such as intrusive thoughts; and (e) behavioral responses such as withdrawing from others and decreasing intimacy with partners (Figure 9.1).

It is significant and encouraging that across themes therapists reported experiencing not only risk factors but also the potential for personal growth, arising from successfully helping others and from witnessing clients' resilience. Opportunities for therapist growth are discussed later in this chapter. First, I identify factors that may increase risk of VT and STS.

FIGURE 9.1. Cognitive Model of Vicarious Trauma and Growth

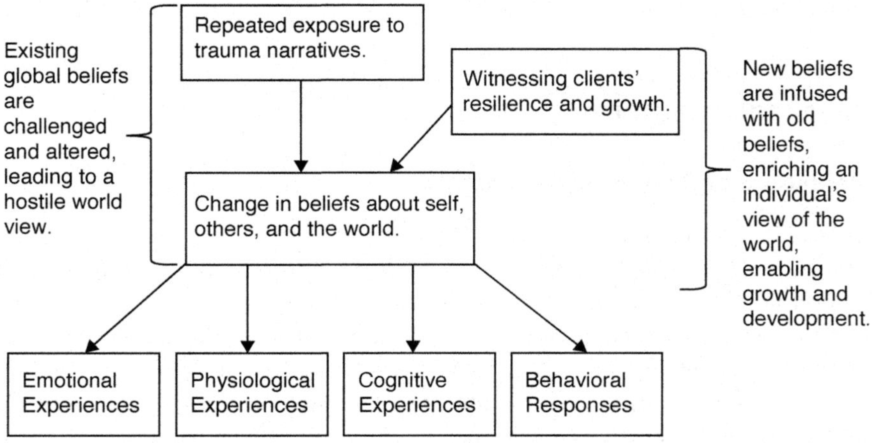

Note. From "Vicarious Trauma in Therapists: A Meta-Ethnographic Review," by N. McNeillie and J. Rose, 2021, *Behavioural and Cognitive Psychotherapy*, *49*(4), p. 11 (https://doi.org/10.1017/S1352465820000776). Copyright 2021 by Cambridge University Press. Reprinted with permission.

The literature on risk factors for therapists is sparse relative to the work on risk factors for clients, with much of the discussion either theoretical or descriptive (Jordan, 2010; McNeillie & Rose, 2021; Sansbury et al., 2015; Voss Horrell et al., 2011). However, existing findings have been relatively consistent. With a few exceptions (DelTosta et al., 2019), investigations have focused on factors internal to therapists (e.g., age, history, coping style). Therapists are more vulnerable to experiencing VT and STS when they are young or new to the field (Aafjes-van Doorn et al., 2020; Adams & Riggs, 2008; Halevi & Idisis, 2018). A sample of social workers, psychologists, and other mental health professionals found that the younger the therapist, the higher the report of symptoms of VT, with more negative perceptions of their personal safety, intimacy, trust, self-esteem, and locus of control (Halevi & Idisis, 2018). A survey of therapists' experiences of VT during the COVID-19 pandemic ($N = 339$) found that being younger, having less experience, and feeling more negatively about telehealth therapy were associated with higher levels of VT symptoms (Aafjes-van Doorn et al., 2020). Therapists' personal experiences of trauma (Adams & Riggs, 2008; Jenkins & Baird, 2002) and the use of avoidant coping styles (M. L. Miller et al., 2020) have also been linked to more severe symptoms of STS.

Because of the particular vulnerability of therapists who are new to the field, some work has focused on identifying specific factors that increase risk among therapists-in-training. Consistent with the experiences of licensed clinicians, therapists' coping styles were associated with VT symptoms among a sample of clinical and counseling psychology trainees. Trainees who had a self-sacrificing style (e.g., attempting to maintain an image as always helpful and never distressed or angry) reported more symptoms than those who had an adaptive style (e.g., using positive coping mechanisms such as humor; Adams & Riggs, 2008). Similarly, trainees' levels of general personal distress in intense interpersonal situations were associated with higher levels of VT (DelTosta et al., 2019).

THERAPIST BURNOUT

Definitions and Contributing Factors

Given all the challenges of working with parents and children, the ongoing emotional engagement required of therapists, and the non-client-related responsibilities of the job such as administrative paperwork, most therapists have experienced periods of dissatisfaction with the work, times when we worry about how to reach a particular family or wonder if what we are doing is making a difference. Such doubt and weariness are not uncommon in day-to-day experiences as a clinician, but typically they resolve after a good night's sleep, a break from the work, or some supportive supervision. The phenomenon of burnout is different from transitory worry. It is a pervasive and sometimes chronic experience that impacts therapists in multiple domains. Considering the complexities and challenges involved in therapeutic work with children and families described earlier, burnout has particular salience for clinicians who treat families. The World Health Organization (2021) included *burnout* in the *International Classification of Diseases–11* as an "occupational phenomenon" that may impact an individual's health or lead to contact with health services. The phenomenon includes three primary dimensions: the experiences of emotional exhaustion, depersonalization of or disengagement from the job (e.g., for mental health professionals, from clients), and a sense of low personal accomplishment/efficacy (Dreison et al., 2018; Maslach et al., 1996). *Emotional exhaustion* describes the depletion of emotional resources, a sense of being overwhelmed and without sufficient coping mechanisms to continue functioning effectively. The *depersonalization* of clients refers to the development of negative attitudes toward families who present for services: viewing families' problems in stereotyped ways, feeling pessimistic about their capacity for change, and perceiving their problems as deserved. *Low personal accomplishment/efficacy* refers to negative feelings about the self and about the ability to work effectively with challenging clients. VT and STS are also related to therapist burnout (Jenkins & Baird, 2002). Although they are conceptualized as specific to work with trauma survivors and less often assessed, their potential consequences make it important to include them in any discussion of therapists' health and well-being.

Much research has been conducted on contributors to burnout among health care providers. Although the factors associated with burnout specifically among mental health professionals have received less study, they have generally reflected the broader literature. Risk factors exist at multiple levels: organization, client, and therapist. At the organization level, number of hours worked—particularly number of hours completing administrative tasks rather than therapy—inadequate supervisory support, low salary, and lack of opportunities for professional development have been associated with burnout (J. Johnson et al., 2018; Martin & Schinke, 1998; Rupert et al., 2015; Tartakovsky, 2016). Therapists who work within institutional settings (e.g., community mental health centers, hospitals) have shown greater risk for experiencing burnout than those who work in private practice (Farber, 1985; Rupert & Kent, 2007). At the client level, working with challenging clients (e.g., those who are aggressive, are resistant, or have diagnoses related to psychoses or personality disorder) is associated with greater emotional exhaustion and depersonalization of clients (Rupert et al., 2015). Therapists who work with parents with significant psychopathology may therefore be at greater risk to experience burnout. For the individual therapist, burnout has been associated with being younger, having less therapy experience, being overly involved with clients (e.g., taking on too much responsibility for change), and having avoidant coping styles (J. Lee et al., 2011; Simionato & Simpson, 2018; Simpson et al., 2019). Some individual therapist characteristics have the potential to contribute to burnout even beyond the contribution of organization and client factors. In a sample of 443 primarily masters-level psychotherapists, an avoidant coping style and maladaptive schemas predicted burnout beyond stressors such as difficult clients, inadequate supervisory support, and lack of professional development opportunities (Simpson et al., 2019).

The study of contributors to burnout among therapists suffers from some of the same limitations as the work on VT and STS. That is, there is a disproportionate number of theoretical articles and narrative reviews relative to rigorous investigations (e.g., Friedman, 1985; J. Johnson et al., 2018; Morse et al., 2012; Rupert et al., 2015). A vast amount (96.3%) of the existing quantitative research on burnout intervention for mental health providers has been based on one self-report measure—the Maslach Burnout Inventory—which includes the three primary dimensions of emotional exhaustion, depersonalization of clients, and low personal accomplishment (Dreison et al., 2018; Maslach et al., 1996). Although an advantage of such consistent measurement is the ability to compare findings regarding associated factors across samples of mental health professionals, conclusions that might be drawn from the findings are limited by methodological flaws. Most studies of burnout are cross-sectional and assess therapists' attitudes and functioning at one time point, making it impossible to establish the direction of the relationships between hypothesized risk factors and burnout; that is, we don't yet know which risk factors actually predict later burnout. Causal relationships have not been tested, and other explanations for the associations cannot yet be ruled out; for example, job dissatisfaction and burnout, which have been found to be associated, may both be predicted by a third factor or factors, perhaps general distress or depression. The literature is further limited by an overwhelming reliance on self-report measures (e.g., online surveys). The strength of the relationships found between risk factors and burnout are therefore likely to be inflated because of shared method variance. In other words, although we have an increasing amount of data about the types of variables that occur along with burnout among mental health professionals, we do not yet have models of causality that are empirically validated.

The lack of high-quality research in this important area is concerning, as it prevents us from developing interventions that attack the causal conditions of burnout. It may also reflect the enduring stigma associated with therapists seeking mental health services. Not until 1981 did the American Psychological Association (APA) publicly discuss the issue of impairment and the need for interventions for psychologists (Smith & Moss, 2009). Even today, a tendency remains for therapists to view self and clients with an "us and them" mindset, described by Good et al. (2009) as "noble us and troubled them" (p. 21). In contrast, the literature on burnout and VT among health care professionals (e.g., physicians, nurses) is larger and more varied than the work related to mental health professionals, supporting the case that discussing the mental health needs of mental health providers remains difficult. Accurate information about the consequences of burnout and the importance of self-care may help to combat the stigma against therapists' expressions of vulnerability and requests for help.

Consequences of Burnout

Studies of mental health professionals put the prevalence of burnout at 21% to 67% (Morse et al., 2012; Simionato & Simpson, 2018). Since the rise of the COVID-19 pandemic, with associated increases in therapist workloads, the severity of families' distress, the complexity of administering services via telehealth or in-person with health safety routines, and the added personal stress impacting therapists, the rates of burnout have likely increased (Rokach & Boulazreg, 2020). These are concerning statistics, as the emotional exhaustion, depersonalization of clients, and low personal efficacy associated with burnout take a toll not only on therapists but also on clients and the health of organizations (Simionato et al., 2019).

At the individual level, burnout has been associated with somatic symptoms such as headaches, backaches, and sleeplessness (Salvagioni et al., 2017; Yang & Hayes, 2020) and psychological distress such as depression and anxiety (Simionato et al., 2019). Disruptions in interpersonal functioning have also been reported, with therapists' experiences of STS symptoms associated with less satisfaction with relationships, poorer social intimacy, and less use of effective communication patterns (Robinson-Keilig, 2014). More recent research has explored the impact of burnout on physiological stress mechanisms. Early evidence suggests that the experience of burnout is related to stress responses that are similar to the physiological responses to other types of chronic stress (Bayes et al., 2021; Salvagioni et al., 2017). Sustained activation of the autonomic nervous system, systemic inflammation, immunosuppression, increased allostatic load (a multidimensional measure of the impact of chronic stress), and cardiovascular disease are some of the consequences that may be related to ongoing experiences of burnout (Bayes et al., 2021).

The sequelae of burnout also impact clients and organizations. Consider, for example, the extremely high rates of turnover in mental health and other human services positions, ranging from 20% to 80% within a span of 1 year (Annie E. Casey Foundation, 2003; Landoll et al., 2018). Such high turnover rates mean disrupted services for families, when the quality of the family–provider relationship is so important to success. At the same time, agencies face costs related to lost productivity, rehiring, and training. Burnout is one of the strongest predictors of both intention to leave a job and actual turnover (Beidas et al., 2016; H. Kim & Kao, 2014; Mor Barak et al., 2001). In a sample of nearly 11,000 mental health professionals working within the Veterans Health Administration, emotional exhaustion was directly related to both intention to leave a position and active plans to leave (Yanchus et al., 2017). Similarly, among 1,786 social workers, burnout was negatively associated with commitment to the organization (A. R. Brown et al., 2019). In one of the few prospective studies exploring predictors of actual turnover among therapists in community agencies, the results were consistent with cross-sectional studies: As level of burnout increased, the odds of leaving the agency 1 year later also increased (Beidas et al., 2016).

In sum, burnout is a prevalent and increasing phenomenon among mental health professionals. It carries with it potential negative outcomes for therapists that can be far-reaching and chronic. At the same time, burnout in therapists also impacts families who are seeking or in the midst of receiving services as well as the healthy functioning of organizations. Effective strategies for the prevention and treatment of burnout could have broad benefits for individuals and society.

Prevention and Treatment of Burnout and Vicarious Trauma

Efforts to reduce the impact of burnout among psychotherapists and other mental health professionals began to grow in the 1980s. Since that time, the development and evaluation of interventions for therapist burnout has crawled behind the development of interventions for other psychological conditions. Treatment approaches generally fall within three categories, depending on the primary focus: "organization-directed" models address factors within the work environment (e.g., employee communication, job training, education; Hayes et al., 2004), "person-directed" models build coping mechanisms within therapists (e.g., cognitive-behavioral stress reduction, mindfulness techniques; Rollins et al., 2016), and "combined" models tackle mechanisms within the work environment and the individual.

A meta-analysis of the existing intervention literature from 1980 through 2015 found that the length and intensity of interventions varies greatly, with programs lasting from 3 to 314 hours (from 1 day to 18 months; Dreison et al., 2018). Most interventions (70.4%) are organization directed. Overall, the impact of the interventions on symptoms of burnout among mental health professionals was positive but very small (Hedges's $g = 0.13$, $p = .006$). Person-directed interventions were somewhat better than organization-directed interventions at reducing emotional exhaustion. However, neither type of intervention improved therapists' sense of personal accomplishment (Dreison et al., 2018). The study of one type of person-directed intervention—models intended to increase therapist mindfulness—demonstrated similar findings, with small, positive effects on burnout (Lomas et al., 2019). Interventions to address VT, like other aspects of burnout, have not always been effective (Bober & Regehr, 2006).

The small effects of existing interventions on symptoms of burnout prove that the work in this field is far from complete. As burnout is a complex and multidimensional phenomenon, it likely requires a multilayered approach to adequately address it (Simionato et al., 2019). Novel interventions must move beyond merely combining organization- and person-directed approaches and instead consider the ways in which the environment and therapist factors interact to develop protective factors and reduce risk.

Given the persistence of burnout symptoms, prevention may be a more effective approach than treatment. Even while still completing graduate training, psychologists may begin to experience burnout (Kaeding et al., 2017).

Exploration of protective factors that may be effective targets to promote therapist resilience has found the supervisory relationship to be particularly significant. Among a sample of clinical and counseling psychologist trainees, the supervisor–trainee alliance predicted the experience of VT, with a stronger working alliance related to fewer symptoms of VT (DelTosta et al., 2019). A study of first responders, including emotional support first responders providing initial trauma intervention, found that self-compassion predicted lower risk for emotional exhaustion, depersonalization, STS, and general distress and increased resilience (McDonald et al., 2021). "Self-compassion" was defined as being accepting of the self in difficult situations, aware that adverse experiences are shared (one is not isolated) and aware, rather than avoidant, of the stress of adverse experiences (Neff, 2003). Recent work has also looked at opportunities for therapists to experience personal growth through work with challenging families, specifically in work with clients who have experienced trauma. Witnessing individuals' resilience in the face of adversity has demonstrated positive effects for therapists (Bartoskova, 2015; Brockhouse et al., 2011; Killian et al., 2017). Fostering therapists' awareness of and attention to a family's strengths may also be protective against experiences of VT.

PERSONAL SELF-CARE: NURTURING BODY AND SELF

Self-care refers to a deliberate and active effort to nurture one's physical, psychological, and spiritual well-being (Norcross & VandenBos, 2018). It is a term heard with increasing regularity, yet our understanding of exactly what it entails and how it can be taught remains elusive. Participating in self-care has been associated with positive outcomes in terms of professional practice (e.g., burnout; Bloomquist et al., 2015; L. D. Butler et al., 2017) and personal life (e.g., Boellinghaus et al., 2013; Valente & Marotta, 2005). However, it is a wide and varied construct: For example, self-care would be expected to decrease the experience of burnout or VT, yet not all self-care strategies target specific risks for burnout or VT. How someone operationalizes self-care depends on the needs and interests of the individuals involved (Bettney, 2017).

The act of self-care has repeatedly been described as an "ethical imperative" for mental health professionals (e.g., J. E. Barnett et al., 2007; Grise-Owens et al., 2018; Norcross & VandenBos, 2018; Wise et al., 2012). The APA and the National Association of Social Workers promote the importance of maintaining professional functioning and competence (Clay, 2020; National Association of Social Workers, 2008), and self-care is a core competency for the training of psychologists (APA, 2011). Yet therapists report that self-care is not routinely taught during training (Bloomquist et al., 2015). A review of the literature from 2006 through 2016 found only four studies that evaluated self-care interventions/curricula for social work students in the United States (Griffiths et al., 2019). The results of the studies were mixed, with some support for mindfulness as a self-care intervention that may increase life satisfaction.

However, interventions did not decrease student stress or increase well-being. None of the studies included measures of actual behavior change, but only self-report, and none included long-term follow-up to determine if changes were maintained. Without effective training within graduate programs, therapists are more likely to enter the workforce unprepared to manage the persistent stressors related to the job. In fact, among a national sample of social workers in child welfare, less experienced clinicians were less likely to engage in self-care (J. J. Miller et al., 2019). This is consistent with the findings that younger therapists are also at greater risk for burnout and VT. Of further concern is the evidence that mental health professionals from marginalized racial and ethnic backgrounds engage in less self-care (J. J. Miller et al., 2019). These findings suggest that differences in self-care may be affected by social and systemic determinants and may play a role in perpetuating health disparities among therapists of different backgrounds.

In sum, we can draw limited conclusions about the elements that lead to successful treatment for therapist burnout or the ways in which self-care can be taught effectively. The need is clear; however, a culture shift is required that places increased value on the well-being of mental health professionals, breaks down the stigma of seeking support, and confronts social factors that increase barriers to self-care for therapists from marginalized backgrounds. Although so far we have been moderately effective at increasing self-care behavior among therapists and therapists-in-training, we do understand the types of strategies that promote physical and psychological health. Many of the strategies included next are those that therapists might very well recommend to stressed parents (Table 9.1).

Although it has been said before, it is essential to remember that as mental health professionals we must nurture ourselves to competently nurture others (Wise et al., 2012).

Awareness

The first step in meeting one's own need for self-care is awareness of the self—being present in the moment, aware of one's physical, emotional, and cognitive responses; being able to reflect on those responses and then to select actions based on them are abilities that can be fostered. Mindfulness interventions support this process (Lomas et al., 2019), as does reflective supervision (Hinshaw-Fusilier et al., 2009; Shea et al., 2016). In the context of maintaining physical and psychological health, it is essential to be able to access one's own states and to use that information to make decisions about the type of self-care that will meet one's needs (Norcross & VandenBos, 2018). To foster self-awareness, consider setting regular times during the day (e.g., morning, lunch, before bed) to explore how your body feels, your self-talk, and your emotional status. After completing therapy session notes, consider making notes on the self-talk that arose during the session. On the way home from work, notice what you do with the day's stress (e.g., increased muscle tension, headaches,

TABLE 9.1. Personal Self-Care Strategies for Mental Health Professionals

Personal self-care	Strategies
Awareness	Develop awareness of internal states. Set routine times to check in with yourself to examine physiological, emotional, and cognitive status. Be aware of stressors and notice your reactions to them. For deeper exploration of self-awareness, consider training in mindfulness.
Self-assessment	If aware of increasing stress responses, conduct a more focused assessment. Identify recent life/job stressors; consider whether your distress has increased over the past several months; assess how personal and professional relationships have been affected; assess feelings of anxiety, depression, emotional exhaustion; identify and seek sources of support.
Sleep hygiene	Chronic deficits in sleep are common. Yet without sufficient sleep, concentration, emotion regulation, and many physiological systems can be disrupted. Check your sleep hygiene and consider areas to change to support health.
Monitor nutrition intake and physical activity	Healthy decisions around food and activity often become a last priority when stress is high. Two simple strategies: (a) Keep fresh fruit and vegetables available. If the healthy choice is the most accessible one, then it's more likely to be selected. (b) Remember that physical activity doesn't have to mean going to the gym or taking a run. Exercise anywhere with anything: dance to your favorite playlist while making dinner; vacuum a bedroom; mow the lawn; take a walk while talking on the phone to a friend.
Seek social connection	Social support is a buffer against stress. Set aside a few minutes each day to say hello to a friend, play with your children, or spend some time with your partner.
Seek professional support	Practice self-compassion: Reach out for support to help manage symptoms of distress and burnout. Use personal therapy to enhance resilience and safely explore issues related to work with parents and children.
Do one thing each day	When anything else seems too much, select just one thing you can do each day to support your psychological, physical, or spiritual health.

positive/negative self-talk). Development of awareness of our own status allows for the early identification of risks and the opportunity to boost resilience.

Self-Assessment

In concert with awareness, therapists can seek to assess their own states with openness and acceptance of the fact that, as human beings working in psychologically strenuous circumstances, we are vulnerable to distress. Early detection of the impact of new life/work stressors is important for effective intervention (Dattilio, 2015). If self-assessment reveals a chronic or escalating state of emotional exhaustion; distress; disengagement from friends, family, and clients; or a sense of anxiety or depression, it is important to delve deeper to assess the issue. Some questions to ask oneself: Have my feelings of distress increased over the past several months? Are these feelings impacting my personal relationships? How have my relationships with clients been impacted? Where can I seek support? With awareness and self-assessment, therapists are in a position to select and take actions to prevent distress from leading to impairment.

Sleep, Nutrition, and Physical Activity

A deeper appreciation exists now than it once did for the influence of physical health on emotional, behavioral, and cognitive functioning, yet for many of us, when stressed, solid sleep, healthy eating, and physical activity are the first things to slip out of our daily routine. For adults to maintain healthy physiological and psychological functioning, at least 7 hours of sleep each night is recommended (Y. Liu et al., 2016). Without sufficient sleep, concentration, emotion regulation, and many physiological systems can be disrupted. In the long term, less than 7 hours of sleep a night is associated with increased risk for a range of negative outcomes such as diabetes, cardiovascular disease, high blood pressure, and high stress. However, chronic deficits in sleep are common among adults in the United States, with as much as 35% of the population sleeping less than 7 hours per night (Y. Liu et al., 2016). To support healthy sleep patterns, check your sleep hygiene and look for opportunities to make improvements. Sleep hygiene includes environmental structure and personal routine: for example, keeping screen devices (television, tablet, smartphone) off or out of the bedroom; creating a quiet and dark sleeping space; discontinuing caffeine, alcohol, and tobacco intake at least 4 hours before bed; and going to bed and getting up at approximately the same time each day (Mastin et al., 2006; C. K. Snyder & Chang, 2019). The keys to making changes in a sleep routine are to determine its relative priority in your self-care practice and focus on feasible changes. If you are not able to increase the length of time available for sleep, focus on improving the quality of your sleep. Better sleep hygiene is associated with better sleep quality (Mastin et al., 2006).

Assessing the priority and feasibility of changes is important in any aspect of the self-care routine. Select inexpensive, simple strategies that can be integrated into your existing routine over expensive, time-consuming, and complex ones. Regarding nutrition and physical activity, it is not necessary to cook at home every night to eat healthier and it is not necessary to join a gym to boost one's physical activity. Two simple strategies can increase health behaviors. The first strategy is related to nutrition: Keep fresh fruit and vegetables readily available—put them in a bowl on the table at home and throw them in a bag to take to work. If the healthy choice is the most accessible one, then it is more likely to be selected. The second strategy is related to physical activity: Reconceptualize healthy movement from something that must be structured and separate from other activities to something that can be woven throughout the day. It is possible to exercise nearly anywhere with nearly anything: take a 10-minute walk around the block outside the clinic at lunch, do stretches in your office in the 5 minutes between sessions, dance to your favorite playlist while making dinner, vacuum a bedroom, mow the lawn, or take a stroll while talking on the phone to a friend.

Seek Social Connection

Since the COVID-19 pandemic, "social connection" often looks different than it did prior to 2020. However, even during times when we are physically distanced from one another, it is important to reach out to others to connect, share struggles, and find moments of mutual enjoyment. Social support buffers us from the negative impact of adverse experiences (Wang et al., 2021). Again, apply the rule of priority and feasibility. Set priorities for the connections you most want to maintain and allocate brief but regular times to check-in. When extended social time is not available, integrate socializing with other activities: talk with a friend on the way home from work, cook dinner together with your child, or run to the grocery store with your partner. Even mundane chores can be opportunities to share positive time.

Make Use of Personal Therapy

Self-compassion has been associated with greater resilience and lower rates of burnout (McDonald et al., 2021). Part of self-compassion is being kind to one's self and accepting one's painful experiences and struggles. Seeking professional support is consistent with an attitude of self-compassion. When distress is high, functioning dips, and self-care is insufficient to return to a state of well-being, it may be necessary to access appropriate services. However, personal therapy offers benefits beyond merely restoring functioning. It provides the opportunity to expand coping mechanisms, enhance resilience, and explore issues of self that are relevant to therapeutic work with families. Within a personal therapeutic relationship, therapists can safely consider the reactions they have to particular family situations and emotions. They can strengthen their capacity to respond effectively to parent anger or address anxiety related to working with reluctant parents. Given the dual needs of therapists for self-care and self-awareness, it makes sense and is encouraging that many more psychologists access services than individuals within the general population (about 75% of psychologists relative to 25% of the general community; Bearse et al., 2013). However, 59% of surveyed psychologists reported not seeking therapy when they thought they might benefit from it; thus, there is still a way to go to optimize the use of services among those of us for whom it is so important. Consider personal therapy not as a luxury or evidence of any deficit but as an important contributor to professional efficacy, an expression of self-compassion, and an opportunity for growth.

Do One Thing Each Day

A mother with whom I worked used to say, "The vegetables you eat are better for you than the vegetables you don't eat, so don't worry about whether there's butter on them." I propose the same principle applies for self-care: The activity you do is better for you than the one you don't. Self-care need not be a burden to be valuable (Dattilio, 2015). If it is overwhelming to take up meditation, participate in a virtual mindfulness class, or make it to yoga every week, then choose something you can do instead: Read a chapter of a fluffy novel before you go to sleep. Stand in your backyard at sunset for 10 minutes and practice deep breathing. Carry out a brief progressive muscle relaxation exercise before getting into bed. Remember once again that self-compassion in itself can be a protective factor in dealing with stress (McDonald et al., 2021).

PROFESSIONAL SELF-CARE: STRATEGIES FOR WORKING WITH CHALLENGING FAMILIES

Working with clients who are challenging or have complex presenting issues is repeatedly associated with therapist burnout, and specifically with emotional exhaustion. As previously discussed, when working with parent–child dyads, complexity and challenge are routine. Enhancing confidence and effectiveness in work with such challenges may therefore lead to positive outcomes not only for families but also for therapists. Adding to one's repertoire of effective intervention strategies is a category of professional self-care that can reduce burnout risk. The following are strategies that address some of the most common challenges of therapeutic work with parents and children.

SETTING PRIORITIES TO ADDRESS FAMILIES' NEEDS

> When a family doesn't have a safe place to sleep or enough food, those needs must take priority, but not every "crisis" really is. Many times, parents come in wanting to vent about an incident—how their preschooler got kicked off the bus—but venting alone doesn't create meaning or build skills. It shouldn't take priority over the therapeutic work. (Community Mental Health Therapist)

This reminder was provided by therapists working in community mental health center settings who often must help parents to avoid getting mired in the crisis of the moment. For some parents, coming into session each week with a lengthy report of the worst parent–child moments is what they expect to do in therapy. They may need help shifting their understanding about the treatment process and how therapists and parents collaborate to support the parents' change and accomplishment of their goals. Other parents may be reluctant to engage in the therapeutic work. Venting frustration about a parent–child interaction can serve to keep it at a distance and keep the responsibility external to the parent. More effort is required—emotionally and cognitively—to consider new ways to conceptualize the conflict (new schema) and new ways to respond to it.

Keep in mind the overarching goal of helping parents to enhance their relationships with their children and to provide responsive parenting in real-world situations. Allowing a parent to go into lengthy descriptions of difficult interactions from the week without moving forward in the treatment process may provide the parent with a fleeting sense of relief. It will not bring about changes in their insight, skills, or interaction patterns.

Instead of letting the parent tell a long story about a problem, help the parent to find meaning in the incident in the context of the treatment model.

- "Even though you were angry, you stayed regulated in the moment. Showing your child that you can control your anger will help him learn to regulate his emotions too."
- "I'm glad you shared your frustration with me. The new interactions you're learning here will reduce those conflicts at home."
- "You really didn't know what to do in the moment. You made the best decision you could. Let's talk about how what you're learning here might help you."

Finding Empathy for Challenging Parents

> When I hear a parent talking negatively about their child, about how badly behaved they are or how they never do anything right, I feel sad, frustrated, and angry. Then I think of what this adult probably heard as a kid from their parents. It makes me realize how important it is for us to work together so that parents can have new ways of being with their children. When I can recognize a parent's vulnerability, then I feel more able to work with their negative emotions. (Licensed Social Worker)

Some days it can be difficult to deal with parents who appear unable or unwilling to make positive changes. Some days parents take out their own anger and frustration on us. Our ability to manage that anger is influenced by our own emotion regulation, but it is also complicated by our hope to bolster children's well-being.

Connect with the vulnerability in the parents. In the harmful messages they give their children, hear the messages they may have received as a child. Find the small strengths and build on those. Identify little steps forward and label those for the family and for yourself.

Dealing With Our Own Emotions in the Room

The emotions that therapists experience in session depend on personal and client factors, such as our own distress, the presentation of the parent, and the way in which our own issues interact with a family's presentation (Soloski & Deitz, 2016). Therapists' expression of emotion in session can be a valuable therapeutic tool when we are mindful of what we are expressing, why we are expressing it, and what it may communicate to a parent. Emotion expression has been positively related to client outcome (Peluso & Freund, 2018). However, therapist emotion should be used in the context of facilitating a client's processing of their own emotions, should not press a client into a defensive position, and should not be about reducing our own stress or discomfort. The ability to understand our own emotional reactions to a family, to recognize when those reactions may impair the therapeutic process, and to seek appropriate supervisory support has been referred to collectively as "reflective skills" (Shea et al., 2016). Appropriate supervision promotes the development of those skills.

Empowering Parents—Avoiding Power Struggles

> When I started paying attention to my language, I realized a lot of times I was saying things in a way that made the work about me instead of about the parent and child. It's something I did so easily, without paying attention. When I say something like "I need you to do this," I'm no longer focusing on what the parent wants or needs from treatment. That must make a difference in a parent's motivation. (Family Therapist)

"I need you to practice this at home." "You need to do this homework." "Make sure you do these things this week." We often say such things to parents in session without really thinking about it. Yet the meaning behind these statements is problematic for us and for the families with whom we work. By giving imperatives such as these, it pulls the focus away from parents' goals, gives the task moral undertones (suggesting, "You need to do this . . . or you're a bad parent/person"), makes the work about us, and takes away parents' self-agency. The most unfortunate thing about such statements is that they are not even true. We do not "need" a parent to practice their skills or to remember their homework. Most parents (even those who have been mandated to treatment) come to us with goals related to their or their children's functioning. Those goals are our foot in the door. They are the most likely motivator of parent behavior.

When reflecting on a session, check your language. Are you staying focused on the parents' goals? Are you connecting the therapeutic strategies to their goals to give them the opportunity to understand the process? Keep the parent, not the therapist, as the primary agent of change. When discussing therapeutic recommendations, such as home practice of new interaction patterns, be positive and honest about what it will take to reach a family's goals. If a parent does not complete the prescribed practice—"This week was too busy!"—it does not facilitate change if the therapist only reflects the experience of a busy week ("I understand. You were so busy"). Neither does it help a parent if a therapist takes a disapproving or critical tone ("You need to do more next week"). Instead, praise the initial attempt ("That's a good start. What made that possible?") and then connect the parent's behavior to the parent's goals ("One of your goals is to help your son get along better at school. When you do X every day you will reach your goal more quickly").

The following examples move away from statements that keep the power with the therapist (e.g., "I need you to" or "You need to") and give the agency back to the parent (Table 9.2):

- "When you practice these strategies daily at home, your child will start to listen better."
- "When you come regularly to session, we'll be able to work together toward your goals."

TABLE 9.2. Language Matters: Empower Parents, Avoid Power-Struggles, and Stay Goal-Focused

Instead of . . .	Try . . .	Why?
"I need you to [practice the new skills at home]."	"When you practice regularly, then you'll see the changes you want."	Helps parents to focus on their own goals. Empowers parents to make their own decisions about change.
"Make sure you [don't forget what I said]."	"Is there something that would help you to remember?"	Is solution-focused and strength-based. Encourages parents to reduce barriers to their success.
"You really need to [come in every week]."	"I notice that when you attend session regularly, you report more improvements at home."	Connects parents' actions to positive change. Builds feelings of self-efficacy.
"Treatment won't work if you don't commit to it."	"Being an active part of the treatment will allow you to reach your goals."	Avoids power struggles. Allows parents to make choices based on their goals.
"You had a chaotic week and didn't get the chance to try the skills. I understand."	"It was a really stressful week. When you use those new skills, you'll start to feel less stressed."	Connects parent engagement to reduction of the current problem. Avoids keeping the family at the same level of dysfunction.
"Don't you want the best for your child?"	"What would you like for your child to be doing five years from now? What would you like to be different in your relationship?"	Avoids shaming parents. Promotes change by helping parents to imagine positive outcomes for their child and family.

- "To reach your goal to increase your child's compliance will require your consistency."
- "I'm glad you were able to practice one day this week. That's a good start! To reach your goals will take practice five to six times a week. How would you like to take the next step?"

Implementing Evidence-Based Interventions

> When I'm implementing [Parent–Child Interaction Therapy], I see positive changes in the parent's and the child's behaviors, not just from session to session, but right there in the room. In the moment. The parent sees it too. Seeing that change really energizes me because I know I'm making a difference for the family. (Family Therapist)

When therapists feel that clients are not improving, they are more likely to experience burnout (von Hippel et al., 2019). Lengthy treatment with little progress may lead to a decrease in therapeutic focus and feelings of emotional exhaustion (Soloski & Deitz, 2016). In contrast, witnessing change within the parent–child relationship from session to session may support a therapist's sense of efficacy, reduce emotional exhaustion, and prevent depersonalization. Implementing interventions in which change can be measured and outcomes are positive, therefore, may have a protective effect for therapists. This suggests that the implementation of evidence-based parent–child interventions may have a positive impact not only on families but also on therapists. Does implementation of evidence-based interventions reduce burnout? Initial exploration of the question reveals that when therapists feel confident in their training within an evidence-based practice, it is a protective factor against emotional exhaustion (J. J. Kim et al., 2018). Organizations play a role as well: When therapists feel that the culture of the organization prioritizes clients' well-being, supports therapists' skill development, and promotes the use of evidence-based treatments, they are less likely to leave their positions (N. J. Williams & Beidas, 2018).

CASE EXAMPLE: SAMANTHA AND MS. R

"I don't know what to do with this parent. She's not making any progress and she's resistant to any recommendations I make." During supervision, a therapist shared her sense of futility about her work with a young parent–child dyad. She had been working with the family for approximately 1 month, after Ms. R, the 20-year-old biological mother of 4-year-old Samantha, was referred for services by her daughter's Head Start teacher, who described Samantha as having poor emotion regulation and frequent minor aggression (e.g., taking others' toys) relative to other children her age. Although Ms. R attended sessions regularly, the therapist reported that she was not following through on the recommended home practice between sessions, and during sessions she continued to be excessively negative about her child, herself, and increasingly with the therapeutic process.

What Happened?

To gain a clearer understanding of the interactions occurring during sessions, the therapist and I reviewed the video of the most recent session. Ms. R's ambivalence about treatment was apparent. At the start of session, she sank into her chair with a sullen-looking expression and made little eye contact with the therapist. She reported being too busy to complete the daily 5 minutes of prescribed parent–child interactions and said her daughter continued to be a "troublemaker" at preschool. During this recitation, the therapist grew increasingly quiet, giving only brief responses that were meant to validate Ms. R's busy week (e.g., "Oh, okay. It sounds like a really busy week"). The therapist said nothing explicitly about the parent's low level of homework completion or ambivalence, but nonverbal signals of her discomfort and disapproval (e.g., frowning, decreased verbalizations, shifting in her seat) were clear. Ms. R responded to the therapist's disapproval with a combination of protective defensiveness (e.g., repeating how busy she was) and continued lack of eye contact that may have been an indication of her feelings of shame or blame for not following through with the recommendations.

Despite the negativity in the session, a number of positive moments occurred that the therapist, already feeling overwhelmed by her own anxiety and disappointment, had missed. Ms. R had completed 2 days of practice of the responsive parenting skills, had expressed wanting things to be different in her interactions with her child, and had expressed having fun one day just playing with blocks with her daughter. Instead of seeing these small but important moments as opportunities to reinforce Ms. R's progress, to build her sense of self-efficacy, and enhance her intention to change, the therapist felt defeated by the lack of large gains and the parent's verbal expressions of reluctance. Supervision focused on helping the therapist to make the most of the positive moments as well as reflecting upon and managing her own negative responses to the parent in session. Upon reflection, the therapist recognized three specific moments that she could have leveraged to support the parent and promote positive change.

Making the Most of the Micromoments

1. Ms. R had completed 2 days of home practice of responsive parent–child interactions. Although not considered the necessary clinical dosage, 2 days is a positive place to start and opened the door for a solution-focused conversation that could lead to additional engagement. Solution-focused questions to build the parent's sense of efficacy and empower her to take responsibility for her own change could include the following: What do you enjoy during your interactions with Samantha on those 2 days? What skills came naturally for you? How did you make it possible to complete 2 days rather than 1 or none?

2. Ms. R expressed wanting things to be different at home and at preschool. Acknowledging a need for change is a precursor to taking action. This is an excellent opportunity to ask the parent what she would like to be different and to connect her goals to the treatment process.

3. Ms. R mentioned a time during the week when her interaction with her child included shared positive affect. This is an essential moment to help the parent to elaborate on her experience of joy and to develop awareness of how her own behavior facilitated the positive parent–child interaction. It is also valuable to (a) connect the parent's behaviors to the achievement of her long-term goals and (b) increase awareness of the importance of the positive time for her child.

SUMMARY

Working therapeutically with parent–child dyads poses unique challenges. These challenges can contribute to experiences of stress among therapists. Working with challenging clients is one factor associated with therapist burnout. Other factors occur at the organization, client, and therapist levels, leading to burnout prevalence rates estimated to be higher than 50% and climbing. This concerning statistic has implications for the well-being of therapists and clients and for the functioning of mental health organizations. Most of the literature on preventing therapist burnout is theoretical and based on correlational research. A host of factors co-occur with burnout and have been labeled as "risk factors," but causal models for burnout among therapists have not been adequately tested. Treatment strategies have been somewhat more carefully evaluated. However, the size of treatment effects for existing models are small to medium. To foster the health of therapists it is recommended that

- education about burnout and self-care is routinely provided in graduate training programs for psychologists, social workers, and other mental health professionals;
- during the training years, a stronger emphasis is placed on building the abilities of therapists to manage challenging clients using evidence-based strategies to increase engagement, and implement evidence-based interventions with fidelity; and
- mental health agencies develop strategies to support therapists, promote their well-being, and decrease the stigma of acknowledging a need for support.

Key Takeaways

1. Burnout is a multidimensional construct that includes emotional exhaustion, depersonalization of clients, and low personal accomplishment.
2. Rates of burnout among mental health professionals are concerning and can have negative consequences for therapists, families, and organizations.
3. Existing treatment strategies for burnout demonstrate only small effect sizes, suggesting that prevention may be a more valuable approach to reduce burnout rates among therapists, but more rigorous testing is necessary.
4. Potential protective factors against burnout and vicarious trauma include supportive supervision, specific training in evidence-based trauma work, opportunities for professional development, and self-compassion.
5. Self-care strategies may help to prevent emotional exhaustion and other aspects of burnout. A culture shift is necessary to train mental health professionals to value self-care, to reduce the stigma for acknowledging a need for support, and to break down systemic barriers that perpetuate health disparities among professionals from marginalized backgrounds.
6. The use of evidence-based parent–child interventions with large positive effects may maintain therapists' sense of efficacy and decrease emotional exhaustion and depersonalization of clients, thus reducing burnout.

Clinical Growth Questions

1. Are there aspects of burnout or vicarious trauma that I have experienced or am experiencing?
2. What factors within my current position, among my clients, and within myself do I think may contribute to my risk for burnout?
3. What is my self-care routine? What strategies could I add to my routine to support my personal well-being?
4. How do I engage with challenging families? Do I find ways to empathize with difficult parents, help to shift parents forward in their readiness to change, and implement effective interventions?
5. Have I checked the language I use with families? Are there things I might adjust in order to continue to empower parents and maintain the focus on families' goals?

Additional Self-Care Resources

- Self-care resources for psychologists: https://www.apa.org/monitor/2014/04/self-care
- Promotion of wellness for psychotherapists and trainees: https://societyforpsychotherapy.org/distress-therapist-burnout-self-care-promotion-wellness-psychotherapists-trainees-issues-implications-recommendations/
- Self-care in social work: https://www.naswpress.org/product/53634/self-care-in-social-work

10

Knocking Down Barriers to Effective Treatment

A Call for Advances and Culture Shifts

We must come to see that social progress never rolls in on the wheels of inevitability. It comes through the tireless efforts and the persistent work of dedicated individuals, and without this hard work, time itself becomes an ally of the primitive forces of social stagnation. And so we must have time, and we must realize that the time is always right to do right.

—MARTIN LUTHER KING, JR. (1967)

My primary goals in writing this book were to promote the importance of strengthening the parent–child relationship in therapy and to provide guidance on effective ways to do so. I have brought together the developmental literature on the influence of the parent–child relationship with the treatment outcome research and offered them in a way I hope will support therapists in their challenging work with parent–child dyads. Responsive and effective parenting is a first domino in a child's lifelong functioning, and as therapists we have the opportunity to help keep that domino standing. It is one critical and demonstrably effective way that we can buffer children against adversity.

During the course of my writing, the significance of buffers in the face of adversity became heart-wrenchingly salient. The COVID-19 pandemic savaged the world, exposing with stark clarity the vast inequities experienced by families within certain racial and ethnic communities across the United States. As of November 2020, incidence and mortality rates among American Indian

https://doi.org/10.1037/0000304-010
Strengthening the Parent–Child Relationship in Therapy: Laying the Foundation for Healthy Development, by L. N. Niec

and Alaskan Native communities were 2.2 and 3.8 times greater, respectively, than among White communities (Williamson et al., 2021). In a sample of COVID-19 patients in Louisiana, 76.9% of those hospitalized, 81.6% of those requiring ventilation, and 70.6% of those who died were Black, although Black individuals made up only 31% of the community (Price-Haywood et al., 2020). Disproportionate incidence and mortality rates are associated with factors caused by structural and systemic marginalization. That is, families from marginalized communities are likely to be exposed to more harmful factors (e.g., less access to education, employment, and health care) and to greater health risks (e.g., obesity, diabetes, heart disease), which increase the likelihood of experiencing negative consequences and reduce the capacity of communities to respond (S. J. Kim & Bostwick, 2020). Due to the additional exposure to harmful factors, negative psychological consequences also occur more often among marginalized families. In June 2020, a study of the mental health symptoms of a representative sample of adults in the United States found that more than 40% of adults were experiencing depression, anxiety, trauma-related symptoms, or increased stress-related substance use (Czeisler et al., 2020). Younger adults and individuals from marginalized racial/ethnic backgrounds were most likely to have seriously considered suicide in the 30 days before the survey. The increased mental health symptoms in adults have repercussions for children as well. In families in which parents lost their jobs because of COVID-19 and were more depressed, children were more likely to be physically and psychologically maltreated (Lawson, Piel, & Simon, 2020).

These are a few of the consequences of the social and structural inequities that were amplified by the pandemic. It will take time before we fully understand the long-term impact of the pandemic on children and parents, but it is evident that within our existing systems—mental health systems, education programs for mental health professionals, and family-related policies within the United States—it will not be possible to achieve health equity. We cannot reach the majority of families who are in need of psychosocial services from where we stand now, for we are mired in structures that often perpetuate the disparities they are meant to relieve. Novel organizational structures and further advances are necessary, within the field and within society, to make significant and lasting changes. Thus, to conclude this volume, which at its essence is a guide to promoting the development of emotionally, behaviorally, and physically healthy children, I must offer a discussion of some of the types of shifts and advances necessary to reduce the burden of mental illness for all families.

Figure 10.1 illustrates key influences on parents' ability to access, use, and benefit from mental health interventions; each outer ring exerts influence on the systems and individuals within it. Risk factors at each level may reduce the likelihood that parents will access effective care, whereas protective factors have the potential to increase access and utilization. Solutions that address only one system or focus solely on downstream factors (e.g., parent stigmatizing beliefs, therapist burnout) are unlikely to make a significant or sustained

FIGURE 10.1. Influences on Parents' Access to, Use of, and Benefit From Mental Health Services

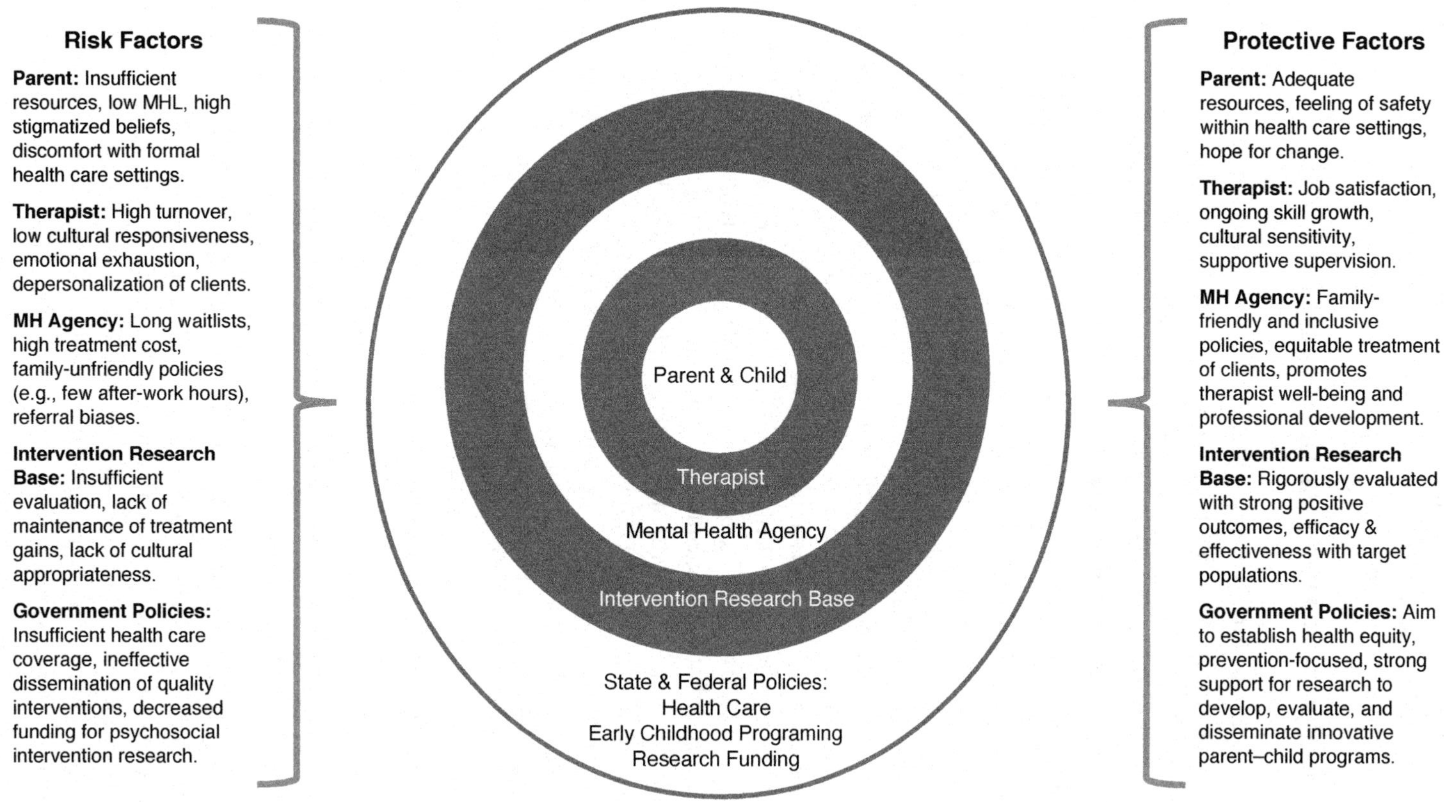

Note. MHL = mental health literacy; MH = mental health.

impact on access to care. However, an integrated approach has the potential to build the capacity within mental health systems and increase families' use and benefits, moving closer to achieving health equity.

VALUING THERAPISTS VALUES FAMILIES

To foster a culture that values its mental health professionals, it is necessary to move away from a deficit-model culture that views treating burnout rather than preventing burnout as the best that can be done for overworked, distressed mental health professionals. Within the current culture, burnout is viewed as an acceptable risk and consequence for therapists. The reflected attitude appears to be something to the effect of "You knew what you were getting into when you decided to be a therapist. . . ." In contrast, a culture that truly values therapists promotes systems structured to maximize health and reduce chronic stressors, aspiring to help therapists thrive (Wise et al., 2012). What would such a culture shift look like? At the most foundational level, therapists would be paid a salary commensurate with their education, their experience, and the value of their contribution to society. In 2016, social workers in the United States earned an average of $46,890 a year, approximately 85% of the salary of kindergarten teachers and 69% of the salary of registered nurses (George Washington University Health Workforce Institute and School of Nursing, 2017). Master of social work (MSW) graduates from 2017 to 2019 reported that the single most common reason they struggled to find a job was the lack of positions with adequate compensation (Fitzhugh Mullan Institute for Health Workforce Equity, 2020). Although practicing psychologists with doctoral degrees make significantly more than MSWs (the 2015 median annual salary was $60,000 for private nonprofit community agencies; American Psychological Association [APA], 2017), the majority of therapists serving families in community mental health settings are MSWs and other master's-level clinicians such as marriage and family therapists and licensed professional counselors. Of the representative sample of MSWs in 2016, 69% reported that more than half of their clients had a household income below the federal poverty level. In other words, some of the lowest paid mental health professionals are engaging in a major portion of the work with many of the most vulnerable families.

A culture shift to value therapists would also design systems in which therapists had more time to work directly with families, necessary administrative duties were directly tied to clients' well-being, and paperwork unrelated to clients' assessment and treatment was minimized (Madsen, 1999). This shift might include hiring more support staff or training support staff to manage some administrative duties previously left to clinicians. Organizations would provide ongoing professional development opportunities—including the development of skills in evidence-based interventions, which have been associated with lower burnout and greater job satisfaction. Training opportunities would be implemented within a context that supported effective learning. For instance, therapists who are spending additional hours in training and consultation would have reduced productivity requirements that facilitate successful program adoption. Finally, to complete a culture shift that values therapists, organizations must identify and change structures and policies that reflect White supremacist attitudes and must adopt antiracist and inclusive policies to create an environment in which therapists of all backgrounds and identities might flourish.

New costs are associated with such a culture shift; for instance, there are costs related to providing training and temporarily reducing productivity expectations. However, the price of not caring for therapists is very high, even if only considering the financial cost to organizations and society. Organizations pay in the form of chronic lost productivity, absenteeism, and rapid turnover (Simionato et al., 2019). Families pay in the form of disrupted therapeutic relationships and disengaged or discontinued services (J. Johnson et al., 2018). A culture shift such as the one just described would have the potential to decrease therapists' emotional exhaustion, depersonalization, and job dissatisfaction, thus reducing stress-related absences and job turnover and thereby increasing the effectiveness and continuity of care for families. Supporting a workforce of therapists who are healthy and satisfied with their jobs also creates space for the successful implementation of training initiatives. An overworked, exhausted, and distressed corps of therapists is unlikely to have the resources to invest in learning new interventions or other advancements in care. When society supports therapists, it supports the welfare of families and children.

REACHING FAMILIES WHO NEED HELP

It remains an unacceptable truth that most families who need mental health services do not receive them, with estimates of between 67% and 80% of children who need services going without them (Kazdin, 2008; Kazdin & Blase, 2011). Barriers to access are higher in some geographical regions and among some communities—for example, in rural areas where mental health provider shortages are more common (Health Resources and Services Administration, 2021), within impoverished communities where families may lack sufficient resources to access care, and among marginalized communities where there may be reasons to distrust formal health care settings (Niec et al., 2014). Additional reasons that families do not use mental health services may include the cost of services, the stigma of acknowledging parenting struggles, a poor understanding of mental health problems in children, and a lack of hope for positive change (Haine-Schlagel & Walsh, 2015).

The social and environmental determinants that affect a family's ability to access mental health services lead to service disparities in which some groups are less likely to have access to care than others. Disparities in access to care perpetuate disparities in health. Although calls have repeatedly gone out to increase access to mental health care, the barriers are complex and multifactored, crossing numerous systems. The following subsections specify three areas that are ripe for growth as components of a comprehensive plan to improve families' access to effective mental health care.

Increasing Mental Health Literacy

A program director within a community mental health center shared her disappointment with me that a new program for parents, which provided psychoeducation about the impact of trauma on young children, was routinely underutilized in her rural county: "What I see in the community is that a lot of parents don't know what trauma is. They don't identify the adverse events in their or their children's lives as traumatic. It's just what life is." With her observation, she touched on the issue of child mental health literacy (MHL) among parents. *Mental health literacy* refers to a basic understanding that mental health symptoms exist, are influenced by an individual's environment and experiences, can impact functioning, and can be treated. MHL has been conceptualized as an essential component of mental health services access and utilization (Tully et al., 2019). In the case of children's mental health, parents must have a basic MHL before they may identify the need for and the possibility of receiving help for their children. Unfortunately, investigations find that, on average, parents' MHL is very low (Hurley et al., 2020). Some evidence suggests that parents may have more literacy regarding mental health issues that receive more attention in the media (e.g., attention deficit hyperactivity disorder; Bonanno et al., 2021). Although the information offered by popular media outlets is not necessarily accurate, the availability and familiarity of information may help to reduce stigma around some disorders.

Stigma and MHL are interrelated. In a culture in which MHL was high, parents would be more likely to believe that reaching out for mental health services was a safe and helpful action to take. Most efforts to increase MHL have targeted adult and adolescent mental health. However, several recent efforts have attempted to promote parents' literacy about children's mental health. To date, brief community-delivered MHL interventions have not consistently demonstrated effectiveness (Hurley et al., 2021). Interventions to build the MHL of professionals who work with children demonstrate increases in knowledge, but it is not clear that increased knowledge leads to increased appropriate help-seeking (O'Connell et al., 2021). Rather than targeting specific groups such as parents or childcare professionals, an argument has been made that a universal intervention to promote child MHL should target all adults, with a goal of reducing population-wide stigma, improving early identification of children's mental health problems, and increasing help-seeking (Tully et al., 2019). Efforts to increase child MHL will be most effective when they are integrated within a broader approach to mental health care access. For instance, increasing parents' help-seeking for their children will increase access to and benefit of care only when sufficient therapists are available who are trained to deliver effective parent–child services.

Telehealth Interventions and Training

Increasing access to mental health care requires that services be available, affordable, and within a family's reach. Telehealth services have been promoted for the past 3 decades as a potential resource through which to increase access to care. However, a lack of infrastructure (e.g., audio/visual equipment), discomfort with the technology, and doubts about the ability to provide effective mental health services via telehealth contributed to the slow uptake of telehealth interventions. The COVID-19 pandemic forced many mental health agencies to rapidly increase their capacity to provide telehealth services and forced many mental health professionals to increase their comfort with providing remote treatment. Now the question becomes, How do we leverage those positive changes to reach more families in underserved areas? Prior to the pandemic, only one of the four parent–child interventions reviewed in Chapter 7 of this volume (parent–child interaction therapy) had conducted any quantitative evaluation of the efficacy of the model when provided via the internet (Comer et al., 2015, 2017). I have hope that with the rapid shifts in service delivery caused by the pandemic, other interventions will investigate outcomes for families who received remote services. Some interventions may be particularly suited to remote delivery, whereas others may not maintain efficacy. To include telehealth as part of the greater solution to increasing access to care, the next necessary steps are (a) to determine which parent–child interventions are effective when delivered via telehealth; (b) to provide therapist training in the delivery of effective parent–child telehealth interventions; and (c) to consider the limits to telehealth interventions, particularly for families from low-resourced backgrounds who do not own sufficient equipment and families living in remote areas with insufficient internet connectivity.

Paraprofessionals and Prevention Interventions

Paraprofessionals—including those referred to as lay health workers, community health workers, natural helpers, and promotoras (lay Hispanic/Latinx community helper)—are interventionists without formal mental health credentials who have had training to support families. Because they do not hold graduate-level degrees, the potential workforce is larger and less costly to develop. Some work has been conducted to assess the feasibility of using natural helpers to (a) serve as a support to therapists in the delivery of parent–child interventions and (b) provide parenting services independently under the supervision of a credentialed therapist (M. L. Barnett et al., 2016; Calzada et al., 2005). Natural helpers have the potential to increase use of, not just access to, mental health services, as families from marginalized backgrounds who are not comfortable in formal health care settings may feel safer or more supported by turning to natural helpers who are trusted within their communities (e.g., teachers, spiritual leaders, elders; Niec et al., 2014). Natural helpers are an undertapped resource. The preliminary research demonstrates that a significant expansion of research on the delivery of interventions by natural helpers would be worthwhile (Teachman et al., 2019). A major culture shift to improve access to care and reduce the impact of adversity on children would include innovations in the recruitment, training, and implementation of natural helpers within communities.

STRENGTHENING RESEARCHER–CLINICIAN RELATIONSHIPS

For decades, researchers and policy makers have bemoaned the glacial-paced transportation of scientific innovations in mental health care into community practice. Through the 1990s and into the early 2000s, a favored theme of psychology conventions was "bridging the gap" from science to practice. The birth of *dissemination and implementation science*—a field focused on identifying best practices to bridge the gap and take interventions to scale—demonstrates that progress has been made. However, significant discrepancies remain between what science tells us about what works to improve the mental health of parents and children and what is done in practice. One core aspect of the problem is that too often the primary drive underlying the bridge-the-gap theme has been the perception that science must more quickly cross the bridge to practitioners. The issue was largely conceptualized as unidirectional, and the bridge seen as a one-way street. Only more slowly did the understanding arise that the street must run both ways: that research must be informed by practice and that society benefits when the relationship between researchers and practitioners is genuinely collaborative. *Community-based participatory research* (CBPR) provides one framework that promotes the equitable partnership of scientists with communities, including practicing therapists (Minkler & Wallerstein, 2003). The principles of CBPR emphasize the importance of establishing long-term relationships between researchers and community members, identifying and building strengths and resources within the community, colearning for all partners, balancing the need for research with the need for action, sharing findings with all community members, and understanding that solutions develop through cyclical processes that involve ongoing communication between researchers and community members (Israel et al., 2012). CBPR supports equitable, respectful engagement with marginalized communities and has been used successfully in some cases to begin to repair trust (Damon et al., 2017; Mitchell, 2018).

Building healthy and mutually beneficial relationships between scientists and practitioners has the potential to reduce the gap by supporting a process in which interventions are created, evaluated, and refined with collaborative input from the community of individuals who will be responsible for implementing them. In other words, issues of feasibility and acceptability can be considered from the early days of intervention development. Social factors that may impact dissemination and implementation can also be considered by researchers, therapists, agency administrators, and families together, decreasing barriers that often slow the move across the bridge. Principles such as those exemplified by the CBPR framework should become a routine way of interacting with therapists and the larger community. They should infuse the process from the development and evaluation of parent–child interventions to the administration of training programs for therapists and the implementation of new services within systems of care.

LIFTING UP VOICES TOO RARELY HEARD

To make meaningful long-term changes for children facing adversity, we must also examine the inequities embedded within three structures relevant to therapeutic work with families: the education of mental health professionals, the provision of mental health services, and the design of research.

Graduate Education for Therapists

The racial, ethnic, and cultural composition of the workforce of psychologists is far less diverse than that of the U.S. population. A national survey of licensed psychologists in 2015 found approximately 86% to be White, whereas 5% were Asian/Pacific Islander, 5% Hispanic/Latinx, 4% Black/African American, and 0.3% American Indian/Alaskan Native (APA, 2016). These figures are in contrast to 2015 U.S. Census data that found the national population to be 62% White and 38% racial/ethnic minority (U.S. Census Bureau, as cited in Lin et al., 2018). The relative lack of racial/ethnic diversity represented in the psychology workforce cannot be explained by disparities in the rates of doctoral degrees conferred across all professions. Data on doctoral degrees earned in the United States from 2008 to 2019 show overall rates much closer to the racial/ethnic distribution of the national population (White = 64%–72%, Asian/Pacific Islander = 12%–13%, Black/African American = 9%–11%, Hispanic/Latinx = 6%–9%, American Indian/Alaskan Native = 0.4%–0.7%), with consistently increasing percentages across the 12 years for individuals from marginalized racial/ethnic backgrounds (U.S. Department of Education, 2020). Of further concern is the report of 47% of surveyed psychologists that they felt only "fairly prepared" to "not at all prepared" to work with clients of diverse cultural backgrounds (APA, 2016). Considering other mental health professionals, representation of racial/ethnic diversity within the psychiatric workforce is even lower than psychologists, with only 10% of practicing psychiatrists identifying as from a marginalized racial or ethnic group (Wyse et al., 2020). In contrast, to the psychological and psychiatric communities, the racial/ethnic composition of master's-level social workers more closely reflects the diversity of the U.S. population and is one of the most diverse mental health disciplines. From 2017 to 2019, 66% of MSW graduates were White, 22% Black/African American, 14% Hispanic/Latinx, 5% Asian/Pacific Islander, and 1% American Indian/Alaskan Native (Fitzhugh Mullan Institute for Health Workforce Equity, 2020).

The racial/ethnic homogeneity of much of the mental health workforce and the gap in preparation to serve a diverse population of families suggest a need to ask probing questions about graduate training in psychology: What structural and systemic barriers impact the enrollment and retention of these students into psychology doctoral programs? What impedes their entry into the workforce? What aspects of the graduate training process reflect implicit attitudes of racism? How can psychologists be better prepared to work with children and families from diverse racial and cultural backgrounds? Although I have focused here on racial/ethnic diversity, similar questions must also be explored regarding the success of individuals from other marginalized groups. Addressing these questions and acting to dismantle barriers to psychological education for students from marginalized backgrounds and identities is a necessary step on the path toward health equity.

Mental Health Systems

Families who experience more individual and household factors associated with marginalization (e.g., low education, young parenthood, low income, diverse racial/ethnic background) are less likely to have access to mental health care (Lê Cook et al., 2017), and if they are able to gain access, they are at increased risk for attrition from parent–child interventions (Jester et al., 2021; Lanier et al., 2011). Solutions to the issue must include the mental health system itself. Consider one hypothetical example of an organizational barrier to equitable access. Imagine a mental health clinic—perhaps in a medical center setting or group practice—in which some types of insurance are favored over others. In this setting, referrals are given priority depending on the source of reimbursement. In particular, one insurance type is privileged above others. The type of insurance a family carries, however, is associated with other factors—employment status, income, education level. The preferred insurance in this case is associated with lower social vulnerability factors. Thus, families with greater social vulnerability who try to access treatment at this clinic face longer wait times for services, are perhaps referred to the less experienced therapists in the practice, and may not be seen for as many sessions as other families. As a result, families are lost from the waitlist, their mental health conditions continue to worsen, and families who make it into services do not demonstrate effects as large as others do.

This situation illustrates just one type of barrier within mental health systems that may be infrequently discussed and that perpetuates health disparities. Another common barrier includes the lengthy intake processes frequently used within community mental health settings in which families who reach out for services may wait days to weeks before they are told whether they meet the criteria to receive services. If they do meet the criteria, they may then wait weeks to months before being seen by a therapist, who is often disconnected from the intake process. Thus, the family is again required to tell their story and to start from the beginning to build a new relationship. Numerous other barriers exist—from the cultural responsiveness of therapists delivering services to the availability of appointments for families needing after-work hours to the lack of childcare for parents with insufficient resources.

In 2001, the U.S. Surgeon General released a report on the disturbing level of disparities in access to mental health care between individuals from marginalized communities and White individuals (U.S. Department of Health and Human Services, 2001). Subsequent to the report came a wave of federal policies intended to decrease disparities (Snowden, 2012). A primary goal of *Healthy People 2020*, a 10-year federal plan to improve the health of the U.S. population, was to "achieve health equity, eliminate disparities, and improve the health of all groups" (U.S. Department of Health and Human Services, 2010, "Overarching Goals"). Despite those goals, from 2004 to 2012, disparities in mental health care access increased for Black/African American and Hispanic/Latinx communities (Lê Cook et al., 2017). In other words, we cannot continue treading in the same direction. A drastic shift is needed in culture and policy at all levels. At the organization and system levels, we must identify the embedded barriers—digging more deeply to uncover the impediments of structural racism—address them, and create safe, welcoming, and effective environments for families.

Research Design

In this chapter, I have discussed some of the changes that will promote novel research to address the needs of children and parents from marginalized communities. To lift up the voices of marginalized families throughout the process of intervention development, I must touch on another key shift. With few exceptions, parent–child interventions designated as evidence-based have little information on the model's efficacy with families from marginalized backgrounds. When information does exist, it is commonly collected later in the development process, after the intervention has been created based primarily on the responses of families within the dominant culture. As mentioned above, the CBPR framework can facilitate a transformation of this process. However, even to identify the CBPR approach as an essential one, researchers must first identify cultural responsiveness as a core goal of intervention development. That is, intervention development should begin with cultural responsiveness rather than considering it an afterthought. This is not to say that different intervention models must be created and tested for every racial/ethnic and cultural group—although for some mental health conditions and for some groups different models may be valuable. Rather, if responsiveness and flexibility is built within an intervention itself, then therapists can tailor language and present strategies in a way that is appropriate for the families before them. The concept of developing modules within an intervention to be selected based on the specific needs of a child or family is not a new one. One example is found in the MATCH program, which was designed to allow therapists to select intervention strategies based on a child's presenting problems (Chorpita et al., 2017). Another example is MY PCIT, a parent–child intervention designed to allow therapists to conduct a cultural assessment of a family—including important family attitudes, beliefs, and behaviors that impact the parent–child relationship—and subsequently to personalize strategies and components to address the family's needs. This personalization of the protocol allows therapists to respond sensitively to each family's beliefs throughout the implementation of parent–child interaction therapy (K. M. McCabe et al., 2020). These examples demonstrate that building flexibility into a standardized intervention protocol to address specific family needs is feasible and effective. An attitude shift among intervention developers is needed now to make cultural responsiveness a priority.

SUMMARY

Fostering the parent–child relationship in therapy is a critical way in which therapists can reduce the negative effects of adversity on children and promote healthy lifelong functioning. Yet, far more children and parents are in need of effective intervention than can access services. For those who do access services, many do not receive sufficient care, and thus they continue to experience the cascading impacts of early adversity. To make population-level improvements for children and families, it is necessary to address the dual problems—to reduce children's adversity exposure and increase access to mental health care—by considering risk and protective factors occurring across multiple systems/structures. Although calls for change have been voiced repeatedly from within one system or another (e.g., education, research, policy), progress seems to have stalled. Health and service disparities are increasing, leaving the children who are experiencing high levels of social vulnerability less likely to receive quality care. The response to this situation requires innovative solutions across all systems, and more: It requires that we delve into the complex network of structures related to the provision of mental health care for parents and children (e.g., academic centers of research, therapist training programs, mental health agencies, child welfare services) to identify and root out embedded attitudes and policies that maintain disparities. When we address the structural issues, then we will be in sight of achieving health equity for all families. As therapists, part of our role includes advocating for social justice. However, as we strive for changes in society-level structures, we can continue to focus on each parent and child who reaches us, knowing that by enhancing the parent–child relationship, we are setting another child on a more positive life trajectory.

Key Takeaways

1. When mental health agencies create a culture that values therapists, they reduce the financial and relational costs associated with therapists' emotional exhaustion, depersonalization of clients, and lowered productivity, creating a more supportive environment for families as well.
2. A majority of families in need of mental health services do not receive them. Increasing access to care and striving toward health equity requires innovative solutions that address barriers at every level from parent to policy maker.
3. Increasing child mental health literacy in the community, leveraging new telehealth options for mental health services, and investigating the potential of natural helpers to deliver parent–child interventions are three ways in which access and utilization may be increased.
4. When relationships between researchers and therapists is collaborative and equitable, then the development, evaluation, and implementation of novel parent–child interventions are likely to "cross the bridge" from research to practice more smoothly.
5. To lift up the voices from marginalized communities, changes are needed within graduate training programs, mental health systems, and academic centers of research.

Clinical Growth Questions

1. How are therapists and families valued within my mental health practice/clinic/agency? Are there areas in which I could advocate for myself and for my clients to shift the organizational culture?
2. How could I help researchers understand challenges to the implementation of parent–child interventions within the communities of families I treat?
3. What questions do I have about child development, interventions, and implementation that I would like researchers to answer?
4. How do I lift up the voices of the families I treat who come from marginalized communities? Are there areas in which I would like to be a stronger advocate?

REFERENCES

Aafjes-van Doorn, K., Békés, V., Prout, T. A., & Hoffman, L. (2020). Psychotherapists' vicarious traumatization during the COVID-19 pandemic. *Psychological Trauma: Theory, Research, Practice, and Policy, 12*(S1), S148–S150. https://doi.org/10.1037/tra0000868

Abidin, R. R. (1995). *Parenting Stress Index: Professional manual*. Psychological Assessment Resources.

Abidin, R. R. (2012). *Parenting Stress Index* (4th ed.). Psychological Assessment Resources.

Abrahamse, M. E., Egan, R., Coelman, F., & Heiner, W. (2018). Transporting PCIT around the world. In L. N. Niec (Ed.), *Handbook of parent–child interaction therapy: Innovations and applications for research and practice* (pp. 269–281). Springer.

Abrahamse, M. E., Junger, M., van Wouwe, M. A. M. M., Boer, F., & Lindauer, R. J. L. (2016). Treating child disruptive behavior in high-risk families: A comparative effectiveness trial from a community-based implementation. *Journal of Child and Family Studies, 25*(5), 1605–1622. https://doi.org/10.1007/s10826-015-0322-4

Adams, S. A., & Riggs, S. A. (2008). An exploratory study of vicarious trauma among therapist trainees. *Training and Education in Professional Psychology, 2*(1), 26–34. https://doi.org/10.1037/1931-3918.2.1.26

Aggarwal, N., & Lewis-Fernández, R. (2020). An introduction to the Cultural Formulation Interview. *Focus, 18*(1), 77–82. (Original work published 2015) https://doi.org/10.1176/appi.focus.18103

Ahnert, L., Pinquart, M., & Lamb, M. E. (2006). Security of children's relationships with nonparental care providers: A meta-analysis. *Child Development, 77*(3), 664–679. https://doi.org/10.1111/j.1467-8624.2006.00896.x

Ainsworth, M. D. S. (1969). *Maternal sensitivity scales*. Johns Hopkins University.

Ainsworth, M. D. S. (1989). Attachments beyond infancy. *American Psychologist, 44*(4), 709–716. https://doi.org/10.1037/0003-066X.44.4.709

Ainsworth, M. D. S., Bell, S. M., & Stayton, D. F. (1974). Infant–mother attachment and social development: Socialization as a product of reciprocal responsiveness to signals. In M. P. M. Richards (Ed.), *The integration of a child into a social world* (pp. 99–135). Cambridge University Press.

Ainsworth, M. D. S., Blehar, M. C., Waters, E., & Wall, S. (1978). *Patterns of attachment: A psychological study of the strange situation*. Lawrence Erlbaum Associates.

Akcinar, B., & Baydar, N. (2014). Parental control is not unconditionally detrimental for externalizing behaviors in early childhood. *International Journal of Behavioral Development, 38*(2), 118–127. https://doi.org/10.1177/0165025413513701

Albers, C. C., Müller, J. M., Mehring, K., & Romer, G. (2020). Is a mother's recalled parental rearing behavior, her attributions of her child's behavior, and her psychopathology associated with her mother–child relationship quality? *Infant Mental Health Journal, 41*(3), 378–392. https://doi.org/10.1002/imhj.21850

Allen, B. (2020). Child–parent relationship therapy for externalizing problems: A meta-analysis and methodological critique. *Evidence-Based Practice in Child and Adolescent Mental Health, 5*(4), 426–436. https://doi.org/10.1080/23794925.2020.1784054

Amato, P. A., & Gilbreth, J. G. (1999). Nonresident fathers and children's well-being: A meta-analysis. *Journal of Marriage and the Family, 61*(3), 557–573. https://doi.org/10.2307/353560

American Academy of Pediatrics. (2018, November 5). *What's the best way to discipline my child?* https://www.healthychildren.org/English/family-life/family-dynamics/communication-discipline/Pages/Disciplining-Your-Child.aspx

American Psychological Association. (2011). *Revised competency benchmarks for professional psychology*. https://www.apa.org/ed/graduate/competency

American Psychological Association. (2016). *2015 Survey of Psychology Health Service Providers*. https://www.apa.org/workforce/publications/15-health-service-providers

American Psychological Association. (2017). *Salaries in psychology: Findings from the National Science Foundation's 2015 National Survey of College Graduates*. https://doi.org/10.1037/e505912017-001

An, D., & Kochanska, G. (2020). Parents' early representations of their children moderate socialization processes: Evidence from two studies. *Development and Psychopathology*. Advance online publication. https://doi.org/10.1017/S0954579420001546

Anderson, S. E., & Keim, S. A. (2016). Parent–child interaction, self-regulation, and obesity prevention in early childhood. *Current Obesity Reports, 5*(2), 192–200. https://doi.org/10.1007/s13679-016-0208-9

Andrade, B. F., Browne, D. T., & Naber, A. R. (2015). Parenting skills and parent readiness for treatment are associated with child disruptive behavior and parent participation in treatment. *Behavior Therapy, 46*(3), 365–378. https://doi.org/10.1016/j.beth.2015.01.004

Annie E. Casey Foundation. (2003). *The unsolved challenge of system reform: The condition of the frontline human services workforce*. https://www.aecf.org/resources/the-unsolved-challenge-of-system-reform

Aoki, Y., Zeanah, C. H., Heller, S. S., & Bakshi, S. (2002). Parent–infant relationship global assessment scale: A study of its predictive validity. *Psychiatry and Clinical Neurosciences, 56*(5), 493–497. https://doi.org/10.1046/j.1440-1819.2002.01044.x

Aracena, M., Gómez, E., Undurraga, C., Leiva, L., Marinkovic, K., & Molina, Y. (2016). Validity and reliability of the Parenting Stress Index Short Form (PSI-SF)

applied to a Chilean sample. *Journal of Child and Family Studies, 25*(12), 3554–3564. https://doi.org/10.1007/s10826-016-0520-8

Asok, A., Bernard, K., Roth, T. L., Rosen, J. B., & Dozier, M. (2013). Parental responsiveness moderates the association between early-life stress and reduced telomere length. *Development and Psychopathology, 25*(3), 577–585. https://doi.org/10.1017/S0954579413000011

Aspland, H., & Gardner, F. (2003). Observational measures of parent–child interaction: An introductory review. *Child and Adolescent Mental Health, 8*(3), 136–143. https://doi.org/10.1111/1475-3588.00061

Atkinson, L., Paglia, A., Coolbear, J., Niccols, A., Parker, K. C., & Guger, S. (2000). Attachment security: A meta-analysis of maternal mental health correlates. *Clinical Psychology Review, 20*(8), 1019–1040. https://doi.org/10.1016/S0272-7358(99)00023-9

Atzaba-Poria, N., Meiri, G., Millikovsky, M., Barkai, A., Dunaevsky-Idan, M., & Yerushalmi, B. (2010). Father–child and mother–child interaction in families with a child feeding disorder: The role of paternal involvement. *Infant Mental Health Journal, 31*(6), 682–698. https://doi.org/10.1002/imhj.20278

Bagner, D. M. (2013). Father's role in parent training for children with developmental delay. *Journal of Family Psychology, 27*(4), 650–657. https://doi.org/10.1037/a0033465

Bagner, D. M., Rodríguez, G. M., Blake, C. A., Linares, D., & Carter, A. S. (2012). Assessment of behavioral and emotional problems in infancy: A systematic review. *Clinical Child and Family Psychology Review, 15*(2), 113–128. https://doi.org/10.1007/s10567-012-0110-2

Bailey, H. N., Bernier, A., Bouvette-Turcot, A. A., Tarabulsy, G. M., Pederson, D. R., & Becker-Stoll, F. (2017). Deconstructing maternal sensitivity: Predictive relations to mother–child attachment in home and laboratory settings. *Social Development, 26*(4), 679–693. https://doi.org/10.1111/sode.12220

Baker, C. E., & Brooks-Gunn, J. (2020). Early parenting and the intergenerational transmission of self-regulation and behavior problems in African American Head Start families. *Child Psychiatry and Human Development, 51*(2), 220–230. https://doi.org/10.1007/s10578-019-00921-5

Bakermans-Kranenburg, M. J., & van IJzendoorn, M. H. (2007). Research review: Genetic vulnerability or differential susceptibility in child development: The case of attachment. *Journal of Child Psychology and Psychiatry, 48*(12), 1160–1173. https://doi.org/10.1111/j.1469-7610.2007.01801.x

Bakermans-Kranenburg, M. J., & van IJzendoorn, M. H. (2016). Attachment, parenting, and genetics. In J. Cassidy & P. R. Shaver (Eds.), *Handbook of attachment: Theory, research, and clinical applications* (3rd ed., pp. 155–179). Guilford Press.

Bakermans-Kranenburg, M. J., van IJzendoorn, M. H., Bokhorst, C. L., & Schuengel, C. (2004). The importance of shared environment in infant–father attachment: A behavioral genetic study of the Attachment Q-Sort. *Journal of Family Psychology, 18*(3), 545–549. https://doi.org/10.1037/0893-3200.18.3.545

Bakermans-Kranenburg, M. J., van IJzendoorn, M. H., & Juffer, F. (2003). Less is more: Meta-analyses of sensitivity and attachment interventions in early childhood. *Psychological Bulletin, 129*(2), 195–215. https://doi.org/10.1037/0033-2909.129.2.195

Barak, A., Hen, L., Boniel-Nissim, M., & Shapira, N. A. (2008). A comprehensive review and a meta-analysis of the effectiveness of internet-based psychotherapeutic interventions. *Journal of Technology in Human Services, 26*(2–4), 109–160. https://doi.org/10.1080/15228830802094429

Barlow, S. E., & the Expert Committee. (2007). Expert committee recommendations regarding the prevention, assessment, and treatment of child and adolescent overweight and obesity: Summary report. *Pediatrics, 120*(Suppl. 4), S164–S192. https://doi.org/10.1542/peds.2007-2329C

Barnett, J. E., Baker, E. K., Elman, N. S., & Schoener, G. R. (2007). In pursuit of wellness: The self-care imperative. *Professional Psychology, Research and Practice, 38*(6), 603–612. https://doi.org/10.1037/0735-7028.38.6.603

Barnett, M. L., Davis, E. M., Callejas, L. M., White, J. V., Acevedo-Polakovich, I. D., Niec, L. N., & Jent, J. F. (2016). The development and evaluation of a natural helpers' training program to increase the engagement of urban, Latina/o families in parent–child interaction therapy. *Children and Youth Services Review, 65,* 17–25. https://doi.org/10.1016/j.childyouth.2016.03.016

Barnett, M. L., Niec, L. N., & Acevedo-Polakovich, I. D. (2014). Assessing the key to effective coaching in parent–child interaction therapy: The therapist–parent interaction coding system. *Journal of Psychopathology and Behavioral Assessment, 36*(2), 211–223. https://doi.org/10.1007/s10862-013-9396-8

Barnett, M. L., Niec, L. N., Peer, S. O., Jent, J. F., Weinstein, A., Gisbert, P., & Simpson, G. (2015). Successful therapist–parent coaching: How in vivo feedback relates to parent engagement in parent–child interaction therapy. *Journal of Clinical Child & Adolescent Psychology, 46*(6), 895–902. https://doi.org/10.1080/15374416.2015.1063428

Barnett, M. L., Sigal, M., Green Rosas, Y., Corcoran, F., Rastogi, M., & Jent, J. F. (2021). Therapist experiences and attitudes about implementing internet-delivered parent–child interaction therapy during COVID-19. *Cognitive and Behavioral Practice, 28*(4), 630–641. https://doi.org/10.1016/j.cbpra.2021.03.005

Barroso, N. E., Hungerford, G. M., Garcia, D., Graziano, P. A., & Bagner, D. M. (2016). Psychometric properties of the Parenting Stress Index-Short Form (PSI-SF) in a high-risk sample of mothers and their infants. *Psychological Assessment, 28*(10), 1331–1335. https://doi.org/10.1037/pas0000257

Bartoskova, L. (2015). Research into post-traumatic growth in therapists: A critical literature review. *Counselling Psychology Review, 30*(3), 57–68.

Batum, P., & Yagmurlu, B. (2007). What counts in externalizing behaviors? The contributions of emotion and behavior regulation. *Current Psychology, 25*(4), 272–294.

Baumrind, D. (1966). Effects of authoritative parental control on child behavior. *Child Development, 37*(4), 887–907. https://doi.org/10.2307/1126611

Baumrind, D. (1971). Current patterns of parental authority. *Developmental Psychology, 4*(1, Pt. 2), 1–103. https://doi.org/10.1037/h0030372

Baumrind, D. (1991). The influence of parenting style on adolescent competence and substance use. *The Journal of Early Adolescence, 11*(1), 56–95. https://doi.org/10.1177/0272431691111004

Bayes, A., Tavella, G., & Parker, G. (2021). The biology of burnout: Causes and consequences. *The World Journal of Biological Psychiatry, 22*(9), 686–698. https://doi.org/10.1080/15622975.2021.1907713

Beardslee, W. R. (2019). Master clinician review: Parental depression and family health and wellness: What clinicians can do and reflections on opportunities for the future. *Journal of the American Academy of Child & Adolescent Psychiatry, 58*(8), 759–767. https://doi.org/10.1016/j.jaac.2019.02.008

Bearse, J. L., McMinn, M. R., Seegobin, W., & Free, K. (2013). Barriers to psychologists seeking mental health care. *Professional Psychology, Research and Practice, 44*(3), 150–157. https://doi.org/10.1037/a0031182

Beckerman, M., van Berkel, S. R., Mesman, J., & Alink, L. R. A. (2017). The role of negative parental attributions in the associations between daily stressors, maltreatment history, and harsh and abusive discipline. *Child Abuse & Neglect, 64*, 109–116. https://doi.org/10.1016/j.chiabu.2016.12.015

Beebe, B., & Steele, M. (2013). How does microanalysis of mother-infant communication inform maternal sensitivity and infant attachment? *Attachment & Human Development, 15*(5–6), 583–602. https://doi.org/10.1080/14616734.2013.841050

Beidas, R. S., Marcus, S., Wolk, C. B., Powell, B., Aarons, G. A., Evans, A. C., Hurford, M. O., Hadley, T., Adams, D. R., Walsh, L. M., Babbar, S., Barg, F., & Mandell, D. S. (2016). A prospective examination of clinician and supervisor turnover within the context of implementation of evidence-based practices in a publicly-funded mental health system. *Administration and Policy in Mental Health, 43*(5), 640–649. https://doi.org/10.1007/s10488-015-0673-6

Belsky, J. (1984). The determinants of parenting: A process model. *Child Development, 55*(1), 83–96. https://doi.org/10.2307/1129836

Bergmeier, H., Paxton, S. J., Milgrom, J., Anderson, S. E., Baur, L., Hill, B., Lim, S., Green, R., & Skouteris, H. (2020). Early mother–child dyadic pathways to childhood obesity risk: A conceptual model. *Appetite, 144*, 104459. https://doi.org/10.1016/j.appet.2019.104459

Berlin, L. J., Ispa, J. M., Fine, M. A., Malone, P. S., Brooks-Gunn, J., Brady-Smith, C., Ayoub, C., & Bai, Y. (2009). Correlates and consequences of spanking and verbal punishment for low-income White, African American, and Mexican American toddlers. *Child Development, 80*(5), 1403–1420. https://doi.org/10.1111/j.1467-8624.2009.01341.x

Bernier, A., Beauchamp, M. H., Carlson, S. M., & Lalonde, G. (2015). A secure base from which to regulate: Attachment security in toddlerhood as a predictor of executive functioning at school entry. *Developmental Psychology, 51*(9), 1177–1189. https://doi.org/10.1037/dev0000032

Bernier, A., Carlson, S. M., Deschênes, M., & Matte-Gagné, C. (2012). Social factors in the development of early executive functioning: A closer look at the caregiving environment. *Developmental Science, 15*(1), 12–24. https://doi.org/10.1111/j.1467-7687.2011.01093.x

Bernier, A., Carlson, S. M., & Whipple, N. (2010). From external regulation to self-regulation: Early parenting precursors of young children's executive functioning. *Child Development, 81*(1), 326–339. https://doi.org/10.1111/j.1467-8624.2009.01397.x

Bettney, L. (2017). Reflecting on self-care practices during clinical psychology training and beyond. *Reflective Practice, 18*(3), 369–380. https://doi.org/10.1080/14623943.2017.1294532

Biringen, Z. (2005). Training and reliability issues with the Emotional Availability Scales. *Infant Mental Health Journal, 26*(4), 404–405. https://doi.org/10.1002/imhj.20060

Biringen, Z., Derscheid, D., Vliegen, N., Closson, L., & Easterbrooks, M. A. (2014). Emotional availability (EA): Theoretical background, empirical research using the EA Scales, and clinical applications. *Developmental Review, 34*(2), 114–167. https://doi.org/10.1016/j.dr.2014.01.002

Biringen, Z., & Easterbrooks, M. A. (2012). Emotional availability: Concept, research, and window on developmental psychopathology. *Development and Psychopathology, 24*(1), 1–8. https://doi.org/10.1017/S0954579411000617

Bjørseth, Å., & Wichstrøm, L. (2016). Effectiveness of parent–child interaction therapy (PCIT) in the treatment of young children's behavior problems. A randomized controlled study. *PLOS ONE, 11*(9), Article e0159845. https://doi.org/10.1371/journal.pone.0159845

Blair, B. L., Perry, N. B., O'Brien, M., Calkins, S. D., Keane, S. P., & Shanahan, L. (2015). Identifying developmental cascades among differentiated dimensions of social competence and emotion regulation. *Developmental Psychology, 51*(8), 1062–1073. https://doi.org/10.1037/a0039472

Blair, C., & Raver, C. C. (2016). Poverty, stress, and brain development: New directions for prevention and intervention. *Academic Pediatrics, 16*(3, Suppl.), S30–S36. https://doi.org/10.1016/j.acap.2016.01.010

Blair, C., Raver, C. C., Berry, D. J., & the Family Life Project Investigators. (2014). Two approaches to estimating the effect of parenting on the development of executive function in early childhood. *Developmental Psychology, 50*(2), 554–565. https://doi.org/10.1037/a0033647

Bloomquist, K. R., Wood, L., Friedmeyer-Trainor, K., & Kim, H. W. (2015). Self-care and professional quality of life: Predictive factors among MSW practitioners. *Advances in Social Work, 16*(2), 292–311. https://doi.org/10.18060/18760

Bluestone, C., & Tamis-LeMonda, C. (1999). Correlates of parenting styles in predominantly working- and middle-class African American mothers. *Journal of Marriage and the Family, 61*(4), 881–893. https://doi.org/10.2307/354010

Bober, T., & Regehr, C. (2006). Strategies for reducing secondary or vicarious trauma: Do they work? *Brief Treatment and Crisis Intervention, 6*(1), 1–9. https://doi.org/10.1093/brief-treatment/mhj001

Boellinghaus, I., Jones, F. W., & Hutton, J. (2013). Cultivating self-care and compassion in psychological therapists in training: The experience of practicing loving-kindness meditation. *Training and Education in Professional Psychology, 7*(4), 267–277. https://doi.org/10.1037/a0033092

Bokhorst, C. L., Bakermans-Kranenburg, M. J., Fearon, R. M., van IJzendoorn, M. H., Fonagy, P., & Schuengel, C. (2003). The importance of shared environment in mother-infant attachment security: A behavioral genetic study. *Child Development, 74*(6), 1769–1782. https://doi.org/10.1046/j.1467-8624.2003.00637.x

Bonanno, G. A. (2004). Loss, trauma, and human resilience: Have we underestimated the human capacity to thrive after extremely aversive events? *American Psychologist, 59*(1), 20–28. https://doi.org/10.1037/0003-066X.59.1.20

Bonanno, R., Sisselman-Borgia, A., & Veselak, K. (2021). Parental mental health literacy and stigmatizing beliefs. *Social Work in Mental Health, 19*(4), 324–344. https://doi.org/10.1080/15332985.2021.1919815

Bornstein, M. H., Tamis-Lemonda, C. S., Hahn, C. S., & Haynes, O. M. (2008). Maternal responsiveness to young children at three ages: Longitudinal analysis of a multidimensional, modular, and specific parenting construct. *Developmental Psychology, 44*(3), 867–874. https://doi.org/10.1037/0012-1649.44.3.867

Borofsky, L. A., Kellerman, I., Baucom, B., Oliver, P. H., & Margolin, G. (2013). Community violence exposure and adolescents' school engagement and academic achievement over time. *Psychology of Violence, 3*(4), 381–395. https://doi.org/10.1037/a0034121

Bos, H. M., Gartrell, N. K., Peyser, H., & van Balen, F. (2008). The USA National Longitudinal Lesbian Family Study (NLLFS): Homophobia, psychological adjustment, and protective factors. *Journal of Lesbian Studies, 12*(4), 455–471. https://doi.org/10.1080/10894160802278630

Bos, H. M., & van Balen, F. (2008). Children in planned lesbian families: Stigmatisation, psychological adjustment and protective factors. *Culture, Health & Sexuality, 10*(3), 221–236. https://doi.org/10.1080/13691050701601702

Bowlby, J. (1973). *Attachment and loss II: Separation*. Basic Books.

Bowlby, J. (1982). *Attachment and loss I: Attachment*. Basic Books. (Original work published 1969)

Bowlby, J. (1988). *A secure base*. Routledge.

Bowlby, J., & World Health Organization. (1952). *Maternal care and mental health: A report prepared on behalf of the World Health Organization as a contribution to the United Nations programme for the welfare of homeless children* (2nd ed.). World Health Organization. https://apps.who.int/iris/handle/10665/40724

Boyd, R. C., & Waanders, C. (2013). Protective factors for depression among African American children of predominantly low-income mothers with depression. *Journal of Child and Family Studies, 22*(1), 85–95. https://doi.org/10.1007/s10826-012-9588-y

Bratton, S., & Landreth, G. (1995). Filial therapy with single parents: Effects on parental acceptance, empathy, and stress. *International Journal of Play Therapy, 4*(1), 61–80. https://doi.org/10.1037/h0089142

Brennan, P. A., Le Brocque, R., & Hammen, C. (2003). Maternal depression, parent–child relationships, and resilient outcomes in adolescence. *Journal of the American Academy of Child & Adolescent Psychiatry, 42*(12), 1469–1477. https://doi.org/10.1097/00004583-200312000-00014

Brestan, E. V., Eyberg, S. M., Boggs, S. R., & Algina, J. (1997). Parent–child interaction therapy: Parents' perceptions of untreated siblings. *Child & Family Behavior Therapy, 19*(3), 13–28. https://doi.org/10.1300/J019v19n03_02

Bretherton, I. (1987). New perspectives on attachment relations: Security, communication, and internal working models. In J. D. Osofsky (Ed.), *Handbook of infant development* (2nd ed., pp. 1061–1100). Wiley.

Bretherton, I. (2005). In pursuit of the internal working model construct and its relevance to attachment relationships. In K. E. Grossmann, K. Grossmann, & E. Waters (Eds.), *Attachment from infancy to adulthood: The major longitudinal studies* (pp. 13–47). Guilford Press.

Bretherton, I. (2010). Fathers in attachment theory and research: A review. *Early Child Development and Care, 180*(1–2), 9–23. https://doi.org/10.1080/03004430903414661

Bretherton, I., Lambert, J. D., & Golby, B. (2006). Modeling and reworking childhood experiences: Involved fathers' representations of being parented and of parenting a preschool child. In O. Mayseless (Ed.), *Parenting representations: Theory, research, and clinical implications* (pp. 177–207). Cambridge University Press. https://doi.org/10.1017/CBO9780511499869.007

Bretherton, I., & Munholland, K. (2016). The internal working model construct in light of contemporary neuroimaging research. In J. Cassidy & P. Shaver (Eds.), *Handbook of attachment: Theory, research, and clinical applications* (3rd ed., pp. 63–90). Guilford Press.

Briegel, W. (2014a). *Checkliste kindliches Beziehungsverhalten* (CKB) [Child Relationship Checklist; unpublished questionnaire]. Leopoldina Hospital, Schweinfurt, Germany.

Briegel, W. (2014b). *Fragebogen zur kindlichen Beziehungsgestaltung* (FKB) [Child Relationship Development Questionnaire; unpublished questionnaire]. Leopoldina Hospital, Schweinfurt, Germany.

Briegel, W., Peer, S. O., Dell'armi, M., & Niec, L. N. (2018). Building resilience through PCIT: Assessing child adaptive functioning and parent–child relationship quality. In L. N. Niec (Ed.), *Handbook of parent–child interaction therapy: Innovations and applications for research and practice* (pp. 341–356). Springer. https://doi.org/10.1007/978-3-319-97698-3_21

Briegel, W., Walter, T., Schimek, M., Knapp, D., & Bussing, R. (2015). Parent–child interaction therapy in in-room-coaching. *Kindheit und Entwicklung, 24*(1), 47–54. https://doi.org/10.1026/0942-5403/a000158

Brockhouse, R., Msetfi, R. M., Cohen, K., & Joseph, S. (2011). Vicarious exposure to trauma and growth in therapists: The moderating effects of sense of coherence, organizational support, and empathy. *Journal of Traumatic Stress, 24*(6), 735–742. https://doi.org/10.1002/jts.20704

Brodd, I., & Niec, L. N. (2021). *Parents' attitudes toward time-out* [Manuscript submitted for publication]. Department of Psychology, Central Michigan University.

Brody, G. H., Gray, J., Yu, T., Barton, A. W., Beach, S. R., Galván, A., MacKillop, J., Windle, M., Chen, E., Miller, G. E., & Sweet, L. H. (2017). Protective prevention effects on the association of poverty with brain development. *JAMA Pediatrics, 171*(1), 46–52. https://doi.org/10.1001/jamapediatrics.2016.2988

Brody, G. H., Murry, V. M., Gerrard, M., Gibbons, F. X., Molgaard, V., McNair, L., Brown, A. C., Wills, T. A., Spoth, R. L., Luo, Z., Chen, Y. F., & Neubaum-Carlan, E. (2004). The Strong African American Families Program: Translating research into prevention programming. *Child Development, 75*(3), 900–917. https://doi.org/10.1111/j.1467-8624.2004.00713.x

Brody, G. H., Yu, T., Chen, E., & Miller, G. E. (2017). Family-centered prevention ameliorates the association between adverse childhood experiences and prediabetes status in young black adults. *Preventive Medicine, 100*, 117–122. https://doi.org/10.1016/j.ypmed.2017.04.017

Brody, G. H., Yu, T., Nusslock, R., Barton, A. W., Miller, G. E., Chen, E., Holmes, C., McCormick, M., & Sweet, L. H. (2019). The protective effects of supportive parenting on the relationship between adolescent poverty and resting-state functional brain connectivity during adulthood. *Psychological Science, 30*(7), 1040–1049. https://doi.org/10.1177/0956797619847989

Bronfenbrenner, U. (2005). Ecological systems theory (1992). In U. Bronfenbrenner (Ed.), *Making human beings human: Bioecological perspectives on human development* (pp. 106–173). Sage Publications.

Brown, A. R., Walters, J. E., & Jones, A. E. (2019). Pathways to retention: Job satisfaction, burnout, & organizational commitment among social workers. *Journal of Evidence-Based Social Work, 16*(6), 577–594. https://doi.org/10.1080/26408066.2019.1658006

Brown, G. L., Mangelsdorf, S. C., & Neff, C. (2012). Father involvement, paternal sensitivity, and father–child attachment security in the first 3 years. *Journal of Family Psychology, 26*(3), 421–430. https://doi.org/10.1037/a0027836

Brown, G. L., McBride, B. A., Shin, N., & Bost, K. K. (2007). Parenting predictors of father–child attachment security: Interactive effects of father involvement and fathering quality. *Fathering, 5*(3), 197–219. https://doi.org/10.3149/fth.0503.197

Bruce, M., Young, D., Turnbull, S., Rooksby, M., Chadwick, G., Oates, C., Nelson, R., Young-Southward, G., Haig, C., & Minnis, H. (2019). Reactive attachment disorder in maltreated young children in foster care. *Attachment & Human Development, 21*(2), 152–169. https://doi.org/10.1080/14616734.2018.1499211

Budd, K. S., & O'Brien, T. P. (1982). Father involvement in behavioral parent training: An area in need of research. *Behavior Therapist, 5*(3), 85–89.

Burchinal, M. R., Roberts, J. E., Zeisel, S. A., & Rowley, S. J. (2008). Social risk and protective factors for African American children's academic achievement and adjustment during the transition to middle school. *Developmental Psychology, 44*(1), 286–292. https://doi.org/10.1037/0012-1649.44.1.286

Bureau, J., Martin, J., Yurkowski, K., Schmiedel, S., Quan, J., Moss, E., Deneault, A. A., & Pallanca, D. (2017). Correlates of child–father and child–mother attachment in the preschool years. *Attachment & Human Development, 19*(2), 130–150. https://doi.org/10.1080/14616734.2016.1263350

Bustamante, A. C., Aiello, A. E., Guffanti, G., Galea, S., Wildman, D. E., & Uddin, M. (2018). FKBP5 DNA methylation does not mediate the association between childhood maltreatment and depression symptom severity in the Detroit Neighborhood Health Study. *Journal of Psychiatric Research, 96*, 39–48. https://doi.org/10.1016/j.jpsychires.2017.09.016

Butler, L. D., Carello, J., & Maguin, E. (2017). Trauma, stress, and self-care in clinical training: Predictors of burnout, decline in health status, secondary traumatic stress symptoms, and compassion satisfaction. *Psychological Trauma: Theory, Research, Practice, and Policy, 9*(4), 416–424. https://doi.org/10.1037/tra0000187

Butler, O., Yang, X. F., Laube, C., Kühn, S., & Immordino-Yang, M. H. (2018). Community violence exposure correlates with smaller gray matter volume and lower IQ in urban adolescents. *Human Brain Mapping, 39*(5), 2088–2097. https://doi.org/10.1002/hbm.23988

Buttitta, K. V., Smiley, P. A., Kerr, M. L., Rasmussen, H. F., Querdasi, F. R., & Borelli, J. L. (2019). In a father's mind: Paternal reflective functioning, sensitive parenting, and protection against socioeconomic risk. *Attachment & Human Development, 21*(5), 445–466. https://doi.org/10.1080/14616734.2019.1582596

Cabrera, N. J., Volling, B. L., & Barr, R. (2018). Fathers are parents, too! Widening the lens on parenting for children's development. *Child Development Perspectives, 12*(3), 152–157. https://doi.org/10.1111/cdep.12275

Calkins, S. D., & Leerkes, E. M. (2004). Early attachment processes and the development of emotional self-regulation. In R. F. Baumeister & K. D. Vohs (Eds.), *Handbook of self-regulation: Research, theory, and applications* (pp. 355–373). Guilford Press.

Callaghan, B. L., & Tottenham, N. (2016). The neuro-environmental loop of plasticity: A cross-species analysis of parental effects on emotion circuitry development following typical and adverse caregiving. *Neuropsychopharmacology, 41*(1), 163–176. https://doi.org/10.1038/npp.2015.204

Calzada, E. J., Caldwell, M. B., Brotman, L. M., Brown, E. J., Wallace, S. A., McQuaid, J. H., Rojas-Flores, L., & O'Neal, C. R. (2005). Training community members to serve as paraprofessionals in an evidence-based, prevention program for parents of preschoolers. *Journal of Child and Family Studies, 14*(3), 387–402. https://doi.org/10.1007/s10826-005-6851-5

Calzada, E. J., Eyberg, S. M., Rich, B., & Querido, J. G. (2004). Parenting disruptive preschoolers: Experiences of mothers and fathers. *Journal of Abnormal Child Psychology, 32*(2), 203–213. https://doi.org/10.1023/B:JACP.0000019771.43161.1c

Caplan, B., Blacher, J., & Eisenhower, A. (2019). Responsive parenting and prospective social skills development in early school-aged children with autism spectrum disorder. *Journal of Autism and Developmental Disorders, 49*(8), 3203–3217. https://doi.org/10.1007/s10803-019-04039-4

Carlson, E. A., Sampson, M. C., & Sroufe, L. A. (2003). Implications of attachment theory and research for developmental-behavioral pediatrics. *Journal of Developmental and Behavioral Pediatrics, 24*(5), 364–379. https://doi.org/10.1097/00004703-200310000-00010

Carnes-Holt, K., & Bratton, S. C. (2014). The efficacy of child parent relationship therapy for adopted children with attachment disruptions. *Journal of Counseling and Development, 92*(3), 328–337. https://doi.org/10.1002/j.1556-6676.2014.00160.x

Carpenter, A. L., Puliafico, A. C., Kurtz, S. M., Pincus, D. B., & Comer, J. S. (2014). Extending parent–child interaction therapy for early childhood internalizing problems: New advances for an overlooked population. *Clinical Child and Family Psychology Review, 17*(4), 340–356. https://doi.org/10.1007/s10567-014-0172-4

Cassidy, J., & Berlin, L. J. (1994). The insecure/ambivalent pattern of attachment: Theory and research. *Child Development, 65*(4), 971–991. https://doi.org/10.2307/1131298

Cassidy, J., Brett, B. E., Gross, J. T., Stern, J. A., Martin, D. R., Mohr, J. J., & Woodhouse, S. S. (2017). Circle of security–parenting: A randomized controlled trial in Head Start. *Development and Psychopathology, 29*(2), 651–673. https://doi.org/10.1017/S0954579417000244

Cassidy, J., Jones, J. D., & Shaver, P. R. (2013). Contributions of attachment theory and research: A framework for future research, translation, and policy. *Development and Psychopathology, 25*(4, Pt. 2), 1415–1434. https://doi.org/10.1017/S0954579413000692

Cassidy, J., & Shaver, P. R. (Eds.). (2016). *Handbook of attachment: Theory, research, and clinical applications* (3rd ed.). Guilford Press.

Cassidy, J., Woodhouse, S. S., Sherman, L. J., Stupica, B., & Lejuez, C. W. (2011). Enhancing infant attachment security: An examination of treatment efficacy and differential susceptibility. *Development and Psychopathology, 23*(1), 131–148. https://doi.org/10.1017/S0954579410000696

Catchpole, R., Young, A., Baer, S., & Salih, T. (2019). Examining a novel, parent child interaction therapy-informed, behavioral treatment of selective mutism. *Journal of Anxiety Disorders, 66*, 102112. https://doi.org/10.1016/j.janxdis.2019.102112

Ceballos, P. L., & Bratton, S. C. (2010). Empowering Latino families: Effects of a culturally responsive intervention for low-income immigrant Latino parents on children's behaviors and parental stress. *Psychology in the Schools, 47*(8), 761–775. https://doi.org/10.1002/pits.20502

Ceballos, P. L., Lin, Y. W., Bratton, S. C., & Lindo, N. (2019). Effects of parenting programs on Latina mothers' parental stress and their children's internalizing behavioral problems. *Journal of Child and Adolescent Counseling, 5*(1), 73–88. https://doi.org/10.1080/23727810.2018.1556983

Cecil, C. A., Viding, E., Fearon, P., Glaser, D., & McCrory, E. J. (2017). Disentangling the mental health impact of childhood abuse and neglect. *Child Abuse & Neglect, 63*, 106–119. https://doi.org/10.1016/j.chiabu.2016.11.024

Centers for Disease Control and Prevention. (2019, November 5). *Using time-out.* https://www.cdc.gov/parents/essentials/timeout/index.html

Centers for Disease Control and Prevention. (2020). *Preventing child abuse and neglect.* https://www.cdc.gov/violenceprevention/pdf/can/CAN-factsheet_2020.pdf

Chacko, A., Fabiano, G. A., Doctoroff, G. L., & Fortson, B. (2018). Engaging fathers in effective parenting for preschool children using shared book reading: A randomized controlled trial. *Journal of Clinical Child and Adolescent Psychology, 47*(1), 79–93. https://doi.org/10.1080/15374416.2016.1266648

Chaffin, M., Funderburk, B., Bard, D., Valle, L. A., & Gurwitch, R. (2011). A combined motivation and parent–child interaction therapy package reduces child welfare recidivism in a randomized dismantling field trial. *Journal of Consulting and Clinical Psychology, 79*(1), 84–95. https://doi.org/10.1037/a0021227

Chaffin, M., Silovsky, J. F., Funderburk, B., Valle, L. A., Brestan, E. V., Balachova, T., Jackson, S., Lensgraf, J., & Bonner, B. L. (2004). Parent–child interaction therapy with physically abusive parents: Efficacy for reducing future abuse reports. *Journal of Consulting and Clinical Psychology, 72*(3), 500–510. https://doi.org/10.1037/0022-006X.72.3.500

Chaffin, M., Valle, L. A., Funderburk, B., Gurwitch, R., Silovsky, J., Bard, D., McCoy, C., & Kees, M. (2009). A motivational intervention can improve retention in PCIT for low-motivation child welfare clients. *Child Maltreatment, 14*(4), 356–368. https://doi.org/10.1177/1077559509332263

Chamberlain, P., Feldman, S. W., Wulczyn, F., Saldana, L., & Forgatch, M. (2016). Implementation and evaluation of linked parenting models in a large urban child welfare system. *Child Abuse & Neglect, 53*, 27–39. https://doi.org/10.1016/j.chiabu.2015.09.013

Chambless, D. L., & Ollendick, T. H. (2001). Empirically supported psychological interventions: Controversies and evidence. *Annual Review of Psychology, 52*(1), 685–716. https://doi.org/10.1146/annurev.psych.52.1.685

Chaudron, L. H., Kitzman, H. J., Peifer, K. L., Morrow, S., Perez, L. M., & Newman, M. C. (2005). Self-recognition of and provider response to maternal depressive symptoms in low-income Hispanic women. *Journal of Women's Health, 14*(4), 331–338. https://doi.org/10.1089/jwh.2005.14.331

Chen, Y. C., & Fortson, B. L. (2015). Predictors of treatment attrition and treatment length in parent–child interaction therapy in Taiwanese families. *Children and Youth Services Review, 59*, 28–37. https://doi.org/10.1016/j.childyouth.2015.10.009

Cherry, K. E., Gerstein, E. D., & Ciciolla, L. (2019). Parenting stress and children's behavior: Transactional models during Early Head Start. *Journal of Family Psychology, 33*(8), 916–926. https://doi.org/10.1037/fam0000574

Cheung, K., & Theule, J. (2019). Paternal depressive symptoms and parenting behaviors: An updated meta-analysis. *Journal of Child and Family Studies, 28*(3), 613–626. https://doi.org/10.1007/s10826-018-01316-1

Chinitz, S., Guzman, H., Amstutz, E., Kohchi, J., & Alkon, M. (2017). Improving outcomes for babies and toddlers in child welfare: A model for infant mental health intervention and collaboration. *Child Abuse & Neglect, 70*, 190–198. https://doi.org/10.1016/j.chiabu.2017.05.015

Chorpita, B. F., Daleiden, E. L., Park, A. L., Ward, A. M., Levy, M. C., Cromley, T., Chiu, A. W., Letamendi, A. M., Tsai, K. H., & Krull, J. L. (2017). Child STEPs in California: A cluster randomized effectiveness trial comparing modular treatment with community implemented treatment for youth with anxiety, depression, conduct problems, or traumatic stress. *Journal of Consulting and Clinical Psychology, 85*(1), 13–25. https://doi.org/10.1037/ccp0000133

Christensen, A., Margolin, G., & Sullaway, M. (1992). Interparental agreement on child behavior problems. *Psychological Assessment, 4*(4), 419–425. https://doi.org/10.1037/1040-3590.4.4.419

Christian, A. S., Niec, L. N., Acevedo-Polakovich, I. D., & Kassab, V. A. (2014). Dissemination of an evidence-based parenting program: Clinician perspectives on training and implementation. *Children and Youth Services Review, 43*, 8–17. https://doi.org/10.1016/j.childyouth.2014.04.005

Christie, H., Hamilton-Giachritsis, C., Alves-Costa, F., Tomlinson, M., & Halligan, S. L. (2019). The impact of parental posttraumatic stress disorder on parenting: A systematic review. *European Journal of Psychotraumatology, 10*(1), 1550345. https://doi.org/10.1080/20008198.2018.1550345

Cicchetti, D., & Handley, E. D. (2019). Child maltreatment and the development of substance use and disorder. *Neurobiology of Stress, 10*, 100144. https://doi.org/10.1016/j.ynstr.2018.100144

Cicchetti, D., Rogosch, F. A., & Toth, S. L. (2006). Fostering secure attachment in infants in maltreating families through preventive interventions. *Development and Psychopathology, 18*(3), 623–649. https://doi.org/10.1017/S0954579406060329

Cicchetti, D., Rogosch, F. A., Toth, S. L., & Sturge-Apple, M. L. (2011). Normalizing the development of cortisol regulation in maltreated infants through preventive interventions. *Development and Psychopathology, 23*(3), 789–800. https://doi.org/10.1017/S0954579411000307

Clark, C. A. C., Massey, S. H., Wiebe, S. A., Espy, K. A., & Wakschlag, L. S. (2019). Does early maternal responsiveness buffer prenatal tobacco exposure effects on young children's behavioral disinhibition? *Development and Psychopathology, 31*(4), 1285–1298. https://doi.org/10.1017/S0954579418000706

Clay, R. A. (2020, June 11). *Are you experiencing compassion fatigue?* American Psychological Association. https://doi.org/10.1037/e505242020-001

Cohen, J. (1988). *Statistical power analysis for the behavioral sciences* (2nd ed.). Lawrence Erlbaum Associates.

Coley, R. L., Kull, M. A., & Carrano, J. (2014). Parental endorsement of spanking and children's internalizing and externalizing problems in African American and Hispanic families. *Journal of Family Psychology, 28*(1), 22–31. https://doi.org/10.1037/a0035272

Colich, N. L., Rosen, M. L., Williams, E. S., & McLaughlin, K. A. (2020). Biological aging in childhood and adolescence following experiences of threat and deprivation: A systematic review and meta-analysis. *Psychological Bulletin, 146*(9), 721–764. https://doi.org/10.1037/bul0000270

Comer, J. S., Furr, J. M., Cooper-Vince, C., Madigan, R. J., Chow, C., Chan, P., Idrobo, F., Chase, R. M., McNeil, C. B., & Eyberg, S. M. (2015). Rationale and considerations for the internet-based delivery of parent–child interaction therapy. *Cognitive and Behavioral Practice, 22*(3), 302–316. https://doi.org/10.1016/j.cbpra.2014.07.003

Comer, J. S., Furr, J. M., Miguel, E. M., Cooper-Vince, C. E., Carpenter, A. L., Elkins, R. M., Kerns, C. E., Cornacchio, D., Chou, T., Coxe, S., DeSerisy, M., Sanchez, A. L., Golik, A., Martin, J., Myers, K. M., & Chase, R. (2017). Remotely delivering real-time parent training to the home: An initial randomized trial of internet-delivered parent–child interaction therapy (I-PCIT). *Journal of*

Consulting and Clinical Psychology, 85(9), 909–917. https://doi.org/10.1037/ccp0000230

Comer, J. S., Puliafico, A. C., Aschenbrand, S. G., McKnight, K., Robin, J. A., Goldfine, M. E., & Albano, A. M. (2012). A pilot feasibility evaluation of the CALM program for anxiety disorders in early childhood. *Journal of Anxiety Disorders, 26*(1), 40–49. https://doi.org/10.1016/j.janxdis.2011.08.011

Comfort, M., & Gordon, P. R. (2006). The Keys to Interactive Parenting Scale (KIPS): A practical observational assessment of parenting behavior. *NHSA Dialog, 9*(1), 22–48. https://doi.org/10.1207/s19309325nhsa0901_4

Comfort, M., Gordon, P. R., & Naples, D. (2011). KIPS: An evidence-based tool for assessing parenting strengths and needs in diverse families. *Infants and Young Children, 24*(1), 56–74. https://doi.org/10.1097/IYC.0b013e3182001bd3

Comfort, M., Gordon, P. R., & Unger, D. G. (2006). Keys to Interactive Parenting Scale: A window into many facets of parenting. *Zero to Three Journal, 26*(5), 37–44.

Compas, B. E., Champion, J. E., Forehand, R., Cole, D. A., Reeslund, K. L., Fear, J., Hardcastle, E. J., Keller, G., Rakow, A., Garai, E., Merchant, M. J., & Roberts, L. (2010). Coping and parenting: Mediators of 12-month outcomes of a family group cognitive–behavioral preventive intervention with families of depressed parents. *Journal of Consulting and Clinical Psychology, 78*(5), 623–634. https://doi.org/10.1037/a0020459

Conway, L. J., Cook, F., Cahir, P., Mensah, F., Reilly, S., Brown, S., Gartland, D., & Giallo, R. (2021). Intimate partner violence, maternal depression, and pathways to children's language ability at 10 years. *Journal of Family Psychology, 35*(1), 112–122. https://doi.org/10.1037/fam0000804

Conyers, C., Miltenberger, R., Maki, A., Barenz, R., Jurgens, M., Sailer, A., Haugen, M., & Kopp, B. (2004). A comparison of response cost and differential reinforcement of other behavior to reduce disruptive behavior in a preschool classroom. *Journal of Applied Behavior Analysis, 37*(3), 411–415. https://doi.org/10.1901/jaba.2004.37-411

Cooper, G., Hoffman, K., & Powell, B. (2017). Circle of security in child care: Putting attachment theory into practice in preschool classrooms. *Zero to Three, 37*(3), 27–34.

Corralejo, S. M., Jensen, S. A., Greathouse, A. D., & Ward, L. E. (2018). Parameters of time-out: Research update and comparison to parenting programs, books, and online recommendations. *Behavior Therapy, 49*(1), 99–112. https://doi.org/10.1016/j.beth.2017.09.005

Cosson, B., & Graham, E. (2012). 'I felt like a third wheel': Fathers' stories of exclusion from the 'parenting team.' *Journal of Family Studies, 18*(2–3), 121–129. https://doi.org/10.5172/jfs.2012.18.2-3.121

Cronin, T. J., Pepping, C. A., & Lyons, A. (2019). Internalized transphobia and well-being: The moderating role of attachment. *Personality and Individual Differences, 143*, 80–83. https://doi.org/10.1016/j.paid.2019.02.018

Cross, D., Vance, L. A., Kim, Y. J., Ruchard, A. L., Fox, N., Jovanovic, T., & Bradley, B. (2018). Trauma exposure, PTSD, and parenting in a community sample of low-income, predominantly African American mothers and children. *Psychological Trauma: Theory, Research, Practice, and Policy, 10*(3), 327–335. https://doi.org/10.1037/tra0000264

Cunningham, C. E., Deal, K., Rimas, H., Buchanan, D. H., Gold, M., Sdao-Jarvie, K., & Boyle, M. (2008). Modeling the information preferences of parents of children with mental health problems: A discrete choice conjoint experiment. *Journal of Abnormal Child Psychology, 36*(7), 1123–1138. https://doi.org/10.1007/s10802-008-9238-4

Cusack, K. J., Frueh, B. C., & Brady, K. T. (2004). Trauma history screening in a community mental health center. *Psychiatric Services, 55*(2), 157–162. https://doi.org/10.1176/appi.ps.55.2.157

Cyr, C., Euser, E. M., Bakermans-Kranenburg, M. J., & Van IJzendoorn, M. H. (2010). Attachment security and disorganization in maltreating and high-risk families: A series of meta-analyses. *Development and Psychopathology, 22*(1), 87–108. https://doi.org/10.1017/S0954579409990289

Czeisler, M. É., Lane, R. I., Petrosky, E., Wiley, J. F., Christensen, A., Njai, R., Weaver, M. D., Robbins, R., Facer-Childs, E. R., Barger, L. K., Czeisler, C. A., Howard, M. E., & Rajaratnam, S. M. W. (2020). Mental health, substance use, and suicidal ideation during the COVID-19 pandemic—United States, June 24–30, 2020. *Morbidity and Mortality Weekly Report, 69*(32), 1049–1057. https://doi.org/10.15585/mmwr.mm6932a1

Dadds, M. R., & Tully, L. A. (2019). What is it to discipline a child: What should it be? A reanalysis of time-out from the perspective of child mental health, attachment, and trauma. *American Psychologist, 74*(7), 794–808. https://doi.org/10.1037/amp0000449

Dagan, O., Asok, A., Steele, H., Steele, M., & Bernard, K. (2018). Attachment security moderates the link between adverse childhood experiences and cellular aging. *Development and Psychopathology, 30*(4), 1211–1223. https://doi.org/10.1017/S0954579417001705

Damon, W., Callon, C., Wiebe, L., Small, W., Kerr, T., & McNeil, R. (2017). Community-based participatory research in a heavily researched inner city neighbourhood: Perspectives of people who use drugs on their experiences as peer researchers. *Social Science & Medicine, 176*, 85–92. https://doi.org/10.1016/j.socscimed.2017.01.027

Danko, C. M., Garbacz, L. L., & Budd, K. S. (2016). Outcomes of parent–child interaction therapy in an urban community clinic: A comparison of treatment completers and dropouts. *Children and Youth Services Review, 60*, 42–51. https://doi.org/10.1016/j.childyouth.2015.11.007

Dattilio, F. M. (2015). The self-care of psychologists and mental health professionals: A review and practitioner guide. *Australian Psychologist, 50*(6), 393–399. https://doi.org/10.1111/ap.12157

Davidov, M., & Grusec, J. E. (2006). Untangling the links of parental responsiveness to distress and warmth to child outcomes. *Child Development, 77*(1), 44–58. https://doi.org/10.1111/j.1467-8624.2006.00855.x

Davis, A. N., Carlo, G., & Crockett, L. J. (2020). The role of economic stress in parents' depression and warmth and adolescents' prosocial behaviors among US Latino/as. *Peace and Conflict, 26*(2), 162–170. https://doi.org/10.1037/pac0000406

Davison, K. K., Charles, J. N., Khandpur, N., & Nelson, T. J. (2017). Fathers' perceived reasons for their underrepresentation in child health research and strategies to increase their involvement. *Maternal and Child Health Journal, 21*(2), 267–274. https://doi.org/10.1007/s10995-016-2157-z

Debowska, A., Willmott, D., Boduszek, D., & Jones, A. D. (2017). What do we know about child abuse and neglect patterns of co-occurrence? A systematic review of profiling studies and recommendations for future research. *Child Abuse & Neglect, 70*, 100–111. https://doi.org/10.1016/j.chiabu.2017.06.014

De Falco, S., Emer, A., Martini, L., Rigo, P., Pruner, S., & Venuti, P. (2014). Predictors of mother–child interaction quality and child attachment security in at-risk families. *Frontiers in Psychology, 5*, 898. https://doi.org/10.3389/fpsyg.2014.00898

De Los Reyes, A., Augenstein, T. M., Wang, M., Thomas, S. A., Drabick, D. A. G., Burgers, D. E., & Rabinowitz, J. (2015). The validity of the multi-informant approach to assessing child and adolescent mental health. *Psychological Bulletin, 141*(4), 858–900. https://doi.org/10.1037/a0038498

DelTosta, J. E., Ellis, M. V., & McNamara, M. L. (2019). Trainee vicarious traumatization: Examining supervisory working alliance and trainee empathy. *Training and Education in Professional Psychology, 13*(4), 300–306. https://doi.org/10.1037/tep0000232

Del Vecchio, T., & Rhoades, K. A. (2010). Bidirectional influences in mother–toddler dyads: An examination of the relative influence of mothers' and children's behaviours. *Infant and Child Development, 19*(5), 516–529. https://doi.org/10.1002/icd.674

DePasquale, C. E., Handley, E. D., & Cicchetti, D. (2019). Investigating multilevel pathways of developmental consequences of maltreatment. *Development and Psychopathology, 31*(4), 1227–1236. https://doi.org/10.1017/S0954579418000834

Derogatis, L. R., & Savitz, K. L. (2000). The SCL–90–R and Brief Symptom Inventory (BSI) in primary care. In M. E. Maruish (Ed.), *Handbook of psychological assessment in primary care settings* (pp. 297–334). Lawrence Erlbaum Associates.

De Wolff, M. S., & van IJzendoorn, M. H. (1997). Sensitivity and attachment: A meta-analysis on parental antecedents of infant attachment. *Child Development, 68*(4), 571–591. https://doi.org/10.1111/j.1467-8624.1997.tb04218.x

Di Bartolo, C. A., & Braun, M. K. (2017). *Pediatrician's guide to discussing research with patients*. Springer. https://doi.org/10.1007/978-3-319-49547-7

DiClemente, C. C., & Prochaska, J. O. (1998). Toward a comprehensive, transtheoretical model of change: Stages of change and addictive behaviors. In W. R. Miller & N. Heather (Eds.), *Treating addictive behaviors* (2nd ed., pp. 3–24). Plenum. https://doi.org/10.1007/978-1-4899-1934-2_1

Diener, M. J., Geenen, R., Koelen, J. A., Aarts, F., Gerdes, V. E., Brandjes, D. P., & Hinnen, C. (2016). The significance of attachment quality for obesity: A meta-analytic review. *Canadian Journal of Behavioural Science, 48*(4), 255–265. https://doi.org/10.1037/cbs0000050

Ding, X., Ansari, A., Li, X., Liu, Y., & Yan, N. (2020). Transactional effects between parental sensitivity and child social adjustment: Specifying trait–state aspects of parenting. *Developmental Psychology, 56*(7), 1331–1342. https://doi.org/10.1037/dev0000963

Ding, Y.-h., Xu, X., Wang, Z.-y., Li, H.-r., & Wang, W.-p. (2012). Study of mother–infant attachment patterns and influence factors in Shanghai. *Early Human Development, 88*(5), 295–300. https://doi.org/10.1016/j.earlhumdev.2011.08.023

Dix, T. (1991). The affective organization of parenting: Adaptive and maladaptive processes. *Psychological Bulletin, 110*(1), 3–25. https://doi.org/10.1037/0033-2909.110.1.3

Domoff, S. E., & Niec, L. N. (2018). Parent–child interaction therapy as a prevention model for childhood obesity: A novel application for high-risk families. *Children and Youth Services Review, 91,* 77–84. https://doi.org/10.1016/j.childyouth.2018.05.024

Doty, J. L., Davis, L., & Arditti, J. A. (2017). Cascading resilience: Leverage points in promoting parent and child well-being. *Journal of Family Theory & Review, 9*(1), 111–126. https://doi.org/10.1111/jftr.12175

Dozier, M., & Rutter, M. (2016). Challenges to the development of attachment relationships faced by children in foster and adoptive care. In J. Cassidy & P. Shaver (Eds.), *Handbook of attachment: Theory, research, and clinical applications* (3rd ed., pp. 696–714). Guilford Press.

Drayton, A. K., Andersen, M. N., Knight, R. M., Felt, B. T., Fredericks, E. M., & Dore-Stites, D. J. (2014). Internet guidance on time out: Inaccuracies, omissions, and what to tell parents instead. *Journal of Developmental and Behavioral Pediatrics, 35*(4), 239–246. https://doi.org/10.1097/DBP.0000000000000059

Drayton, A. K., Byrd, M. R., Albright, J. J., Nelson, E. M., Andersen, M. N., & Morris, N. K. (2017). Deconstructing the time-out: What do mothers understand about a common disciplinary procedure? *Child & Family Behavior Therapy, 39*(2), 91–107. https://doi.org/10.1080/07317107.2017.1307677

Dreison, K. C., Luther, L., Bonfils, K. A., Sliter, M. T., McGrew, J. H., & Salyers, M. P. (2018). Job burnout in mental health providers: A meta-analysis of 35 years of intervention research. *Journal of Occupational Health Psychology, 23*(1), 18–30. https://doi.org/10.1037/ocp0000047

Driscoll, K., & Pianta, R. C. (2011). Mothers' and fathers' perceptions of conflict and closeness in parent–child relationships during early childhood. *Journal of Early Childhood and Infant Psychology, 7,* 1–24.

Drury, S. S., Theall, K., Gleason, M. M., Smyke, A. T., De Vivo, I., Wong, J. Y. Y., Fox, N. A., Zeanah, C. H., & Nelson, C. A. (2012). Telomere length and early severe social deprivation: Linking early adversity and cellular aging. *Molecular Psychiatry, 17*(7), 719–727. https://doi.org/10.1038/mp.2011.53

Dunst, C. J., & Kassow, D. Z. (2008). Caregiver sensitivity, contingent social responsiveness, and secure infant attachment. *Journal of Early and Intensive Behavior Intervention, 5*(1), 40–56. https://doi.org/10.1037/h0100409

Du Rocher Schudlich, T. D., Jessica, N. W., Erwin, S. E., & Rishor, A. (2019). Infants' emotional security: The confluence of parental depression, interparental conflict, and parenting. *Journal of Applied Developmental Psychology, 63,* 42–53. https://doi.org/10.1016/j.appdev.2019.05.006

Dyer, W. J., Kaufman, R., & Fagan, J. (2017). Father–child closeness and conflict: Validating measures for nonresident fathers. *Journal of Family Psychology, 31*(8), 1074–1080. https://doi.org/10.1037/fam0000384

Ebrahimi, L., Amiri, M., Mohamadlou, M., & Rezapur, R. (2017). Attachment styles, parenting styles, and depression. *International Journal of Mental Health and Addiction, 15*(5), 1064–1068. https://doi.org/10.1007/s11469-017-9770-y

Edwards, E. P., Eiden, R. D., & Leonard, K. E. (2006). Behaviour problems in 18- to 36-month old children of alcoholic fathers: Secure mother–infant attachment as a protective factor. *Development and Psychopathology, 18*(2), 395–407. https://doi.org/10.1017/S0954579406060214

Eisenstadt, T. H., Eyberg, S., McNeil, C. B., Newcomb, K., & Funderburk, B. (1993). Parent–child interaction therapy with behavior problem children: Relative effectiveness of two stages and overall treatment outcome. *Journal of Clinical Child Psychology, 22*(1), 42–51. https://doi.org/10.1207/s15374424jccp2201_4

Elsaesser, C. (2018). The longitudinal relations between dimensions of community violence exposure and developmental outcomes among adolescent ethnic minority males. *Psychology of Violence, 8*(4), 409–417. https://doi.org/10.1037/vio0000140

England, M., & Sim, L. (Eds.). (2009). *Depression in parents, parenting, and children: Opportunities to improve identification, treatment, and prevention.* National Academies Press.

Epkins, C. C., & Harper, S. L. (2016). Mothers' and fathers' parental warmth, hostility/rejection/neglect, and behavioral control: Specific and unique relations with parents' depression versus anxiety symptoms. *Parenting, 16*(2), 125–145. https://doi.org/10.1080/15295192.2016.1134991

Epstein, R. A., Fonnesbeck, C., Potter, S., Rizzone, K. H., & McPheeters, M. (2015). Psychosocial interventions for child disruptive behaviors: A meta-analysis. *Pediatrics, 136*(5), 947–960. https://doi.org/10.1542/peds.2015-2577

Eshel, N., Daelmans, B., de Mello, M. C., & Martines, J. (2006). Responsive parenting: Interventions and outcomes. *Bulletin of the World Health Organization, 84*(12), 991–998. https://doi.org/10.2471/BLT.06.030163

Ettekal, I., Eiden, R. D., Nickerson, A. B., Molnar, D. S., & Schuetze, P. (2020). Developmental cascades to children's conduct problems: The role of prenatal substance use, socioeconomic adversity, maternal depression and sensitivity, and children's conscience. *Development and Psychopathology, 32*(1), 85–103. https://doi.org/10.1017/S095457941800144X

Evans, G. W. (2004). The environment of childhood poverty. *American Psychologist, 59*(2), 77–92. https://doi.org/10.1037/0003-066X.59.2.77

Everett, G. E., Hupp, S. D. A., & Olmi, D. J. (2010). Time-out with parents: A descriptive analysis of 30 years of research. *Education & Treatment of Children, 33*(2), 235–259. https://doi.org/10.1353/etc.0.0091

Everett, G. E., Olmi, D. J., Edwards, R. P., Tingstrom, D. H., Sterling-Turner, H. E., & Christ, T. J. (2007). An empirical investigation of time-out with and without escape extinction to treat escape-maintained noncompliance. *Behavior Modification, 31*(4), 412–434. https://doi.org/10.1177/0145445506297725

Ewart-Boyle, S., Manktelow, R., & McColgan, M. (2015). Social work and the shadow father: Lessons for engaging fathers in Northern Ireland. *Child & Family Social Work, 20*(4), 470–479. https://doi.org/10.1111/cfs.12096

Eyberg, S. M., Boggs, S. R., & Algina, J. (1995). Parent–child interaction therapy: A psychosocial model for the treatment of young children with conduct problem behavior and their families. *Psychopharmacology Bulletin, 31*(1), 83–91.

Eyberg, S. M., Chase, R. M., Fernandez, M. A., & Nelson, M. M. (2014). *Dyadic Parent–Child Interaction Coding System (DPICS) clinical manual* (4th ed.). PCIT International.

Eyberg, S. M., & Funderburk, B. (2011). *Parent–child interaction therapy protocol.* Parent–Child Interaction Therapy International.

Eyberg, S. M., Funderburk, B. W., Hembree-Kigin, T. L., McNeil, C. B., Querido, J. G., & Hood, K. K. (2001). Parent–child interaction therapy with behavior problem children: One and two year maintenance of treatment effects in the family. *Child & Family Behavior Therapy, 23*(4), 1–20. https://doi.org/10.1300/J019v23n04_01

Eyberg, S. M., Nelson, M. M., Gin, N. C., Bhuiyan, N., & Boggs, S. R. (2014). *Dyadic Parent–Child Interaction Coding System (DPICS): Comprehensive manual for research and training* (4th ed.). PCIT International.

Eyberg, S. M., & Pincus, D. (1999). *Eyberg Child Behavior Inventory & Sutter-Eyberg Student Behavior Inventory–Revised: Professional manual.* Psychological Assessment Resources.

Eyberg, S. M., & Robinson, E. A. (1982). Parent–child interaction training: Effects on family functioning. *Journal of Clinical Child and Adolescent Psychology, 11*(2), 130–137. https://doi.org/10.1207/s15374424jccp1102_6

Fabiano, G. A., & Caserta, A. (2018). Future directions in father inclusion, engagement, retention, and positive outcomes in child and adolescent research. *Journal of Clinical Child and Adolescent Psychology, 47*(5), 847–862. https://doi.org/10.1080/15374416.2018.1485106

Fabiano, G. A., Pelham, W. E., Jr., Manos, M. J., Gnagy, E. M., Chronis, A. M., Onyango, A. N., Lopez-Williams, A., Burrows-MacLean, L., Cole, E. K., Meichenbaum, D. L., Caserta, D. A., & Swain, S. (2004). An evaluation of three time-out procedures for children with attention-deficit/hyperactivity disorder. *Behavior Therapy, 35*(3), 449–469. https://doi.org/10.1016/S0005-7894(04)80027-3

Farber, B. A. (1985). Clinical psychologists' perceptions of psychotherapeutic work. *The Clinical Psychologist, 38*(1), 10–13.

Fearon, P., Shmueli-Goetz, Y., Viding, E., Fonagy, P., & Plomin, R. (2014). Genetic and environmental influences on adolescent attachment. *Journal of Child Psychology and Psychiatry, 55*(9), 1033–1041. https://doi.org/10.1111/jcpp.12171

Fearon, R. M. P., & Belsky, J. (2016). Precursors of attachment security. In J. Cassidy & P. R. Shaver (Eds.), *Handbook of attachment: Theory, research, and clinical applications* (3rd ed., pp. 291–313). The Guilford Press.

Fearon, R. P., Bakermans-Kranenburg, M. J., van IJzendoorn, M. H., Lapsley, A. M., & Roisman, G. I. (2010). The significance of insecure attachment and disorganization in the development of children's externalizing behavior: A meta-analytic study. *Child Development, 81*(2), 435–456. https://doi.org/10.1111/j.1467-8624.2009.01405.x

Fedewa, A. L., Black, W. W., & Ahn, S. (2015). Children and adolescents with same-gender parents: A meta-analytic approach in assessing outcomes. *Journal of GLBT Family Studies, 11*(1), 1–34. https://doi.org/10.1080/1550428X.2013.869486

Felitti, V. J., Anda, R. F., Nordenberg, D., Williamson, D. F., Spitz, A. M., Edwards, V., Koss, M. P., & Marks, J. S. (1998). Relationship of childhood abuse and household dysfunction to many of the leading causes of death in adults. The Adverse Childhood Experiences (ACE) Study. *American Journal of Preventive Medicine, 14*(4), 245–258. https://doi.org/10.1016/S0749-3797(98)00017-8

Fernandez, M. A., Adelstein, J. S., Miller, S. P., Areizaga, M. J., Gold, D. C., Sanchez, A. L., Rothschild, S. A., Hirsch, E., & Gudiño, O. G. (2015). Teacher–child interaction training: A pilot study with random assignment. *Behavior Therapy, 46*(4), 463–477. https://doi.org/10.1016/j.beth.2015.02.002

Fernandez, M. A., Butler, A. M., & Eyberg, S. M. (2011). Treatment outcome for low socioeconomic status African American families in parent–child interaction therapy: A pilot study. *Child & Family Behavior Therapy, 33*(1), 32–48. https://doi.org/10.1080/07317107.2011.545011

Ferreira, T., Cadima, J., Matias, M., Vieira, J. M., Leal, T., & Matos, P. M. (2016). Preschool children's prosocial behavior: The role of mother–child, father–child and teacher–child relationships. *Journal of Child and Family Studies, 25*(6), 1829–1839. https://doi.org/10.1007/s10826-016-0369-x

Figley, C. R. (1995). Compassion fatigue as secondary traumatic stress disorder: An overview. In C. R. Figley (Ed.), *Compassion fatigue: Coping with secondary traumatic stress disorder in those who treat the traumatized* (pp. 1–20). Brunner-Rutledge.

Finkelhor, D., Turner, H., Ormrod, R., & Hamby, S. L. (2009). Violence, abuse, and crime exposure in a national sample of children and youth. *Pediatrics, 124*(5), 1411–1423. https://doi.org/10.1542/peds.2009-0467

Fitzhugh Mullan Institute for Health Workforce Equity. (2020, August). *The social work profession: Findings from three years of surveys of new social workers*. https://www.socialworkers.org/LinkClick.aspx?fileticket=1_j2EXVNspY%3D&portalid=0

Flouri, E., Papachristou, E., Midouhas, E., Ploubidis, G. B., Lewis, G., & Joshi, H. (2019). Developmental cascades of internalising symptoms, externalising problems and cognitive ability from early childhood to middle adolescence. *European Psychiatry, 57*, 61–69. https://doi.org/10.1016/j.eurpsy.2018.12.005

Forehand, R., Thigpen, J. C., Parent, J., Hardcastle, E. J., Bettis, A., & Compas, B. E. (2012). The role of parent depressive symptoms in positive and negative parenting in a preventive intervention. *Journal of Family Psychology, 26*(4), 532–541. https://doi.org/10.1037/a0028406

Fowler, P. J., Tompsett, C. J., Braciszewski, J. M., Jacques-Tiura, A. J., & Baltes, B. B. (2009). Community violence: A meta-analysis on the effect of exposure and mental health outcomes of children and adolescents. *Development and Psychopathology, 21*(1), 227–259. https://doi.org/10.1017/S0954579409000145

Fraiberg, S. (1980). *Clinical studies in infant mental health: The first year of life*. Basic Books.

Fraley, R. C. (2002). Attachment stability from infancy to adulthood: Meta-analysis and dynamic modeling of developmental mechanisms. *Personality and Social Psychology Review, 6*(2), 123–151. https://doi.org/10.1207/S15327957PSPR0602_03

Frank, T. J., Keown, L. J., Dittman, C. K., & Sanders, M. R. (2015). Using father preference data to increase father engagement in evidence-based parenting programs. *Journal of Child and Family Studies, 24*(4), 937–947. https://doi.org/10.1007/s10826-014-9904-9

Frank, T. J., Keown, L. J., & Sanders, M. R. (2015). Enhancing father engagement and interparental teamwork in an evidence-based parenting intervention: A randomized-controlled trial of outcomes and processes. *Behavior Therapy, 46*(6), 749–763. https://doi.org/10.1016/j.beth.2015.05.008

Freedenfeld, R. N., Ornduff, S. R., & Kelsey, R. M. (1995). Object relations and physical abuse: A TAT analysis. *Journal of Personality Assessment, 64*(3), 552–568. https://doi.org/10.1207/s15327752jpa6403_12

Friedman, R. (1985). Making family therapy easier for the therapist: Burnout prevention. *Family Process, 24*(4), 549–553. https://doi.org/10.1111/j.1545-5300.1985.00549.x

Frosch, C. A., Mangelsdorf, S. C., & McHale, J. L. (2000). Marital behavior and the security of preschooler-parent attachment relationships. *Journal of Family Psychology, 14*(1), 144–161. https://doi.org/10.1037/0893-3200.14.1.144

Fuertes, M., Faria, A., Beeghly, M., & Lopes-dos-Santos, P. (2016). The effects of parental sensitivity and involvement in caregiving on mother–infant and father–infant attachment in a Portuguese sample. *Journal of Family Psychology, 30*(1), 147–156. https://doi.org/10.1037/fam0000139

Funderburk, B. W., Eyberg, S. M., Newcomb, K., McNeil, C. B., Hembree-Kigin, T., & Capage, L. (1998). Parent–child interaction therapy with behavior problem children: Maintenance of treatment effects in the school setting. *Child & Family Behavior Therapy, 20*(2), 17–38. https://doi.org/10.1300/J019v20n02_02

Funk, M., Drew, N., & Knapp, M. (2012). Mental health, poverty and development. *Journal of Public Mental Health, 11*(4), 166–185. https://doi.org/10.1108/17465721211289356

Galanter, R., Self-Brown, S., Valente, J. R., Dorsey, S., Whitaker, D. J., Bertuglia-Haley, M., & Prieto, M. (2012). Effectiveness of parent–child interaction therapy delivered to at-risk families in the home setting. *Child & Family Behavior Therapy, 34*(3), 177–196. https://doi.org/10.1080/07317107.2012.707079

Galatzer-Levy, I. R., Huang, S. H., & Bonanno, G. A. (2018). Trajectories of resilience and dysfunction following potential trauma: A review and statistical evaluation. *Clinical Psychology Review, 63*, 41–55. https://doi.org/10.1016/j.cpr.2018.05.008

Galdas, P. M., Cheater, F., & Marshall, P. (2005). Men and health help-seeking behaviour: Literature review. *Journal of Advanced Nursing, 49*(6), 616–623. https://doi.org/10.1111/j.1365-2648.2004.03331.x

Ganong, L., Jensen, T., Sanner, C., Russell, L., & Coleman, M. (2019). Stepfathers' affinity-seeking with stepchildren, stepfather–stepchild relationship quality, marital quality, and stepfamily cohesion among stepfathers and mothers. *Journal of Family Psychology, 33*(5), 521–531. https://doi.org/10.1037/fam0000518

Garbacz, L. L., Zychinski, K. C., Feuer, R., Carter, J. S., & Budd, K. S. (2014). The impact of Teacher–Child Interaction Training on teachers' skills and children's behaviors. *Psychology in the Schools, 51*, 850–865. https://doi.org/10.1002/pits.21788

García, J. I. R., Manongdo, J. A., & Ozechowski, T. J. (2014). Depression symptoms among Mexican American youth: Paternal parenting in the context of maternal parenting, economic stress, and youth gender. *Cultural Diversity & Ethnic Minority Psychology, 20*(1), 27–36. https://doi.org/10.1037/a0033350

Gardner, M. J., Thomas, H. J., & Erskine, H. E. (2019). The association between five forms of child maltreatment and depressive and anxiety disorders: A systematic review and meta-analysis. *Child Abuse & Neglect, 96*, 104082. https://doi.org/10.1016/j.chiabu.2019.104082

Garner, A., & Saul, R. (2018). *Thinking developmentally: Nurturing wellness in childhood to promote lifelong health*. American Academy of Pediatrics.

Gaylord-Harden, N. K., Bai, G. J., So, S., & Tolan, P. H. (2018). Impact of maternal support and involvement on coping in adolescent males of color. *Journal of Child and Family Studies, 27*(10), 3262–3276. https://doi.org/10.1007/s10826-018-1166-5

George Washington University Health Workforce Institute and School of Nursing. (2017, October). *Profile of the social work workforce*. https://www.socialworkers.org/LinkClick.aspx?fileticket=wCttjrHq0gE%3d&portalid=0

Gerhart, J. I., Sanchez Varela, V., Burns, J. W., Hobfoll, S. E., & Fung, H. C. (2015). Anger, provider responses, and pain: Prospective analysis of stem cell transplant patients. *Health Psychology, 34*(3), 197–206. https://doi.org/10.1037/hea0000095

Gershoff, E. T. (2002). Corporal punishment by parents and associated child behaviors and experiences: A meta-analytic and theoretical review. *Psychological Bulletin, 128*(4), 539–579. https://doi.org/10.1037/0033-2909.128.4.539

Gewirtz, A. H., Erbes, C. R., Polusny, M. A., Forgatch, M. S., & Degarmo, D. S. (2011). Helping military families through the deployment process: Strategies to support parenting. *Professional Psychology, Research and Practice, 42*(1), 56–62. https://doi.org/10.1037/a0022345

Ginn, N. C., Clionsky, L. N., Eyberg, S. M., Warner-Metzger, C., & Abner, J. P. (2017). Child-directed interaction training for young children with autism spectrum disorders: Parent and child outcomes. *Journal of Clinical Child and Adolescent Psychology, 46*(1), 101–109. https://doi.org/10.1080/15374416.2015.1015135

Glover, G. J., & Landreth, G. L. (2000). Filial therapy with Native Americans on the Flathead reservation. *International Journal of Play Therapy, 9*(2), 57–80. https://doi.org/10.1037/h0089436

Glynn, L., & Dale, M. (2015). Engaging dads: Enhancing support for fathers through parenting programmes. *Aotearoa New Zealand Social Work, 27*(1–2), 59–72. https://doi.org/10.11157/anzswj-vol27iss1-2id17

Gold, C. (2015). Quantitative psychotherapy outcome research: Methodological issues. In O. C. G. Gelo, A. Pritz, & B. Ricken (Eds.), *Psychotherapy research: Foundations, process, and outcome* (pp. 537–558). Springer.

Golm, D., Maughan, B., Barker, E. D., Hill, J., Kennedy, M., Knights, N., Kreppner, J., Kumsta, R., Schlotz, W., Rutter, M., & Sonuga-Barke, E. J. S. (2020). Why does early childhood deprivation increase the risk for depression and anxiety in adulthood? A developmental cascade model. *Journal of Child Psychology and Psychiatry, 61*(9), 1043–1053. https://doi.org/10.1111/jcpp.13205

Golombok, S., Mellish, L., Jennings, S., Casey, P., Tasker, F., & Lamb, M. E. (2014). Adoptive gay father families: Parent–child relationships and children's psychological adjustment. *Child Development, 85*(2), 456–468. https://doi.org/10.1111/cdev.12155

Gonzales, N. A., Liu, Y., Jensen, M., Tein, J. Y., White, R. M. B., & Deardorff, J. (2017). Externalizing and internalizing pathways to Mexican American adolescents' risk taking. *Development and Psychopathology, 29*(4), 1371–1390. https://doi.org/10.1017/S0954579417000323

Gonzalez, M. A., & Jones, D. J. (2016). Cascading effects of BPT for child internalizing problems and caregiver depression. *Clinical Psychology Review, 50*, 11–21. https://doi.org/10.1016/j.cpr.2016.09.007

Good, G. E., Khairallah, T., & Mintz, L. B. (2009). Wellness and impairment: Moving beyond noble us and troubled them. *Clinical Psychology: Science and Practice, 16*(1), 21–23. https://doi.org/10.1111/j.1468-2850.2009.01139.x

Goodman, R. (1997). The Strengths and Difficulties Questionnaire: A research note. *Journal of Child Psychology and Psychiatry, 38*(5), 581–586. https://doi.org/10.1111/j.1469-7610.1997.tb01545.x

Goodman, S. H., Rouse, M. H., Connell, A. M., Broth, M. R., Hall, C. M., & Heyward, D. (2011). Maternal depression and child psychopathology: A meta-analytic review. *Clinical Child and Family Psychology Review, 14*(1), 1–27. https://doi.org/10.1007/s10567-010-0080-1

Gordon, M. S. (2016). Community disadvantage and adolescent's academic achievement: The mediating role of father influence. *Journal of Child and Family Studies, 25*(7), 2069–2078. https://doi.org/10.1007/s10826-016-0380-2

Graceffo, R. A., Mihura, J. L., & Meyer, G. J. (2014). A meta-analysis of an implicit measure of personality functioning: The Mutuality of Autonomy Scale. *Journal of Personality Assessment, 96*(6), 581–595. https://doi.org/10.1080/00223891.2014.919299

Granic, I., & Patterson, G. R. (2006). Toward a comprehensive model of antisocial development: A dynamic systems approach. *Psychological Review, 113*(1), 101–131. https://doi.org/10.1037/0033-295X.113.1.101

Greene, C. A., McCarthy, K. J., Estabroo, R., Wakschlag, L. S., & Briggs-Gowa, M. J. (2020). Responsive parenting buffers the impact of maternal PTSD on young children. *Parenting, 20*(2), 141–165. https://doi.org/10.1080/15295192.2019.1707623

Griffiths, A., Royse, D., Murphy, A., & Starks, S. (2019). Self-care practice in social work education: A systematic review of interventions. *Journal of Social Work Education, 55*(1), 102–114. https://doi.org/10.1080/10437797.2018.1491358

Grise-Owens, E., Miller, J. J., Escobar-Ratliff, L., & George, N. (2018). Teaching note—Teaching self-care and wellness as a professional practice skill: A curricular case example. *Journal of Social Work Education, 54*(1), 180–186. https://doi.org/10.1080/10437797.2017.1308778

Groh, A. M., Fearon, R. P., van IJzendoorn, M. H., Bakermans-Kranenburg, M. J., & Roisman, G. I. (2017). Attachment in the early life course: Meta-analytic evidence for its role in socioemotional development. *Child Development Perspectives, 11*(1), 70–76. https://doi.org/10.1111/cdep.12213

Groh, A. M., Roisman, G. I., van Ijzendoorn, M. H., Bakermans-Kranenburg, M. J., & Fearon, R. P. (2012). The significance of insecure and disorganized attachment for children's internalizing symptoms: A meta-analytic study. *Child Development, 83*(2), 591–610. https://doi.org/10.1111/j.1467-8624.2011.01711.x

Grossman, J. M., Black, A. C., Richer, A. M., & Lynch, A. D. (2019). Parenting practices and emerging adult sexual health: The role of residential fathers. *The Journal of Primary Prevention, 40*(5), 505–528. https://doi.org/10.1007/s10935-019-00560-5

Guild, D. J., Toth, S. L., Handley, E. D., Rogosch, F. A., & Cicchetti, D. (2017). Attachment security mediates the longitudinal association between child–parent psychotherapy and peer relations for toddlers of depressed mothers. *Development and Psychopathology, 29*(2), 587–600. https://doi.org/10.1017/S0954579417000207

Gunnar, M., & Quevedo, K. (2007). The neurobiology of stress and development. *Annual Review of Psychology, 58*(1), 145–173. https://doi.org/10.1146/annurev.psych.58.110405.085605

Gurwitch, R. H., Salem, H., Nelson, M. M., & Comer, J. S. (2020). Leveraging parent–child interaction therapy and telehealth capacities to address the unique needs of young children during the COVID-19 public health crisis. *Psychological Trauma: Theory, Research, Practice, and Policy, 12*(S1), S82–S84. https://doi.org/10.1037/tra0000863

Gustafsson, H. C., Coffman, J. L., & Cox, M. J. (2015). Intimate partner violence, maternal sensitive parenting behaviors, and children's executive functioning. *Psychology of Violence, 5*(3), 266–274. https://doi.org/10.1037/a0037971

Gutman, L. M. (2019). Do conduct problem pathways differ for Black and minority ethnic children in the UK? An examination of trajectories from early childhood to adolescence. *Journal of Youth and Adolescence, 48*(10), 1967–1979. https://doi.org/10.1007/s10964-019-01116-w

Hackman, D. A., O'Brien, J. R., & Zalewski, M. (2018). Enduring association between parenting and cortisol: A meta-analysis. *Child Development, 89*(5), 1485–1503. https://doi.org/10.1111/cdev.13077

Hagan, M. J., Browne, D. T., Sulik, M., Ippen, C. G., Bush, N., & Lieberman, A. F. (2017). Parent and child trauma symptoms during child–parent psychotherapy: A prospective cohort study of dyadic change. *Journal of Traumatic Stress, 30*(6), 690–697. https://doi.org/10.1002/jts.22240

Haine-Schlagel, R., & Walsh, N. E. (2015). A review of parent participation engagement in child and family mental health treatment. *Clinical Child and Family Psychology Review, 18*(2), 133–150. https://doi.org/10.1007/s10567-015-0182-x

Halevi, E., & Idisis, Y. (2018). Who helps the helper? Differentiation of self as an indicator for resisting vicarious traumatization. *Psychological Trauma: Theory, Research, Practice, and Policy, 10*(6), 698–705. https://doi.org/10.1037/tra0000318

Haller, M., Handley, E., Chassin, L., & Bountress, K. (2010). Developmental cascades: Linking adolescent substance use, affiliation with substance use promoting peers, and academic achievement to adult substance use disorders. *Development and Psychopathology, 22*(4), 899–916. https://doi.org/10.1017/S0954579410000532

Hamby, S., Finkelhor, D., Turner, H., & Ormrod, R. (2011, October). *Children's exposure to intimate partner violence and other family violence.* U.S. Department of Justice. https://doi.org/10.1037/e725322011-001

Handley, E. D., Michl-Petzing, L. C., Rogosch, F. A., Cicchetti, D., & Toth, S. L. (2017). Developmental cascade effects of interpersonal psychotherapy for depressed mothers: Longitudinal associations with toddler attachment, temperament, and maternal parenting efficacy. *Development and Psychopathology, 29*(2), 601–615. https://doi.org/10.1017/S0954579417000219

Handley, E. D., Russotti, J., Rogosch, F. A., & Cicchetti, D. (2019). Developmental cascades from child maltreatment to negative friend and romantic interactions in emerging adulthood. *Development and Psychopathology, 31*(5), 1649–1659. https://doi.org/10.1017/S095457941900124X

Hardy, D. F., Power, T. G., & Jaedicke, S. (1993). Examining the relation of parenting to children's coping with everyday stress. *Child Development, 64*(6), 1829–1841. https://doi.org/10.2307/1131472

Haskett, M. E., Smith Scott, S., Grant, R., Ward, C. S., & Robinson, C. (2003). Child-related cognitions and affective functioning of physically abusive and comparison parents. *Child Abuse & Neglect, 27*(6), 663–686. https://doi.org/10.1016/S0145-2134(03)00103-0

Hatchel, T., Polanin, J. R., & Espelage, D. L. (2021). Suicidal thoughts and behaviors among LGBTQ youth: Meta-analyses and a systematic review. *Archives of Suicide Research, 25*(1), 1–37. https://doi.org/10.1080/13811118.2019.1663329

Hatzinikolaou, K., Karveli, V., Skoubourdi, A., Zarokosta, F., Antonucci, G., Visci, G., Calheiros, M. M., MagalhÃes, E., Essau, C., Allan, S., Pithia, J., Walji, F., Ezpeleta, L., Perez-Robles, R., Fanti, K. A., Katsimicha, E., Hadjicharambous, M. Z., Nikolaidis, G., & Reddy, V. (2016). Using the parent–infant relationship global assessment scale to identify caregiver–infant/toddler dyads with abusive relationship patterns in six European countries. *Infant Mental Health Journal, 37*(4), 335–355. https://doi.org/10.1002/imhj.21577

Hayes, S. C., Bissett, R., Roget, N., Padilla, M., Kohlenberg, B. S., Fisher, G., Masuda, A. A., Pistorello, J., Rye, A. K., Berry, K., & Niccolls, R. (2004). The impact of acceptance and commitment training and multicultural training on the stigmatizing attitudes and professional burnout of substance abuse counselors. *Behavior Therapy, 35*(4), 821–835. https://doi.org/10.1016/S0005-7894(04)80022-4

Health Resources and Services Administration. (2021). *Designated health professional shortage areas statistics: Second quarter of fiscal year 2021 designated HPSA quarterly summary as of March 2021.*

Henry, L. M., Forehand, R., Watson, K. H., Gruhn, M., Bettis, A. H., McKee, L. G., & Compas, B. E. (2018). Parental depressive symptoms and parenting: Associations with children's coping in families of depressed parents. *Parenting, 18*(4), 281–296. https://doi.org/10.1080/15295192.2018.1529453

Hesse, E. (2016). The Adult Attachment Interview: Protocol, method of analysis, and empirical studies: 1985–2015. In J. Cassidy & P. Shaver (Eds.), *Handbook of attachment: Theory, research, and clinical applications* (3rd ed., pp. 553–597). Guilford Press.

Hicks, B., & Baggerly, J. (2017). The effectiveness of child parent relationship therapy in an online format. *International Journal of Play Therapy, 26*(3), 138–150. https://doi.org/10.1037/pla0000033

Hill, C., Maskowitz, K., Danis, B., & Wakschlag, L. (2008). Validation of a clinically sensitive, observational coding system for parenting behaviors: The Parenting Clinical Observation Schedule. *Parenting: Science and Practice, 8*(2), 153–185. https://doi.org/10.1080/15295190802045469

Hinshaw-Fusilier, S., Zeanah, P. D., & Larrieu, J. (2009). Training in infant mental health. In C. Zeanah (Ed.), *Handbook of infant mental health* (3rd ed., pp. 533–548). Guilford Press.

Hobbs, S. A., Forehand, R., & Murray, R. G. (1978). Effects of various durations of timeout on the noncompliant behavior of children. *Behavior Therapy, 9*(4), 652–656. https://doi.org/10.1016/S0005-7894(78)80142-7

Hoffman, K. T., Marvin, R. S., Cooper, G., & Powell, B. (2006). Changing toddlers' and preschoolers' attachment classifications: The circle of security intervention. *Journal of Consulting and Clinical Psychology, 74*(6), 1017–1026. https://doi.org/10.1037/0022-006X.74.6.1017

Holden, G. W., Grogan-Kaylor, A., Durrant, J. E., & Gershoff, E. T. (2017). Researchers deserve a better critique: Response to Larzelere, Gunnoe, Roberts, and Ferguson (2017). *Marriage & Family Review, 53*(5), 465–490. https://doi.org/10.1080/01494929.2017.1308899

Hood, K. K., & Eyberg, S. M. (2003). Outcomes of parent–child interaction therapy: Mothers' reports of maintenance three to six years after treatment. *Journal of Clinical Child and Adolescent Psychology, 32*(3), 419–429. https://doi.org/10.1207/S15374424JCCP3203_10

Hosogane, N., Kodaira, M., Kihara, N., Saito, K., & Kamo, T. (2018). Parent–child interaction therapy (PCIT) for young children with attention-deficit hyperactivity disorder (ADHD) in Japan. *Annals of General Psychiatry, 17*(1), Article 9. https://doi.org/10.1186/s12991-018-0180-8

Howell, K. H., Graham-Bermann, S. A., Czyz, E., & Lilly, M. (2010). Assessing resilience in preschool children exposed to intimate partner violence. *Violence and Victims, 25*(2), 150–164. https://doi.org/10.1891/0886-6708.25.2.150

Hu, N., Taylor, C. L., Li, J., & Glauert, R. A. (2017). The impact of child maltreatment on the risk of deliberate self-harm among adolescents: A population-wide cohort study using linked administrative records. *Child Abuse & Neglect, 67*, 322–337. https://doi.org/10.1016/j.chiabu.2017.03.012

Huber, A., Hicks, A. M., Ball, M., & McMahon, C. (2021). Postintervention and follow-up changes in caregiving behavior and representations after individually or group delivered hybrid circle of security-intensive intervention with New Zealand caregiver–child dyads. *Attachment & Human Development, 23*(6), 931–952. https://doi.org/10.1080/14616734.2020.1809057

Huber, A., McMahon, C. A., & Sweller, N. (2015). Efficacy of the 20-week circle of security intervention: Changes in caregiver reflective functioning, representations, and child attachment in an Australian clinical sample. *Infant Mental Health Journal, 36*(6), 556–574. https://doi.org/10.1002/imhj.21540

Hurley, D., Allen, M. S., Swann, C., & Vella, S. A. (2021). A matched control trial of a mental health literacy intervention for parents in community sports clubs. *Child Psychiatry and Human Development, 52*(1), 141–153. https://doi.org/10.1007/s10578-020-00998-3

Hurley, D., Swann, C., Allen, M. S., Ferguson, H. L., & Vella, S. A. (2020). A systematic review of parent and caregiver mental health literacy. *Community Mental Health Journal, 56*(1), 2–21. https://doi.org/10.1007/s10597-019-00454-0

Iruka, I. U. (2009). Ethnic variation in the association between family structures and practices on child outcomes at 36 months: Results from early head start. *Early Education and Development, 20*(1), 148–173. https://doi.org/10.1080/10409280802206916

Israel, B. A., Eng, E., Schulz, A. J., & Parker, E. A. (2012). Introduction to methods of community-based participatory research for health. In B. A. Israel, E. Eng, A. J. Schulz, & E. A. Parker (Eds.), *Methods in community-based participatory research for health* (2nd ed., pp. 3–26). Jossey-Bass.

Jaffe, M., Gullone, E., & Hughes, E. K. (2010). The roles of temperamental dispositions and perceived parenting behaviours in the use of two emotion regulation strategies in late childhood. *Journal of Applied Developmental Psychology, 31*(1), 47–59. https://doi.org/10.1016/j.appdev.2009.07.008

Jenkins, S. R., & Baird, S. (2002). Secondary traumatic stress and vicarious trauma: A validational study. *Journal of Traumatic Stress, 15*(5), 423–432. https://doi.org/10.1023/A:1020193526843

Jeon, S., & Neppl, T. K. (2019). Economic pressure, parent positivity, positive parenting, and child social competence. *Journal of Child and Family Studies, 28*(5), 1402–1412. https://doi.org/10.1007/s10826-019-01372-1

Jester, J., Rosenblum, K., Muzik, M., Niec, L., Stringer, M., Handelzalts, J., Brophy-Herb, H., Stacks, A., Weatherston, D., Torres, C., Julian, M., Lawler, J., & The Michigan Collaborative for Infant Mental Health Research. (2021). *Demographic and psychological factors that predict retention in infant mental health home visiting* [Manuscript submitted for publication]. University of Michigan.

Jin, M. K., Jacobvitz, D., Hazen, N., & Jung, S. H. (2012). Maternal sensitivity and infant attachment security in Korea: Cross-cultural validation of the Strange Situation. *Attachment & Human Development, 14*(1), 33–44. https://doi.org/10.1080/14616734.2012.636656

John, R. M., & Rougeulle, C. (2018). Developmental epigenetics: Phenotype and the flexible epigenome. *Frontiers in Cell and Developmental Biology, 6*, 130. https://doi.org/10.3389/fcell.2018.00130

Johnson, J., Hall, L. H., Berzins, K., Baker, J., Melling, K., & Thompson, C. (2018). Mental healthcare staff well-being and burnout: A narrative review of trends, causes, implications, and recommendations for future interventions. *International Journal of Mental Health Nursing, 27*(1), 20–32. https://doi.org/10.1111/inm.12416

Johnson, S. B., Riis, J. L., & Noble, K. G. (2016). State of the art review: Poverty and the developing brain. *Pediatrics, 137*(4), Article e20153075. https://doi.org/10.1542/peds.2015-3075

Jones, T. L., & Prinz, R. J. (2005). Potential roles of parental self-efficacy in parent and child adjustment: A review. *Clinical Psychology Review, 25*(3), 341–363. https://doi.org/10.1016/j.cpr.2004.12.004

Jones, T. M., Hill, K. G., Epstein, M., Lee, J. O., Hawkins, J. D., & Catalano, R. F. (2016). Understanding the interplay of individual and social-developmental factors in the progression of substance use and mental health from childhood to adulthood. *Development and Psychopathology, 28*(3), 721–741. https://doi.org/10.1017/S0954579416000274

Jonson-Reid, M., Kohl, P. L., & Drake, B. (2012). Child and adult outcomes of chronic child maltreatment. *Pediatrics, 129*(5), 839–845. https://doi.org/10.1542/peds.2011-2529

Jordan, K. (2010). Vicarious trauma: Proposed factors that impact clinicians. *Journal of Family Psychotherapy, 21*(4), 225–237. https://doi.org/10.1080/08975353.2010.529003

Jouriles, E. N., & McDonald, R. (2015). Intimate partner violence, coercive control, and child adjustment problems. *Journal of Interpersonal Violence, 30*(3), 459–474. https://doi.org/10.1177/0886260514535099

Julian, M., Lawler, J., & Rosenblum, K. (2017). Caregiver–child relationships in early childhood: Interventions to promote well-being and reduce risk for psychopathology. *Child and Developmental Psychiatry, 4*(2), 87–98. https://doi.org/10.1007/s40473-017-0110-0

Kaeding, A., Sougleris, C., Reid, C., van Vreeswijk, M. F., Hayes, C., Dorrian, J., & Simpson, S. (2017). Professional burnout, early maladaptive schemas, and physical health in clinical and counselling psychology trainees. *Journal of Clinical Psychology, 73*(12), 1782–1796. https://doi.org/10.1002/jclp.22485

Kaehler, L. A., Jacobs, M., & Jones, D. J. (2016). Distilling common history and practice elements to inform dissemination: Hanf-model BPT programs as an example. *Clinical Child and Family Psychology Review, 19*(3), 236–258. https://doi.org/10.1007/s10567-016-0210-5

Kakinami, L., Barnett, T. A., Séguin, L., & Paradis, G. (2015). Parenting style and obesity risk in children. *Preventive Medicine, 75*, 18–22. https://doi.org/10.1016/j.ypmed.2015.03.005

Kaminski, J. W., Valle, L. A., Filene, J. H., & Boyle, C. L. (2008). A meta-analytic review of components associated with parent training program effectiveness. *Journal of Abnormal Child Psychology, 36*(4), 567–589. https://doi.org/10.1007/s10802-007-9201-9

Kamphaus, R. W., & Reynolds, C. R. (2006). *Parenting Relationship Questionnaire (PRQ): manual*. Pearson.

Kauffman Best Practices Project. (2004). *Kauffman Best Practices Project Final Report: Closing the quality chasm in child abuse treatment; identifying and disseminating best practices*.

Kazdin, A. E. (2008). Evidence-based treatments and delivery of psychological services: Shifting our emphases to increase impact. *Psychological Services, 5*(3), 201–215. https://doi.org/10.1037/a0012573

Kazdin, A. E., & Blase, S. L. (2011). Rebooting psychotherapy research and practice to reduce the burden of mental illness. *Perspectives on Psychological Science, 6*(1), 21–37. https://doi.org/10.1177/1745691610393527

Keller, H., Lohaus, A., Völker, S., Cappenberg, M., & Chasiotis, A. (1999). Temporal contingency as an independent component of parenting behavior. *Child Development, 70*(2), 474–485. https://doi.org/10.1111/1467-8624.00034

Kelly-Irving, M., & Delpierre, C. (2019). A critique of the adverse childhood experiences framework in epidemiology and public health: Uses and misuses. *Social Policy and Society, 18*(3), 445–456. https://doi.org/10.1017/S1474746419000101

Kelmanson, I. A. (2012). Separation anxiety and bedtime resistance in eight-month-old infants. *Early Child Development and Care, 182*(11), 1455–1464. https://doi.org/10.1080/03004430.2011.619659

Killian, K., Hernandez-Wolfe, P., Engstrom, D., & Gangsei, D. (2017). Development of the Vicarious Resilience Scale (VRS): A measure of positive effects of working with trauma survivors. *Psychological Trauma: Theory, Research, Practice, and Policy, 9*(1), 23–31. https://doi.org/10.1037/tra0000199

Kim, H., & Kao, D. (2014). A meta-analysis of turnover intention predictors among US child welfare workers. *Children and Youth Services Review, 47*, 214–223. https://doi.org/10.1016/j.childyouth.2014.09.015

Kim, J. J., Brookman-Frazee, L., Gellatly, R., Stadnick, N., Barnett, M. L., & Lau, A. S. (2018). Predictors of burnout among community therapists in the sustainment phase of a system-driven implementation of multiple evidence-based practices in children's mental health. *Professional Psychology, Research and Practice, 49*(2), 132–141. https://doi.org/10.1037/pro0000182

Kim, P., Evans, G. W., Angstadt, M., Ho, S. S., Sripada, C. S., Swain, J. E., Liberzon, I., & Phan, K. L. (2013). Effects of childhood poverty and chronic stress on emotion regulatory brain function in adulthood. *Proceedings of the National Academy of Sciences of the United States of America, 110*(46), 18442–18447. https://doi.org/10.1073/pnas.1308240110

Kim, S., & Kochanska, G. (2015). Mothers' power assertion; children's negative, adversarial orientation; and future behavior problems in low-income families: Early maternal responsiveness as a moderator of the developmental cascade. *Journal of Family Psychology, 29*(1), 1–9. https://doi.org/10.1037/a0038430

Kim, S., & Kochanska, G. (2021). Family sociodemographic resources moderate the path from toddlers' hard-to-manage temperament to parental control to disruptive behavior in middle childhood. *Development and Psychopathology, 33*(1), 160–172. https://doi.org/10.1017/S0954579419001664

Kim, S. J., & Bostwick, W. (2020). Social vulnerability and racial inequality in COVID-19 deaths in Chicago. *Health Education & Behavior, 47*(4), 509–513. https://doi.org/10.1177/1090198120929677

Kimonis, E. R., Frick, P. J., & McCahon, R. J. (2014). Conduct and oppositional defiant disorders. In E. Mash & R. Barkley (Eds.), *Child psychopathology* (pp. 145–179). Guilford Press.

King, M. L., Jr. (1967, April 14). *"The other America" speech transcript*. Stanford University. https://www.rev.com/blog/transcripts/the-other-america-speech-transcript-martin-luther-king-jr

Kitzmann, K. M., Gaylord, N. K., Holt, A. R., & Kenny, E. D. (2003). Child witnesses to domestic violence: A meta-analytic review. *Journal of Consulting and Clinical Psychology, 71*(2), 339–352. https://doi.org/10.1037/0022-006X.71.2.339

Klimes-Dougan, B., & Kopp, C. (1999). Children's conflict tactics with mothers: A longitudinal investigation of the toddler and preschool years. *Merrill-Palmer Quarterly, 45*(2), 226–242.

Knight, R. M., Albright, J., Deling, L., Dore-Stites, D., & Drayton, A. K. (2020). Longitudinal relationship between time-out and child emotional and behavioral functioning. *Journal of Developmental and Behavioral Pediatrics, 41*(1), 31–37. https://doi.org/10.1097/DBP.0000000000000725

Kochanska, G., & Thompson, R. A. (1997). The emergence and development of conscience in toddlerhood and early childhood. In J. Grusec & L. Kuczysnki (Eds.), *Parenting and children's internalization of values: A handbook of contemporary theory* (pp. 53–77). Wiley.

Koehn, A. J., & Kerns, K. A. (2018). Parent–child attachment: Meta-analysis of associations with parenting behaviors in middle childhood and adolescence.

Attachment & Human Development, 20(4), 378–405. https://doi.org/10.1080/14616734.2017.1408131

Kohlhoff, J., Morgan, S., Briggs, N., Egan, R., & Niec, L. (2021). Parent–child interaction therapy with toddlers: A community-based randomized controlled trial with children aged 14–24 months. *Journal of Clinical Child and Adolescent Psychology, 50*(3), 411–426. https://doi.org/10.1080/15374416.2020.1723599

Kolko, D. J., Baumann, B. L., Herschell, A. D., Hart, J. A., & Wisniewski, S. (2012). Dissemination of AF-CBT to community practitioners serving mental health and child welfare: A randomized trial. *Child Maltreatment, 17*(1), 32–46. https://doi.org/10.1177/1077559511427346

Kundakovic, M., & Champagne, F. A. (2015). Early-life experience, epigenetics, and the developing brain. *Neuropsychopharmacology, 40*(1), 141–153. https://doi.org/10.1038/npp.2014.140

Laganière, J., Tessier, R., & Nadeau, L. (2003). Attachement dans le cas de prématurité: Un lien médiatisé par les perceptions maternelles [Attachment in the case of prematurity: A link mediated by maternal perceptions]. *Enfance, 55*(2), 101–117. https://doi.org/10.3917/enf.552.0101

Laible, D. J., & Thompson, R. A. (2000). Mother–child discourse, attachment security, shared positive affect, and early conscience development. *Child Development, 71*(5), 1424–1440. https://doi.org/10.1111/1467-8624.00237

Lamb, M. E. (1975). Fathers: Forgotten contributors to child development. *Human Development, 18*(4), 245–266. https://doi.org/10.1159/000271493

Lamb, M. E., & Lewis, C. (2010). The development and significance of father–child relationships in two-parent families. In M. E. Lamb (Ed.), *The role of the father in child development* (5th ed., pp. 94–153). Wiley. (Original work published 1976)

Lambert, J. E., Holzer, J., & Hasbun, A. (2014). Association between parents' PTSD severity and children's psychological distress: A meta-analysis. *Journal of Traumatic Stress, 27*(1), 9–17. https://doi.org/10.1002/jts.21891

Landoll, R. R., Nielsen, M. K., & Waggoner, K. K. (2018). Factors affecting behavioral health provider turnover in US Air Force primary care behavioral health services. *Military Psychology, 30*(5), 398–403. https://doi.org/10.1080/08995605.2018.1478549

Landreth, G. L. (2002). Therapeutic limit setting in the play therapy relationship. *Professional Psychology, Research and Practice, 33*(6), 529–535. https://doi.org/10.1037/0735-7028.33.6.529

Landreth, G. L., & Bratton, S. C. (2006). *Child parent relationship therapy: A 10-session filial therapy model*. Routledge.

Landreth, G. L., & Lobaugh, A. F. (1998). Filial therapy with incarcerated fathers: Effects on parental acceptance of child, parental stress, and child adjustment. *Journal of Counseling and Development, 76*(2), 157–165. https://doi.org/10.1002/j.1556-6676.1998.tb02388.x

Landry, S. H., Smith, K. E., & Swank, P. R. (2006). Responsive parenting: Establishing early foundations for social, communication, and independent problem-solving skills. *Developmental Psychology, 42*(4), 627–642. https://doi.org/10.1037/0012-1649.42.4.627

Landry, S. H., Smith, K. E., Swank, P. R., Assel, M. A., & Vellet, S. (2001). Does early responsive parenting have a special importance for children's development or is consistency across early childhood necessary? *Developmental Psychology, 37*(3), 387–403. https://doi.org/10.1037/0012-1649.37.3.387

Lanier, P., Kohl, P. L., Benz, J., Swinger, D., Moussette, P., & Drake, B. (2011). Parent–child interaction therapy in a community setting: Examining outcomes, attrition, and treatment setting. *Research on Social Work Practice, 21*(6), 689–698. https://doi.org/10.1177/1049731511406551

Lanier, P., O'Brien, J. E., Rizo, C. F., Welch, H., & Macy, R. (2016). Examining parenting quality and dyad interactions between female CPS-and/or court-involved partner violence survivors and their young children using observational methods. *Journal of Child Custody, 13*(1), 30–51. https://doi.org/10.1080/15379418.2016.1132025

Lansford, J. E., Godwin, J., McMahon, R. J., Crowley, M., Pettit, G. S., Bates, J. E., Coie, J. D., & Dodge, K. A. (2021). Early physical abuse and adult outcomes. *Pediatrics, 147*(1), Article e20200873. https://doi.org/10.1542/peds.2020-0873

Larzelere, R. E., Gunnoe, M. L., Roberts, M. W., Lin, H., & Ferguson, C. J. (2020). Causal evidence for exclusively positive parenting and for timeout: Rejoinder to Holden, Grogan-Kaylor, Durrant, and Gershoff (2017). *Marriage & Family Review, 56*(4), 287–319. https://doi.org/10.1080/01494929.2020.1712304

Larzelere, R. E., Knowles, S. J., Henry, C. S., & Ritchie, K. L. (2018). Immediate and long-term effectiveness of disciplinary tactics by type of toddler noncompliance. *Parenting, 18*(3), 141–171. https://doi.org/10.1080/15295192.2018.1465304

Lawson, M., Piel, M. H., & Simon, M. (2020). Child maltreatment during the COVID-19 pandemic: Consequences of parental job loss on psychological and physical abuse towards children. *Child Abuse & Neglect, 110*(Pt. 2), Article 104709. https://doi.org/10.1016/j.chiabu.2020.104709

Lawson, M., Speidel, R., Fondren, K., Cummings, E. M., & Valentino, K. (2020). Intimate partner violence and maltreated preschoolers' internal representations of conflict. *Journal of Family Psychology, 34*(4), 425–435. https://doi.org/10.1037/fam0000627

Lechowicz, M. E., Jiang, Y., Tully, L. A., Burn, M. T., Collins, D. A., Hawes, D. J., Lenroot, R. K., Anderson, V., Doyle, F. L., Piotrowska, P. J., Frick, P. J., Moul, C., Kimonis, E. R., & Dadds, M. R. (2019). Enhancing father engagement in parenting programs: Translating research into practice recommendations. *Australian Psychologist, 54*(2), 83–89. https://doi.org/10.1111/ap.12361

Leckman-Westin, E., Cohen, P. R., & Stueve, A. (2009). Maternal depression and mother–child interaction patterns: Association with toddler problems and continuity of effects to late childhood. *Journal of Child Psychology and Psychiatry, 50*(9), 1176–1184. https://doi.org/10.1111/j.1469-7610.2009.02083.x

Lê Cook, B. L., Trinh, N. H., Li, Z., Hou, S. S. Y., & Progovac, A. M. (2017). Trends in racial-ethnic disparities in access to mental health care, 2004–2012. *Psychiatric Services, 68*(1), 9–16. https://doi.org/10.1176/appi.ps.201500453

LeCuyer, E. A., & Swanson, D. P. (2017). A within-group analysis of African American mothers' authoritarian attitudes, limit-setting and children's self-regulation. *Journal of Child and Family Studies, 26*(3), 833–842. https://doi.org/10.1007/s10826-016-0609-0

Lee, A. A., James, A. S., & Hunleth, J. M. (2020). Waiting for care: Chronic illness and health system uncertainties in the United States. *Social Science & Medicine, 264*, 113296. https://doi.org/10.1016/j.socscimed.2020.113296

Lee, J., Lim, N., Yang, E., & Lee, S. M. (2011). Antecedents and consequences of three dimensions of burnout in psychotherapists: A meta-analysis. *Professional Psychology, Research and Practice, 42*(3), 252–258. https://doi.org/10.1037/a0023319

Lee, S. J., Gopalan, G., & Harrington, D. (2016). Validation of the Parenting Stress Index–Short Form with minority caregivers. *Research on Social Work Practice, 26*(4), 429–440. https://doi.org/10.1177/1049731514554854

Leen-Feldner, E. W., Feldner, M. T., Knapp, A., Bunaciu, L., Blumenthal, H., & Amstadter, A. B. (2013). Offspring psychological and biological correlates of parental posttraumatic stress: Review of the literature and research agenda. *Clinical Psychology Review, 33*(8), 1106–1133. https://doi.org/10.1016/j.cpr.2013.09.001

Leidy, M. S., Schofield, T. J., & Parke, R. D. (2013). Fathers' contributions to children's social development. In N. J. Cabrera & C. S. Tamis-LeMonda (Eds.), *Handbook of father involvement: Multidisciplinary perspectives* (2nd ed., pp. 151–167). Routledge.

Leijten, P., Gardner, F., Landau, S., Harris, V., Mann, J., Hutchings, J., Beecham, J., Bonin, E.-M., & Scott, S. (2018). Research review: Harnessing the power of individual participant data in a meta-analysis of the benefits and harms of the Incredible Years parenting program. *Journal of Child Psychology and Psychiatry, 59*(2), 99–109. https://doi.org/10.1111/jcpp.12781

Leijten, P., Gardner, F., Melendez-Torres, G. J., Knerr, W., & Overbeek, G. (2018). Parenting behaviors that shape child compliance: A multilevel meta-analysis. *PLOS ONE, 13*(10), Article e0204929. https://doi.org/10.1371/journal.pone.0204929

Leijten, P., Gardner, F., Melendez-Torres, G. J., van Aar, J., Hutchings, J., Schulz, S., Knerr, W., & Overbeek, G. (2019). Meta-analyses: Key parenting program components for disruptive child behavior. *Journal of the American Academy of Child & Adolescent Psychiatry, 58*(2), 180–190. https://doi.org/10.1016/j.jaac.2018.07.900

Leijten, P., Melendez-Torres, G. J., Gardner, F., van Aar, J., Schulz, S., & Overbeek, G. (2018). Are relationship enhancement and behavior management "the golden couple" for disruptive child behavior? Two meta-analyses. *Child Development, 89*(6), 1970–1982. https://doi.org/10.1111/cdev.13051

LeMoult, J., Humphreys, K. L., Tracy, A., Hoffmeister, J. A., Ip, E., & Gotlib, I. H. (2020). Meta-analysis: Exposure to early life stress and risk for depression in childhood and adolescence. *Journal of the American Academy of Child & Adolescent Psychiatry, 59*(7), 842–855. https://doi.org/10.1016/j.jaac.2019.10.011

Lenze, S. N., Pautsch, J., & Luby, J. (2011). Parent–child interaction therapy emotion development: A novel treatment for depression in preschool children. *Depression and Anxiety, 28*(2), 153–159. https://doi.org/10.1002/da.20770

Letourneau, N. L., Duffett-Leger, L., Levac, L., Watson, B., & Young-Morris, C. (2013). Socioeconomic status and child development: A meta-analysis. *Journal of Emotional and Behavioral Disorders, 21*(3), 211–224. https://doi.org/10.1177/1063426611421007

Letourneau, N. L., Fedick, C. B., & Willms, J. D. (2007). Mothering and domestic violence: A longitudinal analysis. *Journal of Family Violence, 22*(8), 649–659. https://doi.org/10.1007/s10896-007-9099-6

Leung, C., Tsang, S., Heung, K., & Yiu, I. (2009). Effectiveness of parent–child interaction therapy (PCIT) among Chinese families. *Research on Social Work Practice, 19*(3), 304–313. https://doi.org/10.1177/1049731508321713

Leung, C., Tsang, S., Ng, G. S., & Choi, S. Y. (2017). Efficacy of parent–child interaction therapy with Chinese ADHD children: Randomized controlled trial. *Research on Social Work Practice, 27*(1), 36–47. https://doi.org/10.1177/1049731516643837

Leung, C., Tsang, S., Sin, T. C., & Choi, S. Y. (2015). The efficacy of parent–child interaction therapy with Chinese families: Randomized controlled trial. *Research on Social Work Practice, 25*(1), 117–128. https://doi.org/10.1177/1049731513519827

Levine, L. V., & Tuber, S. B. (1993). Measures of mental representation: Clinical and theoretical considerations. *Bulletin of the Menninger Clinic, 57*(1), 69–87.

Lewallen, A. C., & Neece, C. L. (2015). Improved social skills in children with developmental delays after parent participation in MBSR: The role of parent–child relational factors. *Journal of Child and Family Studies, 24*(10), 3117–3129. https://doi.org/10.1007/s10826-015-0116-8

Lieberman, A. F., Ghosh Ippen, C., & Van Horn, P. (2006). Child–parent psychotherapy: 6-month follow-up of a randomized controlled trial. *Journal of the American Academy of Child & Adolescent Psychiatry, 45*(8), 913–918. https://doi.org/10.1097/01.chi.0000222784.03735.92

Lieberman, A. F., Ghosh Ippen, C., & Van Horn, P. (2015). *Don't hit my mommy* (2nd ed.). National Center for Clinical Infant Programs.

Lieberman, A. F., & Van Horn, P. (2005). *Don't hit my mommy*. Zero to Three Press.

Lieberman, A. F., & Van Horn, P. (2008). *Psychotherapy with infants and young children: Repairing the effects of stress and trauma on early attachment*. Guilford Press.

Lieberman, A. F., Van Horn, P., & Ippen, C. G. (2005). Toward evidence-based treatment: Child-parent psychotherapy with preschoolers exposed to marital violence. *Journal of the American Academy of Child & Adolescent Psychiatry, 44*(12), 1241–1248. https://doi.org/10.1097/01.chi.0000181047.59702.58

Lieberman, A. F., Weston, D. R., & Pawl, J. H. (1991). Preventive intervention and outcome with anxiously attached dyads. *Child Development, 62*(1), 199–209. https://doi.org/10.2307/1130715

Lieneman, C. C., Girard, E. I., Quetsch, L. B., & McNeil, C. B. (2020). Emotion regulation and attrition in parent–child interaction therapy. *Journal of Child and Family Studies, 29*(4), 978–996. https://doi.org/10.1007/s10826-019-01674-4

Lin, L., Stamm, K., & Christidis, P. (2018). How diverse is the psychology workforce? *Datapoint, 49*(2), 19. https://www.apa.org/monitor/2018/02/datapoint

Lin, Y. W., & Bratton, S. C. (2015). A meta-analytic review of child-centered play therapy approaches. *Journal of Counseling and Development, 93*(1), 45–58. https://doi.org/10.1002/j.1556-6676.2015.00180.x

Lindo, N. A., Bratton, S. C., & Landreth, G. L. (2016). Child parent relationship therapy: Theory, research and intervention process. In L. A. Reddy, T. M. Files-Hall, & C. E. Schaefer (Eds.), *Empirically based play interventions for children* (2nd ed., pp. 241–261). American Psychological Association. https://doi.org/10.1037/14730-013

Litchford, A., Savoie Roskos, M. R., & Wengreen, H. (2020). Influence of fathers on the feeding practices and behaviors of children: A systematic review. *Appetite, 147*, 104558. Advance online publication. https://doi.org/10.1016/j.appet.2019.104558

Liu, R. T., Sheehan, A. E., Walsh, R. F. L., Sanzari, C. M., Cheek, S. M., & Hernandez, E. M. (2019). Prevalence and correlates of non-suicidal self-injury among lesbian, gay, bisexual, and transgender individuals: A systematic review and meta-analysis. *Clinical Psychology Review, 74*, 101783. https://doi.org/10.1016/j.cpr.2019.101783

Liu, Y., Wheaton, A. G., Chapman, D. P., Cunningham, T. J., Lu, H., & Croft, J. B. (2016). Prevalence of healthy sleep duration among adults—United States, 2014. *Morbidity and Mortality Weekly Report, 65*(6), 137–141. https://doi.org/10.15585/mmwr.mm6506a1

Lomas, T., Medina, J. C., Ivtzan, I., Rupprecht, S., & Eiroa-Orosa, F. J. (2019). A systematic review and meta-analysis of the impact of mindfulness-based interventions on the well-being of healthcare professionals. *Mindfulness, 10*(7), 1193–1216. https://doi.org/10.1007/s12671-018-1062-5

Loncar, H., Wilson, D. K., Sweeney, A. M., Quattlebaum, M., & Zarrett, N. (2021). Associations of parenting factors and weight related outcomes in African American adolescents with overweight and obesity. *Journal of Behavioral Medicine, 44*(4), 541–550. https://doi.org/10.1007/s10865-021-00208-y

Lovejoy, M. C., Graczyk, P. A., O'Hare, E., & Neuman, G. (2000). Maternal depression and parenting behavior: A meta-analytic review. *Clinical Psychology Review, 20*(5), 561–592. https://doi.org/10.1016/S0272-7358(98)00100-7

Lovejoy, M. C., Weis, R., O'Hare, E., & Rubin, E. C. (1999). Development and initial validation of the Parent Behavior Inventory. *Psychological Assessment, 11*(4), 534–545. https://doi.org/10.1037/1040-3590.11.4.534

Lowe, K. N., Adams, K. S., Browne, B. L., & Hinkle, K. T. (2012). Impact of military deployment on family relationships. *Journal of Family Studies, 18*(1), 17–27. https://doi.org/10.5172/jfs.2012.2003

Lucassen, N., Tharner, A., van IJzendoorn, M. H., Bakermans-Kranenburg, M. J., Volling, B. L., Verhulst, F. C., Lambregtse-Van den Berg, M. P., & Tiemeier, H. (2011). The association between paternal sensitivity and infant–father attachment security: A meta-analysis of three decades of research. *Journal of Family Psychology, 25*(6), 986–992. https://doi.org/10.1037/a0025855

Lundahl, B. W., Tollefson, D., Risser, H., & Lovejoy, M. C. (2008). A meta-analysis of father involvement in parent training. *Research on Social Work Practice, 18*(2), 97–106. https://doi.org/10.1177/1049731507309828

Lunkenheimer, E., Ram, N., Skowron, E. A., & Yin, P. (2017). Harsh parenting, child behavior problems, and the dynamic coupling of parents' and children's positive behaviors. *Journal of Family Psychology, 31*(6), 689–698. https://doi.org/10.1037/fam0000310

Lux, U., & Walper, S. (2019). A systemic perspective on children's emotional insecurity in relation to father: Links to parenting, interparental conflict and children's social well-being. *Attachment & Human Development, 21*(5), 467–484. https://doi.org/10.1080/14616734.2019.1582597

Lyon, A. R., Gershenson, R. A., Farahmand, F. K., Thaxter, P. J., Behling, S., & Budd, K. S. (2009). Effectiveness of teacher–child interaction training (TCIT) in a preschool setting. *Behavior Modification, 33*(6), 855–884. https://doi.org/10.1177/0145445509344215

Maccoby, E. E., & Martin, J. A. (1983). Socialization in the context of the family: Parent–child interaction. In P. H. Mussen & E. M. Hetherington (Eds.), *Handbook of child psychology: Vol. 4. Socialization, personality, and social development* (4th ed., pp. 1–101). John Wiley & Sons.

MacDonald, K. (1992). Warmth as a developmental construct: An evolutionary analysis. *Child Development, 63*(4), 753–773. https://doi.org/10.2307/1131231

Madsen, W. C. (1999). *Collaborative therapy with multi-stressed families.* Guilford Press.

Main, M., Hesse, E., & Kaplan, N. (2005). Predictability of attachment behavior and representational processes at 1, 6, and 19 years of age. In K. E. Grossmann, K. Grossmann, & E. Waters (Eds.), *Attachment from infancy to adulthood: The major longitudinal studies* (pp. 245–304). Guilford Press.

Main, M., & Solomon, J. (1990). Procedures for identifying infants as disorganized/disoriented during the Ainsworth Strange Situation. In M. T. Greenberg, D. Cicchetti, & E. M. Cummings (Eds.), *Attachment in the preschool years* (pp. 121–160). University of Chicago Press.

Main, M., & Weston, D. R. (1981). The quality of the toddler's relationship to mother and to father: Related to conflict behavior and the readiness to establish new relationships. *Child Development, 52*(3), 932–940. https://doi.org/10.2307/1129097

Malmberg, L. E., Lewis, S., West, A., Murray, E., Sylva, K., & Stein, A. (2016). The influence of mothers' and fathers' sensitivity in the first year of life on children's cognitive outcomes at 18 and 36 months. *Child: Care, Health and Development, 42*(1), 1–7. https://doi.org/10.1111/cch.12294

Martin, U., & Schinke, S. P. (1998). Organizational and individual factors influencing job satisfaction and burnout of mental health workers. *Social Work in Health Care, 28*(2), 51–62. https://doi.org/10.1300/J010v28n02_04

Martinez-Torteya, C., Dayton, C. J., Beeghly, M., Seng, J. S., McGinnis, E., Broderick, A., Rosenblum, K., & Muzik, M. (2014). Maternal parenting predicts infant biobehavioral regulation among women with a history of childhood maltreatment. *Development and Psychopathology, 26*(2), 379–392. https://doi.org/10.1017/S0954579414000017

Marvin, R., Cooper, G., Hoffman, K., & Powell, B. (2002). The Circle of Security project: Attachment-based intervention with caregiver–pre-school child dyads. *Attachment & Human Development, 4*(1), 107–124. https://doi.org/10.1080/14616730252982491

Marvin, R. S., Britner, P. A., & Russell, B. S. (2016). Normative development: The ontogeny of attachment in childhood. In J. Cassidy & P. Shaver (Eds.), *Handbook of attachment: Theory, research, and clinical applications* (3rd ed., pp. 273–290). Guilford Press.

Maslach, C., Jackson, S. E., & Leiter, M. P. (1996). *Maslach Burnout Inventory* (3rd ed.). Consulting Psychologists Press.

Masten, A. S., & Cicchetti, D. (2010). Developmental cascades. *Development and Psychopathology, 22*(3), 491–495. https://doi.org/10.1017/S0954579410000222

Masten, A. S., Roisman, G. I., Long, J. D., Burt, K. B., Obradović, J., Riley, J. R., Boelcke-Stennes, K., & Tellegen, A. (2005). Developmental cascades: Linking academic achievement and externalizing and internalizing symptoms over 20 years. *Developmental Psychology, 41*(5), 733–746. https://doi.org/10.1037/0012-1649.41.5.733

Mastin, D. F., Bryson, J., & Corwyn, R. (2006). Assessment of sleep hygiene using the Sleep Hygiene Index. *Journal of Behavioral Medicine, 29*(3), 223–227. https://doi.org/10.1007/s10865-006-9047-6

Matos, M., Bauermeister, J. J., & Bernal, G. (2009). Parent–child interaction therapy for Puerto Rican preschool children with ADHD and behavior problems: A pilot efficacy study. *Family Process, 48*(2), 232–252. https://doi.org/10.1111/j.1545-5300.2009.01279.x

Maupin, A. N., Samuel, E. E., Nappi, S. M., Heath, J. M., & Smith, M. V. (2017). Disseminating a parenting intervention in the community: Experiences from a multi-site evaluation. *Journal of Child and Family Studies, 26*(11), 3079–3092. https://doi.org/10.1007/s10826-017-0804-7

Mavranezouli, I., Megnin-Viggars, O., Daly, C., Dias, S., Stockton, S., Meiser-Stedman, R., Trickey, D., & Pilling, S. (2020). Research review: Psychological and psychosocial treatments for children and young people with post-traumatic stress disorder: A network meta-analysis. *Journal of Child Psychology and Psychiatry, 61*(1), 18–29. https://doi.org/10.1111/jcpp.13094

McBride, B. A., Schoppe-Sullivan, S. J., & Ho, M. H. (2005). The mediating role of fathers' school involvement on student achievement. *Journal of Applied Developmental Psychology, 26*(2), 201–216. https://doi.org/10.1016/j.appdev.2004.12.007

McCabe, J. E. (2014). Maternal personality and psychopathology as determinants of parenting behavior: A quantitative integration of two parenting literatures. *Psychological Bulletin, 140*(3), 722–750. https://doi.org/10.1037/a0034835

McCabe, K., & Yeh, M. (2009). Parent–child interaction therapy for Mexican Americans: A randomized clinical trial. *Journal of Clinical Child and Adolescent Psychology, 38*(5), 753–759. https://doi.org/10.1080/15374410903103544

McCabe, K., Yeh, M., Lau, A., & Argote, C. B. (2012). Parent–child interaction therapy for Mexican Americans: Results of a pilot randomized clinical trial at follow-up. *Behavior Therapy, 43*(3), 606–618. https://doi.org/10.1016/j.beth.2011.11.001

McCabe, K. M., Shanley, J. R., Niec, L. N., Naaf, M., Yeh, M., & Lau, A. S. (2013). Cultural differences in the parenting of young children: An observational study of low-income Mexican American and European American families. *Child & Family Behavior Therapy, 35*(4), 307–326. https://doi.org/10.1080/07317107.2013.846680

McCabe, K. M., Yeh, M., Garland, A. F., Lau, A. S., & Chavez, G. (2005). The GANA program: A tailoring approach to adapting parent child interaction therapy for Mexican Americans. *Education & Treatment of Children, 28*(2), 111–129.

McCabe, K. M., Yeh, M., & Zerr, A. A. (2020). Personalizing behavioral parent training interventions to improve treatment engagement and outcomes for culturally diverse families. *Psychology Research and Behavior Management, 13*, 41–53. https://doi.org/10.2147/PRBM.S230005

McCabe, P. C., Dragowski, E. A., & Rubinson, F. (2013). What is homophobic bias anyway? Defining and recognizing microaggressions and harassment of LGBTQ youth. *Journal of School Violence, 12*(1), 7–26. https://doi.org/10.1080/15388220.2012.731664

McConnachie, A. L., Ayed, N., Jadva, V., Lamb, M., Tasker, F., & Golombok, S. (2020). Father–child attachment in adoptive gay father families. *Attachment & Human Development, 22*(1), 110–123. https://doi.org/10.1080/14616734.2019.1589067

McDonald, M. A., Meckes, S. J., & Lancaster, C. L. (2021). Compassion for oneself and others protects the mental health of first responders. *Mindfulness, 12*(3), 1–13. https://doi.org/10.1007/s12671-020-01527-y

McFarlane, E., Burrell, L., Duggan, A., & Tandon, D. (2017). Outcomes of a randomized trial of a cognitive behavioral enhancement to address maternal distress in home visited mothers. *Maternal and Child Health Journal, 21*(3), 475–484. https://doi.org/10.1007/s10995-016-2125-7

McGoron, L., Gleason, M. M., Smyke, A. T., Drury, S. S., Nelson, C. A., III, Gregas, M. C., Fox, N. A., & Zeanah, C. H. (2012). Recovering from early deprivation: Attachment mediates effects of caregiving on psychopathology. *Journal of the American Academy of Child & Adolescent Psychiatry, 51*(7), 683–693. https://doi.org/10.1016/j.jaac.2012.05.004

McGuffin, P. W. (1991). The effect of timeout duration on frequency of aggression in hospitalized children with conduct disorders. *Behavioral Interventions, 6*(4), 279–288. https://doi.org/10.1002/bin.2360060405

McGuire, J. K., Anderson, C. R., Toomey, R. B., & Russell, S. T. (2010). School climate for transgender youth: A mixed method investigation of student experiences and school responses. *Journal of Youth and Adolescence, 39*(10), 1175–1188. https://doi.org/10.1007/s10964-010-9540-7

McHale, J. P., & Lindahl, K. M. (Eds.). (2011). *Coparenting: A conceptual and clinical examination of family systems.* American Psychological Association. https://doi.org/10.1037/12328-000

McIntosh, J. E., Schnabel, A., Youssef, G. J., & Olsson, C. A. (2021). Preconception and perinatal predictors of offspring attachment disorganization: Advancing the replicated evidence. *Development and Psychopathology, 33*(1), 240–251. https://doi.org/10.1017/S095457941900172X

McLaughlin, K. A., Sheridan, M. A., Tibu, F., Fox, N. A., Zeanah, C. H., & Nelson, C. A., III. (2015). Causal effects of the early caregiving environment on development of stress response systems in children. *Proceedings of the National Academy of Sciences of the United States of America, 112*(18), 5637–5642. https://doi.org/10.1073/pnas.1423363112

McNeillie, N., & Rose, J. (2021). Vicarious trauma in therapists: A meta-ethnographic review. *Behavioural and Cognitive Psychotherapy, 49*(4), 426–440. https://doi.org/10.1017/S1352465820000776

McWayne, C., Downer, J. T., Campos, R., & Harris, R. D. (2013). Father involvement during early childhood and its association with children's early learning: A meta-analysis. *Early Education and Development, 24*(6), 898–922. https://doi.org/10.1080/10409289.2013.746932

Measelle, J. R., & Ablow, J. C. (2018). Contributions of early adversity to pro-inflammatory phenotype in infancy: The buffer provided by attachment security. *Attachment & Human Development, 20*(1), 1–23. https://doi.org/10.1080/14616734.2017.1362657

Merz, E. C., Landry, S. H., Montroy, J. J., & Williams, J. M. (2017). Bidirectional associations between parental responsiveness and executive function during early childhood. *Social Development, 26*(3), 591–609. https://doi.org/10.1111/sode.12204

Merz, E. C., Zucker, T. A., Landry, S. H., Williams, J. M., Assel, M., Taylor, H. B., Lonigan, C. J., Phillips, B. M., Clancy-Menchetti, J., Barnes, M. A., Eisenberg, N., de Villiers, J., & the School Readiness Research Consortium. (2015). Parenting predictors of cognitive skills and emotion knowledge in socioeconomically disadvantaged preschoolers. *Journal of Experimental Child Psychology, 132,* 14–31. https://doi.org/10.1016/j.jecp.2014.11.010

Mesman, J., & Emmen, R. A. (2013). Mary Ainsworth's legacy: A systematic review of observational instruments measuring parental sensitivity. *Attachment & Human Development, 15*(5–6), 485–506. https://doi.org/10.1080/14616734.2013.820900

Miller, J. E., Kim, S., Boldt, L. J., Goffin, K. C., & Kochanska, G. (2019). Long-term sequelae of mothers' and fathers' mind-mindedness in infancy: A developmental path to children's attachment at age 10. *Developmental Psychology, 55*(4), 675–686. https://doi.org/10.1037/dev0000660

Miller, J. J., Donohue-Dioh, J., Niu, C., Grise-Owens, E., & Poklembova, Z. (2019). Examining the self-care practices of child welfare workers: A national perspective. *Children and Youth Services Review, 99,* 240–245. https://doi.org/10.1016/j.childyouth.2019.02.009

Miller, M. L., Gerhart, J. I., Maffett, A. J., Lorbeck, A., England, A. E., & O'Mahony, S. (2020). Experiential avoidance and post-traumatic stress symptoms among child abuse counselors and service workers: A brief report. *Journal of Interpersonal Violence.* Advance online publication. https://doi.org/10.1177/0886260520976225

Miller, W. R., & Rollnick, S. (2002). *Motivational interviewing: Preparing people for change* (2nd ed.). Guilford Press.

Minkler, M., & Wallerstein, N. (2003). Introduction to community based participatory research. In M. Minkler & N. Wallerstein (Eds.), *Community-based participatory research for health* (pp. 3–26). Jossey-Bass.

Minnis, H., Macmillan, S., Pritchett, R., Young, D., Wallace, B., Butcher, J., Sim, F., Baynham, K., Davidson, C., & Gillberg, C. (2013). Prevalence of reactive attachment disorder in a deprived population. *The British Journal of Psychiatry, 202*(5), 342–346. https://doi.org/10.1192/bjp.bp.112.114074

Mitchell, F. M. (2018). Engaging in Indigenous CBPR within academia: A critical narrative. *Affilia, 33*(3), 379–394. https://doi.org/10.1177/0886109918762570

Moffitt, T. E., Caspi, A., Harrington, H., & Milne, B. J. (2002). Males on the life-course-persistent and adolescence-limited antisocial pathways: Follow-up at age 26 years. *Development and Psychopathology, 14*(1), 179–207. https://doi.org/10.1017/S0954579402001104

Moran, P., Ghate, D., & Van der Merwe, A. (2004). *What works in parenting support? A review of the international evidence* (Research Report No. 574). Department for Education and Skills, Policy Research Bureau.

Mor Barak, M. E., Nissly, J. A., & Levin, A. (2001). Antecedents to retention and turnover among child welfare, social work, and other human service employees: What can we learn from past research? A review and metanalysis. *The Social Service Review, 75*(4), 625–661. https://doi.org/10.1086/323166

Morris, A. S., Robinson, L. R., Hays-Grudo, J., Claussen, A. H., Hartwig, S. A., & Treat, A. E. (2017). Targeting parenting in early childhood: A public health approach to improve outcomes for children living in poverty. *Child Development, 88*(2), 388–397. https://doi.org/10.1111/cdev.12743

Morse, G., Salyers, M. P., Rollins, A. L., Monroe-DeVita, M., & Pfahler, C. (2012). Burnout in mental health services: A review of the problem and its remediation. *Administration and Policy in Mental Health, 39*(5), 341–352. https://doi.org/10.1007/s10488-011-0352-1

Mountain, G., Cahill, J., & Thorpe, H. (2017). Sensitivity and attachment interventions in early childhood: A systematic review and meta-analysis. *Infant Behavior and Development, 46*, 14–32. https://doi.org/10.1016/j.infbeh.2016.10.006

Murray, A. L., Obsuth, I., Speyer, L., Murray, G., McKenzie, K., Eisner, M., & Ribeaud, D. (2021). Developmental cascades from aggression to internalizing problems via peer and teacher relationships from early to middle adolescence. *Journal of Youth and Adolescence, 50*(4), 663–673. https://doi.org/10.1007/s10964-021-01396-1

Muzik, M., Morelen, D., Hruschak, J., Rosenblum, K. L., Bocknek, E., & Beeghly, M. (2017). Psychopathology and parenting: An examination of perceived and observed parenting in mothers with depression and PTSD. *Journal of Affective Disorders, 207*, 242–250. https://doi.org/10.1016/j.jad.2016.08.035

Myers, W., Turanovic, J. J., Lloyd, K. M., & Pratt, T. C. (2020). The victimization of LGBTQ students at school: A meta-analysis. *Journal of School Violence, 19*(4), 421–432. https://doi.org/10.1080/15388220.2020.1725530

Narendorf, S. C., Munson, M. R., Ben-David, S., Cole, A. R., & Scott, L. D., Jr. (2018). Race and gender differences in attitudes toward help seeking among marginalized young adults with mood disorders: A mixed-methods investigation. *Psychiatric Rehabilitation Journal, 41*(4), 277–289. https://doi.org/10.1037/prj0000312

National Association of Social Workers. (2008). *Code of ethics of the National Association of Social Workers.* https://www.socialworkers.org/LinkClick.aspx?fileticket=KZmmbz15evc%3D&portalid=0

National Children's Traumatic Stress Network. (2019, March). *Parent–child interaction therapy (PCIT).* https://www.nctsn.org/sites/default/files/interventions/pcit_general_031419.pdf

National Human Genome Research Institute. (n.d.). *Telomere.* https://www.genome.gov/genetics-glossary/Telomere

National Scientific Council on the Developing Child. (2014). *Excessive stress disrupts the architecture of the developing brain: Working paper no. 3* (Updated ed.). https://developingchild.harvard.edu/resources/wp3/ (Original work published 2005)

NCD Risk-Factor Collaboration. (2017). Worldwide trends in body-mass index, underweight, overweight, and obesity from 1975 to 2016: A pooled analysis of 2416 population-based measurement studies in 128·9 million children, adolescents, and adults. *The Lancet, 390*(10113), 2627–2642. https://doi.org/10.1016/S0140-6736(17)32129-3

Neff, K. D. (2003). The development and validation of a scale to measure self-compassion. *Self and Identity, 2*(3), 223–250. https://doi.org/10.1080/15298860309027

Nelson, M. M., & Olsen, B. (2018). Dyadic Parent–Child Interaction Coding System (DPICS): An adaptable measure of parent and child behavior during dyadic interactions. In L. N. Niec (Ed.), *Handbook of parent–child interaction therapy: Innovations and applications for research and practice* (pp. 285–302). Springer. https://doi.org/10.1007/978-3-319-97698-3_18

Nicolson, S., Judd, F., Thomson-Salo, F., & Mitchell, S. (2013). Supporting the adolescent mother-infant relationship: Preliminary trial of a brief perinatal attachment intervention. *Archives of Women's Mental Health, 16*(6), 511–520. https://doi.org/10.1007/s00737-013-0364-9

Niec, L. N. (Ed.). (2018a). *Handbook of parent–child interaction therapy: Innovations and applications for research and practice.* Springer. https://doi.org/10.1007/978-3-319-97698-3

Niec, L. N. (2018b). Parent–child interaction therapy: A transdiagnostic intervention to enhance family functioning. In L. N. Niec (Ed.), *Handbook of parent–child interaction therapy: Innovations and applications for research and practice* (pp. 3–15). Springer. https://doi.org/10.1007/978-3-319-97698-3_1

Niec, L. N. (2018c). Parent–child interaction therapy: Taking the next steps. In L. N. Niec (Ed.), *Handbook of parent–child interaction therapy: Innovations and applications for research and practice* (pp. 409–413). Springer. https://doi.org/10.1007/978-3-319-97698-3_25

Niec, L. N., Abrahamse, M. E., Egan, R., Coelman, F. J., & Heiner, W. D. (2018). Global dissemination of parent–child interaction therapy: The perspectives of Dutch trainees. *Children and Youth Services Review, 94,* 485–492. https://doi.org/10.1016/j.childyouth.2018.08.019

Niec, L. N., Acevedo-Polakovich, I. D., Abbenante-Honold, E., Christian, A. S., Barnett, M. L., Aguilar, G., & Peer, S. O. (2014). Working together to solve disparities: Latina/o parents' contributions to the adaptation of a preventive intervention for childhood conduct problems. *Psychological Services, 11*(4), 410–420. https://doi.org/10.1037/a0036200

Niec, L. N., Barnett, M. L., Schoonover, C., & Brodd, I. (2019). *Comprehensive manual of the Therapist–Parent Interaction Coding System.* CMU Center for Children, Families, and Communities.

Niec, L. N., Barnett, M. L., Gering, C. L., Triemstra, K., & Solomon, D. T. (2015). Differences in mothers' and fathers' readiness for change in parent training. *Child & Family Behavior Therapy, 37*(3), 224–235. https://doi.org/10.1080/07317107.2015.1071980

Niec, L. N., Barnett, M. L., Prewett, M. S., & Shanley Chatham, J. R. (2016). Group parent–child interaction therapy: A randomized control trial for the treatment of conduct problems in young children. *Journal of Consulting and Clinical Psychology, 84*(8), 682–698. https://doi.org/10.1037/a0040218

Niec, L. N., Brestan, E. V., & Valle, L. A. (2008). Violence on the screen: Psychological perspectives on child abuse in American popular film 1992–2001. In R. Fisher & N. Billias (Series Eds.) and T. Levin (Vol. Ed.), *Violence: 'Mercurial gestalt'* (pp. 91–110). Rodopi B. V. Press.

Niec, L. N., Hemme, J. M., Yopp, J. M., & Brestan, E. V. (2005). Parent–child interaction therapy: The rewards and challenges of a group format. *Cognitive and Behavioral Practice, 12*(1), 113–125. https://doi.org/10.1016/S1077-7229(05)80046-X

Niec, L. N., & Russ, S. W. (2002). Children's internal representations, empathy, and fantasy play: A validity study of the SCORS-Q. *Psychological Assessment, 14*(3), 331–338. https://doi.org/10.1037/1040-3590.14.3.331

Niec, L. N., Shanley, J. R., Barnett, M. L., Baker, S. E., & Solomon, D. T. (2015). Optimal or typical performance? The impact of instructional set on the behavioral assessment of parent–child interactions. *Child & Family Behavior Therapy, 37*(2), 105–113. https://doi.org/10.1080/07317107.2015.1035981

Niec, L. N., Todd, M., Brodd, I., & Domoff, S. E. (2022). PCIT-Health: Preventing childhood obesity by strengthening the parent–child relationship. *Cognitive and Behavioral Practice, 29*(2), 335–347. https://doi.org/10.1016/j.cbpra.2020.07.001

Nixon, R. D., Sweeney, L., Erickson, D. B., & Touyz, S. W. (2004). Parent–child interaction therapy: One- and two-year follow-up of standard and abbreviated treatments for oppositional preschoolers. *Journal of Abnormal Child Psychology, 32*(3), 263–271. https://doi.org/10.1023/B:JACP.0000026140.60558.05

Nogueira-de-Almeida, C. A., Del Ciampo, L. A., Ferraz, I. S., Del Ciampo, I. R. L., Contini, A. A., & Ued, F. D. V. (2020). COVID-19 and obesity in childhood and adolescence: A clinical review. *Jornal de Pediatria, 96*(5), 546–558. https://doi.org/10.1016/j.jped.2020.07.001

Noonan, C. B., & Pilkington, P. D. (2020). Intimate partner violence and child attachment: A systematic review and meta-analysis. *Child Abuse & Neglect, 109*, 104765. https://doi.org/10.1016/j.chiabu.2020.104765

Norcross, J. C., & VandenBos, G. R. (2018). *Leaving it at the office: A guide to psychotherapist self-care.* Guilford Press.

Nunes, F., & Mota, C. P. (2017). Parenting styles and suicidal ideation in adolescents: Mediating effect of attachment. *Journal of Child and Family Studies, 26*(3), 734–747. https://doi.org/10.1007/s10826-016-0611-6

Nuttall, A. K., Froyen, L. C., Skibbe, L. E., & Bowles, R. P. (2019). Maternal and paternal depressive symptoms, home learning environment, and children's early literacy. *Child Psychiatry and Human Development, 50*(4), 681–691. https://doi.org/10.1007/s10578-019-00872-x

O'Connell, J., Pote, H., & Shafran, R. (2021). Child mental health literacy training programmes for professionals in contact with children: A systematic review. *Early Intervention in Psychiatry, 15*(2), 234–247. https://doi.org/10.1111/eip.12964

O'Connor, E. E., Scott, M. A., McCormick, M. P., & Weinberg, S. L. (2014). Early mother–child attachment and behavior problems in middle childhood: The role of the subsequent caregiving environment. *Attachment & Human Development, 16*(6), 590–612. https://doi.org/10.1080/14616734.2014.937817

O'Connor, T. G., Woolgar, M., Humayun, S., Briskman, J. A., & Scott, S. (2019). Early caregiving predicts attachment representations in adolescence: Findings from two longitudinal studies. *Journal of Child Psychology and Psychiatry, 50*(9), 944–952. https://doi.org/10.1111/jcpp.12936

O'Dor, S. L., Grasso, D. J., Forbes, D., Bates, J. E., McCarthy, K. J., Wakschlag, L. S., & Briggs-Gowan, M. J. (2017). The Family Socialization Interview–Revised (FSI-R): A comprehensive assessment of parental disciplinary behaviors. *Prevention Science, 18*(3), 292–304. https://doi.org/10.1007/s11121-016-0707-7

Ogden, C. L., Carroll, M. D., Kit, B. K., & Flegal, K. M. (2014). Prevalence of childhood and adult obesity in the United States, 2011–2012. *Journal of the American Medical Association, 311*(8), 806–814. https://doi.org/10.1001/jama.2014.732

Olds, D. L., Robinson, J., O'Brien, R., Luckey, D. W., Pettitt, L. M., Henderson, C. R., Jr., Ng, R. K., Sheff, K. L., Korfmacher, J., Hiatt, S., & Talmi, A. (2002). Home visiting by paraprofessionals and by nurses: A randomized, controlled trial. *Pediatrics, 110*(3), 486–496. https://doi.org/10.1542/peds.110.3.486

Olvera, N., & Power, T. G. (2010). Brief report: parenting styles and obesity in Mexican American children: A longitudinal study. *Journal of Pediatric Psychology, 35*(3), 243–249. https://doi.org/10.1093/jpepsy/jsp071

Opie, J. E., McIntosh, J. E., Esler, T. B., Duschinsky, R., George, C., Schore, A., Kothe, E. J., Tan, E. S., Greenwood, C. J., & Olsson, C. A. (2021). Early childhood attachment stability and change: A meta-analysis. *Attachment & Human Development, 23*(6), 897–930. https://doi.org/10.1080/14616734.2020.1800769

Ouellet-Morin, I., Robitaille, M. P., Langevin, S., Cantave, C., Brendgen, M., & Lupien, S. J. (2019). Enduring effect of childhood maltreatment on cortisol and heart rate responses to stress: The moderating role of severity of experiences. *Development and Psychopathology, 31*(2), 497–508. https://doi.org/10.1017/S0954579418000123

Pallini, S., Baiocco, R., Schneider, B. H., Madigan, S., & Atkinson, L. (2014). Early child-parent attachment and peer relations: A meta-analysis of recent research. *Journal of Family Psychology, 28*(1), 118–123. https://doi.org/10.1037/a0035736

Pallini, S., Chirumbolo, A., Morelli, M., Baiocco, R., Laghi, F., & Eisenberg, N. (2018). The relation of attachment security status to effortful self-regulation: A meta-analysis. *Psychological Bulletin, 144*(5), 501–531. https://doi.org/10.1037/bul0000134

Pancsofar, N., & Vernon-Feagans, L. (2006). Mother and father language input to young children: Contributions to later language development. *Early Childhood Research Quarterly, 27*(6), 571–587. 10.1016/j.appdev.2006.08.003

Pancsofar, N., Vernon-Feagans, L., & The Family Life Project Investigators. (2010). Fathers' early contributions to children's language development in families from low-income rural communities. *Early Childhood Research Quarterly, 25*(4), 450–463. https://doi.org/10.1016/j.ecresq.2010.02.001

Panter-Brick, C., Burgess, A., Eggerman, M., McAllister, F., Pruett, K., & Leckman, J. F. (2014). Practitioner review: Engaging fathers—Recommendations for a game change in parenting interventions based on a systematic review of the global evidence. *Journal of Child Psychology and Psychiatry, 55*(11), 1187–1212. https://doi.org/10.1111/jcpp.12280

Parent, J., Forehand, R., Pomerantz, H., Peisch, V., & Seehuus, M. (2017). Father participation in child psychopathology research. *Journal of Abnormal Child Psychology, 45*(7), 1259–1270. https://doi.org/10.1007/s10802-016-0254-5

Paris, R., Herriott, A., Holt, M., & Gould, K. (2015). Differential responsiveness to a parenting intervention for mothers in substance abuse treatment. *Child Abuse & Neglect, 50*, 206–217. https://doi.org/10.1016/j.chiabu.2015.09.007

Parker, K., & Livingston, G. (2019, June 12). *8 facts about American dads.* Pew Research Center. https://www.pewresearch.org/fact-tank/2019/06/12/fathers-day-facts/

Parolin, Z., Collyer, S., Curran, M. A., & Wimer, C. (2021, March). *The American Rescue Plan could cut child poverty by more than half.* Center on Poverty & Social Policy. https://www.povertycenter.columbia.edu/news-internal/2021/presidential-policy/biden-economic-relief-proposal-poverty-impact

Parpal, M., & Maccoby, E. E. (1985). Maternal responsiveness and subsequent child compliance. *Child Development, 56*(5), 1326–1334. https://doi.org/10.2307/1130247

Passini, C. M., Pihet, S., & Favez, N. (2014). Assessing specific discipline techniques: A mixed-methods approach. *Journal of Child and Family Studies, 23*(8), 1389–1402. https://doi.org/10.1007/s10826-013-9796-0

Patterson, G. R. (1982). *Coercive family process* (Vol. 3). Castalia Publishing Company.

Patterson, G. R. (2002). The early development of coercive family process. In J. B. Reid, G. R. Patterson, & J. Snyder (Eds.), *Antisocial behavior in children and adolescents: A developmental analysis and model for intervention* (pp. 25–44). American Psychological Association. https://doi.org/10.1037/10468-002

Patterson, G. R., & Forgatch, M. S. (1995). Predicting future clinical adjustment from treatment outcome and process variables. *Psychological Assessment, 7*(3), 275–285. https://doi.org/10.1037/1040-3590.7.3.275

Patterson, G. R., Reid, J., & Dishion, T. J. (1992). *Antisocial boys.* Castalia.

Pauli-Pott, U., Schloß, S., & Becker, K. (2018). Maternal responsiveness as a predictor of self-regulation development and attention-deficit/hyperactivity symptoms across preschool ages. *Child Psychiatry and Human Development, 49*(1), 42–52. https://doi.org/10.1007/s10578-017-0726-z

Pearl, E., Thieken, L., Olafson, E., Boat, B., Connelly, L., Barnes, J., & Putnam, F. (2012). Effectiveness of community dissemination of parent–child interaction therapy. *Psychological Trauma: Theory, Research, Practice, and Policy, 4*(2), 204–213. https://doi.org/10.1037/a0022948

Pearlman, L. A., & Mac Ian, P. S. (1995). Vicarious traumatization: An empirical study of the effects of trauma work on trauma therapists. *Professional Psychology, Research and Practice, 26*(6), 558–565. https://doi.org/10.1037/0735-7028.26.6.558

Pearson, J., & Wilkinson, L. (2013). Family relationships and adolescent well-being: Are families equally protective for same-sex attracted youth? *Journal of Youth and Adolescence, 42*(3), 376–393. https://doi.org/10.1007/s10964-012-9865-5

Peluso, P. R., & Freund, R. R. (2018). Therapist and client emotional expression and psychotherapy outcomes: A meta-analysis. *Psychotherapy: Theory, Research, & Practice, 55*(4), 461–472. https://doi.org/10.1037/pst0000165

Pemberton, J. R., Borrego, J., Jr., & Sherman, S. (2013). Differential attention as a mechanism of change in parent–child interaction therapy: Support from time-series analysis. *Journal of Psychopathology and Behavioral Assessment, 35*(1), 35–44. https://doi.org/10.1007/s10862-012-9312-7

Perry, R. E., Finegood, E. D., Braren, S. H., Dejoseph, M. L., Putrino, D. F., Wilson, D. A., Sullivan, R. M., Raver, C. C., Blair, C., & the Family Life Project Key

Investigators. (2019). Developing a neurobehavioral animal model of poverty: Drawing cross-species connections between environments of scarcity-adversity, parenting quality, and infant outcome. *Development and Psychopathology, 31*(2), 399–418. https://doi.org/10.1017/S095457941800007X

Peterson, N. J., Drotar, D., Olness, K., Guay, L., & Kiziri-Mayengo, R. (2001). The relationship of maternal and child HIV infection to security of attachment among Ugandan infants. *Child Psychiatry and Human Development, 32*(1), 3–17. https://doi.org/10.1023/A:1017581412328

Peterson, R., & Krivo, L. (2010). *Divergent social worlds: Neighborhood crime and the racial-spatial divide*. Russell Sage Foundation.

Pezzella, F. S., Thornberry, T. P., & Smith, C. A. (2016). Race socialization and parenting styles: Links to delinquency for African American and White adolescents. *Youth Violence and Juvenile Justice, 14*(4), 448–467. https://doi.org/10.1177/1541204015581390

Pfitzner, N., Humphreys, C., & Hegarty, K. (2017). Research review: Engaging men: A multi-level model to support father engagement. *Child & Family Social Work, 22*(1), 537–547. https://doi.org/10.1111/cfs.12250

Pianta, R. C. (1992). *Child–Parent Relationship Scale*. https://education.virginia.edu/faculty-research/centers-labs-projects/castl/measures-developed-robert-c-pianta-phd

Picardi, A., Fagnani, C., Nisticò, L., & Stazi, M. A. (2011). A twin study of attachment style in young adults. *Journal of Personality, 79*(5), 965–992. https://doi.org/10.1111/j.1467-6494.2010.00707.x

Picardi, A., Giuliani, E., & Gigantesco, A. (2020). Genes and environment in attachment. *Neuroscience and Biobehavioral Reviews, 112*, 254–269. https://doi.org/10.1016/j.neubiorev.2020.01.038

Pilkington, P., Rominov, H., Brown, H. K., & Dennis, C. L. (2019). Systematic review of the impact of coparenting interventions on paternal coparenting behaviour. *Journal of Advanced Nursing, 75*(1), 17–29. https://doi.org/10.1111/jan.13815

Pilling, S., Fonagy, P., Allison, E., Barnett, P., Campbell, C., Constantinou, M., Gardner, T., Lorenzini, N., Matthews, H., Ryan, A., Sacchetti, S., Truscott, A., Ventura, T., Watchorn, K., Whittington, C., & Kendall, T. (2020). Long-term outcomes of psychological interventions on children and young people's mental health: A systematic review and meta-analysis. *PLOS ONE, 15*(11), Article e0236525. https://doi.org/10.1371/journal.pone.0236525

Pincus, D. B., Santucci, L. C., Ehrenreich, J. T., & Eyberg, S. M. (2008). The implementation of modified parent–child interaction therapy for youth with separation anxiety disorder. *Cognitive and Behavioral Practice, 15*(2), 118–125. https://doi.org/10.1016/j.cbpra.2007.08.002

Pinderhughes, E. E., Dodge, K. A., Bates, J. E., Pettit, G. S., & Zelli, A. (2000). Discipline responses: Influences of parents' socioeconomic status, ethnicity, beliefs about parenting, stress, and cognitive-emotional processes. *Journal of Family Psychology, 14*(3), 380–400. https://doi.org/10.1037/0893-3200.14.3.380

Pinquart, M. (2014). Associations of general parenting and parent–child relationship with pediatric obesity: A meta-analysis. *Journal of Pediatric Psychology, 39*(4), 381–393. https://doi.org/10.1093/jpepsy/jst144

Pinquart, M. (2016). Associations of parenting styles and dimensions with academic achievement in children and adolescents: A meta-analysis. *Educational Psychology Review, 28*(3), 475–493. https://doi.org/10.1007/s10648-015-9338-y

Pinquart, M. (2017). Associations of parenting dimensions and styles with externalizing problems of children and adolescents: An updated meta-analysis. *Developmental Psychology, 53*(5), 873–932. https://doi.org/10.1037/dev0000295

Pinquart, M., Feussner, C., & Ahnert, L. (2013). Meta-analytic evidence for stability in attachments from infancy to early adulthood. *Attachment & Human Development, 15*(2), 189–218. https://doi.org/10.1080/14616734.2013.746257

Pinquart, M., & Kauser, R. (2018). Do the associations of parenting styles with behavior problems and academic achievement vary by culture? Results from a meta-analysis. *Cultural Diversity & Ethnic Minority Psychology, 24*(1), 75–100. https://doi.org/10.1037/cdp0000149

Piotrowska, P. J., Tully, L. A., Lenroot, R., Kimonis, E., Hawes, D., Moul, C., Frick, P. J., Anderson, V., & Dadds, M. R. (2017). Mothers, fathers, and parental systems: A conceptual model of parental engagement in programmes for child mental health—Connect, Attend, Participate, Enact (CAPE). *Clinical Child and Family Psychology Review, 20*(2), 146–161. https://doi.org/10.1007/s10567-016-0219-9

Piskernik, B., & Ahnert, L. (2019). What does it mean when fathers are involved in parenting? *Monographs of the Society for Research in Child Development, 84*(1), 64–78. https://doi.org/10.1002/mono.12404

Powell, B., Cooper, G., Hoffman, K., & Marvin, B. (2014). *Circle of security: Enhancing attachment in early parent–child relationships*. Guilford Press.

Price-Haywood, E. G., Burton, J., Fort, D., & Seoane, L. (2020). Hospitalization and mortality among Black patients and White patients with Covid-19. *The New England Journal of Medicine, 382*(26), 2534–2543. https://doi.org/10.1056/NEJMsa2011686

Prochaska, J. O., Redding, C. A., & Evers, K. E. (2002). The transtheoretical model and stages of change. In K. Glanz, B. Rimer, & F. Lewis (Eds.), *Health behavior and health education* (3rd ed., pp. 99–120). Jossey-Bass.

Pruett, M. K., Pruett, K. D., Cowan, C. P., & Cowan, P. A. (2017a). Enhancing father involvement in low-income families: A couples group approach to preventive intervention. *Child Development, 88*(2), 398–407. https://doi.org/10.1111/cdev.12744

Pruett, M. K., Pruett, K. D., Cowan, C. P., & Cowan, P. A. (2017b). Enhancing paternal engagement in a coparenting paradigm. *Child Development Perspectives, 11*(4), 245–250. https://doi.org/10.1111/cdep.12239

Purewal Boparai, S. K., Au, V., Koita, K., Oh, D. L., Briner, S., Burke Harris, N., & Bucci, M. (2018). Ameliorating the biological impacts of childhood adversity: A review of intervention programs. *Child Abuse & Neglect, 81*, 82–105. https://doi.org/10.1016/j.chiabu.2018.04.014

Querido, J. G., Warner, T. D., & Eyberg, S. M. (2002). Parenting styles and child behavior in African American families of preschool children. *Journal of Clinical Child and Adolescent Psychology, 31*(2), 272–277. https://doi.org/10.1207/S15374424JCCP3102_12

Raikes, H. A., & Thompson, R. A. (2005). Efficacy and social support as predictors of parenting stress among families in poverty. *Infant Mental Health Journal, 26*(3), 177–190. https://doi.org/10.1002/imhj.20044

Ramsauer, B., Mühlhan, C., Lotzin, A., Achtergarde, S., Mueller, J., Krink, S., Tharner, A., Becker-Stoll, F., Nolte, T., & Romer, G. (2020). Randomized controlled trial of the circle of security-intensive intervention for mothers with postpartum depression: Maternal unresolved attachment moderates changes in sensitivity. *Attachment & Human Development, 22*(6), 705–726. https://doi.org/10.1080/14616734.2019.1689406

Rasing, S. P. A., Braam, M. W. G., Brunwasser, S. M., Janssens, J. M. A. M., Creemers, D. H. M., & Scholte, R. H. J. (2020). Depression and anxiety symptoms in female adolescents: Relations with parental psychopathology and parenting behavior. *Journal of Research on Adolescence, 30*(1), 298–313. https://doi.org/10.1111/jora.12525

Ravindran, N., Berry, D., & McElwain, N. L. (2019). Dynamic bidirectional associations in negative behavior: Mother–toddler interaction during a snack delay. *Developmental Psychology, 55*(6), 1191–1198. https://doi.org/10.1037/dev0000703

Reyes, L. M., Jaekel, J., Heuser, K. M., & Wolke, D. (2019). Developmental cascades of social inhibition and friendships in preterm and full-term children. *Infant and Child Development, 28*(6), Article e2165. https://doi.org/10.1002/icd.2165

Reynolds, C. R., & Kamphaus, R. W. (2015). *Behavior assessment for children: Third edition. (BASC-3).* Circle Pines.

Ridout, K. K., Levandowski, M., Ridout, S. J., Gantz, L., Goonan, K., Palermo, D., Price, L. H., & Tyrka, A. R. (2018). Early life adversity and telomere length: A meta-analysis. *Molecular Psychiatry, 23*(4), 858–871. https://doi.org/10.1038/mp.2017.26

Ridout, S. J., Ridout, K. K., Kao, H. T., Carpenter, L. L., Philip, N. S., Tyrka, A. R., & Price, L. H. (2015). Telomeres, early-life stress, and mental illness. In R. Balon & T. N. Wise (Eds.), *Clinical challenges in the biopsychosocial interface* (pp. 92–108). Karger. https://doi.org/10.1159/000369088

Riley, A. R., Wagner, D. V., Tudor, M. E., Zuckerman, K. E., & Freeman, K. A. (2017). A survey of parents' perceptions and use of time-out compared to empirical evidence. *Academic Pediatrics, 17*(2), 168–175. https://doi.org/10.1016/j.acap.2016.08.004

Rispoli, K. M., McGoey, K. E., Koziol, N. A., & Schreiber, J. B. (2013). The relation of parenting, child temperament, and attachment security in early childhood to social competence at school entry. *Journal of School Psychology, 51*(5), 643–658. https://doi.org/10.1016/j.jsp.2013.05.007

Robinson, J., Little, C., & Biringen, Z. (1993). Emotional communication in mother-toddler relationships: Evidence for early gender differentiation. *Merrill-Palmer Quarterly, 39*(4), 496–517.

Robinson-Keilig, R. A. (2014). Secondary traumatic stress and disruptions to interpersonal functioning among mental health therapists. *Journal of Interpersonal Violence, 29*(8), 1477–1496. https://doi.org/10.1177/0886260513507135

Robson, D. A., Allen, M. S., & Howard, S. J. (2020). Self-regulation in childhood as a predictor of future outcomes: A meta-analytic review. *Psychological Bulletin, 146*(4), 324–354. https://doi.org/10.1037/bul0000227

Rodriguez, C. M. (2010). Parent–child aggression: Association with child abuse potential and parenting styles. *Violence and Victims, 25*(6), 728–741. https://doi.org/10.1891/0886-6708.25.6.728

Roisman, G. I., & Fraley, R. C. (2008). A behavior-genetic study of parenting quality, infant attachment security, and their covariation in a nationally representative sample. *Developmental Psychology, 44*(3), 831–839. https://doi.org/10.1037/0012-1649.44.3.831

Rokach, A., & Boulazreg, S. (2020). The COVID-19 era: How therapists can diminish burnout symptoms through self-care. *Current Psychology*. https://doi.org/10.1007/s12144-020-01149-6

Rollins, A. L., Kukla, M., Morse, G., Davis, L., Leiter, M., Monroe-DeVita, M., Flanagan, M. E., Russ, A., Wasmuth, S., Eliacin, J., Collins, L., & Salyers, M. P. (2016). Comparative effectiveness of a burnout reduction intervention for behavioral health providers. *Psychiatric Services, 67*(8), 920–923. https://doi.org/10.1176/appi.ps.201500220

Rosen, A. L., Handley, E. D., Cicchetti, D., & Rogosch, F. A. (2018). The impact of patterns of trauma exposure among low income children with and without histories of child maltreatment. *Child Abuse & Neglect, 80,* 301–311. https://doi.org/10.1016/j.chiabu.2018.04.005

Rosenthal, D. (1963). A suggested conceptual framework. In D. Rosenthal (Ed.), *The Genain quadruplets: A case study and theoretical analysis of heredity and environment in schizophrenia* (pp. 505–511). Basic Books. https://doi.org/10.1037/11420-031

Roskam, I., Brassart, E., Loop, L., Mouton, B., & Schelstraete, M. A. (2015). Stimulating parents' self-efficacy beliefs or verbal responsiveness: Which is the best way to decrease children's externalizing behaviors? *Behaviour Research and Therapy, 72,* 38–48. https://doi.org/10.1016/j.brat.2015.06.012

Rothenberg, W. A., Weinstein, A., Dandes, E. A., & Jent, J. F. (2019). Improving child emotion regulation: Effects of parent–child interaction-therapy and emotion socialization strategies. *Journal of Child and Family Studies, 28*(3), 720–731. https://doi.org/10.1007/s10826-018-1302-2

Rubinic, D., & Schwickrath, H. (2010). Test review: Kamphaus, R. W., & Reynolds, C. R. (2006). Parenting Relationship Questionnaire. Minneapolis, MN: NCS Pearson. *Journal of Psychoeducational Assessment, 28*(3), 270–275. https://doi.org/10.1177/0734282909346718

Rupert, P. A., & Kent, J. S. (2007). Gender and work setting differences in career-sustaining behaviors and burnout among professional psychologists. *Professional Psychology, Research and Practice, 38*(1), 88–96. https://doi.org/10.1037/0735-7028.38.1.88

Rupert, P. A., Miller, A. O., & Dorociak, K. E. (2015). Preventing burnout: What does the research tell us? *Professional Psychology, Research and Practice, 46*(3), 168–174. https://doi.org/10.1037/a0039297

Saltzman, J. A., Fiese, B. H., Bost, K. K., & McBride, B. A. (2018). Development of appetite self-regulation: Integrating perspectives from attachment and family systems theory. *Child Development Perspectives, 12*(1), 51–57. https://doi.org/10.1111/cdep.12254

Salvagioni, D. A. J., Melanda, F. N., Mesas, A. E., González, A. D., Gabani, F. L., & Andrade, S. M. D. (2017). Physical, psychological and occupational consequences of job burnout: A systematic review of prospective studies. *PLOS ONE, 12*(10), Article e0185781. https://doi.org/10.1371/journal.pone.0185781

Sameroff, A. (Ed.). (2009). *The transactional model of development. How children and contexts shape each other*. American Psychological Association. https://doi.org/10.1037/11877-000

Sanders, M. R. (2008). Triple P-Positive Parenting Program as a public health approach to strengthening parenting. *Journal of Family Psychology, 22*(4), 506–517. https://doi.org/10.1037/0893-3200.22.3.506

Sanders, M. R., Kirby, J. N., Tellegen, C. L., & Day, J. J. (2014). The Triple P-Positive Parenting Program: A systematic review and meta-analysis of a multi-level system of parenting support. *Clinical Psychology Review, 34*(4), 337–357. https://doi.org/10.1016/j.cpr.2014.04.003

Sanders, M. R., & Turner, K. M. T. (2019). The Triple P System: Parenting support for every family. In B. H. Fiese, M. Celano, K. Deater-Deckard, E. N. Jouriles, & M. A. Whisman (Eds.), *APA handbook of contemporary family psychology: Family therapy and training* (pp. 409–424). American Psychological Association. https://doi.org/10.1037/0000101-025

Sanetti, L. M. H. (2017). Increasing equitable care for youth through coordinated school health. *Psychology in the Schools, 54*(10), 1312–1318. https://doi.org/10.1002/pits.22081

Sansbury, B. S., Graves, K., & Scott, W. (2015). Managing traumatic stress responses among clinicians: Individual and organizational tools for self-care. *Trauma, 17*(2), 114–122. https://doi.org/10.1177/1460408614551978

Schiltz, H. K., McVey, A. J., Magnus, B., Dolan, B. K., Willar, K. S., Pleiss, S., Karst, J., Carson, A. M., Caiozzo, C., Vogt, E., & Van Hecke, A. V. (2018). Examining the links between challenging behaviors in youth with ASD and parental stress, mental health, and involvement: Applying an adaptation of the family stress model to families of youth with ASD. *Journal of Autism and Developmental Disorders, 48*(4), 1169–1180. https://doi.org/10.1007/s10803-017-3446-0

Schuhmann, E. M., Foote, R. C., Eyberg, S. M., Boggs, S. R., & Algina, J. (1998). Efficacy of parent–child interaction therapy: Interim report of a randomized trial with short-term maintenance. *Journal of Clinical Child Psychology, 27*(1), 34–45. https://doi.org/10.1207/s15374424jccp2701_4

Scourfield, J., Culpin, I., Gunnell, D., Dale, C., Joinson, C., Heron, J., & Collin, S. M. (2016). The association between characteristics of fathering in infancy and depressive symptoms in adolescence: A UK birth cohort study. *Child Abuse & Neglect, 58*, 119–128. https://doi.org/10.1016/j.chiabu.2016.06.013

Shafi, R. M. A., Bieber, E. D., Shekunov, J., Croarkin, P. E., & Romanowicz, M. (2019). Evidence based dyadic therapies for 0-to 5-year-old children with emotional and behavioral difficulties. *Frontiers in Psychiatry, 10*(677), 677. https://doi.org/10.3389/fpsyt.2019.00677

Shalev, I., Moffitt, T. E., Sugden, K., Williams, B., Houts, R. M., Danese, A., Mill, J., Arseneault, L., & Caspi, A. (2013). Exposure to violence during childhood is associated with telomere erosion from 5 to 10 years of age: A longitudinal study. *Molecular Psychiatry, 18*(5), 576–581. https://doi.org/10.1038/mp.2012.32

Shanley, J. R., & Niec, L. N. (2010). Coaching parents to change: The impact of in vivo feedback on parents' acquisition of skills. *Journal of Clinical Child and Adolescent Psychology, 39*(2), 282–287. https://doi.org/10.1080/15374410903532627

Shannon, J. D., Tamis-LeMonda, C. S., & Cabrera, N. J. (2006). Fathering in infancy: Mutuality and stability between 8 and 16 months. *Parenting, 6*(2–3), 167–188. https://doi.org/10.1080/15295192.2006.9681304

Shapiro, C. J., Kilburn, J., & Hardin, J. W. (2014). Prevention of behavior problems in a selected population: Stepping Stones Triple P for parents of young children with disabilities. *Research in Developmental Disabilities, 35*(11), 2958–2975. https://doi.org/10.1016/j.ridd.2014.07.036

Shea, S. E., Goldberg, S., & Weatherston, D. J. (2016). A community mental health professional development model for the expansion of reflective practice and supervision: Evaluation of a pilot training series for infant mental health professionals. *Infant Mental Health Journal, 37*(6), 653–669. https://doi.org/10.1002/imhj.21611

Sherman, L. J., Rice, K., & Cassidy, J. (2015). Infant capacities related to building internal working models of attachment figures: A theoretical and empirical review. *Developmental Review, 37*, 109–141. https://doi.org/10.1016/j.dr.2015.06.001

Shih, M., Dumke, K. A., Goran, M. I., & Simon, P. A. (2013). The association between community-level economic hardship and childhood obesity prevalence in Los Angeles. *Pediatric Obesity, 8*(6), 411–417. https://doi.org/10.1111/j.2047-6310.2012.00123.x

Shirk, S. R., & Russell, R. L. (1996). *Change processes in child psychotherapy: Revitalizing treatment and research*. Guilford Press.

Shivers, E. M. (2008). Using the emotional availability scales along the child care continuum. *Journal of Early Childhood and Infant Psychology, 4*, 27–38.

Shloim, N., Edelson, L. R., Martin, N., & Hetherington, M. M. (2015). Parenting styles, feeding styles, feeding practices, and weight status in 4–12 year-old children: A systematic review of the literature. *Frontiers in Psychology, 6*, 1849. https://doi.org/10.3389/fpsyg.2015.01849

Shmueli-Goetz, Y., Target, M., Fonagy, P., & Datta, A. (2008). The Child Attachment Interview: A psychometric study of reliability and discriminant validity. *Developmental Psychology, 44*(4), 939–956. https://doi.org/10.1037/0012-1649.44.4.939

Shonkoff, J. P., Garner, A. S., the Committee on Psychosocial Aspects of Child and Family Health, Committee on Early Childhood, Adoption, and Dependent Care, & Section on Developmental and Behavioral Pediatrics. (2012). The lifelong effects of early childhood adversity and toxic stress. *Pediatrics, 129*(1), e232–e246. https://doi.org/10.1542/peds.2011-2663

Shonkoff, J. P., & Richmond, J. B. (2009, December). Investment in early childhood development lays the foundation for a prosperous and sustainable society. *Encyclopedia on Early Childhood Development*. https://www.child-encyclopedia.com/pdf/expert/importance-early-childhood-development/according-experts/investment-early-childhood-development-lays

Shreffler, J., & Huecker, M. R. (2021, March). Diagnostic testing accuracy: Sensitivity, specificity, predictive values and likelihood ratios. *StatPearls*. https://www.ncbi.nlm.nih.gov/books/NBK557491/

Siegel, D. J., & Bryson, T. P. (2014a). *No-drama discipline*. Mind Your Brain.

Siegel, D. J., & Bryson, T. P. (2014b, September 23). 'Time-outs' are hurting your child. *Time*. http://time.com/3404701/discipline-time-out-is-not-good/

Silovsky, J. F., & Niec, L. (2002). Characteristics of young children with sexual behavior problems: A pilot study. *Child Maltreatment, 7*(3), 187–197. https://doi.org/10.1177/1077559502007003002

Simionato, G. K., & Simpson, S. (2018). Personal risk factors associated with burnout among psychotherapists: A systematic review of the literature. *Journal of Clinical Psychology, 74*(9), 1431–1456. https://doi.org/10.1002/jclp.22615

Simionato, G. K., Simpson, S., & Reid, C. (2019). Burnout as an ethical issue in psychotherapy. *Psychotherapy: Theory, Research, & Practice, 56*(4), 470–482. https://doi.org/10.1037/pst0000261

Simpson, S., Simionato, G., Smout, M., van Vreeswijk, M. F., Hayes, C., Sougleris, C., & Reid, C. (2019). Burnout amongst clinical and counselling psychologist: The role of early maladaptive schemas and coping modes as vulnerability factors. *Clinical Psychology & Psychotherapy, 26*(1), 35–46. https://doi.org/10.1002/cpp.2328

Skinner, A. C., Perrin, E. M., & Skelton, J. A. (2016). Prevalence of obesity and severe obesity in US children, 1999–2014. *Obesity, 24*(5), 1116–1123. https://doi.org/10.1002/oby.21497

Slagt, M., Dubas, J. S., Deković, M., & van Aken, M. A. (2016). Differences in sensitivity to parenting depending on child temperament: A meta-analysis. *Psychological Bulletin, 142*(10), 1068–1110. https://doi.org/10.1037/bul0000061

Smith, P. L., & Moss, S. B. (2009). Psychologist impairment: What is it, how can it be prevented, and what can be done to address it? *Clinical Psychology: Science and Practice, 16*(1), 1–15. https://doi.org/10.1111/j.1468-2850.2009.01137.x

Snowden, L. R. (2012). Health and mental health policies' role in better understanding and closing African American–White American disparities in treatment access and quality of care. *American Psychologist, 67*(7), 524–531. https://doi.org/10.1037/a0030054

Snyder, C. K., & Chang, A. (2019). Mobile technology, sleep, and circadian disruption. In M. A. Grandner (Ed.), *Sleep and health* (pp. 159–170). Elsevier Academic Press. https://doi.org/10.1016/B978-0-12-815373-4.00013-7

Snyder, J., Gewirtz, A., Schrepferman, L., Gird, S. R., Quattlebaum, J., Pauldine, M. R., Elish, K., Zamir, O., & Hayes, C. (2016). Parent–child relationship quality and family transmission of parent posttraumatic stress disorder symptoms and child externalizing and internalizing symptoms following fathers' combat-trauma exposure. *Development and Psychopathology, 28*(4, Pt. 1), 947–969. https://doi.org/10.1017/S095457941600064X

Society of Clinical Child and Adolescent Psychology. (2014, September 29). *Outrageous claims regarding appropriateness of time out have no basis in science.* https://effectivechildtherapy.org/outrageous-claims-regarding-appropriateness-time-no-basis-science/

Soloski, K. L., & Deitz, S. L. (2016). Managing emotional responses in therapy: An adapted EFT supervision approach. *Contemporary Family Therapy, 38*(4), 361–372. https://doi.org/10.1007/s10591-016-9392-8

Spinrad, T. L., Eisenberg, N., Silva, K. M., Eggum, N. D., Reiser, M., Edwards, A., Iyer, R., Kupfer, A. S., Hofer, C., Smith, C. L., Hayashi, A., & Gaertner, B. M. (2012). Longitudinal relations among maternal behaviors, effortful control and young children's committed compliance. *Developmental Psychology, 48*(2), 552–566. https://doi.org/10.1037/a0025898

Spoth, R., Redmond, C., Haggerty, K., & Ward, T. (1995). A controlled parenting skills outcome study examining individual difference and attendance effects. *Journal of Marriage and the Family, 57*(2), 449–464. https://doi.org/10.2307/353698

Sroufe, L. A. (2005). Attachment and development: A prospective, longitudinal study from birth to adulthood. *Attachment & Human Development, 7*(4), 349–367. https://doi.org/10.1080/14616730500365928

Stacks, A. M., Oshio, T., Gerard, J., & Roe, J. (2009). The moderating effect of parental warmth on the association between spanking and child aggression: A longitudinal approach. *Infant and Child Development, 18*(2), 178–194. https://doi.org/10.1002/icd.596

Starks, T. J., Newcomb, M. E., & Mustanski, B. (2015). A longitudinal study of interpersonal relationships among lesbian, gay, and bisexual adolescents and young adults: Mediational pathways from attachment to romantic relationship quality. *Archives of Sexual Behavior, 44*(7), 1821–1831. https://doi.org/10.1007/s10508-015-0492-6

Steele, E. H., & McKinney, C. (2019). Emerging adult psychological problems and parenting style: Moderation by parent–child relationship quality. *Personality and Individual Differences, 146*, 201–208. https://doi.org/10.1016/j.paid.2018.04.048

Steele, H., & Steele, M. (Eds.). (2018). *Handbook of attachment-based interventions*. Guilford Press.

Sturge-Apple, M. L., Davies, P. T., Cicchetti, D., Hentges, R. F., & Coe, J. L. (2017). Family instability and children's effortful control in the context of poverty: Sometimes a bird in the hand is worth two in the bush. *Development and Psychopathology, 29*(3), 685–696. https://doi.org/10.1017/S0954579416000407

Sullivan, R., Perry, R., Sloan, A., Kleinhaus, K., & Burtchen, N. (2011). Infant bonding and attachment to the caregiver: Insights from basic and clinical science. *Clinics in Perinatology, 38*(4), 643–655. https://doi.org/10.1016/j.clp.2011.08.011

Tamis-LeMonda, C. S., Shannon, J. D., Cabrera, N. J., & Lamb, M. E. (2004). Fathers and mothers at play with their 2- and 3-year-olds: Contributions to language and cognitive development. *Child Development, 75*(6), 1806–1820. https://doi.org/10.1111/j.1467-8624.2004.00818.x

Tartakovsky, E. (2016). Personal value preferences and burnout of social workers. *Journal of Social Work, 16*(6), 657–673. https://doi.org/10.1177/1468017315589872

Teachman, B. A., McKay, D., Barch, D. M., Prinstein, M. J., Hollon, S. D., & Chambless, D. L. (2019). How psychosocial research can help the National Institute of Mental Health achieve its grand challenge to reduce the burden of mental illnesses and psychological disorders. *American Psychologist, 74*(4), 415–431. https://doi.org/10.1037/amp0000361

Thomas, J. M., Benham, A. L., Gean, M., Luby, J., Minde, K., Turner, S., Wright, H. H., & the American Academy of Child and Adolescent Psychiatry. (1997). Practice parameters for the psychiatric assessment of infants and toddlers (0–36 months). *Journal of the American Academy of Child & Adolescent Psychiatry, 36*(10, Suppl.), 21S–36S. https://doi.org/10.1097/00004583-199710001-00003

Thomas, R., Abell, B., Webb, H. J., Avdagic, E., & Zimmer-Gembeck, M. J. (2017). Parent–child interaction therapy: A meta-analysis. *Pediatrics, 140*(3), Article e20170352. https://doi.org/10.1542/peds.2017-0352

Thomas, R., & Zimmer-Gembeck, M. J. (2007). Behavioral outcomes of parent–child interaction therapy and Triple P—Positive Parenting Program: A review and meta-analysis. *Journal of Abnormal Child Psychology, 35*(3), 475–495. https://doi.org/10.1007/s10802-007-9104-9

Thomas, R., & Zimmer-Gembeck, M. J. (2011). Accumulating evidence for parent–child interaction therapy in the prevention of child maltreatment. *Child Development, 82*(1), 177–192. https://doi.org/10.1111/j.1467-8624.2010.01548.x

Thompson, A., Hollis, C., & Dagger, D. R. (2003). Authoritarian parenting attitudes as a risk for conduct problems: Results from a British national cohort study. *European Child & Adolescent Psychiatry, 12*(2), 84–91. https://doi.org/10.1007/s00787-003-0324-4

Thompson, R. A. (2016). Early attachment and later development: Reframing the questions. In J. Cassidy & P. R. Shaver (Eds.), *Handbook of attachment: Theory, research, and clinical applications* (3rd ed., pp. 330–348). Guilford Press.

Tiberio, S. S., Capaldi, D. M., Kerr, D. C., Bertrand, M., Pears, K. C., & Owen, L. (2016). Parenting and the development of effortful control from early childhood to early adolescence: A transactional developmental model. *Development and Psychopathology, 28*(3), 837–853. https://doi.org/10.1017/S0954579416000341

Timmer, S. G., Thompson, D., Culver, M. A., Urquiza, A. J., & Altenhofen, S. (2012). Mothers' physical abusiveness in a context of violence: Effects on the mother–child relationship. *Development and Psychopathology, 24*(1), 79–92. https://doi.org/10.1017/S0954579411000678

Timmer, S. G., Urquiza, A. J., Zebell, N. M., & McGrath, J. M. (2005). Parent–child interaction therapy: Application to maltreating parent–child dyads. *Child Abuse & Neglect, 29*(7), 825–842. https://doi.org/10.1016/j.chiabu.2005.01.003

Tompson, M. C., Asarnow, J. R., Mintz, J., & Cantwell, D. P. (2015). Parental depression risk: Comparing youth with depression, attention deficit hyperactivity disorder and community controls. *Journal of Psychology & Psychotherapy, 5*(4), 1–9. https://doi.org/10.4172/2161-0487.1000193

Toth, S. L., Maughan, A., Manly, J. T., Spagnola, M., & Cicchetti, D. (2002). The relative efficacy of two interventions in altering maltreated preschool children's representational models: Implications for attachment theory. *Development and Psychopathology, 14*(4), 877–908. https://doi.org/10.1017/S095457940200411X

Toth, S. L., Michl-Petzing, L. C., Guild, D., & Lieberman, A. F. (2018). Child-parent psychotherapy: Theoretical bases, clinical applications, and empirical support. In H. Steele & M. Steele (Eds.), *Handbook of attachment-based interventions* (pp. 296–317). Guilford Press.

Toth, S. L., Rogosch, F. A., Manly, J. T., & Cicchetti, D. (2006). The efficacy of toddler-parent psychotherapy to reorganize attachment in the young offspring of mothers with major depressive disorder: A randomized preventive trial. *Journal of Consulting and Clinical Psychology, 74*(6), 1006–1016. https://doi.org/10.1037/0022-006X.74.6.1006

Treyvaud, K., Doyle, L. W., Lee, K. J., Ure, A., Inder, T. E., Hunt, R. W., & Anderson, P. J. (2016). Parenting behavior at 2 years predicts school-age performance at 7 years in very preterm children. *Journal of Child Psychology and Psychiatry, 57*(7), 814–821. https://doi.org/10.1111/jcpp.12489

Triemstra, K. T., Niec, L. N., Peer, S. O., & Christian-Brandt, A. S. (2017). The influence of conventional masculine gender role norms on parental attitudes toward seeking psychological services for children. *Psychology of Men & Masculinity, 18*(4), 311–320. https://doi.org/10.1037/men0000055

Trub, L., Quinlan, E., Starks, T. J., & Rosenthal, L. (2017). Discrimination, internalized homonegativity, and attitudes toward children of same-sex parents: Can secure attachment buffer against stigma internalization? *Family Process, 56*(3), 701–715. https://doi.org/10.1111/famp.12255

Tully, L. A., Collins, D. A. J., Piotrowska, P. J., Mairet, K. S., Hawes, D. J., Moul, C., Lenroot, R. K., Frick, P. J., Anderson, V. A., Kimonis, E. R., & Dadds, M. R. (2018). Examining practitioner competencies, organizational support and barriers to engaging fathers in parenting interventions. *Child Psychiatry and Human Development, 49*(1), 109–122. https://doi.org/10.1007/s10578-017-0733-0

Tully, L. A., Hawes, D. J., Doyle, F. L., Sawyer, M. G., & Dadds, M. R. (2019). A national child mental health literacy initiative is needed to reduce childhood mental health disorders. *The Australian and New Zealand Journal of Psychiatry, 53*(4), 286–290. https://doi.org/10.1177/0004867418821440

Urist, J. (1980). Object relations. In R. W. Woody (Ed.), *Encyclopedia of clinical assessment* (Vol. 2, pp. 821–833). Jossey-Bass.

U.S. Department of Education. (2020, June). *Table 324.20. Doctor's degrees conferred by postsecondary institutions, by race/ethnicity and sex of student: Selected years,*

1976–77 through 2018–19. National Center for Education Statistics. https://nces.ed.gov/programs/digest/d20/tables/dt20_324.20.asp

U.S. Department of Health and Human Services. (2001). *Mental health: Culture, race, and ethnicity: A supplement to Mental health: A report of the surgeon general*. https://www.ncbi.nlm.nih.gov/books/NBK44243/

U.S. Department of Health and Human Services. (2010). *About healthy people*. https://www.healthypeople.gov/2020/About-Healthy-People

Valdez, C. R., Shewakramani, V., Goldberg, S., & Padilla, B. (2013). Parenting influences on Latino children's social competence in the first grade: Parental depression and parent involvement at home and school. *Child Psychiatry and Human Development, 44*(5), 646–657. https://doi.org/10.1007/s10578-013-0358-x

Valente, V., & Marotta, A. (2005). The impact of yoga on the professional and personal life of the psychotherapist. *Contemporary Family Therapy, 27*(1), 65–80. https://doi.org/10.1007/s10591-004-1971-4

van Beusekom, G., Bos, H. M. W., Overbeek, G., & Sandfort, T. G. M. (2015). Same-sex attraction, gender nonconformity, and mental health: The protective role of parental acceptance. *Psychology of Sexual Orientation and Gender Diversity, 2*(3), 307–312. https://doi.org/10.1037/sgd0000118

Van Den Dries, L., Juffer, F., Van Ijzendoorn, M. H., Bakermans-Kranenburg, M. J., & Alink, L. R. (2012). Infants' responsiveness, attachment, and indiscriminate friendliness after international adoption from institutions or foster care in China: Application of Emotional Availability Scales to adoptive families. *Development and Psychopathology, 24*(1), 49–64. https://doi.org/10.1017/S0954579411000654

van Ee, E., Kleber, R. J., & Jongmans, M. J. (2016). Relational patterns between caregivers with PTSD and their nonexposed children: A review. *Trauma, Violence & Abuse, 17*(2), 186–203. https://doi.org/10.1177/1524838015584355

van Ee, E., Kleber, R. J., & Mooren, T. T. M. (2012). War trauma lingers on: Associations between maternal posttraumatic stress disorder, parent–child interaction, and child development. *Infant Mental Health Journal, 33*(5), 459–468. https://doi.org/10.1002/imhj.21324

van Eldik, W. M., de Haan, A. D., Arends, L. R., Belsky, J., & Prinzie, P. (2019). Personality, depressive symptoms, the interparental relationship and parenting: Prospective associations of an actor-partner interdependency model. *Journal of Family Psychology, 33*(6), 671–681. https://doi.org/10.1037/fam0000553

van Gelderen, L., Gartrell, N. N., Bos, H. M., & Hermanns, J. M. (2013). Stigmatization and promotive factors in relation to psychological health and life satisfaction of adolescents in planned lesbian families. *Journal of Family Issues, 34*(6), 809–827. https://doi.org/10.1177/0192513X12447269

van IJzendoorn, M. H. (1995). Adult attachment representations, parental responsiveness, and infant attachment: A meta-analysis on the predictive validity of the Adult Attachment Interview. *Psychological Bulletin, 117*(3), 387–403. https://doi.org/10.1037/0033-2909.117.3.387

van IJzendoorn, M. H., & Bakermans-Kranenburg, M. J. (2012). A sniff of trust: Meta-analysis of the effects of intranasal oxytocin administration on face recognition, trust to in-group, and trust to out-group. *Psychoneuroendocrinology, 37*(3), 438–443. https://doi.org/10.1016/j.psyneuen.2011.07.008

van IJzendoorn, M. H., Dijkstra, J., & Bus, A. G. (1995). Attachment, intelligence, and language: A meta-analysis. *Social Development, 4*(2), 115–128. https://doi.org/10.1111/j.1467-9507.1995.tb00055.x

van IJzendoorn, M. H., Rutgers, A. H., Bakermans-Kranenburg, M. J., Swinkels, S. H., van Daalen, E., Dietz, C., Naber, F. B., Buitelaar, J. K., & van Engeland, H. (2007). Parental sensitivity and attachment in children with autism spectrum disorder: Comparison with children with mental retardation, with language delays, and with typical development. *Child Development, 78*(2), 597–608. https://doi.org/10.1111/j.1467-8624.2007.01016.x

van IJzendoorn, M. H., Schuengel, C., & Bakermans-Kranenburg, M. J. (1999). Disorganized attachment in early childhood: Meta-analysis of precursors, concomitants, and sequelae. *Development and Psychopathology, 11*(2), 225–250. https://doi.org/10.1017/S0954579499002035

Vaughn, B., Egeland, B., Sroufe, L. A., & Waters, E. (1979). Individual differences in infant-mother attachment at twelve and eighteen months: Stability and change in families under stress. *Child Development, 50*(4), 971–975. https://doi.org/10.2307/1129321

Venuti, P., de Falco, S., Giusti, Z., & Bornstein, M. H. (2008). Play and emotional availability in young children with Down syndrome. *Infant Mental Health Journal, 29*(2), 133–152. https://doi.org/10.1002/imhj.20168

Verhage, M. L., Fearon, R. M. P., Schuengel, C., van IJzendoorn, M. H., Bakermans-Kranenburg, M. J., Madigan, S., Roisman, G. I., Oosterman, M., Behrens, K. Y., Wong, M. S., Mangelsdorf, S., Priddis, L. E., Brisch, K. H., & the Collaboration on Attachment Transmission Synthesis. (2018). Examining ecological constraints on the intergenerational transmission of attachment via individual participant data meta-analysis. *Child Development, 89*(6), 2023–2037. https://doi.org/10.1111/cdev.13085

Verhage, M. L., Schuengel, C., Madigan, S., Fearon, R. M. P., Oosterman, M., Cassibba, R., Bakermans-Kranenburg, M. J., & van IJzendoorn, M. H. (2016). Narrowing the transmission gap: A synthesis of three decades of research on intergenerational transmission of attachment. *Psychological Bulletin, 142*(4), 337–366. https://doi.org/10.1037/bul0000038

Vieira, J. M., Matias, M., Ferreira, T., Lopez, F. G., & Matos, P. M. (2016). Parents' work-family experiences and children's problem behaviors: The mediating role of the parent–child relationship. *Journal of Family Psychology, 30*(4), 419–430. https://doi.org/10.1037/fam0000189

Vogel, S., & Schwabe, L. (2016). Learning and memory under stress: Implications for the classroom. *npj/Science of Learning, 1*(1), 1–10. https://doi.org/10.1038/npjscilearn.2016.11

von Hippel, C., Brener, L., Rose, G., & von Hippel, W. (2019). Perceived inability to help is associated with client-related burnout and negative work outcomes among community mental health workers. *Health & Social Care in the Community, 27*(6), 1507–1514. https://doi.org/10.1111/hsc.12821

von Suchodoletz, A., Trommsdorff, G., & Heikamp, T. (2011). Linking maternal warmth and responsiveness to children's self-regulation. *Social Development, 20*(3), 486–503. https://doi.org/10.1111/j.1467-9507.2010.00588.x

Voss Horrell, S. C., Holohan, D. R., Didion, L. M., & Vance, G. T. (2011). Treating traumatized OEF/OIF veterans: How does trauma treatment affect the clinician? *Professional Psychology, Research and Practice, 42*(1), 79–86. https://doi.org/10.1037/a0022297

Vu, N. L., Jouriles, E. N., McDonald, R., & Rosenfield, D. (2016). Children's exposure to intimate partner violence: A meta-analysis of longitudinal associations with child adjustment problems. *Clinical Psychology Review, 46*, 25–33. https://doi.org/10.1016/j.cpr.2016.04.003

Vygotsky, L. S. (1978). *Mind in society*. Harvard University Press.

Waisbren, S. E., Rones, M., Read, C. Y., Marsden, D., & Levy, H. L. (2004). Brief report: Predictors of parenting stress among parents of children with biochemical genetic disorders. *Journal of Pediatric Psychology, 29*(7), 565–570. https://doi.org/10.1093/jpepsy/jsh058

Waldinger, R. J., Toth, S. L., & Gerber, A. (2001). Maltreatment and internal representations of relationships: Core relationship themes in the narratives of abused and neglected preschoolers. *Social Development, 10*(1), 41–58. https://doi.org/10.1111/1467-9507.00147

Wang, Y., Chung, M. C., Wang, N., Yu, X., & Kenardy, J. (2021). Social support and posttraumatic stress disorder: A meta-analysis of longitudinal studies. *Clinical Psychology Review, 85*, 101998. Advance online publication. https://doi.org/10.1016/j.cpr.2021.101998

Ward, M. A., Theule, J., & Cheung, K. (2016). Parent–child interaction therapy for child disruptive behaviour disorders: A meta-analysis. *Child and Youth Care Forum, 45*(5), 675–690. https://doi.org/10.1007/s10566-016-9350-5

Washington State Institute for Public Policy. (2019, December). *Child–parent psychotherapy: Children's mental health: Trauma*. https://www.wsipp.wa.gov/BenefitCost/ProgramPdf/263/Child-Parent-Psychotherapy

Waters, E. (1978). The reliability and stability of individual differences in infant–mother attachment. *Child Development, 49*(2), 483–494. https://doi.org/10.2307/1128714

Waters, E., Posada, G., Crowell, J. A., & Lay, K. L. (1994). The development of attachment: From control system to working models. *Psychiatry, 57*(1), 32–42. https://doi.org/10.1080/00332747.1994.11024666

Waters, H. S., & Waters, E. (2006). The attachment working models concept: Among other things, we build script-like representations of secure base experiences. *Attachment & Human Development, 8*(3), 185–197. https://doi.org/10.1080/14616730600856016

Weaver, I. C., Cervoni, N., Champagne, F. A., D'Alessio, A. C., Sharma, S., Seckl, J. R., Dymov, S., Szyf, M., & Meaney, M. J. (2004). Epigenetic programming by maternal behavior. *Nature Neuroscience, 7*(8), 847–854. https://doi.org/10.1038/nn1276

Weaver, I. C., Meaney, M. J., & Szyf, M. (2006). Maternal care effects on the hippocampal transcriptome and anxiety-mediated behaviors in the offspring that are reversible in adulthood. *Proceedings of the National Academy of Sciences of the United States of America, 103*(9), 3480–3485. https://doi.org/10.1073/pnas.0507526103

Webster-Stratton, M. S. (2016). The Incredible Years series: A developmental approach. In M. J. VanRyzin, K. Kumpfer, G. Fosco, & M. T. Greenberg (Eds.), *Family-based prevention programs for children and adolescents: Theory, research, and large-scale dissemination* (pp. 42–67). Psychology Press.

Weissman, D. G., Bitran, D., Miller, A. B., Schaefer, J. D., Sheridan, M. A., & McLaughlin, K. A. (2019). Difficulties with emotion regulation as a transdiagnostic mechanism linking child maltreatment with the emergence of psychopathology. *Development and Psychopathology, 31*(3), 899–915. https://doi.org/10.1017/S0954579419000348

Wesarg, C., Van Den Akker, A. L., Oei, N. Y., Hoeve, M., & Wiers, R. W. (2020). Identifying pathways from early adversity to psychopathology: A review on dysregulated HPA axis functioning and impaired self-regulation in early childhood. *European Journal of Developmental Psychology, 17*(6), 808–827. https://doi.org/10.1080/17405629.2020.1748594

Westen, D. (1991). Social cognition and object relations. *Psychological Bulletin, 109*(3), 429–455. https://doi.org/10.1037/0033-2909.109.3.429

Westen, D. (1995). *Social cognition and object relations scale: Q-sort for projective stories (SCORS–Q)* [Unpublished manual]. Cambridge Hospital and Harvard Medical School.

Westen, D., Klepser, J., Ruffins, S. A., Silverman, M., Lifton, N., & Boekamp, J. (1991). Object relations in childhood and adolescence: The development of working representations. *Journal of Consulting and Clinical Psychology, 59*(3), 400–409. https://doi.org/10.1037/0022-006X.59.3.400

Whitcomb, S. A. (2017). *Behavioral, social, and emotional assessment of children and adolescents* (5th ed.). Routledge. https://doi.org/10.4324/9781315747521

White, G. D., Nielsen, G., & Johnson, S. M. (1972). Timeout duration and the suppression of deviant behavior in children. *Journal of Applied Behavior Analysis, 5*(2), 111–120. https://doi.org/10.1901/jaba.1972.5-111

Wilkes-Gillan, S., Cantrill, A., Parsons, L., Smith, C., & Cordier, R. (2017). The pragmatic language, communication skills, parent–child relationships, and symptoms of children with ADHD and their playmates 18-months after a parent-delivered play-based intervention. *Developmental Neurorehabilitation, 20*(5), 317–322. https://doi.org/10.1080/17518423.2016.1188861

Williams, L. R. (2020). The impact of infant carrying on adolescent mother–infant interactions during the still-face task. *Infant and Child Development, 29*(3), Article e2169. https://doi.org/10.1002/icd.2169

Williams, N. J., & Beidas, R. S. (2018). Navigating the storm: How proficient organizational culture promotes clinician retention in the shift to evidence-based practice. *PLOS ONE, 13*(12), Article e0209745. https://doi.org/10.1371/journal.pone.0209745

Williamson, L. L., Harwell, T. S., Koch, T. M., Anderson, S. L., Scott, M. K., Murphy, J. S., Holzman, G. S., & Tesfai, H. F. (2021). COVID-19 incidence and mortality among American Indian/Alaska Native and White persons—Montana, March 13–November 30, 2020. *Morbidity and Mortality Weekly Report, 70*(14), 510–513. https://doi.org/10.15585/mmwr.mm7014a2

Wilson, S., & Durbin, C. E. (2010). Effects of paternal depression on fathers' parenting behaviors: A meta-analytic review. *Clinical Psychology Review, 30*(2), 167–180. https://doi.org/10.1016/j.cpr.2009.10.007

Winnicott, D. (1971). *Playing and reality*. Tavistock Publications.

Wise, E. H., Hersh, M. A., & Gibson, C. M. (2012). Ethics, self-care and well-being for psychologists: Reenvisioning the stress-distress continuum. *Professional Psychology, Research and Practice, 43*(5), 487–494. https://doi.org/10.1037/a0029446

Wittig, S. M. O., & Rodriguez, C. M. (2019). Emerging behavior problems: Bidirectional relations between maternal and paternal parenting styles with infant temperament. *Developmental Psychology, 55*(6), 1199–1210. https://doi.org/10.1037/dev0000707

Woodhouse, S. S., Powell, B., Cooper, G., Hoffman, K., & Cassidy, J. (2018). The circle of security intervention: Design, research, and implementation. In H. Steele & M. Steele (Eds.), *Handbook of attachment-based interventions* (pp. 50–78). Guilford Press.

Woodhouse, S. S., Scott, J. R., Hepworth, A. D., & Cassidy, J. (2020). Secure base provision: A new approach to examining links between maternal caregiving and infant attachment. *Child Development, 91*(1), e249–e265. https://doi.org/10.1111/cdev.13224

World Health Organization. (2021). *International classification of diseases for mortality and morbidity statistics* (11th rev.). https://icd.who.int/browse11/l-m/en

Wünsche, S., & Brisch, K. H. (2010). Emotional availability of VLBW infants and their mothers in post-stress and play situations. *Infant Mental Health Journal, 32*(Suppl.), 183–184.

Wyse, R., Hwang, W. T., Ahmed, A. A., Richards, E., & Deville, C., Jr. (2020). Diversity by race, ethnicity, and sex within the US psychiatry physician workforce. *Academic Psychiatry, 44*(5), 523–530. https://doi.org/10.1007/s40596-020-01276-z

Yaholkoski, A., Hurl, K., & Theule, J. (2016). Efficacy of the circle of security intervention: A meta-analysis. *Journal of Infant, Child, and Adolescent Psychotherapy, 15*(2), 95–103. https://doi.org/10.1080/15289168.2016.1163161

Yanchus, N. J., Periard, D., & Osatuke, K. (2017). Further examination of predictors of turnover intention among mental health professionals. *Journal of Psychiatric and Mental Health Nursing, 24*(1), 41–56. https://doi.org/10.1111/jpm.12354

Yang, Y., & Hayes, J. A. (2020). Causes and consequences of burnout among mental health professionals: A practice-oriented review of recent empirical literature. *Psychotherapy: Theory, Research, & Practice, 57*(3), 426–436. https://doi.org/10.1037/pst0000317

Yoshikawa, H., Aber, J. L., & Beardslee, W. R. (2012). The effects of poverty on the mental, emotional, and behavioral health of children and youth: Implications for prevention. *American Psychologist, 67*(4), 272–284. https://doi.org/10.1037/a0028015

Yousafzai, A. K., Rasheed, M. A., Rizvi, A., Armstrong, R., & Bhutta, Z. A. (2015). Parenting skills and emotional availability: An RCT. *Pediatrics, 135*(5), e1247–e1257. https://doi.org/10.1542/peds.2014-2335

Yule, K., Houston, J., & Grych, J. (2019). Resilience in children exposed to violence: A meta-analysis of protective factors across ecological contexts. *Clinical Child and Family Psychology Review, 22*(3), 406–431. https://doi.org/10.1007/s10567-019-00293-1

Zeanah, C. H. (2000). Disturbances of attachment in young children adopted from institutions. *Journal of Developmental and Behavioral Pediatrics, 21*(3), 230–236.

Zeegers, M. A. J., Colonnesi, C., Stams, G. J. M., & Meins, E. (2017). Mind matters: A meta-analysis on parental mentalization and sensitivity as predictors of infant-parent attachment. *Psychological Bulletin, 143*(12), 1245–1272. https://doi.org/10.1037/bul0000114

Zero to Three. (2005). *Diagnostic classification of mental health and developmental disorders of infancy and early childhood* (Rev. ed.). Zero to Three Press.

Zevalkink, J., Riksen-Walraven, J. M., & Van Lieshout, C. F. (1999). Attachment in the Indonesian caregiving context. *Social Development, 8*(1), 21–40. https://doi.org/10.1111/1467-9507.00078

Zhang, J., Palmer, A., Zhang, N., & Gewirtz, A. H. (2020). Coercive parenting mediates the relationship between military fathers' emotion regulation and children's adjustment. *Journal of Abnormal Child Psychology, 48*(5), 633–645. https://doi.org/10.1007/s10802-020-00625-8

Zimmer-Gembeck, M. J., Kerin, J. L., Webb, H. J., Gardner, A. A., Campbell, S. M., Swan, K., & Timmer, S. G. (2019). Improved perceptions of emotion regulation and reflective functioning in parents: Two additional positive outcomes of parent–child interaction therapy. *Behavior Therapy, 50*(2), 340–352. https://doi.org/10.1016/j.beth.2018.07.002

Zimmermann, P., & Iwanski, A. (2015). Attachment in middle childhood: Associations with information processing. *New Directions for Child and Adolescent Development, 2015*(148), 47–61. https://doi.org/10.1002/cad.20099

Ziv, Y., Aviezer, O., Gini, M., Sagi, A., & Koren-Karie, N. (2000). Emotional availability in the mother–infant dyad as related to the quality of infant–mother attachment relationship. *Attachment & Human Development, 2*(2), 149–169. https://doi.org/10.1080/14616730050085536

INDEX

B

C

F

S

W

ABOUT THE AUTHOR

Larissa N. Niec, PhD, is a professor of psychology and the director of the Center for Children, Families, and Communities at Central Michigan University. As a clinician, trainer, and researcher, Dr. Niec seeks to improve health equity for families by increasing access to effective parent–child interventions. Dr. Niec is involved in national and international efforts to disseminate parent–child interaction therapy to community therapists. She has written extensively on the evidence-based use of play in clinical practice and parent–child interaction therapy. For more information about her research and creative work, see her website (https://www.LarissaNiec.com).